The Global New Deal

PRAISE FOR THE FIRST EDITION

"Student friendly. . . . The questions addressed in each chapter are introduced clearly, and there are useful boxes detailing key information. Yet, *The Global New Deal* is a sophisticated and succinct text."—*Millennium: Journal of International Studies*

"The central value of the volume is its discussion of the variety of existing institutions and laws that potentially can be harnessed to address global poverty. Recommended."—*Choice*

"This book amounts to that rare beast: an intelligent text that, as it informs, makes an interesting argument of its own. It also advances a set of specific proposals that could inspire lively class discussion and debate."—**Michael J. Smith, University of Virginia**

"Felice's well-conceived proposals for enhanced benevolent global governance offer the only practical solutions to the social cancer of mass poverty, which is undermining world stability. His proposals are likely to dominate the ongoing debate concerning the means for achieving a more humane and sustainable globalization."—**Maurice Williams, former assistant secretary-general, United Nations**

"Through knowledge and imagination, solid evidence and insightful analysis, William Felice demonstrates that a global new deal is a viable alternative to the untenable status quo. He shows how getting there is a well-informed, deliberate process of 'globalization from below,' not a jump of faith! This book is a valuable resource for scholars and students of international relations and human rights, and an inspiring and empowering challenge to practitioners, local activists, and global citizens everywhere."—**Abdullahi A. An-Na'im, Emory University**

"In this groundbreaking book, William Felice demonstrates the necessity of approaching human rights in its full complexity, and how a comprehensive approach to the subject may bring about real change for people suffering from severe human rights violations."—**Sigrun I. Skogly, Lancaster University Law School**

"*The Global New Deal* makes a real contribution in presenting a coherent agenda for international action in a form which, I suspect and hope, will appeal to many students."—**Sir Richard Jolly, Institute of Development Studies, Sussex, United Kingdom**

NEW MILLENNIUM BOOKS
IN INTERNATIONAL STUDIES

Series Editors

Eric Selbin
Southwestern University

Vicki Golich
Metropolitan State College of Denver

Founding Editor

Deborah J. Gerner
University of Kansas

NEW MILLENNIUM BOOKS issue out of the unique position of the global system at the beginning of a new millennium in which our understandings about war, peace, terrorism, identity, sovereignty, security, and sustainability—whether economic, environmental, or ethical—are likely to be challenged. In the new millennium of international relations, new theories, new actors, and new policies and processes are all bound to be engaged. Books in the series are of three types: compact core texts, supplementary texts, and readers.

Titles in the Series

Global Backlash
Edited by Robin Broad

Globalization and Belonging
Sheila Croucher

The Global New Deal, 2nd ed.
William F. Felice

The Information Revolution and World Politics
Elizabeth C. Hanson

Sword & Salve
Peter J. Hoffman and Thomas G. Weiss

International Law in the 21st Century
Christopher C. Joyner

Elusive Security
Laura Neack

The New Foreign Policy, 2nd ed.
Laura Neack

International Negotiation in a Complex World, 3rd ed.
Brigid Starkey, Mark A. Boyer, and Jonathan Wilkenfeld

Global Politics as if People Mattered, 2nd ed.
Mary Ann Tétreault and Ronnie D. Lipschutz

Military-Civilian Interactions, 2nd ed.
Thomas G. Weiss

The Global New Deal

Economic and Social Human Rights in World Politics

Second Edition

William F. Felice

ROWMAN & LITTLEFIELD PUBLISHERS, INC.
Lanham • Boulder • New York • Toronto • Plymouth, UK

Published by Rowman & Littlefield Publishers, Inc.
A wholly owned subsidiary of The Rowman & Littlefield Publishing Group, Inc.
4501 Forbes Boulevard, Suite 200, Lanham, Maryland 20706
http://www.rowmanlittlefield.com

Estover Road, Plymouth PL6 7PY, United Kingdom

British Library Cataloguing in Publication Information Available

Library of Congress Cataloging-in-Publication Data

Felice, William F., 1950–
   The global new deal : economic and social human rights in world politics /
William F. Felice. — 2nd ed.
      p.   cm. — (New millennium books in international studies)
   Includes bibliographical references and index.
   ISBN 978-0-7425-6726-9 (cloth : alk. paper) — ISBN 978-0-7425-6727-6 (pbk. :
alk. paper) — ISBN 978-0-7425-6728-3 (electronic)
   1. Human rights. 2. Social rights. I. Title.
JC571.F424 2010
330—dc22

                                                                   2009043888

∞ ™ The paper used in this publication meets the minimum requirements of
American National Standard for Information Sciences—Permanence of Paper
for Printed Library Materials, ANSI/NISO Z39.48-1992.

Printed in the United States of America

Contents

Illustrations

Tables

Boxes

Acknowledgments to Second Edition

This second edition of *The Global New Deal* significantly develops the ideas presented in the first volume. In particular, the economic analysis of global public goods, economic equality, the capablities approach, and excessive military spending in relation to economic and social human rights fulfillment are more fully elaborated and explained. This noteworthy enrichment of the text was made possible by the insights and hard work of my friend and colleague Diana Fuguitt. As a professor of economics, Diana was able to articulate and analyze the economic arguments swirling around economic and social human rights. Diana not only spent hours with me debating these concepts, but significantly helped with editing and writing the text. She was of tremendous assistance on the entire manuscript, but in particular on chapters two and seven where she is the co-author. It has been a joy and privilege to work so closely with Diana Fuguitt, an economist of great depth and skill.

I am very grateful for the critical feedback and assistance I received from Tony Brunello on the entire manuscript. Tony's comments and suggestions in relation to the issues of environmental sustainability and ecological balance were particularly useful. I also want to thank Brent Pickett for his insightful critical review and his ongoing support and friendship.

I also wish to thank Rowman & Littlefield Publishers for pursuing the publication of this second edition. Editorial Director Susan McEachern has been an ongoing source of support. In addition, Editorial Assistant Carrie Broadwell-Tkach and Assistant Managing Editor Janice Braunstein guided the manuscript through the various stages in the production process. I am grateful to Susan, Carrie, and Janice for their professionalism and skilled editorial supervision.

I wish to acknowledge with gratitude permission to draw on the following previously published work: "Human Rights Disparities between

Europe and the United States: Conflicting Approaches to Poverty Prevention and the Alleviation of Suffering," *Cambridge Review of International Affairs* 19, no. 1 (March 2006); "Can World Poverty Be Eliminated," *Human Righs & Human Welfare* 3 (2003).

Acknowledgments to First Edition

It is a joy to publicly thank some of the many people who have helped me prepare this manuscript. My gratitude to all of them is immeasurable.

Robert L. Sanderson has been instrumental through every stage in the creation of this book. Only a loyal best friend would read and reread drafts and revisions of every chapter. Bob's wise counsel and advice provided the critical support needed to push the project to completion. He is a fountain of ideas and his recommendations enhanced and invigorated the manuscript.

Sigrun I. Skogly read each chapter with great thoughtfulness and care. I was the beneficiary of her expertise in international human rights law which informed her exceptional and constructive feedback.

Maurice Williams helped me sharpen my argument and strengthen the manuscript. His insights, drawn from his years of experience at the United Nations and at the U.S. State Department, helped me ground the ideas of *The Global New Deal* in the reality of real world politics.

My dear friend Nancy Mitchell also read the manuscript with care and provided critical editorial feedback. Nancy's continued interest in my work gives me inspiration and direction.

Michael J. Smith is not only one of the leading scholars in ethics and international affairs, but also selfless in his willingness to help train and teach others in the profession. His critique of the manuscript helped me to clarify some of the central ideas in *The Global New Deal* and present the thesis in a manner that will (hopefully) be accessible to a wide audience.

The staff of the Office of the High Commissioner for Human Rights in Geneva were extremely helpful to me in researching the UN human rights system. For their time and assistance, I wish to thank Päivikki Aaku, Virginia Dandan, Stefanie Grant, Cecilia Möller, Sylvie Saddier, and Kitty Arambulo Wilson.

It is my good fortune to work at a wonderful liberal arts college committed to its students. Eckerd College's devotion to creative pedagogy is unrivaled. This book was enriched through my interaction with my colleagues and, most importantly, with my students. I, in particular, appreciate the support I received from Dean Lloyd Chapin and my colleagues in political science and international relations and global affairs. I am indebted to Becky Blitch for her outstanding editing of the final draft.

Most of the research for this book was presented at the annual meetings of the International Studies Association (ISA). I am grateful to my ISA colleagues, in particular Mary B. Geske, Catherine V. Scott, and Michael Windfuhr, for providing substantial feedback and direction.

Jennifer Knerr, executive editor at Rowman & Littlefield, was a tremendous source of support from the very beginning of this project. I thank her for her professionalism and skilled editorial supervision. Editorial assistant Renee Legatt was also of enormous assistance in helping to sharpen the draft for publication. I am also indebted to production editor Jehanne Schweitzer for her hard work finalizing the manuscript. I am honored for the inclusion of this book in the distinguished Rowman & Littlefield series "New Millennium Books in International Studies."

I wish to acknowledge with gratitude permission to draw on the following previously published work: "The UN Committee on the Elimination of All Forms of Racial Discrimination: Race and Economic and Social Human Rights," *Human Rights Quarterly* 24, no. 1 (February 2002), "The Viability of the United Nations Approach to Economic and Social Human Rights in a Globalized Economy," *International Affairs* 75, no. 3 (July 2000), and "Militarism and Human Rights," *International Affairs* 74, no. 1 (January 1998).

It has taken over six years to write this book. My partner, Dale Lappe, has stood by me every step of this journey. I thank him for his patience and support.

A Note to the Reader on Terminology and Acronyms

As with any specialized field of study, International Relations has developed its own language of terms with specific meanings known only to those immersed in the discipline. To most readers, however, these expressions (e.g., rational choice, international regimes, structural constructivism, and so on) are often unintelligible and undecipherable. Compounding these communication difficulties are the dozens of specific acronyms used by scholars of international politics, including IGO, NGO, IFI, TNC, MNC, WTO, IMF, and so on. This problem is particularly acute in studies of the United Nations. Experts on the UN routinely refer to the numerous UN committees and treaties by their acronyms, including UNCTAD, ECOSOC, CESCR, CERD, CEDAW, CRC, CCPR, and so on. These references are clear to those working in the UN system and to experts in the field, but to the rest of the world, they are incomprehensible—or nearly so.

To reach beyond the academy, I have minimized the use of specialized terminology and acronyms. A list of all acronyms used in the book is provided here for easy reference. In addition, I refer to key UN human rights treaties and committees by subject matter and not acronym, as follows:

The Covenant on Economic, Social, and Cultural Rights (CESCR) becomes the Economic Rights Treaty. The CESCR Committee becomes the Economic Rights Committee.

The Covenant on Civil and Political Rights (CCPR) becomes the Political Rights Treaty. Its treaty body is the Human Rights Committee.

The Convention on the Elimination of All Forms of Racial Discrimination (CERD) becomes the Minority Rights Treaty. The CERD Committee becomes the Minority Rights Committee.

The Convention on the Elimination of All Forms of Discrimination against Women (CEDAW) becomes the Women's Rights Treaty. The CEDAW Committee becomes the Women's Rights Committee.

References to the UN's Women's Rights, Minority Rights, and Economic Rights Committees clarify the subjects under discussion. This eliminates confusing references to the CEDAW, CERD, and CESCR Committees.

KEY INTERNATIONAL TREATIES AND UN COMMITTEES

Treaty	Abbreviated Treaty Name	UN Treaty Body	Individual Complaint Mechanism
Covenant on Economic, Social and Cultural Rights (CESCR)	Economic Rights Treaty	Economic Rights Committee	Pending
Covenant on Civil and Political Rights (CCPR)	Political Rights Treaty	Human Rights Committee	Yes
Convention on the Elimination of All Forms of Racial Discrimination (CERD)	Minority Rights Treaty	Minority Rights Committee	Yes
Convention on the Elimination of All Forms of Discrimination against Women (CEDAW)	Women's Rights Treaty	Women's Rights Committee	Yes

Abbreviations and Acronyms

CCA	Common Country Assessments
CFA	Comprehensive Freshwater Assessment
CITES	Convention on International Trade in Endangered Species
CPM	capability poverty measure
CRS	Congressional Research Service
CSD	Commission on Sustainable Development
CSW	Commission on the Status of Women
CTBT	Comprehensive Test Ban Treaty
CWC	Convention on the Prohibition of the Development, Production, Stockpiling and Use of Chemical Weapons and their Destruction
DAWN	Development Alternatives with Women for a New Era
ECOSOC	Economic and Social Council of the United Nations
ESC	Economic Security Council
FAO	Food and Agriculture Organization
GAD	Gender and Development
GATT	General Agreement on Tariffs and Trade
GDI	Gender Development Index
GDP	gross domestic product
GEF	Global Environment Facility
GEM	Gender Empowerment Measure
GEMS	Global Environmental Monitoring System
GNI	gross national income
GNP	gross national product
HDI	Human Development Index
HPI	Human Poverty Index
HURIST	Human Rights Strengthening Project
ICFTU	International Confederation of Free Trade Unions
IFI	international financial institution
IGO	intergovernmental organization

ILO   International Labor Organization
IMF   International Monetary Fund
IPCC   Intergovernmental Panel on Climate Change
IPE   international political economy
IPF   Intergovernmental Panel on Forests
LDC   less developed country
MDGs   Millennium Development Goals
MNC   multinational corporation
NAFTA   North American Free Trade Agreement
NGO   nongovernmental organization
OHCHR   Office of the High Commissioner for Human Rights
OPCW   Organization for the Prohibition of Chemical Weapons
PPP   purchasing power parity
SAPs   structural adjustment programs
TNC   transnational corporation
UDHR   Universal Declaration of Human Rights
UN   United Nations
UNCTAD   UN Conference on Trade and Development
UNDAF   UN Development Assistance Framework
UNDP   UN Development Program
UNEP   UN Environment Program
UNESCO   UN Educational, Scientific, and Cultural Organization
UNHCR   UN High Commissioner for Refugees
UNHCHR   UN High Commissioner for Human Rights
UNICEF   UN Children's Fund
UNIFEM   UN Development Fund for Women
USTR   US Trade Representative
WAD   Women and Development
WCED   World Commission on Environment and Development
WEDO   Women's Environment and Development Organization
WEO   World Environment Organization
WHO   World Health Organization
WID   Women in Development
WTO   World Trade Organization
WWF   World Wide Fund for Nature

Introduction to Second Edition

The Elimination of World Poverty

In March 2009, British Prime Minister Gordon Brown called for a "global new deal whose impact can stretch from the villages of Africa to reforming the financial institutions of London and New York—and giving security to hard-working families in every country." The prime minister proclaimed the need to "work for a more stable world where we defeat not only global terrorism but global poverty, hunger and disease."[1] It was indeed refreshing to see the leader of Great Britain endorse the need for a "global new deal" to overcome preventable suffering. In many respects, Gordon Brown's speech continues a history of similar endorsements.

Since its founding, the member states of the United Nations have again and again, often with great flourish, declared their commitment to the elimination of global poverty. In its *Millennium Declaration* of September 2000, for example, the states of the UN declared that they would "spare no effort to free our fellow men, women and children from the abject and dehumanizing conditions of extreme poverty, to which more than a billion of them are currently subjected."[2] To realize this, these states adopted eight ambitious "Millennium Development Goals" (Mdgs) pledging by 2015 to cut income poverty and hunger in half, achieve universal primary education, eliminate gender disparity in primary and secondary schools, reduce child mortality by two-thirds, reduce maternal mortality by three-quarters, halt and reverse the spread of HIV/AIDS and malaria, halve the proportion of people without consistent access to safe drinking water, integrate principles of sustainable development, and open up a new global partnership for development which would include debt relief and increased aid. On 25 September 2008, world leaders again came together in New York to renew their commitments to achieve these MDGs by 2015.[3]

Similar commitments were earlier made at the 1995 World Summit for Social Development meeting in Copenhagen where the United Nations

1

Development Program (UNDP) presented "A World Social Charter," which included the following: "We are convinced that it is possible to overcome the worst aspects of poverty in our lifetime through collective effort. We jointly affirm that our first step towards this goal will be to design a global compact that ensures that no child goes without an education [and] no human being is denied primary health care or safe drinking water."[4] Other leading international organizations make similar declarations. For example, the institutional motto for the World Bank states, "Our dream is a world without poverty."[5] Conservatives, liberals and radicals all appear united in a commitment to end the massive suffering that is currently plaguing millions of innocents.

The UN has gone beyond merely declaring abstract, rhetorical and aspirational goals to alleviate suffering. There is now in place a large corpus of international law negotiated through the UN which seeks to define economic and social human rights. Through its "General Comments," the UN Committee on Economic, Social and Cultural Rights (hereafter Economic Rights Committee) has valiantly struggled to elaborate the core content of these often controversial rights claims. (These "General Comments" are summarized in chapter three.) These treaties and legal documents plainly enunciate states' obligations and legal duties toward their most vulnerable populations. This international human rights law is designed to prod states to take actions to end poverty. Despite this institutional framework, however, poverty persists. This book's goals are first, to clarify the huge distance between what international law (and morality) demand, on the one hand, and what is actually occurring among the poor and defenseless of the world, on the other. And second, I advance a series of specific recommendations, the "Global New Deal," for institutional reforms to reduce this chasm.

As discussed in chapter three, the UN makes the following distinction between economic and social rights: economic rights refer to the right to property, the right to work, and the right to social security. Social rights are those rights necessary for an adequate standard of living, including rights to education, health, shelter, and food. The right to education affirms free and compulsory primary education and equal access to secondary and higher education. The right to health ensures access to adequate health care, nutrition, sanitation, clean water and uncontaminated air. The right to shelter provides guarantees against forced eviction and access to a safe, habitable, and affordable home. The right to food requires that states cooperate in the equitable distribution of world food supplies and respect and assure the ability of people to feed themselves.

Despite global treaties and declarations affirming these economic and social human rights, I argue that too little has actually been done by states and international institutions to uphold the legal (and moral) obligations to improve the conditions faced by those trapped at the bottom of the global division of labor. The UN, other international organizations, non-state actors, and the states themselves have failed to implement workable public policies to meet the duties and obligations outlined in international law to respect, protect, and aid the deprived. In Latin America, for example, in the first years of the twenty-first century, 44 percent still live in poverty, and the number of unemployed workers more than doubled in a decade. Tens of millions of people in Latin American countries barely survive in the "informal economy" working as street vendors, begging and so on.[6] This lack of action by states and international organizations leads to cynicism about the UN, the World Bank, and other intergovernmental agencies. Normative proclamations and declarations to alleviate suffering seem to be continually ignored. This type of diplomatic inconsistency led Sartre to call such high-sounding principles as liberty, equality, and fraternity little more than "chatter, chatter."[7]

It is difficult to see, for example, how the UN will meet the 2015 deadline for the MDGs. In most areas of the world it will be impossible to achieve the overarching goal of reducing absolute poverty in half by 2015. The UN reported in 2008 that almost half of the developing world's population, some 2.5 billion people, lived without any improved sanitation, and more than one-third of the booming urban population in these countries lived in slum conditions. Despite all efforts thus far, one-quarter of all children in developing countries are "considered to be underweight and are at risk of having a future blighted by the long-term effects of undernourishment."[8]

The 2009 global economic recession has deepened the misery of the poor. The International Monetary Fund (IMF) estimates that this crisis will cost developing countries $1 trillion in lost growth. The World Bank believes that this will add more than 50 million people to the 2.6 billion currently struggling on less than $2 a day. Half of humanity, over 3 billion people, already live on less than $2.50 a day.[9] The World Bank predicted that the global economy would shrink in 2009 for the first time since the 1940s. The impact on the developing nations will be to squeeze them out of the credit markets, creating "massive financial shortfalls that could turn back the clock on poverty reduction by years." The bank report said that 94 out of 116 developing countries were hit by economic slowdowns in 2009 which created a wave of job losses.[10]

The global recession also led to higher food prices which, according to the UN World Food Program, pushed another 105 million people into hunger in the first half of 2009. Josette Sheeran, the food program's executive director, said the world faced "a human catastrophe" as the total number of hungry people around the world now totaled more than one billion. "This year [2009], we are clocking in, on average, four million new hungry people a week—urgently hungry," Ms. Sheeran said. Yet, despite these desperate conditions, the World Food Program had to cut food aid rations and shut down some operations in Africa and Asia because of the credit crunch.[11]

Is Global Poverty Getting Worse, or Better?

Nevertheless, despite the accuracy of these dismal outcomes, some analysts believe that the successes in poverty alleviation over the past few decades imply that the global community is on the right track and that a global new deal is thus not needed. The World Bank captured this sentiment in the title of their policy research working paper, "The Developing World Is Poorer Than We Thought, But No Less Successful in the Fight against Poverty."[12] The bank, highlighting overall trend lines which they believe indicate a proportional improvement in lowering poverty rates, argues that the international economic order is slowly working to improve the conditions of the most vulnerable. The World Bank estimated, for example, that the average proportion of people in developing countries living on less than $1 per day fell from 43 percent to 25 percent between 1990 and 1999. Extrapolating this trend to the year 2015, the Bank claims that the world appears to be on target to reach the UN goal of halving poverty between 1990 and 2015.[13] Some mainstream economists agree and argue that, although there is still too much economic suffering in the world, the global capitalist system is slowly helping both the rich and poor nations.[14] By implication, the types of institutional reforms advocated in *The Global New Deal* may not seem urgent. Perhaps, according to this viewpoint, such reforms could be supported as a means to speed up the process of poverty alleviation, but given the overall improvement in the condition of life for the most vulnerable populations, dramatic change in development planning and economic relations may not seem essential.

In fact, other economists go even further than the analysis of the World Bank in touting the success of economic globalization in poverty alleviation. For example, in a controversial study, Columbia University Professor Xavier Sala-i-Martin attempts to assess the standard of living that $1 and $2 per day provide in different developing countries. His estimates of actual purchasing power parity (PPP) differ dramatically from those of the World Bank. From his PPP estimates, Sala-i-Martin finds that the proportion of people living on what amounts to $1 per day fell from 20 percent of the world's population a quarter-century ago to just 5 percent at the beginning of the twenty-first century, while the $2 per day poverty rate fell from 44 percent to 19 percent.[15]

How are we to understand all of these statistics? Are conditions overall improving for the most vulnerable? And, most importantly, what does this $1 per day standard really indicate? Is it an accurate measure or does it fail to reflect the true depths of global poverty? The World Bank poverty analysis lends support to the current policy approaches toward economic globalization—often labeled the "Washington consensus" and/or "neo-liberalism." On the other hand, if conditions are either getting worse for the poor or improving at an intolerably slow rate, then this consensus should be challenged and new policies articulated.

In 2008, the World Bank itself issued a series of reports and statements that raised significant questions and concerns about their methodology for measuring global poverty. The World Bank has defined poverty as the inability to attain a minimum standard of living. The bank established the extreme poverty line of about $1 a day based on PPP—that is, after adjusting for cost of living differences, $1 a day was the average minimum consumption required for subsistence in the developing world. Keep in mind that this $1 a day figure did NOT mean what that $1 would buy when converted into a local currency. Rather, it was the equivalent of what $1 would buy in the United States—a local bus ride, a quart of milk, and so on. The World Bank claimed that this $1 a day figure captured the minimum subsistence levels across developing countries. This led to the 2000 estimate (published in the first edition of this book) of 1.2 billion people living in extreme poverty, on or below the minimum subsistence level of $1 a day.[16]

In 2008, the World Bank revealed that their methodology and analysis of global poverty over the years had been inaccurate, and significantly underestimated the numbers of people suffering severe deprivations. The bank claimed to have improved its economic estimates of global poverty because it could rely on more precise comparable price data which theoretically produced a more accurate picture of the cost of living in developing countries. It was this new data that led the Bank to establish a new poverty line of $1.25 a day, not $1.00 a day. In other words, it would take at least $1.25 a day, instead of $1.00 a day, to provide a poor person with minimum subsistence. This obviously meant that there were more poor people around the world than previously thought. In its report, the bank stated that in 2005 1.4 billion people, one in four in the developing world, were living on less than $1.25 a day in extreme poverty. Perhaps even more alarming, however, was that the Bank reported that half of humanity, 3.1 billion people, was living on less than $2.50 a day.

Yet, after acknowledging that the actual numbers of the poor were greater than previously thought, the World Bank went on to claim big successes in overcoming extreme poverty. While 1.4 billion people in the developing world were said to live below $1.25 a day in 2005, this was down from 1.9 billion in 1981. Chief Economist and Senior Vice President of Development Economics at the World Bank, Justin Lin, thus concluded: "The new data confirm that the world will likely reach the first Millennium Development Goal of halving the 1990 level of poverty by 2015 and that poverty has fallen by about one percentage point a year since 1981."[17]

Upon release of this data in 2008, the bank noted that the new estimates did "not yet reflect the potentially large adverse effects on poor people of rising food and fuel prices since 2005."[18] The bank thus wants us to look at trends that suggest success, rather than absolute numbers which may indicate a substantial and entrenched problem.

The critical issue, however, is the accuracy and utility of the World Bank's methodology for measuring global poverty. Is the $1.25 per day norm valid for comparing poverty among countries? Does it accurately establish a universal poverty line that permits cross-country comparisons?

Jan Vandemoortele states that the main problem with this World Bank international poverty norm is that it violates the standard definition of income poverty—that is, "a person is considered poor when he/she does not reach a minimum level of economic wellbeing set *by society*."[19] Economic and social human rights depend upon the realization of a basket of basic necessities and public goods, such as clean water, electricity, urban transport, and essential medicines. As a result, more affluent countries set a higher poverty line as that basket is more expensive. The poverty line cannot be disassociated from the average standard of living of a society.

David Gordon explains that the World Bank acknowledges this approach through its statements that a measure of poverty must comprise two elements: "the expenditure necessary to buy a minimum standard of nutrition and other basic necessities and a further amount that varies from country to country, reflecting the cost of participating in the everyday life of society." The first element is relatively straightforward and can be calculated by "looking at the prices of foods that make up the diets of the poor." But the second element is much more subjective. For example, "in some countries indoor plumbing is a luxury, but in others it is a 'necessity.'" Despite this acknowledgment, the World Bank does not take this "second element" into account in its $1.25 per day determination of poverty.[20]

Thus, the World Bank's global estimates are misleading. Vandemoortele states that the use of the $1 per day (now $1.25 per day) poverty norm "underestimates the extent of global poverty; at the same time it overestimates progress in reducing income poverty." He argues that these distortions could be avoided by using national poverty lines which provide more meaningful information.[21] As a result, Wolfgang Sachs and others reject the formulations of "poverty" and "development" as defined and elaborated by the World Bank.[22]

Thomas Pogge also believes that the poverty estimates provided by the World Bank and Xavier Sala-i-Martin are misleading. Pogge, Howard Nye, and Sanjay Reddy note that the general PPP's utilized by the World Bank and Sala-i-Martin are related to average price levels for all commodities, weighted by their share in international expenditure. However, a poor person is not concerned with commodities such as airline tickets or pedicures. A low-income household must concentrate on basic foodstuffs and other necessities. A household should be determined "poor" not in relation to the local price level of commodities in general, but to the local cost of a basket of necessities (food, water, shelter and so on).[23] Complete figures do not exist to give us an accurate view of the costs of what poor people actually buy. However, based on the cost of bread and cereals, Reddy and Pogge estimate that the World Bank's analysis may underestimate the number of the world's people living in absolute poverty by some 32 to 59 percent.[24]

In addition, scholars note that the World Bank's figures used to support the claim of overall "success" in the fight against poverty are highly influenced by China. According to the bank, rapid economic growth in China has reduced income poverty, with 650 million fewer people in extreme poverty in 2005 than in 1980. Yet, according to Roberto Bissio, "Since those tables also say that the total number of extremely poor people in the world decreased by 600 million, in reality, according to the World Bank, the absolute number of extremely poor (but not its proportion to the growing total population) actually increased in the rest of the world." The reliability and significance of the World Bank's income poverty statistics from China are also questioned. For example, during a transition to a market economy, Bissio notes that income may grow without peoples' lives changing. "Think of a commune system where millions of peasants were self-sufficient. They now receive a salary and have an income, but they also have to pay for the food they used to get free." In fact, from a perspective of economic and social human rights, the rapid overall decline in basic health and education services in modern China is disturbing and a potential violation of international law. Such trends make it difficult to point to China as a successful model of economic development.[25]

Furthermore, including China in the global averaging hides the fact that poverty and inequalities are either remaining static or increasing elsewhere on the planet. During the first decade of the twenty-first century, the rate of progress to meet the MDGs slowed down and the targets that seemed perhaps achievable earlier are now seemingly impossible to attain. It is thus difficult to accept the World Bank's optimistic view on the developing world's success in the fight against poverty.

In fact, the overall utility and usefulness of the World Bank's statistics on global poverty must be questioned. In 2000, the bank declared that 1.2 billion people lived on less than $1 a day, and this figure became the global yardstick to measure poverty. The "$1 a day" approach, and the figure of 1.2 billion, was massively circulated and utilized in countless PhD dissertations and masters theses. As late as June 2008, the World Bank continued to endorse this approach and stated that "progress has been made. Fifteen years ago, one of every three people lived on less than one dollar a day; today, that figure has been reduced to one in five. Yet one billion people still live in extreme poverty." Then suddenly in August 2008 the bank announced that their poverty estimates had been wrong and that there were really 1.4 billion extremely poor people in 2005, an increase of almost 50 percent! Despite this shocking announcement, no serious call for a reassessment of poverty programs ensued; no emergency plea for a global new deal or special measures was heard. Few criticisms of the World Bank entered the mainstream press. Yet, had a government made a 50 percent error in reported unemployment or inflation rates, it is hard not to envision that the consequences would have been swift and severe.[26]

If the $1.25 per day norm is both inaccurate and misleading, thus overestimating poverty reduction and underestimating actual preventable suffering, is there an alternative, more promising, measure of poverty? (This suffering is termed "preventable" since, as discussed throughout *The Global New Deal*, there are workable and feasible policies to overcome global poverty, hunger, and disease, and thus this human pain and agony can be prevented.) The UNDP's "human development approach" (discussed in chapter three) has been particularly helpful in designing new indices and measurements of basic economic and social human rights. Drawing on the work of Nobel laureate Amartya Sen, the human development approach incorporates a capabilities perspective—that is, poverty is the absence of opportunities to develop some basic capabilities to function. Sen's capability functions include being well nourished, adequately clothed and sheltered, able to avoid preventable morbidity, and able to partake in the life of the community (see chapter two below). Poverty thus cannot be reduced to a single dimension, like a $1.25 per day norm. This change in focus dramatically challenges the argument that "progress" is being made in defeating preventable poverty. For example, in 1996 the World Bank estimated that approximately 900 million people in the developing world—21 percent of the total—were income-poor and lived below the poverty line. The UNDP, on the other hand, calculated the percentage of people who lacked basic human capabilities in health, nourishment, and education. The corresponding figure for capability poverty in 1996 was 1.6 billion, or 37 percent of the people in the developing countries. In Pakistan in 1996, only one-third of the population was income poor, but more than three-fifths were capability poor. That same year in Bangladesh, 55 million people were income poor, but 89 million were capability poor.[27] In 2000 the UNDP estimated that in over a third of surveyed developing countries, more than 33 percent of the people suffered from conditions of extreme human poverty.[28] And in 2006, the UNDP reported for all developing countries that one in two people—2.6 billion in all—lacked access to adequate sanitation.[29] These statistics unfortunately seem to indicate that contrary to the optimism expressed by the World Bank, the global trend is for mass poverty to persist.

Poverty and Economic and Social Human Rights

The Global New Deal is framed within the world movement to establish international economic and social human rights. Scholars have linked economic and social rights claims to meeting basic human needs and the alleviation of global poverty. Johan Galtung, for example, locates human needs inside individual human beings, whereas human rights are situated between them. He justifies economic and social rights by their relationship to fulfilling human needs. To identify human needs, he asks, "What is it you cannot do without?" This human needs approach places the economic human rights debate firmly among the suffering, where the nonsatisfaction of minimum subsistence needs has drastic consequences.[30] In a similar vein, Christian Bay uses the analogy of any reputable hospital which would serve the most severely injured and in need first. The claims of those in global poverty deserve preferred treatment. Basic human needs are powerful facts, not just philosophical speculation, and should inform the content of economic and social human rights. Bay writes, "Provided we take the universality of basic human needs and of need-based rights seriously enough, we may envisage an expanding world-wide human rights movement as a viable third way toward a more human and sustainable world, post-liberal and post-Marxist."[31]

With the development of the idea of "basic rights," Henry Shue presented perhaps the most influential case for economic and social human rights. Shue argues passionately and effectively for "subsistence" as a basic right. All development programs and economic theories must ensure a minimum floor of economic security for all citizens. In fact, all human rights are contingent upon these development rights being respected. All people are entitled to make minimum reasonable demands upon the rest of humanity to have basic rights met. Shue writes, "Basic rights are the morality of the depths. They specify the line beneath which no one is to be allowed to sink." Subsistence rights meet basic human needs and are essential because without them other rights cannot be realized. For all human beings to be able to fully function in today's world, their subsistence rights must be respected. Shue calls this the transitivity principle for rights: "If everyone has a right to y, and the enjoyment of x is necessary for the enjoyment of y, then everyone also has a right to x."[32]

Arguing along similar lines, Thomas Pogge links human rights fulfillment to the alleviation of poverty. "Piercing together the current global record, we find that most of the current massive underfulfillment of human rights is more or less directly connected to poverty. The connection is direct in the case of basic social and economic rights, such as the right to a standard of living adequate for the health and well-being of oneself and one's family, including food, clothing, housing and medical care."[33] Pogge also situates the problem of global poverty within a framework of international human rights. He links human flourishing and well-being to global economic justice and moral universalism. Eradicating systemic poverty, he argues, will involve acting on a new understanding of global responsibility and breaking out of stifling conceptions of "sovereignty" and nationalism, and enacting a series of modest and feasible reforms in international law and organization. He documents, for example, the ways in which the current global structures reinforce and perpetuate undemocratic and elitist practices in the less-developed countries (LDCs). He cites two "international privileges" that benefit the developed countries and the elites in the LDCs at the expense of the poor populations of resource-rich developing countries: an international borrowing privilege and an international resource privilege. When a legitimate or corrupt regime comes to power in an LDC, it is immediately given the privilege to borrow in the county's name (international borrowing privilege) and freely dispose of the country's natural resources (international resource privilege). In fact, the mere existence of these international privileges provides powerful incentives to corrupt local elites to seize power arbitrarily.[34]

The international borrowing privilege is, perhaps, the most insidious. It puts a country's full credit and borrowing at the disposal of even the most ruthless rulers. This privilege is indifferent to how these rulers came to power, thus providing a strong incentive for coup attempts. And even when the dictatorship is overthrown, the new government is saddled with the huge debts of their former oppressors. Pogge convincingly demonstrates the ways in which the global economic order, through the granting of these two "privileges," promotes authoritarian rulers and contributes to the persistence of severe poverty and the denial of economic and social human rights to the world's poorest people. The history of international interactions with the Congo, Nigeria, and São Tomé and Príncipe provide dramatic evidence to support Pogge's analysis.[35]

Pogge's moral critique of the global economic system is compelling and demonstrates many ways in which the structure of international economics and politics causes suffering. With this knowledge, it is hard to deny the moral and legal duty to act to end that suffering. Yet how do we motivate the nations of the world to end the unjust "international borrowing privilege" and the "international resource privilege"? How do we generate the political will and action to implement the many bold global initiatives necessary to end preventable suffering? The argument presented in *The Global New Deal* is that there is currently no adequate institutional framework for world economic and social governance. Neither markets nor national governments satisfactorily take into account what happens beyond individual state borders. However, the success of local and national policy proposals to alleviate poverty often depends, to a significant extent, upon the international regulation of markets, capital and labor. Interest rates, commodity prices, and capital flows, for example, often cannot be controlled nationally and frequently disrupt local efforts to alleviate poverty. *The Global New Deal* thus calls for a strengthening of the existing human rights monitoring and enforcement mechanisms in Geneva (outlined in chapter 3) and the creation of a new Economic Security Council (ESC) (outlined in chapter 9). These international organizations could focus like a laser on economic and social human rights and could act on sensible ideas like those proposed by Pogge and others. The Office of the High Commissioner for Human Rights and the ESC could demand that states and international institutions be more attentive to the human rights implications of their policies. In the world today, there are serious consequences to states that violate the rules of global trade as established and enforced by the World Trade Organization. The ESC could establish similar viable enforcement mechanisms to create real motivations for states to implement policies which respect, protect, and fulfill economic and social human rights.

The MDGs provide a clear example of why such institutional reforms and actions are needed. As noted above, the UN has pledged to work toward the alleviation of poverty through the adoption of the MDGs. The Millennium Project, a large network of policy makers, practitioners, and experts led by Professor Jeffrey Sachs, was established to monitor and promote these goals. A Millennium Campaign was launched to mobilize civil society and efforts were made to produce national MDG reports in LDCs. Furthermore, every major development agency and International Financial Institutions (IFI) focused on the MDGs as did the developed nations with a renewed commitment to increase aid to and lower the debt of LDCs.

Tremendous overlap exists between this MDG effort and the variety of poverty reduction strategies integrated into development planning at the international level, often monitored by the UNDP, the World Bank, and the IMF. Concern has been expressed about the need for better coordination between agencies and enhanced monitoring. Yet, as Philip Alston points out, "none of these reviews takes account of the fact that there already exists a relatively sophisticated and comprehensive system of monitoring linked to the international human rights regime."[36] Indeed, the current human rights reporting mechanisms established in Geneva, combined with a new ESC, could effectively move the MDG agenda forward.

As demonstrated in chapters 3, 5 and 6, the Economic Rights Committee, Minority Rights Committee, and Women's Rights Committee have all established reasonably effective monitoring procedures in relation to major human rights treaties. The institutional framework is now in place to hold governments accountable to follow through on their human rights legal obligations and the MDGs. *The Global New Deal* calls for a variety of measures to strengthen these committees and the Office of the High Commissioner for Human Rights. Instead of creating new bureaucracies, these existing international bodies are the logical place for effective monitoring of state efforts to achieve the MDGs. These human rights committees, for example, already examine each state's individual efforts in the areas of economic and social rights, minority rights, and women's rights. The information on MDG progress could be placed in the core document that each country already submits to the treaty bodies. Such a procedure would ensure not only that these UN committees follow up on national strategies to achieve the MDGs, but would open up this process to civil society and NGOs. These professional human rights committees have come to rely heavily on input and accurate information from the NGO community. The utilization of this human rights machinery would attach an appropriate degree of urgency for states to fulfill the MDGs.[37]

Since 2015 is around the corner, it is probably too late to strengthen the UN human rights regime in these ways to strongly guide the realization of the MDG agenda to meet the time goal. But, the MDG project provides a clear example of how, through the institutional reforms advocated in *The Global New Deal*, progress toward the alleviation of suffering could perhaps be both better measured and attained.

The Global New Deal focuses on practical and doable policies and actions that state and non-state actors can take to respect, protect, and fulfill economic and social human rights. These policy directions flow from an appreciation and understanding of the link between these human rights claims and key economic arguments justifying governmental intervention in the market. In chapter two, this new edition contains an extensive discussion of the following economic and social human rights as global public goods: basic education, a healthy environment, food and water, primary health care and sanitation, and housing. As discussed below, market mechanisms alone often fail to provide socially optimal quantities of these public goods. The well-recognized and accepted logic justifying government action to provide for such public goods as national defense and police protection should also apply to these economic and social human needs as well.

The fundamental premise underlining *The Global New Deal* is that through a legal rights-based, sustainable development framework, the global community has the means and measures to alleviate global poverty. This book is an attempt to articulate the linkages between international human rights law, international organization, and economic policy at the global and national levels. The "Global New Deal," outlined in chapter 9, articulates the policies and programs states can undertake to end preventable suffering and preventable deaths.

1

Global Policy Choices

There Are Alternatives

I have a privileged life; I am a teacher. It is hard to imagine a more rewarding and fulfilling job. It is a joy to go to work. As a teacher of International Relations, I am able to engage young women and men on the crucial issues confronting the planet. My students are demanding and will not accept shallow explanations or superficial theories. They challenge me to be clear, relevant, and thoughtful. Their contemporary and fresh approaches to life and knowledge continuously force me to reevaluate my thinking and to modify my understandings. This ongoing intellectual and human colloquy with students enriches my life immeasurably.

To my dismay, however, over the last eighteen years I have also witnessed a very disturbing phenomenon. The vitality and richness of youth that these students bring to the classroom is tempered by an overwhelming cynicism and despair about the possibility of bringing about positive fundamental change. Conservative, liberal, and radical students express again and again the futility of challenging an economic and political system dominated by corporate power. To these students, the corruption of our political system is beyond repair. The students search in vain for a Kantian "moral politician" who is not groveling before the wealthy class; a politician not eager to serve elite interests.

Students recognize the real problems that confront humanity. They are outraged by the callous destruction of our ecosystem. They are shocked by the needless suffering occurring in every country as a result of preventable poverty, preventable malnutrition, and preventable disease. Yet, many of these students believe that nothing can be done to stop this anguish. These students believe that the current economic and political system, responsible for a great deal of human misery, will never really change. They argue that perhaps some small steps can be taken and some examples of gross maleficence can be exposed, but nothing beyond minor reform is possible. Nothing can be done to change the system overall. These students are profoundly cynical and see little hope in working for fundamental structural change. There is too much money involved, and these powerful interests are committed to the status quo. These students, therefore, consider it utopian and foolish to talk about creating policy to end world hunger, create global peace, or maintain ecological balance. There is no room for such dreamy "idealist" and "utopian" thinking in the "realist" minds of many of today's college students.

As a teacher, I am frustrated by this pessimism. It limits the imagination. It prevents one from looking at feasible policy options to create necessary change. It can block true understanding. Let me give an example.

According to the World Bank, in 2005 half of the world's people—3.1 billion—lived on less than $2.50 a day, and 1.4 billion—close to one-fourth—lived on less than $1.25 a day. In poor countries, as many as 50 percent of all children are malnourished.[1] The United Nations Children's Fund (UNICEF) in 2008 noted with dismay that the deaths of more than 26,000 children every day from mainly preventable causes go largely unnoticed.[2]

Now imagine that 26,000 people died every day from plane crashes or buildings collapsing. The outrage would be palpable! Demands would be made for the government to intervene to stop the slaughter. Public policy would be quickly enacted to make planes and buildings safer. Corporations manufacturing planes and construction companies erecting buildings would be held legally accountable to higher standards. These public policy changes would happen quickly and lives would be saved. These attempts to craft public policy to guarantee the construction of safer planes and buildings would not be labeled "idealist" nor "utopian." Instead, they would be viewed as "realistic" approaches to ending a tragic loss of life and essential to the security of the society.

Yet, the attempts today to craft public policy to end the daily deaths of 26,000 children from preventable causes is labeled "idealist" and "utopian." There is no sense of urgency to end the pain and suffering of these innocents. This lethargy stems in part from ingrained, comfortable, "common sense" ideology—that is, the poor will always be with us, we are doing all we can, scarcity is a fact, there is nothing that can be done, and so on. But more disturbing, this acceptance of unnecessary human misery comes from an overwhelming sense of the futility of challenging existing structures of economic and political power. This sense of the impotence and uselessness of challenging enduring arrangements of power and wealth infects many young people today.

At the end of his final exam in my International Political Economy course, a student wrote to me the following note:

> You have taught me that solving the problems of economic globalization will involve "thinking outside the box." Global priorities have to include ensuring that human rights apply to all (ending all forms of discrimination!), demilitarization of the planet, and the preservation of the environment. But I don't honestly see how we can make the jump from here to there. Economic principles of efficiency and order will never be sacrificed or compromised to achieve common global public goods like human rights and environmental balance. The Bretton Woods system and the great powers would have to restructure their economic and foreign policies to allow for such change. Unfortunately, I don't see that happening. I will try to cling onto the hope your class gave me, but I fear I will lose it very quickly.

This student clearly wanted to believe in humane alternatives, but he feared that these options were probably not viable. But at least he was open to looking at alternatives. Many other students quickly reject such global reforms as utopian nonsense. When I try to show that in fact we can end needless suffering in the world, these students look at me as if I am a relic from the 1960s. The demise of "socialism" in the former Soviet Union reinforced the perception among many that current economic and political models of development are the only game in town. The daily message too often absorbed from the *New York Times* and the *Wall Street Journal* is that "there is no alternative"[3] to the neoliberal economic model (discussed in chapter 2) dominating the post–Cold War world. Students are bombarded with this message: *There is no alternative to the existing global economic system and model of development. It is fool-hardy and counterproductive to challenge the fundamentals of the current economic development model. Unfortunately, there are some who won't benefit from the "creative destruction" that accompanies economic globalization. But since there are more winners than losers—and particularly since we are among the winners—we should all support this process. The protestors in Seattle against globalization and the World Trade Organization (WTO) should stop fighting history. And besides, no one has come up with anything better. The system may not be perfect, but it's the best that human beings have created.* This is the message that our young people are indoctrinated with over and over. It preaches the wisdom of accepting the status quo and of working for only small, minor reforms. It teaches the folly of conceiving of, let alone promoting, fundamental change.

Students recognize the failures of the current system. They are concerned about economic and social human rights, ecological balance, and peace. They speak out and act for equal rights for women, ethnic minorities, and gays and lesbians. They volunteer by the thousands to help the homeless and feed the needy. Yet beneath these noble actions is a quiet acceptance of the way things are. Since there are no alternatives to existing structures, the most that can be done is individual action to try to protect the vulnerable. Volunteering for Habitat for Humanity or the local soup kitchen is to be applauded. But if we are serious about ending suffering we must go beyond volunteerism and charity.

So let me scream out: There are alternatives! There are policy options. There are ways in which we as a global community can end needless suffering. The goal of this book is to address the quandary of my political economy student who could not see the path from here to there. This book hopefully provides a direction for viable structural reform to protect those left behind by the global economy. There are policy options for states to implement to protect the vulnerable and to end needless suffering. This book attempts to define that global public policy and to articulate the conditions for the fulfillment of economic and social human rights for all.

Quoting Albert Einstein, a poster on campus recently proclaimed, "Imagination is more important than knowledge." Yes, imagination is vital. We do need to expand our imaginations to break out of the limitations of the current era. We need to open our minds and imaginations to the idea that as a human species we can do better. It is unfortunate that the "great debates" of the twentieth century, including the viability and validity of liberation theology, socialist humanism, and moral incentives, seem to have ended with the end of the century. Few people living in developed countries now imagine a world different from the present. A recent exposition at the New York Public Library on visionaries, futurology, and imaginative alternative lifestyles ended in the 1980s. This must change. The creation of a pathway toward global humane governance will require us to rediscover our creativity and break open our imaginations.

Nevertheless, the poster is misleading: Imagination is not more important than knowledge. Rather, imagination and knowledge are equally vital. Knowledge provides the means to achieve our visions and inspirations. Our ability to craft effective public policy depends on our knowledge of the successes and limitations of existing policies and programs. On a global level, this means examining the work of the existing international organizations committed to ending human suffering. The work of the specialized agencies of the UN is a particular focus of this book because of these agencies' stated commitment to the protection and fulfillment of economic and social human rights. The insights gained from a critique of the development experience of the UN will enhance the proposals for global policy reform. Imagination alone can be utopian. Knowledge and imagination combined can produce results.

What are some of the problems in the global economy that public policy must address to protect economic and social human rights? The examples leap out from the daily news:

- Slavery has become a defining characteristic of the new global economy. The organization Anti-Slavery International defines the common characteristics of a slave as someone "forced to work—through physical or mental threat; owned or controlled by an 'employer', usually through mental or physical abuse or threatened abuse; dehumanised, treated as a commodity or bought and sold as 'property'; and physically constrained or has restrictions placed on his/her freedom of movement." These slaves receive no pay (or very little), their movements are monitored, and they have no say over working hours, holidays, or rest. Using this definition, the International Labor Organization (ILO) estimates that that there are approximately 12.3 million people enslaved today, while the NGO Free the Slaves puts the figure at 27 million. In addition, tens of thousands of children are transported from country to country in West Africa to fill a demand for cheap labor. The ILO reported in 2004 that at least 218 million children, instead of receiving schooling, worked in mines, factories, and plantations, with 126 million of them doing dangerous jobs, often in conditions of slavery.[4]
- Bangladesh offers the global economy some of the world's cheapest labor. The 3,300 garment factories in the country are inadequately regulated and are among "the worst sweatshops ever to haunt the human conscience." It is the "wretched of the earth who do the world's tailoring." Workers toil from twelve to eighteen hours a day with few breaks. Holidays and overtime pay are a myth. Workers are expected to work virtually every day of the year. Most wages range from $25 to $50 a month—or as little as 6 cents an hour, with children earning less. If workers complain, they are locked out of the factories. A fire at one of these garment factories in November 2000 killed 52 workers, as 1,250 people hurried to a stairway to escape the flames. At the bottom of the stairs was a locked folding gate. The fifty-two victims were trapped in the dark stairway amid screaming, pushing, and frantic men, women, and children fleeing the inferno. The National Garment Workers' Association (NGWA) reports in 2009 that conditions in these factories remain brutal. Approximately 1.5 million jobs remain dependent on export-oriented textile and garment industries producing goods for the European and North American markets. Yet, according to the NGWA, unskilled workers in the garment sector receive a mere 800 taka a month, about $14 and are still forced to work 14–16 hours a day, and often throughout the night. Bangladesh has reportedly received a $4.3 billion economic

boost from its apparel industry. Yet, this "economic boost" has not trickled down to the people of Bangladesh. These sweatshops consolidate poverty and brutalize human beings. This is exploitation, not "development."[5]

- As China enters the global economy and meets the demands of the G8 and the WTO to liberalize its economy, it is dismantling state-supported social services. As a result, huge numbers of China's 800 million rural residents are in a medical free fall. A side effect of the market-oriented changes is that the free rural clinics have disintegrated, and the famous system of "barefoot doctors" has vanished. According to the UN, health costs in China increased between 400 and 500 percent from 1990 to 1997. Medical care is now so costly rural citizens have stopped seeing doctors altogether, enduring pain, chronic infection, and the risks of childbirth at home. Health statistics are now beginning to reflect this lack of access to basic health care. Infant mortality, which had been declining for almost forty years, is beginning to creep up. The UN reports that the number of tuberculosis cases has quadrupled in the last fifteen years. A simple hospital stay could cost more than the yearly income of most peasants. *The Economist* reported in 2007 that these alarming trends have continued throughout the first decade of the twenty-first century, with the public health system in rural China "now in tatters." Riots have now become commonplace as the rural poor face prohibitive costs for health care and education. "In some parts of China, more than 60% of those in dire poverty have been driven there by medical expenses."[6]

- UNICEF reported in 2008 that the number of children worldwide dying before reaching their fifth birthday totaled 9.7 million. In the developing world, these millions of children die every year from ailments that are easily treatable and rarely fatal in developed societies. "One in five child deaths—2 million annually—are due to pneumonia . . . , and diarrheal diseases account for another 2 million. Forty percent of child deaths occur among newborns, most from severe infections, birth asphyxia (difficulty breathing), or complications due to preterm birth. Measles, malaria, and HIV/AIDS together account for 15 percent of child deaths. The interventions necessary to prevent these deaths are well established."[7]

- The ILO reported in 2000 that 75 percent of the world's estimated 150 million unemployed workers have no jobless benefits. By 2007 the ILO estimated that the number of unemployed workers had risen to 190 million. As economic globalization has accelerated, even the most generous countries have been cutting assistance to the unemployed. The ILO notes that these cutbacks represent a significant threat to economic development because they undermine the financial security of employed workers. These trends worsened with the global recession of 2008–2009, with the ILO Director-General Juan Somavia estimating that the number of unemployed could rise to 210 million by early 2010.[8]

* How is one to react to the pharmaceutical companies' attempts to prevent the distribution of life-saving drug therapy to the millions of people with AIDS in developing countries? In December 2000, the UN reported that 25.3 million people in sub-Saharan Africa had AIDS or HIV, the virus that causes AIDS. In 2000, 2.4 million people in the region died of AIDS. Yet, the Agreement on Trade-Related Aspects of Intellectual Property Rights prevents states from distributing cheaper generic AIDS drugs. The big pharmaceutical companies claimed that this patent protection, which enabled them to charge exorbitantly high prices, was essential to cover start-up costs and pay for innovation. Yet, many drugs are initially developed with government money with no risk to the transnational corporation (TNC). These huge pharmaceutical TNCs, after taking little or no financial risk, are then able to gouge AIDS patients for incredible profits. The sick in poor countries where these drugs are unaffordable are left to die. Only a sustained effort by nongovernmental organizations and AIDS activists forced the pharmaceutical industry to drop its effort to prevent South Africa from importing cheaper anti-AIDS drugs and other medicines.[9] These pharmaceutical TNCs seemed more concerned with profits and marketing than research and innovation. Just examine the distribution of revenues of GlaxoSmithKline in 2000, the world's largest manufacturer of AIDS medicines: 37.9 percent on marketing and administrative costs, 27.8 percent on profits, 20.4 percent on manufacturing, raw materials, and related production expenses, and 13.9 percent on research.[10] After significant pressure from the South African government, the European Parliament, and hundreds of thousands of individuals from around the world, GlaxoSmithKline backed down and granted permission for the production of a major South African generic alternative to AIDS drugs, including AZT. And, more recently, UNITAID, an international drug purchase facility, partnered with the Clinton Foundation in 2006 and began negotiating with manufacturers to lower the price of AIDS drugs and supply them to 70 developing countries. By 2009, they announced the successful reduction in the price of a convenient one-daily pill by 30 percent compared to the price they had negotiated in 2008. These groups have also managed to reduce the price of the leading child HIV treatment regimens by 64 percent and the leading adult regimens by 43 percent in low-income countries.[11]

This list could go on and on. Pick up today's newspaper and add to this list yourself. Chances are you will quickly find another example of the

negative impact of economic globalization on the lives of the most vulnerable. You will probably also find numerous examples of the destruction of
such global public goods as clean air and clean water accompanying economic development and industrialization on all continents (see chapters 2
and 4). Our leaders seem unwilling either to aid the vulnerable or to protect our fragile ecosystem from the onslaught of destructive global forces.

Perhaps we need to modify the criteria we use to evaluate our public
officials. Politicians should be judged on the basis of their actions to
protect the most weak and vulnerable. Those politicians who let child
poverty and homelessness rise on their watch or who do nothing while
controllable diseases devastate poor communities should be voted out of
office. Leaders who ignore the negative impacts of globalization on the
weak while continuing to subsidize the rich and powerful should be sent
packing. Economic and social human rights should apply to all and not
just to the winners in the global economy. In addition, our leaders should
act to protect global public goods, including environmental sustainability
and the preservation of the global commons. It is in the self-interest of
all (all classes, all races, and all states) for these global public goods to
be realized. It is not an exaggeration to state that the very survival of the
human species is linked to the protection of global public goods.

International Economic and Social Human Rights

International human rights law defines economic and social human rights
(see chapter 3). Economic rights refer to the right to property, the right to
work, and the right to security of income. Social rights, on the other hand,
are those necessary for an adequate standard of living, including rights to
food, shelter, health, and education.

During the Cold War, many Western countries considered economic
and social human rights to be socialist propaganda. Since the end of the
Cold War, the category of economic and social human rights is still often
criticized by academics and practitioners in the developed world for its
supposed "vague" content and "unrealistic" claims. The U.S. government, for example, refuses to ratify the International Covenant on Economic, Social and Cultural Rights (hereafter Economic Rights Treaty).
Many of these critics contend that these economic and social claims are
merely aspirational goals achievable only in some future, utopian world.
It is thus misleading, according to these critics, to argue that these economic and social objectives represent valid human rights claims.

The UN Committee on Economic, Social and Cultural Rights (hereafter
Economic Rights Committee) has spent a great deal of time defining the
core content of the claims articulated in the Economic Rights Treaty.[12] The
Economic Rights Committee attempts to establish a minimum threshold

of compliance that should be achieved by all states regardless of their economic situation. The burden of proof lies with the state. States must prove to the Economic Rights Committee that they have mobilized their resources to meet the needs of the most vulnerable, and that any remaining poverty, destitution, and hunger are due to factors beyond their control. The Economic Rights Committee thus works to establish universal criteria to hold states accountable for the economic and social rights of their citizens.

Yet problems persist. It is exceedingly difficult to establish minimum thresholds and standards for economic and social rights at the international level. Are different criteria to be applied to resource-poor as opposed to resource-rich countries? Should the minimum level be raised in those countries that have the ability to meet a higher level of demand? And which actors are responsible to meet these rights obligations? In a globalized economy, the behavior of transnational actors—TNCs, international financial institutions (IFIs), and so on—often has a direct impact on the well-being and/or destitution of a population.

The Global New Deal focuses on the practical steps that state and nonstate actors can take to fulfill their duties under the Economic Rights Treaty to protect the vulnerable and to respect, protect, and fulfill economic and social human rights. Chapter 2 examines economic and social rights through the lens of international political economy (IPE) and introduces three concepts central to the achievement of these rights: global public goods, economic equality, and the capabilities approach. Chapter 3 reviews the UN's approach to economic and social human rights, with a particular focus on the work of the Economic Rights Committee. Chapter 4 discusses the priority of ecosystem protection and sustainability within all growth strategies. The debates surrounding a human rights approach to ecological balance are summarized and the work of the UN Environment Program, the Commission on Sustainable Development, and the Global Environment Facility are reviewed. Chapter 5 analyzes the degree of racial bias in global economics and reviews the work of the UN Committee on the Elimination of All Forms of Racial Discrimination (hereafter Minority Rights Committee). Chapter 6 turns to issues of gender and women's rights and the work of the UN Committee on the Elimination of All Forms of Discrimination against Women (hereafter Women's Rights Committee). Feminist theories of IPE are critiqued in relation to approaches to women's rights in international law. Chapter 7 addresses the impact of military spending on economic growth and the achievement of economic and social human rights. Chapter 8 examines the negative impact on the poor caused by the resistance of the United States to adopting economic and social human rights. And finally, the public policy proposals of the Global New Deal are presented in chapter 9. The Global New Deal is a set of recommendations for global public policy designed to facilitate the achievement of economic and social human rights. Such action at the global level, through international law and international organization, is needed to help all individual states adjust policies to protect the vulnerable from the often negative externalities that accompany economic globalization.

The Global New Deal identifies the policies that state and nonstate actors (TNCs, IFIs, and so on) can pursue in these specific arenas—IPE, the UN and international organizations, the environment, race, gender, military spending, and the US and human rights law—to implement economic and social human rights. Achieving economic and social human rights depends on addressing all of these areas as progress in one is dependent on progress in the others. There is a symbiotic, interdependent relationship among them. Under international human rights law, governments have a legal duty to take actions to alleviate suffering and provide for human security. State and nonstate actors have the responsibility to respect, protect, and fulfill their economic and social human rights obligations. The Global New Deal presents a roadmap for action and demonstrates that these rights are more than aspirations: They are a legal and practical framework to guide public policy. The project combines legal and economic approaches to achieve sustainable economic and social public policies. Through a comprehensive evaluation of the successes and failures of both legal and economic avenues to social protection, clear policy directions for rights fulfillment are articulated.

Current international economic structures are unresponsive to the approximately 1.4 billion impoverished people on our planet. These human beings are so poor that they are irrelevant to international markets. Between the 1970s and the mid-1990s, world food prices dropped by one-half, yet millions of people still do not receive an adequate caloric intake in their diet. They are economically invisible. They can neither participate in world commodity markets, nor buy internationally traded food. They cannot compete with the market demand for grain to feed the cattle of the world's wealthy people.[13] Many of the desperately poor have been denied the means to farm their own food. The structures of the global market economy entrench rather than alleviate this suffering. Equal freedom from hunger has not been respected. Tragically, as noted above, the 2009 global financial recession pushed the ranks of the world's hungry to a record 1 billion, with hunger affecting one in six people. UN officials stated that this grim milestone posed a threat to peace and security, as war, drought, political instability, high food prices, poverty, and hunger all intersect.[14]

I believe that all thoughtful scholars and practitioners want destitution on this extreme level ended and that the disagreements are over the most effective means to achieve this goal. The post–Cold War period should give us an opportunity to innovate. We cannot remain fossilized in limited theories that offer bleak hope to those millions on the bottom. We have the ability to end massive destitution.[15] The means are available. The global community can face this moral imperative and find imaginative methods to guarantee everyone basic economic and social human rights. The Global New Deal takes on this challenge and charts a clear direction for economic and social rights fulfillment.

The Global New Deal

The Global New Deal draws its inspiration from Franklin Delano Roosevelt's New Deal for America. The negative impact of economic globalization has brought forth a number of calls for global reform.[16] As a global community, we can summon strength from Roosevelt's attempt to create a government responsive to the needs of the victims of economic development. We can act for the global public welfare and enact a new global covenant.

Eliminating slavery, combating AIDS in Africa, abolishing sweatshops in Bangladesh, and protecting children from preventable diseases will require multilateral action through international organization and international law. These examples dramatize the clear links between economic and social rights protection and the global economy. An individual state often has limited ability to counteract the negative consequences of globalization. Global problems require reforms at the global level.

The public policy proposals of the Global New Deal, described in detail in chapter 9, are *realistic and doable*. In addition to new ideas, I also incorporate into the Global New Deal many specific recommendations for change proposed over the last decade by activists and scholars concerned about global social justice. The Global New Deal is my attempt to bring together a comprehensive program for structural reform to create the conditions for the fulfillment of economic and social human rights.

A great deal of progress has been made in (1) defining economic and social human rights in international law and (2) documenting the impact of economic globalization on the poor. Not enough attention has been paid, however, to the development of public policy to meet basic human needs in this economically interdependent world system. This project is designed to close this gap through an approach that combines theories of economic development with international human rights law.

Scholars have inadequately elaborated the link between IPE and international human rights law. The UN has attempted to relate IPE strategies with human rights through the right to development. In 1986, the UN General Assembly defined the right to development as the right of "every human person and all peoples . . . to participate in, contribute to and enjoy economic, social and cultural and political development, in which all human rights and fundamental freedoms can be fully realized." But the

General Assembly did not define what states must do to fulfill this right. What are the human rights obligations of state and nonstate actors under the right to development?[17] In its 1998 publication *Integrating Human Rights with Sustainable Human Development*, the UNDP called for a rights-based approach to economic planning. But again, the responsibilities of state and nonstate actors remained vague. The Global New Deal develops this approach more fully by defining the economic policies that governments and nonstate actors (TNCs and IFIs) have a duty to implement in order to respect, protect, and fulfill economic and social human rights.

Implementing the Global New Deal involves strengthening the UN and its related agencies (see chapters 3, 4, 5, and 6). The well-publicized flaws and weaknesses of the UN have led many to question the viability and utility of the organization. While I recognize the political and structural deficiencies of the UN system, I do not believe that the system is beyond repair. Many of the reforms of the Global New Deal thus focus on making the UN system responsive to the needs of the vulnerable and the weak. The UN system, to a large extent, is the only forum of international cooperation in existence. Rather than start over, the attempt here is to rehabilitate and transform the UN structure to be able to meet the challenges of economic and social rights implementation.

At this point, you may be thinking that given the current political environment there is little or no chance of implementing a Global New Deal. To many, proposals to strengthen international law and international organizations are unrealistic. They think that these ideas, although appealing to moral and ethical sensibilities, are not based in the realities of power politics and thus have no chance of moving forward. For the last forty plus years, for example, the UN has been put in a defensive posture and has struggled to just survive. You may thus be skeptical that new programs to strengthen human rights enforcement and the UN system would be either adopted or implemented.

I urge you to set aside this "realist" logic for a moment (at least while you are reading this book). Our knowledge of the current international system allows us to imagine a more just future—knowledge and imagination. Each proposal of the Global New Deal is based on a comprehensive evaluation of the successes and failures of current efforts to address economic and social human rights. The analysis undergirding the proposals of the Global New Deal is presented throughout each chapter of this book. The logic and practicality of these reforms will be clear to all readers, I hope, by the end of the book.

Both empathy and self-interest are central to the human condition and are found within each individual human being and collectively within the community of states. The Global New Deal appeals to both of these human characteristics. On the one hand, the Global New Deal provides a means to show compassion for those who suffer. Its programs are a concrete means for people in all states on all continents to act to protect the vulnerable, end destitution, and save our ecosystem. For millions of people, compassionate action on behalf of the community is central to their sense of self and key to what it means to be a human being. On the other hand, the Global New Deal appeals to individual self-interest. It is not a platform of charity. The rich and the poor, the strong and the weak, all need clean drinking water, unpolluted air, and a demilitarized planet. All communities and states suffer from the destabilizing consequences of massive economic and environmental refugee flows, deepening global poverty, and diseases that cross borders. Global warming and the loss of the earth's biodiversity will harm not only the weak, but the powerful as well. It is thus in everyone's self-interest to enact the Global New Deal. From a purely "national-interest" perspective, the United States should take the lead and push this reform program forward. The citizens of the United States depend on the protection of global public goods and will benefit from programs focused on economic equality. Each state's national security depends on attention to the issues addressed in the Global New Deal.

History teaches us that profound change can happen quite quickly and often when least expected. As late as 2007, the overwhelming majority of U.S. citizens thought it impossible for an African American to be elected President of the United States. Furthermore, our theories of how the world works have proven unable to predict change. For example, not one theory of International Relations predicted the end of the Cold War. Scholars were unable to decipher the currents at work within the former Soviet Union that undermined the state and brought about its rapid demise. Today, in countries around the world there are forces for change at work within civil society, beneath the level of the state, promoting the normative principles underlining the Global New Deal. Hundreds of thousands of people on every continent are working for environmental preservation, human rights protection, and the provision of basic human needs. There is growing recognition and appreciation in many countries of the importance of international organization and cooperation to resolve global issues. None of us knows where all of these efforts will lead. They may lead to a more relevant and powerful UN or they may go nowhere. Current economic and political structures are strong and resilient and will resist change. Political realists thus have us believe that these reform efforts are doomed. But I believe that more modesty is in order. Those theorists who were so wrong about the former Soviet Union should be a bit hesitant before labeling the Global New Deal "utopian idealism." The currents at work behind these ideas are strong and vibrant. None of us knows how or when change will occur. If history is our guide, change happens quite abruptly.

2

International Political
Economy and Economic and
Social Human Rights

How do theories of international political economy (IPE) address economic and social human rights? Are there public policies that flow from each theory that would help protect the economic and social human rights of the most vulnerable? What is the impact of economic globalization on the attainment of these rights? What are "global public goods"? How do the ideas of "economic equality" and the "capabilities approach" help provide a direction for economic and social policy formation?

Theories of international political ecomony (IPE) attempt to articulate comprehensive frameworks for organizing efficient and fair systems of production and consumption on a global basis. Each theory of IPE is based on certain normative values and ethical assumptions. This has unfortunately resulted in advocates of competing theories pushing their perspective as the most moral choice with debates taking on a religious fervor. But economics should not be confused with theology. The idea is not to adopt a new belief system. Rather, through the study of IPE it should be possible to structure public policy to better meet basic human needs and alleviate needless human suffering. Since there are aspects of truth found in all theories, it is unhelpful to limit policy debates and options to one framework. The utility of IPE lies in its ability to demonstrate how insights from a variety of perspectives can help direct and guide the formation of a just economic system.

This chapter was coauthored with Diana Fuguitt, professor of economics, Eckerd College.

The goal of IPE is to articulate policies that work, understand why other policies fail, and predict which policies hold more promise for the future. This work is ongoing. Since the world does not stand still, new factors must be constantly integrated into successful policy analysis. Thus, even relatively effective policies must be modified over time, especially in a period of rapid technological and scientific change. In this era of expanding economic globalization, it is foolish to cling to a single model of IPE as the solution to our deepening social and environmental quandaries.

This chapter examines economic and social human rights through the lens of IPE. Three different concepts from IPE central to the achievement of economic and social human rights are global public goods, economic equality, and the capabilities approach. These ideas are explored in the following sections by relating economic and social human rights with:

- theories of IPE,
- global public goods,
- economic equality, and
- the capabilities approach.

Economic and Social Human Rights and Theories of IPE

IPE is the study of the interaction and tension between (1) the market and the state and (2) the market and international economic entities—including transnational corporations (TNCs), international financial institutions (IFIs) such as the International Monetary Fund (IMF) and the World Bank, and global and regional trade organizations, such as the World Trade Organization (WTO). Central principles of IPE include efficiency, autonomy, equity, and order. States try to create economic efficiency, protect their sovereign autonomy, respond to demands for the equitable distribution of goods and services, and follow the rules of IFIs and trade organizations that create a degree of order in international economic relations.

However, in the real world these principles often conflict, and states are forced to make trade-offs between these principles. A state, for example, may act to regulate the market and sacrifice efficiency in order to address issues of equity and autonomy. States' interests in fact frequently collide with market and IFI priorities. State action is often advocated to monitor the market and patrol actions of TNCs and IFIs. However, these policies of state modification of market mechanisms are controversial and often produce unforeseen side effects. This chapter explores these tensions through the lens of human rights. What is the proper balance between the state and the market to guarantee human rights protection for the vulnerable? Are regulations and controls needed on the actions of IFIs and trade organizations to promote economic and social rights fulfillment?

Economic and social human rights are fully defined and articulated in international law (as described in chapter 3). Economic rights include the right to property, the right to work, and the right to social security. Social rights include those rights necessary for an adequate standard of living, including rights to food, health, shelter, and education. The following is a brief review of the major IPE theories, summarizing their strengths and weaknesses in relation to the fulfillment of economic and social human rights.

Conflicting approaches to IPE and economic and social human rights can be roughly summarized as follows:

1. conservative/realist/libertarian,
2. liberal/globalist/utilitarian, and
3. structuralist/dependency/egalitarian.

Conservative/Realist/Libertarian

The combination of the demise of statist Soviet totalitarian economic models with the perceived poor economic performance of "welfare state" social-democratic governments in Europe resulted in a resurgence of conservative economic theories and practices in the 1990s. The logic of conservative economics is well known. Human beings—as aggressive, self-centered, and calculating individuals—need positive (wage raises) and negative (threats of unemployment) material incentives to be productive. A competitive, free enterprise economy allows each individual to achieve maximum personal liberty and material well-being. If individual decision-making units (individuals, households, or firms) are allowed to act freely and rationally through the market, society as a whole will develop and move forward. Open and free competition breeds efficiency by driving the inefficient out of business. Conservatives claim that government interference in this free market process impedes economic growth.[1]

Conservative thinkers thus stress libertarian rights: freedom from the state, individual liberty, and private ownership of material resources and property. Libertarian conservatives oppose taxation and favor a laissez-faire economic system. In general, conservatives call for limited government and a minimalist state. The most important functions of the state are to provide for national security and to maintain social order. Laws for the protection of private property and contracts are necessary for capitalism to operate freely.

Individual effort and competition is at the core of the conservative paradigm. Human rights, according to these thinkers, should focus on individual freedoms and property rights. Wealth is often considered the reward for a person's superior natural abilities. Poverty, on the other hand, is often seen as the result of a person's laziness or inadequacy. The

---

THEORIES OF INTERNATIONAL POLITICAL ECONOMY: STRENGTHS AND WEAKNESSES IN RELATION TO ECONOMIC AND SOCIAL HUMAN RIGHTS

	Conservative	Liberal	Structuralist
Approach to world politics	Realism	Globalism	Dependency
Ethical framework	Libertarian	Utilitarian	Egalitarian
Strength	Understanding of market efficiency	Understanding of global integration	Understanding of global economic structures
Weakness	Limited protection for the vulnerable	Lack of recognition of structural violence	Lack of a theory of incentives
Attitude toward public goods	Provide through market-based solutions	Provide through state action only when the market fails	Provide through state action and remove from the market altogether

---

best government from this perspective is one that governs the least. Competition for wealth and power is natural and necessary. Conservative economic thought has been cast as a form of social Darwinism—for example, the "natural" ability of some to succeed, while others "naturally" fail.[2]

There is a strong overlap between conservative economics and realist political theory. Realist theory depicts states acting in a world of anarchy. There is little possibility for cooperative action between states. The view of human nature is similar to that of conservative theory: people are aggressive, competitive, and egotistical. We exist in a world of insecurity and must struggle and compete with others to survive. According to theologian Reinhold Niebuhr, human beings project a "will to power" in an attempt to transcend this insecurity and control their destiny. "Man is insecure and involved in natural contingency; he seeks to overcome his insecurity by a will-to-power which overreaches the limits of human creatureliness."[3] This desperate search for security leads to relations of power and domination among all human beings. As Niebuhr writes, translating this to the political sphere, men and women seek to fulfill this search for security by projecting the drive for power to the collective plane. They thus pledge their loyalty to the nation. For Niebuhr, the politics of nations is a fight for power and security. Altruism and morality are absent. In the jungle that is international relations, each nation must concern itself with its power position vis-à-vis every other nation. The most that can be hoped for is a balance of power between states.[4]

How does this realist conservative framework provide for economic and social human rights?

Advantages: A much discussed advantage of the conservative economic model is that it provides incentives toward efficient production and personal productiveness. The profit motive encourages entrepreneurs to work hard, innovate, and move ahead in a theoretically free market economy. Furthermore, these economic incentives affect those far beyond the level of the owners and managers of firms. Jennifer L. Hochschild documents how the belief that an individual can attain success and virtue through strenuous effort is the essence of the American dream and the very soul of the United States.[5] She shows how the poor of all races hold this dream, even when it remains an unattainable myth. The dream thus provides strong motivational incentives.

Conservatives argue that progress is the result of individual effort and competition. Competition is a natural process to determine who is the most fit, efficient, and best. The result will be the most goods and services for the most numbers of people—Pareto optimum.[6] Governmental economic controls and planning, as well-known British economist Friedrich A. von Hayek argues, disrupt this system. Hayek envisions private property and individual economic freedom as the basis of democratic government.[7] Thus, the human rights focused on by conservatives are libertarian principles of individual freedoms and property rights.

Disadvantages: The economic and social human rights of those who succeed in this competitive environment are protected. However, the major disadvantage of conservative economic theory is that it provides limited protections for those who fail and for the weak who cannot compete. The theory does not recognize the principle of social injustice—that is, that unemployment and suffering may be the result of the economic structures of a market economy. In fact, on a global scale the causes of human suffering can often be traced to the impact of economic structures on states and societies, which override individual effort, hard work, and natural abilities. From a perspective of economic and social human rights, the "safety net" for those who don't end up on the winning side has too many holes. Thus, the major flaw of conservative theory is its lack of recognition of structural injustice and the lack of protection for the most vulnerable.

Liberal/Globalist/Utilitarian

The depression of the 1930s appeared to discredit the conservative laissez-faire approach. In response to the economic catastrophe of the time, John Maynard Keynes argued that the capitalist economic system was

not self-correcting and would not generate a high enough level of investment to maintain full employment. He felt strongly that the government
had the responsibility to borrow and spend money to prevent economic
depressions. The economy in general, however, should be left free to
respond to the profit-maximizing producers and the welfare-maximizing
consumers. Keynes's correctives were meant to stimulate, not overthrow,
the market.

Unlike conservatives, however, liberals believe that governmental
intervention in the economy can achieve some goals of social justice.
Liberals share with conservatives a basic faith in the capitalist system.
However, they believe that inequalities based on wealth and power
should and can be reduced through state action. The state can assist the
poor when market mechanisms fail. The state has a role in providing basic
human needs to help those who (for whatever reason) cannot compete
fairly in the market system.[8]

Conservative economists argued that markets will inherently tend
toward a socially beneficial equilibrium (*pareto optimum*). Keynes contended that this was not the case. Rather, production and consumption
can balance while unemployment remains at a relatively high level.
The state must therefore intervene to stimulate both employment and
investment. Keynes challenged the basic argument of laissez-faire: that
economic prosperity can best be gained without state management.
Keynes argued that government intervention was necessary to achieve
full employment.[9]

There are basic unities between liberal economists and globalist
approaches to international relations. While both conservatives and liberals embrace a market economy, they differ over the role of the state in the
interdependent global economy. Conservatives focus on the economic
and political interests of the territorial state, adopting a realist framework.
Liberals, on the other hand, prioritize the market needs of transnational
business and financial institutions, embracing a globalist perspective.[10]

Globalists thus explain the politics of interdependence much better than
the realists. Globalists strongly support the activities of TNCs as "engines
of development" and "transmission belts" of free enterprise, efficiency,
and good management. To avoid disruptions in TNC activity and threats
to "orderly growth," some globalists have responded sympathetically to
calls from the South for reforms of international economic governance
that benefit the less developed countries (LDCs). While realists believe
the international system is defined by competition alone, globalists have
pushed for the creation of new international monetary and trade regimes
to facilitate economic cooperation.[11]

For globalists, therefore, as for liberals, governments have a role to
play. The state should direct these reforms so that the TNCs can secure
and distribute the benefits from a global economy. Furthermore, global-

ists repudiate state action (often taken on "realist," conservative grounds) that interferes with transnational management, such as imposing tariffs and surcharges on imports, subsidizing home industries, placing embargoes on trade with particular countries, and so on. For the globalist, as for the liberal, the world is a more interdependent place than that described by a conservative realist. In this world, cooperation is not only possible but necessary.

Globalists and liberals acknowledge the emergence of a global society and argue for the development of a true global economy. Growing trade, investment, and monetary ties are a part of global "interdependence" that challenges old conceptions of national economic autonomy.

How does a globalist liberal framework provide for economic and social human rights?

Advantages: Globalists argue that the alleviation of hunger will come through the benefits of world economic integration. Integrating diverse and separate economies will result in an overall gain of output from which, over time, everyone could potentially benefit. Joel Cohen gives the following hypothetical example to demonstrate the benefits from economic integration and international trade: Countries A and B each have 1,000 acres of land. Country A has 1,000 workers and 100 mules. Country B has 100 workers and 1,000 mules. Neither a worker alone nor a mule alone can cultivate anything. However, one worker together with one mule can cultivate one acre per year. The advantages of integration are clear. Only 100 acres could be cultivated in Countries A and B if neither workers nor mules can move between countries. If, however, Country B could ship 900 mules to Country A, then combined the two countries could cultivate 1,100 acres. Or, instead of shipping mules, the migration of 900 workers from Country A to Country B would equally increase the total cultivated land.[12]

Liberal globalists thus stress ethics of utilitarianism, in that they jump to consequences, the final results. Utilitarian ethics argues for policies, institutions, and actions that improve the welfare of the most people. To act morally in the world today is to act in a way that improves the well-being of the most people. Globalists argue that in our imperfect world, the greatest number of people can benefit from an integrated, globalized economy. It may be messy getting there. The transition from a "backward" localized economy to a full merger into the international market may cause pain to many. But, over the long run, positive net gains for most people will be achieved.

Disadvantages: Critics argue that the globalist perspective refuses to recognize the structural dimension of the world economy that plays a significant role in the creation of hunger and deprivation. The world economy is filled with national and international inequities in power, wealth, and consumption. Unfortunately, TNCs have often been more interested in transferring wealth out of the LDCs than in the developmental needs of the poorest sectors. For example, examine the impact of logging by Japanese TNCs on the Philippines: Since 1945, Japanese TNCs have logged and brought back to Japan a significant percentage of the Filipino forest. By 1989, only 1 million hectares remained of the original 17 million hectares of tropical forests in the Philippines. As a result of the actions of the Japanese TNCs, including Mitsubishi, Mitshi, C. Itoh, and Sumitomo, the Philippines has one of the most severe deforestation problems of any developing country.[13] Rather than serving as "engines of development," TNCs too often focus on short-term gain over sustainability and long-term optimal resource use. These actions are often detrimental to the economic well-being of LDCs, as evidenced here (and, unfortunately, in numerous other examples).

TNCs produce goods and services for those consumers in LDCs who have purchasing power and create a demand for TNC products. However, the poor in these nations lack the money to purchase these products and are thus unable to express their preferences in the marketplace. They become either invisible or a nuisance. A system built on the profit incentive alone has continuously failed to meet the basic human needs of those who fall behind. In the end, economic globalism creates and perpetuates enormous economic and social inequalities. The economic and social human rights of the most vulnerable are violated.

In addition, economic globalization has shifted power away from elected governments and given it to a handful of corporations and financial institutions. These organizations exist for short-term financial gain. As a result, Harvard professor Stanley Hoffmann argues that the global economy is literally out of control. There are no rules of accountability; instead, there is a huge zone of irresponsibility.[14]

Structuralist/Dependency/Egalitarian

Many structuralists believe that human beings are naturally cooperative and productive. The positive (wage increases) and negative (unemployment) incentives that liberals and conservatives advocate are considered for the most part unnecessary. Humans have the ability to mold their own destinies. Traits such as aggression, competition, passivity, uncooperativeness, and egoism are not natural. Rather, they emerge in response to an inhumane and fundamentally immoral economic system. Surviving in a capitalist economy often means becoming selfish and oblivious to the needs of others.[15]

Equality of opportunity is a myth in a society where power and wealth is in the hands of the few. According to structuralists, liberals and conservatives do not go to the root of the problem. A capitalist economy creates classes and institutional structures. All aspects of life, including personal relationships, are shaped by the pursuit of profit and human needs are subordinated to the needs of the market. According to Karl Marx, "exchange value" replaces "use value." For example, food is distributed to those who can buy it (exchange value) and not distributed on the basis of need (use value). The result is that food surpluses in the global economy often do not reach the hungry.

Structuralists see an inherent conflict between the rich and the poor. This inequality of wealth and power is the result of a system that is based on the exploitation of one class by another. Private ownership of the means of production has created a vicious system filled with contradictions and class conflict. Individual freedom to accumulate has unfortunately interfered with the freedom of the many to survive. For the liberal promise of freedom to have real meaning for the majority, socioeconomic inequality must be overcome.[16]

Structuralists thus strongly embrace egalitarian principles and critique the economic structures of capitalism that prohibit true equality of opportunity. Food, shelter, education, and medicine are essential human needs, not abstract concepts. It is a mockery to offer only political rights to people who are underfed or diseased. Individual freedom may not always be everyone's primary need. As a nineteenth-century Russian radical is believed to have proclaimed: There are situations in which boots are superior to the works of William Shakespeare.

Dependency theories extend the internal dynamics of the capitalist mode of production, as originally outlined by Marx, to the world as a whole. These theorists argue that capitalism created underdevelopment in the past and generates it in the present. The world is divided between a powerful developed center and an underdeveloped periphery and semiperiphery which is vulnerable to the actions of the core states. The economic gap widens over time between the center and the periphery, which is reduced to a state of dependence. The position of the countries in the periphery is seen as analogous to the proletariat's situation in relation to the capitalist, as the weaker states are dependent upon the decisions of the powerful, rich states for access to world markets and resources. André Gunder Frank and others maintain that underdevelopment is an essential condition for the survival and maintenance of the capitalist world system as a whole.[17] Samir Amin argues that these LDCs should thus "delink" from the centers of capitalism.[18] Cutting ties with the centers of capitalism is seen as perhaps the only chance the LDCs have of breaking out of the tragedy of underdevelopment. Dependency theory thus veers toward an autarkic, self-sufficient model of development.

How does a structuralist framework provide for economic and social human rights?

Advantages: The structuralist critique brings issues of class and power out of the shadows and into the open. There is a huge discrepancy

---

IPE CONCEPTS CENTRAL TO ECONOMIC AND SOCIAL HUMAN RIGHTS

Global Public Goods

Global public goods refer to those products and necessities that all people enjoy in common that are nonexcludable and nonrivalrous in consumption. Nonrivalry in consumption refers to those goods that any number of consumers may enjoy without detracting from the enjoyment of others. Nonexcludability means that no one can be excluded from enjoying the good. Clean air, for example, is a pure public good. Global public goods are outcomes that benefit all countries, population groups, and generations. Global public goods include the following: international peace and the prevention of deadly conflict; primary health care and the eradication of disease; and environmental sustainability and the preservation of the global commons.*

Economic Equality

Economic equality signifies universal and equal access to essential public goods, including basic education, a healthy environment,

---

*See Inge Kaul, Isabelle Grunberg, and Marc A. Stern, eds., *Global Public Goods: International Cooperation in the 21st Century* (New York: Oxford University Press, 1999).

---

between the normative framework of liberal freedom and the realities of global life in the twenty-first century. Global economic structures are responsible for a great deal of human suffering. The moral message is that this human agony is unjust. We must not delude ourselves. For those on the bottom of the global division of labor, things are getting much worse, not better. We can do better.

Disadvantages: Many conclude from the experience of "socialism" in Russia and Eastern Europe that a major weakness in socialist theory is the lack of a theory of incentives. If the totalitarian states of Eastern Europe had been less corrupt, then perhaps the original humanist vision of a society of true equality could have provided continuous "moral incentives." But with the corrupt "nomenclature" recreating an elite class, the vast majority of the working class in these countries had no possibility for a better life. No matter how hard they worked, their families would not see an improvement in their living conditions. The result was that a general malaise, obvious to the naked eye of even the most untrained observer, gripped these nations,

food and water, primary health care and sanitation, and housing. Economic equality, as distinct from income equality, forms the foundation for achieving economic and social human rights. Economic equality is contingent on public policy to ameliorate deprivations and create equal opportunity for all. Such public policy measures would focus on assuring access for all to health care, sanitation, clean water, food, affordable housing, public education, and so on.†

Capabilities Approach

A way to consider real equality of opportunity is through equality of capabilities. A person's capability for adequate functioning, and ability to participate in the life of the community, depends on being well nourished and having access to basic education, medical care, and affordable housing. The capabilities approach allows us to look at the actual ways in which individuals and groups are given the freedom to achieve adequate functioning. The capabilities approach examines the differences in social conditions that affect human capabilities, including public education, habitable and affordable homes, primary health care, access to essential nutrition and clean water, and an ecologically sound and sustainable environment.‡

---

†See Amartya Sen, *Development As Freedom* (New York: Knopf, 1999).
‡See Amartya Sen, *Inequality Reexamined* (Cambridge, Mass.: Harvard University Press, 1992).

resulting in economic stagnation. There appeared to be no motivation or incentive to work hard and innovate under these conditions.

In sum, it does not appear that there is one approach in IPE theory that fully addresses the economic and social human rights claims embraced by international law. Effective global public policy must therefore take into account the advantages and disadvantages found within each paradigm. To a significant extent, the debates between these IPE theories is over the provision of what economists call "public goods."

Economic and Social Human Rights and Global Public Goods

Pure Public Goods

Paul Samuelson defines a public good as a product "which all enjoy in common in the sense that each individual's consumption of that good leads to no subtraction from any other individual's consumption of that good."[19]

A clean and healthy environment is a pure public good. Individual enjoyment of the environment does not distract from the pleasure of others in
clean air and water. Yet, as the environmental crisis so tragically illustrates,
public goods are often neglected and suffer from underprovision.

To set up a business, an entrepreneur depends on critical factors such
as a peaceful society, clean air, clean water, and so on. A businessper-
son's ability to produce "private goods" or services to sell in the market
depends on these other "public goods" being provided. The benefits of
these public goods are clearly not limited to a single producer or buyer;
once provided for a single individual, many can enjoy the benefits without payment. Market mechanisms have historically failed to provide for
these types of goods.

The theory of market failure explains the necessity for government
action to protect public goods. In some areas, the market seems to meet
the needs of consumers, but in others it clearly fails. Why, for example,
does the market continuously fail to provide the ecological balance—from
nature preservation and wildlife conservation to clean air and water—that
consumers (citizens) unquestionably crave? Economists call this inability
of the market to provide socially optimal quantities of certain goods
"market failure." Market failure occurs due to insufficient financial incentives for the production of public goods. As a result, without government
action, these public goods will be underproduced and threatened.

There are two qualities of public goods and services that are recognized
as limiting financial incentives and contributing to market failure: nonrivalry in consumption and nonexcludability. Nonrivalry in consumption
refers to those goods that any number of consumers may enjoy without
detracting from the enjoyment of others. Or, using alternative wording,
once a nonrivalrous good is provided to one individual, as Paul Samuelson notes, the (marginal) cost of providing it to an additional individual
is zero. Nonexcludability means that no one can be excluded from enjoying the good—that is, the seller is unable (or finds it impractical due to
prohibitively high costs) to prevent nonpayers from consuming the good.
Some examples help to clarify these concepts. Peace and national defense
are often said to be pure public goods. When peace exists in a country, all
citizens enjoy it; one citizen's consumption does not detract from others,
and it is impossible to prevent nonpayers from benefitting from a peaceful
society. Clean air is another pure public good. One cannot exclude nonpayers from enjoying the benefits of clean air, and one person's breathing
(consumption) does not detract from the consumption of others.[20]

Nonexcludability and nonrivalrous consumption mean that there are
insufficient market incentives to provide allocatively efficient quantities
of public goods like peace or clean air. Why? Because nonexcludability
results in what is called the "free-rider problem." A free rider is someone
who benefits from a good without paying to support the good's produc-

tion. It is not possible to charge the occupants of one household for the clean air they breathe if their neighbors breathe it for free. The issue of nonexcludability has long been noted. Adam Smith writes that government would have to erect and maintain "those public works, which, though they may be in the highest degree advantageous to a great society, are, however, of such a nature, that the profit could never repay the expense to any individual or small number of individuals."[21] In other words, when market incentives fail, the government must maintain those public works clearly "advantageous to a great society," such as clean air.

Mixed Goods (with Public and Private Characteristics)

The pure public good characterized by nonrivalry and nonexcludability is one "polar case," and at the other end of the spectrum are pure private goods that are both rivalrous and exclusionary. In between these pure polar ends is a wide continuum for what Samuelson identified as the "mixed case [that] has elements of both in it."[22]

Indeed, there are a relatively small number of truly "pure" public goods. Many more goods combine a mixture of public and private good characteristics.

- Often nonrivalrous goods allow for some level of excludability. For instance, a highway is nonrivalrous by providing consumption benefits to multiple users, and it can be a pure public good provided to all with no exclusion. However, toll booths can exclude vehicles from using the roadway. With a toll, still the highway is nonrivalrous, as once it is built and maintained for one vehicle, the marginal cost of providing the roadway to other vehicles (up to the highway's capacity) is zero.[23]
- Alternatively, goods can be characterized by a mixture of nonexcludability with rivalrous consumption. For example, urban or nature parks are provided without exclusion and, at low levels of community usage, can be enjoyed by a visitor without detracting from any other visitor's experience (i.e., nonrivalrous consumption). Yet, if the park becomes crowded or congested, then one person's visit to the park detracts from or even precludes another's visit and thus park consumption becomes characterized by rivalry.

In reality, a good's classification in terms of public and private characteristics can vary by time and place. For instance, a highway's use (whether or not excluded by toll) can be nonrivalrous under uncrowded conditions; however, during popular use times of the day (e.g., rush hour) or if located in densely populated cities, highway use can be congested and thus rivalrous. Likewise, a park (nonrivalrous at low usage levels and becoming rivalrous if crowded) can have differing levels of excludability—depending, for example, on the degree to which it is surrounded by natural enclosures that limit visitor entry to a small number of easily restricted points of entry.

Common Resources

Common resources (included in table 2.1) are defined as resources characterized by non-excludability (it is prohibitively expensive if not impossible to exclude others from access to the resource), yet rivalry (one person's use of the resource detracts from the quantity or quality available to others).[24] For example, fishing on the high seas outside territorial limits is characterized by open access, but catching a fish is rivalrous, reducing the stock available to others—and as rapidly declining fish populations suggest, not only for current but also future generations of fishers.[25]

Garrett Hardin's treatise on "The Tragedy of the Commons" demonstrates the problem for common resources. He considered the example of "a pasture open to all." As Hardin described, under open access each rational herdsman will see it as in his interest to graze as many cattle as possible on the pasture, given the increased private return he will receive from each additional well-fed cow, while not taking into account the full social costs incurred by all of the herdsmen (from the environmental destruction rendered by his cattle's consumption in the overgrazed pasture). Hardin wrote, "this is the conclusion reached by each and every rational herdsman sharing a commons. Therein is the tragedy. Each man is locked into a system that compels him to increase his herd without limit—in a world that is limited. Ruin is the destination toward which all men rush, each pursuing his own best interest in a society that believes in the freedom of the commons."[26] Extending this analogy to an international regional common resource, Mendez notes, "this is essentially the tragedy of the Sahel, where the overgrazing of rangelands had contributed to the desertification of the region."[27]

Likewise, the global "commons"—the oceans, air, and outer space—are used without regard to the full social costs imposed. No one is excluded

Table 2.1. Public, Private, and Mixed Goods

	Rivalrous	*Nonrivalrous*
Excludable	Pure private goods	Mixed goods: nonrivalrous goods with exclusion
Nonexcludable	Mixed goods: nonexcludable goods subject to congestion; common resources	Pure public goods

Note: Mixed goods have both public and private characteristics.

from utilizing these natural resources. Although regulatory progress has been made in international environmental law, the global commons remain threatened and endangered. The right to a healthy environment is jeopardized (see chapter 4).

Elinor Ostrom (2009 Nobel laureate in economics), Daniel Bromley, and others have compiled substantial evidence of alternative institutional arrangements and governance systems that can effectively manage the use of a common resource and successfully avoid the tragedy.[28] These experiences offer lessons that can guide international common resource management. With careful thought and international cooperation, proper and effective management of the global commons is feasible. What is needed is the international political commitment and action to implement effective systems.

Externalities

An additional form of market failure is externalities. Externalities refer to outcomes that occur "when an individual or firm takes an action but does not bear all the costs (negative externalities) or receive all the benefits (positive externalities)."[29] The action generates a divergence between private and social costs (or benefits) because the market failed to price all of the action's effects. The non-priced effects are said to be external to the market (i.e., extramarket effects or externalities). These externalities generate nonexcludable consumption, as others can receive the external benefits or find they must bear the burden of external costs. Thus, a "free-rider" problem arises. As a result, when externalities exist, markets tend to yield non-optimal (i.e., allocatively inefficient) quantities of production and consumption.

A wide spectrum of goods generates externalities. At one end of the spectrum are pure public goods; given their characteristic of nonexcludability, positive externalities are, according to Samuelson, "basic to the very notion."[30] Even more significant, along the spectrum the many mixed goods that are characterized by some degree of nonexcludability generate positive and negative externalities that are pervasive throughout the economy. Consider, for example, the role of education. The individual person who invests in a solid education receives lifelong benefits, and also provides nonexcludable benefits to society as a whole. Educated individuals are able to increase their labor productivity, comply with written laws and norms, and participate in the civil life of the country—all of which benefits a society and strengthens a nation. Pollution, on the other hand, is a negative externality and can be described as a "public bad."[31]

Approaching the other end of the public-private spectrum, externalities are also prevalent. Many goods commonly considered to be private (characterized by rivalry and exclusion), really are not "pure" private goods.

Indeed, there are relatively few *pure* private goods in existence. Consider, for example, food. The consumption of a hamburger is rivalrous; if someone consumes a hamburger, it is no longer available for anyone else to consume. Also, a fast-food restaurant can exclude individuals from consuming their famous hamburger. But, an individual consuming food to be nourished and well-fed also generates external benefits to others in society. If a person is not hungry, he or she will be more productive on the job, show greater aptitude in learning new information, and will function more effectively as a human being—all of which generates benefits to society.

The challenge is that there is little incentive in a market economy for individual rational actors to take into account the positive external benefits they provide to others in society; thus individuals tend to underinvest in providing the socially beneficial good. Likewise, the market provides little incentive to the polluting firm, for example, to incur the higher expense of reducing the external costs their productive activity imposes on others; thus they tend to overproduce (from a social efficiency perspective).

As externalities become international in reach, the issue of providing the socially optimal level of the positive externality becomes even more problematic. And, if there is no incentive for individual businesses within global capitalism to stem negative externalities, how will the global environment and global social welfare be protected? Given the "free-rider" problem, it is not in the interest of any individual business to pay to protect our endangered oceans, atmosphere, and forests. It is also not in the narrow, immediate self-interest of any individual nation to be concerned with externalities beyond its borders. Yet to achieve social efficiency when international externalities exist, concerted efforts by both state and nonstate actors around the globe are needed.

The Global Dimension of Public Goods

As the discussion so far suggests, a range of goods classifications (i.e., pure public goods, mixed goods, common resources, externalities) entail some degree of nonrivalry and/or nonexcludability. Goods fitting these categories either are entirely public or have elements of public characteristics. But what makes any of these goods with public characteristics "global" is their universal dimensions and the global reach of their positive or negative externalities.

In our interdependent world, many public goods have these universal and global aspects and thus can no longer be seen as only national in character. Inge Kaul, Isabelle Grunberg, and Marc Stern define a global public good as "a public good with benefits that are strongly universal in terms of countries (covering more than one group of countries), people (accruing to several, preferably all, population groups) and generations (extending to both current and future generations, or at least meeting the needs of current generations without foreclosing development options for future generations." They continue, "A maximal definition" of a global public good would thus be a public good "marked by its universality, that is, it benefits all countries, peoples and generations." In comparison, "a minimal definition" of a global public good would be a public good that tended "towards universality in that it would benefit more than one group of countries, and would not discriminate against any population segment or set of generations."[32]

Kaul, Grunberg, and Stern include the following as global public goods: international peace and the prevention of deadly conflict; health and the eradication of disease; financial stability and debt abatement; equitable development and poverty alleviation; refugee and migrant worker protections; and environmental sustainability and the preservation of the global commons.[33] Aspects of these goods are nonexcludable and nonrivalrous and, overall, these goods are frighteningly undersupplied. Furthermore, acting alone, individual nations cannot provide for these global public goods, which will be fulfilled only through multilateral action in international law and international organization.

We believe that the fulfillment of economic and social human rights at the national level depends on the protection and promotion of global public goods internationally. There is a class of goods and services to which all people in all countries can make human rights claims, including basic education, a healthy environment, food and water, primary health care and sanitation, and housing. If our concern is avoiding destitution and achieving equality based on the freedom to achieve and the capability to function (see the discussion of Amartya Sen later in this chapter), access to these goods should be guaranteed by state and international actors. This category of economic and social human rights deserves special attention in public policy making.[34]

Fundamental needs of all human beings include basic education, a healthy environment, food and water, primary health care and sanitation, and housing. We believe that these economic and social human needs should be classified as global public goods as aspects of these goods are nonexcludable and/or nonrivalrous. This classification provides a clear economic justification for government intervention in the market to ensure their provision. The satisfaction of these public goods makes life possible. The human needs these public goods fulfill are universal to all humanity. Economic and social human rights are in essence claims for the fulfillment of these human needs which are global public goods.

It is true that there is a difference in excludability between, for example, health care and clean air. It is impossible to withhold clean air from the rich and the poor alike. Health care, on the other hand, can be provided only to those with money. But there are more similarities than differences between these goods in their many public good characteristics. They are essential for the well-being of the individual, the stability of society, and the efficient functioning of the economy overall. Their consumption generates social (global) benefits far greater than the private benefits to the individual consumer. Classifying these basic human needs—basic education; a healthy environment; food and water; primary health care and sanitation; and housing—as global public goods clarifies their central importance.

Appendix 2.1 explains in detail the global public goods dimensions of basic education, a healthy environment, food and water, primary health care and sanitation, and housing. While economic and social human rights claims have been clearly articulated, the economic justifications for government intervention to promote and protect these public goods remains obscure. This discussion of the public goods component to each of these human rights will help to clarify these issues.

Assuring the Provision of Public Goods

A central divergence in IPE theory between conservatives, liberals, and structuralists is over the degree to which market mechanisms can provide for these basic public goods. Conservatives often seek market-based solutions with minimal state intervention.[35] Liberals, while not wanting to disrupt market efficiency, frequently argue for state action when confronted with market failure. Meanwhile, structuralists regularly assert that basic public goods should be taken out of the market altogether and, with structural reforms of global governance, guaranteed to all people.

As discussed in detail above, market mechanisms alone will most likely fail to provide a socially optimal quantity of these public goods. In addition to the free-rider problem, it is questionable whether the market alone is the right resource allocation mechanism. Our concern is with creating a system that meets basic human needs and allows each individual to live a life of human dignity. An individual with few financial resources should not be denied health care, sanitation, clean water, and so on. Is it possible to live a life of dignity with perpetual fear of homelessness, hunger, and sickness? Examine the right to food. The private market cannot be solely relied on to distribute food to all. The poor and hungry may not be able to command the required purchasing power and are thus denied a life of dignity. Access to adequate and affordable food and clean water should not be subject to market fluctuations.[36]

There are certain public goods that governments are now empowered to assure, including providing security from external threats and protecting citizens against crime and violence. It is generally understood that the market is the wrong mechanism to provide national defense or police protection. Defense and police protection are public goods, nonexcludable and nonrivalrous in consumption. Basic education, a healthy environment, food and water, primary health care and sanitation, and housing should be added to this list of public goods that the state has the legal responsibility to protect. The economic arguments for state involvement in the provision of public goods are compelling.[37]

A government should be judged on the degree to which its citizens have access to these basic human rights and public goods. Satisfaction of these basic needs simply makes life possible. It creates the possibility of living a life of dignity. Defining the fulfillment of basic human needs as global public goods clarifies the urgent stakes at risk. Human needs are a prerequisite for the continuation of life. Their fulfillment makes living possible.[38]

The proposals for the Global New Deal in chapter 9 demonstrate the ways in which states can act through international organization and international law to protect global public goods. There are a variety of reforms and measures that can be implemented in international organizations to guarantee the provision of global public goods. Global public goods are the foundation of the Global New Deal. It is not utopian to imagine a world where these global public goods are adequately supplied. There are clear policy options to secure their attainment.

For example, in the midst of the overall negative trends in LDCs in income distribution and other key economic indicators in the 1980s and 1990s, there were some success stories. There are a number of key economic lessons that can be extrapolated from these cases that point to the continued centrality of the state in economic policy making. While there is no universal blueprint that states can follow to guarantee growth, equity, and justice in their development models, there are policies that can be utilized to meet the obligations found in international law to protect, respect, and fulfill economic and social human rights and, by doing so, shield the most vulnerable.

One of the most striking facets of UN statistics is that the link between economic growth and meeting basic human needs is often not very close. Human development continues to advance around the world despite periodic economic decline and worsening gross national income (GNI). This was even true in the 1980s, the "lost decade," which had a devastating impact on the lives and living standards of 1.5 billion people. The 1980s were marked by severe drops in incomes and living standards in many countries. Yet, despite these conditions in two-thirds of the developing countries, there was an acceleration in the rate at which child mortality was reduced. Richard Jolly writes: "For nearly seventy countries, child mortality was reduced at a faster rate in the 1980s than in the 1960s or 1970s. Moreover, the regions with acceleration in the rate of reduction of child mortality were the regions of economic decline—while countries with slow rates of improvement in child mortality were those of accelerating economic growth."[39]

One conclusion to be drawn is that there is no reason to wait for improvements in economic growth to attack child mortality or other dimensions of social development, such as expanding basic education, access to clean water and sanitation, and improvements in nutrition. Economic policies of social development need to be linked to the duties of states to meet their legal obligations in economic and social human rights law (outlined in chapter 3).

It is now abundantly clear that crucial aspects of social development can occur despite low income levels and limited industrialization and modernization. Low-income countries can achieve levels of health and education comparable to industrialized states. The low-income success stories include Kerala (India), Botswana, Barbados, and Costa Rica. In all cases, state action for social development was a priority and necessary policies were implemented regardless of the pace of economic growth.

Santosh Mehrotra outlines the common successful policies of these countries as including

- state-supported basic public services,
- investment in health and education before economic take-off,
- resource allocation to health and education well above the average for developing countries,
- investment in basic education that preceded the improvement in the health status,
- interventions that favored the status of women, and
- attempts at ensuring a nutritional floor for the population, and specific health and education interventions to ensure the effectiveness of these services.[40]

Rich and poor states have legal obligations to make every effort to assure public goods provision and respect, protect, and fulfill economic and social human rights. This task is clearly more difficult for resource-poor states. But resource scarcity does not relieve a state from conscientiously striving to meet minimum obligations, including minimum levels of essential foodstuffs, primary health care, basic shelter and housing, and basic education. If the state of Kerala—with one of the lowest rates of economic growth in the world and very little industrialization amid a decline in agricultural production—can ensure access to basic health care and primary education to all its citizens, then there is absolutely no reason why other states cannot equally guarantee these economic and social human rights. The UN's Economic Rights Committee is absolutely correct in its evaluation of resources and rights. The lack of resources should not be an excuse to fail to implement public policies to protect and provide basic economic and social human rights.

A key component to the success stories in human development has been the education of women (as discussed in chapter 6). Amartya Sen focuses on the notion of women's agency, which is the freedom women have to engage in work outside the home, receive an education, have ownership rights, and earn an independent income. When these economic and social rights are protected, women's well-being is enhanced.[41] Mehrotra demonstrated the links between female adult literacy and positive health outcomes, as female education preceded health breakthroughs. The education of women strengthened their earning capacity, their caretaking capacity, and their control over resources.

> Women's resource control and caretaking capacity comprise one of the conditions for adequate nutrition, along with household food security, access to health services, and a healthy environment. . . . Maternal literacy and schooling is known to be associated with a more efficient management of limited household resources, greater utilization of available health services, better health-care practices, lower fertility, and more child-centered caring behavior. Moreover, it raises the awareness of the means to overcome problems and generates effective political demand. In general, therefore, women's education has an enormous effect on nutrition and health, in the long run probably one of the most important.[42]

According to Mehrotra, countries that were committed to a program of social development dedicated approximately 5 to 8 percent of their gross domestic product (GDP) to health and education.[43] Defense expenditures were not significant in most of the high-achieving countries.[44] Throughout the crises of the 1980s, government expenditures in health and education as a proportion of GDP held up in all these countries. The global economic recession and structural adjustment did not interrupt macroeconomic priority given to health and education.[45]

These conclusions were further confirmed in the 2008 Social Watch report published by the Instituto Del Tercer Mundo in Montevideo, Uruguay. Social Watch is a transnational coalition of organizations that gathers data on governments' compliance with their social commitments made during UN conferences, including the 1995 Copenhagen Summit on Social Development, the 1995 Beijing Women's Conference, and the 2000 Millennium Summit. The Social Watch country-by-country analyses provide useful information to assess methods of meeting economic and social human rights. These reports demonstrate again the importance of public policy and investment in human capital in any strategy to alleviate poverty. Public spending on health and education are once again demonstrated to be key ingredients to successful social development. Strategies that stress the full utilization of human resources have proven to be a sound path to poverty reduction.[46]

Examine, for example, Costa Rica, which has a tradition of universal coverage of basic social services. Even in economic recessions, suitable resource allocations for preventive health care and primary education are made so that these services continue to reach the poor effectively. Social Watch Reports over the years have documented the ways in which Costa Rica has supported labor-intensive development in agriculture and tourism that effectively integrated peasants and unskilled workers into the formal economy. While Social Watch is critical of recent changes which have weakened the country's political and financial capability to sustain social reform, Costa Rica's social indicators are still substantially above most Central American and Latin American countries.[47] In 2008, for example, the UNDP reported that a child born in Guatemala had a 12.5 percent probability of not surviving to age 40, while in Costa Rica the probability was only 3.7 percent. Both Brazil and the U.S. in 2008, despite a much larger per capita income, had a lower average life expectancy rate than Costa Rica. Why? Because Costa Rica implemented a successful public action plan for social development. (As did Mauritius, a country with a per capita income similar to Costa Rica, which has managed to increase the life expectancy for its population to over seventy-two years.[48]) The example of Costa Rica reaffirms key lessons from Southeast Asia. Many observers have concluded that the rapid reduction of poverty in Southeast Asia was fundamentally due to public provision of social services including public education and basic health care.

The state thus can take the lead in promoting social development and providing public goods. Economic growth, poverty reduction, and social development cannot be left solely to the forces of the market and globalization. The state can institute policies to address all aspects of human development. Human rights law (as outlined in chapter 3) can be used to hold states accountable to basic norms designed to protect human dignity. And furthermore, as we will see later, states can act through international organizations to provide global public goods.

The state's role in implementing public policies to protect the economic and social rights of its citizens is clear. Policy options exist and have proven successful. Yet debates continue and areas of unclarity linger. Disagreements remain particularly strong over the issue of equality and the relationship of equality to the fulfillment of economic and social human rights. Should state policies focus on strategies to achieve income equality? What is the difference between "income equality" and "economic equality"? We thus turn now to the relationship between equality and economic and social human rights.

Economic and Social Human Rights and Economic Equality

It is of extreme significance, as Amartya Sen notes, that all the major ethical and political proposals of the twentieth century in some form or another are justified on the basis of equality,[49] from conservative theories of equality in libertarian rights,[50] to liberal theories of equality in liberty and distribution of primary goods,[51] to Marxist theories of equality in class power and wealth.[52] Article 1 of the Universal Declaration of Human Rights declares, "All human beings are born free and equal in dignity and rights." It is in fact hard to imagine an ethical theory or a viable political program in the current period not embracing some form of equality.

Yet, differences clearly remain over conceptions of the proper subject of this equality norm. What is to be evaluated equally? How is equality in "dignity and rights" determined? What does it mean to argue in favor of equality for all? Equality of what? Resources? Abilities? Access to power? Happiness? Liberty? Property?

Human beings are not created equal. Some of us are born with physical or mental limitations while others are blessed with athletic or mental prowess and ability. Most of us are "average" or below in intelligence measurements while others score brilliantly. A lucky few have households of abundance with few monetary worries while the majority of us organize our lives around the cash nexus. Some of us are more spiritually inclined than others. Significant differences exist over requirements to achieve happiness. This list could go on and on. Combine the never-ending ways in which equality could be evaluated with the fact that we are a heterogeneous species, and the utility of the norm must be questioned. Is the concept of any use beyond rhetorical exuberance?[53]

International human rights law, drafted and adopted at the UN and ratified by states, embraces norms of equality. Certain key economic rights are to be implemented with equity and equality among all member states of the UN.

Economic and social human rights, as adopted in international law, attempt to be responsive to egalitarian, utilitarian, and libertarian ethical perspectives. Egalitarian principles rely on the ethical axiom that all human beings are to be treated as morally equal. Utilitarians seek to maximize the well-being of all people, even if in the short term that means sacrificing equal treatment and equal opportunity. Libertarians aspire to fairness in the procedures by which the world functions (e.g., no theft, no fraud, and so on), whatever the equity resulting.

The Universal Declaration of Human Rights embraces all ethical frameworks and explicitly avoids identifying with any particular moral philosophy. For example, as already noted, article 1 is clearly responsive to egalitarian principles: "All human beings are born free and equal in dignity and rights." A utilitarian, on the other hand, could point to principles in articles 25, 26, and 28 that present economic and social claims for the well-being of all peoples. And libertarian principles can be found in article 12, with regard to "privacy, family, home or correspondence," and in article 17, concerning private property rights. Moral philosophers could make deontological and consequential arguments for each, or all, of the UDHR's articles.

While the UDHR thus helps to frame the morals underlying these human rights claims, the document does not clarify or resolve the conflicts between ethical frameworks. For example, national development strategies could focus on egalitarian principles and invest in their poorest regions. An egalitarian could argue that those regions lagging behind in roads, industry, communication facilities, and agriculture should be the center of investments. Yet, from a utilitarian perspective this might not make sense. And thus, a utilitarian could argue that investment in more advanced regions might result in more rapid growth that would potentially make all areas better off. From this perspective, public investments should be made where they yield the highest return.[54]

Human rights discourse can, therefore, take us only so far. It does not help us resolve these conflicts. Egalitarians, utilitarians, and libertarians can all refer to human rights law to support their particular ethical paradigm. All base their ethical framework on some principles of "equality." The politician's personal value system—no matter what it is—can most likely find some validation somewhere in human rights law.

We believe that Sen's formulation of "economic equality" provides a framework for resolving these ethical conflicts in relation to development planning. Sen emphasizes the distinction between income inequality and economic inequality. He believes that policy debates have been distorted by an overemphasis on income poverty and income inequality "to the neglect of deprivations that relate to other variables, such as unemployment, ill health, lack of education, and social exclusion." Many of the criticisms of egalitarian schemes for income equality do not apply to the broader notions of economic equality. "For example, giving a larger share of income to a person with more needs—say, due to a disability—can be seen as militating against the principle of equalizing incomes, but it does not go against the broader precepts of economic equality, since the greater need for economic resources due to the disability must be taken into account in judging the requirements of economic equality." Economic equality is contingent on "public policy issues with strong economic components: the financing of health care and insurance, provision of public education, arrangements for local security and so on."[55]

This idea of "economic equality" helps us to determine what is absolutely fundamental to the principle of equality—that is, what constitutes its base. For example, philosopher Peter Singer developed the moral principle of "equal consideration of interests" based on the premise that all affected interests should be considered equally in the determination of the rightness of an action. As Singer writes, "The essence of the principle of equal consideration of interests is that we give equal weight in our moral deliberations to the like interests of all those affected by our actions.

This means that if only X and Y would be affected by a possible act, and if X stands to lose more than Y stands to gain, it is better not to do the act."[56] We would suggest that for the equal consideration of any human interest to have true meaning, economic equality, as distinct from income equality, must be upheld. Equal access to affordable food, health care, and shelter are fundamental to the realization of any equal consideration of interests. Economic and social human rights fulfillment is central to the idea of economic equality.

Economic equality can be defined as universal and equal access to global public goods, including basic education, a healthy environment, food and water, primary health care and sanitation, and housing. The enlargement of access to these public goods through state action creates the foundation for achieving economic equality and protecting economic and social human rights for all. International and national public policy should thus focus on measures that seek to guarantee these public goods and achieve true economic equality.

Why have individual nations and the global community been unable to create a world that protects and provides economic equality? We now turn to these issues and explore avenues states can take to achieve global social justice and economic equality.

Global Social Injustice: Preventing Economic Equality

In international relations, issues of economic equality are often tied to arguments for "distributive justice." Justice usually implies a set of claims. Equity (fairness) and equality represent one set of claims that are said to be necessary for true justice. Human rights represent other types of claims to a certain kind of treatment that are also tied to conceptions of justice. Claims have also been based on such precepts as merit, need, fairness, and duty. These claims are said to be applicable to all and impose obligations of action.

If social and economic structures produce unfair disadvantages for some while benefitting others, then claims to distributive action can be justified. The redistribution of economic benefits throughout society is sometimes seen as necessary to ameliorate actions of injustice and unfairness toward individuals and groups within society. Yet, few today argue that true respect for equality requires a total egalitarian distribution of all economic goods. In fact, instead of focusing on the redistribution of wealth, perhaps a more productive approach is to work for the equal access for all to national and global public goods—that is, economic equality.

Claims for distributive justice often are the result of what has been called "social injustice." Social injustice refers to unfair and inequitable structures and policies of the political, legal, economic, and social institutions of a society. When these structures favor some individuals or groups over other individuals and groups, a situation of social injustice exists. It is not just the case of individual action, but of the overall structures and policies of a society or state. The term "structural violence" refers to the denial of subsistence rights to the most vulnerable sectors as a result of the workings of economic and social institutions. For example, a corrupt business executive who embezzles funds and abuses his or her labor force may be committing an egregious action. But this would not be a case of social injustice, or structural violence, unless the economic and legal system promoted and encouraged such behavior (Mobutu's Zaire comes to mind).[57]

The distribution of economic benefits is often tied to issues of social justice. Disparity of wealth itself may not be a case of injustice. However, worldwide poverty and malnutrition as a result of national and international policies and structures are a moral issue of social injustice and structural violence. There is a relation between human suffering and the structures of the international economic system (i.e., the rules and institutions governing world trade, finance, and investment). An unfair outcome is produced; a right is violated. Economic equality thus involves issues of the justice of national and international economic institutions which can perpetuate structural violence.

As we have seen, a minimum agenda of economic and social rights includes the right to basic education, a healthy environment, food and water, primary health care and sanitation, and housing. This "core" of rights establishes the minimum standard necessary to achieve economic equality. Unfortunately, however, these basic human needs are often unintentionally undermined by structural forces within the global economy.

Global Social Justice: Creating Economic Equality

To be classified as a human right, according to David Beetham, economic and social rights claims must be fundamental, universal, and clearly specifiable. "Fundamental" refers to the protection of a minimally decent, rather than a maximally comfortable, life. "Universal" implies that the right should be applicable to all, regardless of the level of development a country has reached. And "specifiable" means it is possible to determine whether a right has been upheld or violated.[58]

There has been a great deal of debate as to the "core" of economic and social rights. The UN Economic Rights Committee has set itself the task of defining a minimum core under each right, which all countries will be obliged to uphold (see chapter 3). There are certain grounds on which all human beings deserve equal respect. Beetham argues the need to specify the most general preconditions required for a decent life. One such precondition is the material means of existence (others would include physical integrity or security and the enjoyment of basic liberties). "These necessary conditions of human agency constitute the basis of human rights."[59]

In a similar vein, as previously noted, Henry Shue develops a framework of "basic rights." He argues that it is fraudulent to guarantee someone a right they are unable to realize.[60] Basic rights, including subsistence, are essential because without them other rights cannot be fulfilled.[61] Rosa Luxemburg articulated a similar concern. She argued that to promise the working class the right to self-determination was equal to telling them they had the right to eat off of gold plates. She believed that those whose lives were at the mercy of the dictates of capital had little real control (or self-determination) over their futures.[62]

A further distinction also helps to clarify the human rights approach: obligations of conduct and of result. Obligations of conduct (active or passive) point "to behavior which the dutyholder should follow or abstain from." For example, the obligation not to torture is an obligation of conduct. Obligations of result are more concerned with achievements than with the choice of a line of action. For example, the elimination of the occurrence of hunger is an obligation of result. However, neither obligation necessarily requires state activity. The objective circumstances, the context, will determine the nature of state involvement. For example, in the case of food distribution it may be that by not interfering with market incentives and individual control over resources, the state can best avoid hunger. Yet, whether active or passive, the obligations of conduct and result require that the state uphold equal freedom from hunger.[63]

The antithesis of this human rights approach to food can be found in Emperor Haile Selassie's comments during the Ethiopian famines of 1973, explaining the absence of famine relief measures undertaken by his government: "We have said wealth has to be gained through hard work. We have said those who don't work starve." Others quote the Bible: "If any would not work neither should he eat."[64] The emperor's comments may seem extreme today. In times of famine, there are probably very few conservatives, liberals, or radicals who would argue against charitable aid of some form.

However, the reality of today's world is that acute poverty afflicts at least 1.4 billion people in the developing world. Is this destitution and poverty the result of laziness and refusal to work? It is perhaps easy to scoff at Emperor Selassie's comments since the plight of the tens of thousands affected in the 1970s in Ethiopia was obviously not the result of their refusal to work. Rather, the world witnessed the complete breakdown of the economic and legal structures within Ethiopia. Because of this, the obligations of conduct and obligations of result were clear. So why are the obligations of conduct and result toward the victims of structural violence in today's world not clear?

Many argue that, unfortunately, there are no alternatives to a system that produces winners and losers. Others maintain that international and local state action to address issues of economic equality will, in the end, only make things worse. These arguments, marshaled against distributive justice and economic equality, often include the following points:

- Any large-scale redistribution would produce disincentives to production. If this occurred, the position of those on the bottom would in fact be lowered instead of raised.
- Such policies would impact negatively on capital accumulation, stifling future economic diversification and growth.
- An economic system that is centrally planned and directed by the state stifles the creativity of individuals.
- The content of economic and social rights remains extremely vague and thus not legally enforceable. As a consequence, the obligations that flow from these rights are not even rhetorically acknowledged, let alone acted on.
- Universal coverage does not restrict the benefit to those who are truly needy (i.e., those who are poor for reasons beyond their control), and it thus dulls the incentive to work.

However, these arguments are perhaps more vulnerable than they initially appear for the following reasons:

- Meeting basic human needs does not limit economic growth. On the contrary, attaining minimum economic rights for all can reinforce development objectives and strengthen patterns of growth (as demonstrated in the Republic of Korea, Japan, Sweden, and elsewhere).
- It is a myth that there must be a trade-off between growth and equity. For example, investment in human capital—that is, policies based on principles of economic equality—can have a very positive impact on growth. Japan and Sweden have combined rapid growth with programs to meet the basic needs of all their citizens. Key to many of the economic success stories is attention to economic equality through land reform, sanitation, primary and secondary education, health care, and so on. Investments in human capital can generate income. For example, scholars have noted how Brazil's GDP has been slowed as a result of its inattention to the many dimensions of equality. One study concluded that if in 1960 the Republic of Korea had had Brazil's inequality, its GDP in 1985 would have been 15 percent lower.[65]
- The only incentive for a person who lacks freedom from hunger is to find food. One's life is consumed with survival needs. Achieving minimum economic rights creates motivational incentives because,

often for the first time, the person who was destitute is now able to consider life options.

- Furthermore, special treatment to achieve economic equality will enhance motivational incentives for people with disabilities, the elderly, and groups continuously denied equal opportunity (women, minorities, and so on). Sen documents how inequality of capability is often the result of gender and age. In these situations, special treatment to create economic equality would therefore generate new opportunities and motivational incentives for these disadvantaged groups.[66]
- It is possible to establish and meet a minimum threshold for the realization of economic and social rights. Bard-Anders Andreassen proposes that all governments establish a nationwide system of identifying local needs and opportunities for the enjoyment of economic and social rights. In particular, the needs of groups that have the greatest difficulties in the enjoyment of these rights should be addressed. Different approaches most suitable to local conditions should be explored.[67] There is no general model applicable to all settings. This approach was affirmed in the "Limburg Principles" (defined and explained in chapter 3) which state, "The achievement of economic, social and cultural rights may be realized in a variety of political settings. There is no single road to their full realization. Successes and failures have been registered in both market and non-market economies, in both centralized and decentralized political structures."[68]

John Kenneth Galbraith's proposal in 1964 for "popular consumption criteria" to be the anchor of development strategies of the LDCs has considerable merit today. He argued that development should be organized around the living standards (consumption requirements) of the present and prospective typical citizen. Development would then concentrate on consumption that is purchasable by people with a low income. A major emphasis would be placed on food, clothing, shelter, education, and medicines—the dominant items of the low-income family. The same rule then would operate equally against automobiles, expensive dwellings, and luxury consumer goods. As a result, economic planning would be concentrated on the needs of the most numerous citizens. Those who are hungry would have a special claim on resources. Galbraith is not arguing for agriculture or for industry or even for light industry as opposed to heavy industry. Rather, he is arguing for whatever approach provides for the supplies of the typical citizen.[69]

Sen's capabilities approach deepens this discussion of economic equality and the achievement of global social justice. The capabilities approach is a clear normative framework useful for resolving some of the dilemmas in ethical theory and human rights law concerning equality and justice. It further provides a pathway for the creation of public policy to realize economic and social human rights.

Economic and Social Human Rights
and the Capabilities Approach

Mary Robinson, the former high commissioner for human rights, acknowledged the impact of Sen's capabilities approach in her remarks to the delegates attending the UN's Copenhagen Plus Five Conference in June 2000:

> A new dialogue is taking place between development and human rights experts which has brought about convergences and given added depth to the law-based approaches of traditional human rights thinking. It has been enriched by Amartya Sen's work on capability rights. This approach recognizes that human development and human rights are mutually reinforcing in that they expand capabilities by protecting rights. This dialogue has contributed to the development of people-centered sustainable development.[70]

The link between human development and human rights was also clearly articulated in the *Human Development Report 2000*, published for the UNDP. "If human development focuses on the enhancement of the capabilities and freedoms that the members of a community enjoy, human rights represent the claims that individuals have on the conduct of individual and collective agents and on the design of social arrangements to facilitate or secure these capabilities and freedoms."[71]

Sen's capabilities approach provides a framework for the realization of economic and social human rights. Sen cogently argues that an adequate way of considering "real" equality of opportunities is through equality of capabilities. The focus is not on outcomes, but on the ability to function and the freedom to achieve. He argues that a person's capability to achieve functions that he or she has reason to value provides us with a general approach to assess equality and inequality. Functions include being well nourished, avoiding escapable morbidity and premature mortality, having self-respect, and being able to take part in the life of the community.[72]

Capability is directly related to the freedom to achieve valuable functionings. Sen believes that by concentrating directly on freedom as such rather than on the means to achieve freedom, we can better identify the real alternatives we have. Capability reflects a person's freedom to achieve well-being. "In the capability-based assessment of justice, individual claims are not to be assessed in terms of the resources or primary goods the persons respectively hold, but by the freedoms they actually enjoy to choose the lives that they have reason to value." Capability is thus distinguished from both the distribution of primary goods (and other resources) and final achievements.[73]

Why is this important? A person with a disability could have more primary goods, yet less capability and freedom than an individual without a disability. Or take another example from Sen: "A person may have more income and more nutritional intake, but less freedom to live a well-nourished existence because of a higher basal metabolic rate, greater vulnerability to parasitic diseases, larger body size, or simply because of pregnancy. . . . Neither primary goods, nor resources more broadly defined, can represent the capability a person actually enjoys."[74] What a person needs to achieve this freedom may vary.

To have the "freedom to achieve" means having certain needs met in one way or another. Sen mentions well nourishment and avoidance of escapable morbidity. Poverty is a result of a deprivation of "some minimum fulfillment of elementary capabilities." As a result, equality does not refer to equal incomes or even equal resources. Rather, equality is based on the equal freedom to achieve. Everyone equally should have freedom of choice and freedom to achieve. One cannot assume the same results would be obtained by looking at the resources a person commands. Valuing freedom imposes more "exacting claims."[75] To be able to live as one would value, desire, and choose requires freedom from hunger, malaria, and other maladies. Inequalities across the world lead to a loss of basic freedoms such as preventable morbidity and escapable hunger.

The relationship between income and capability is affected by age, location, race, gender, and other social factors. Sen believes that no matter what foundational structure we opt for, the reorientation from an income-centered to capability-centered view gives us a better understanding of what is involved in the challenge of poverty.[76] An African American male in Harlem may have more "resources" and live in a country with a higher overall standard of living than a citizen of the state of Costa Rica. Yet, due to social achievements in Costa Rica (or Mauritius or Kerala, India), the citizen from the LDC may have more freedom to achieve and capability to function.[77] These relatively poor countries may suffer income poverty, yet their focus on communal health services, medical care, and basic education has led to remarkable average life expectancies. These insights can inform public policy for development and poverty alleviation. A country, even with a relatively low income, that guarantees health care and education to all can achieve remarkable results in terms of the length and quality of life of their population.

Policy makers interested in achieving economic and social human rights can find direction through the capabilities approach. IPE theories can be evaluated through this lens. How do these theories promote and protect individual access to public goods, creating opportunities for adequate functioning for all peoples? Which of these theories promote economic equality, creating the base for each individual to have the opportunity to actualize his or her capabilities?

Some critics have argued that Sen's proposals do not address hard practical questions. For example, one analyst felt that Sen's arguments overall were too broad, with unfocused ethical calls for individuals and states to address human suffering everywhere. Yet, "[e]ach person cannot carry a burden of responsibility for every ill, missed opportunity, or obvious injustice. To what relevant 'community' should people chiefly belong, and which one should command the most attention?"[78] Another critic wrote that "Sen does not take account of the huge global enterprises that dominate the world economy today" and how these huge economic actors work against the protection and promotion of human capablities and, often, human freedom.[79] These analyists wonder how Sen's ideas can be translated into concrete proposals to alleviate suffering.

Yet, Sen's capabilities approach does provide the analysis and the tools necessary for policy formation to address economic and social human rights. The capabilities approach helps us focus on what individuals need for adequate functioning. Sen asks us not to merely look at low income to determine "poverty," but rather examine the "deprivation of basic capabilities," reflected in "premature mortality, significant undernourishment (especially of children), persistent morbidity, widespread illiteracy and other failures." This shift in focus also allows us to tailor public policy to meet the needs of specific groups within societies who are denied basic capabilities and, thus, denied the freedom to achieve. This approach is thus of value to women and racial minorities who often face unequal conditions, discrimination, and lack of real opportunity.[80]

The capabilities approach allows us to look at the actual ways in which individuals and groups are given the freedom to achieve adequate functioning. What are the differences between peoples and groups in their social conditions, including public education, health care and infectious disease, and affordable shelter? Public policy can then address these shortcomings.

In sum, the capabilities approach is a vehicle to expose and challenge structural violence and oppression. With the capabilities approach, human societies can be judged in terms of how well their members are able to achieve global public goods, such as basic education, a healthy environment, food and water, primary health care and sanitation, and housing. Sen argues that development is more than industrialization and GDP growth. More fundamentally, human development involves an increase in the basic capabilities of millions in the developing world.

"Development," Sen writes, "requires the removal of major sources of unfreedom: poverty as well as tyranny, poor economic opportunities as well as systematic social deprivation, neglect of public facilities as well as intolerance or overactivity of repressive states."[81] A person's capability is severely diminished if he or she is chronically ill and ignorant. The practical policy implications of Sen's thesis are radical and offer a direction to governments and international organizations that promote economic development.

These measures to enhance and protect human capabilities require attention to the provision of public goods. As discussed earlier, the globalized nature of our economy and society require that we now focus on global public goods. Since markets have historically failed to provide either sufficient or socially optimal quantities of global public goods, they can be safeguarded through actions by governments and international organizations. The enhancement of human capabilities is fundamentally linked to the protection of global public goods. We now will turn to policies to protect human capabilities, global public goods, and economic equality.

The Global New Deal and IPE

Summary Observations

The Global New Deal is based on the premise that international organization is needed now more than ever. Due to the problems of "market failure," global public goods and economic equality will be continuously underprovided unless international mechanisms are created for their protection. Every nation and every citizen is vulnerable to forces they cannot individually control. It is only through cooperative action at the global level that these public goods will be safeguarded and provided. States acting alone are no longer solely responsible for their fate in the global economy. State leaders can certainly make matters worse through greed, corruption, and wasteful spending on prestigious construction projects and bloated military budgets. But even the most fiscally disciplined, democratic,

Global New Deal Proposals

Global public goods, economic equality, and the capabilities approach are integral to the protection and fulfillment of economic and social human rights in our interdependent globalized economy. There is no one theory of IPE that successfully incorporates these essential ideas into its approach. The proposals of the Global New Deal in chapter 9 attempt to fill this gap and formulate policy to provide global public goods, generate economic equality, and create real equality of opportunity through equality of capabilities.

The Global New Deal calls for the establishment of a UN Economic Security Council to promote economic equality and a Global Public Goods Fund to finance these underprovided necessities. The Economic Security Council could hold states accountable to their pledges to

and responsible governments cannot control things like terms of
trade, interest rates, exchange rates,
commodity prices, market access,
and so on. Thus, despite their focus
on national local economic policy,
the IMF and the World Bank admit
that to an extent, globalization
undermines national policy.

It is thus necessary to strengthen
international organization and
global governance if we are serious about ending global suffering.
International policy coordination
is a minimum requirement necessary to address the "externalities"
of the global economy and assure
universal access to global public
goods, including basic education,
a healthy environment, food and
water, primary health care and sanitation, and housing.

provide safe drinking water, primary health care, a clean environment and access to basic education,
adequate nutrition, and affordable housing. The Economic Security Council and the Global Public
Goods Fund are reforms recommended in global governance to
protect, respect, and fulfill economic
and social human rights (see chapter 9).

These proposed reforms can help
mobilize state and civil society to
shape economic policy to promote
human development and enhance
human capabilities. This belief in
the utility and promise of international organization and international law informs the proposals of
the Global New Deal. These policy
proposals link human rights and
IPE strategies to overcome global
suffering.

* * *

Appendix 2.1 Economic and Social Human Rights as Global Public Goods: Economic Justifications for Government Intervention in the Economy

- Human Right to Basic Education
- Human Right to a Healthy Environment
- Human Right to Food and Water
- Human Right to Primary Health Care and Sanitation
- Human Right to Housing

Human Right to Education

Legal Claim:
Basic education = Free and
  compulsory primary education;
  Equal access to affordable
  secondary and higher education

Economic Justification for Government Intervention:
Education as a global public good
  with positive externalities

Education as a Public Good

The human right to education contains characteristics of public goods. Joseph Stiglitz maintains that knowledge itself is nonrivalrous as there is "zero marginal cost from an additional individual enjoying the benefits of the knowledge." "[A] mathematical theorem is as true in Russia as it is in the United States, in Africa as it is in Australia." A person anywhere in the world learning this theorem does not subtract from the theorem's knowledge for someone else. Thus, from an allocative efficiency perspective, the knowledge ideally should be made available at zero price. However, as Stiglitz notes, "there may be significant costs associated with transmission of knowledge."[82] For example, the provision of schools and teachers to teach students this theorem (as well as other essential knowledge) entails positive resource costs. Here too, though, there is some degree of nonrivalry. Once these educational services (classroom and teacher) are provided for one student, there is zero marginal cost of adding other students to the class, up to the size of the classroom. A parallel statement can be made about the overall school facility: once the physical facility and staff of teachers are provided, consumption by additional students (up to the facility/staff's capacity) is nonrivalrous.

Nonexcludability, on the other hand, means that no one can be excluded from the public good. As is well known, some forms of knowledge and training can be made excludable. Private school systems can make education and knowledge available only to those with money, excluding the poor. Furthermore, the high value of certain types of knowledge has led to a system of patent protections and "trade secrets" with information appropriated to an individual or a firm for private gain. The positive dimension to this privatization of knowledge is that it creates great incentives for innovative activity. Thus, both education and knowledge in these cases are mixed goods characterized by nonrivalry and excludability.

Negative and Positive Externalities

Basic education is essential to the enjoyment of all public and private goods. The negative externalities of inadequate public education provisioning include difficulties disseminating information through newspapers or the written word, problems in communicating and enforcing laws, difficulties spreading information on combating infectious diseases, and so on.

Positive externalities that occur with the provision of public education and the creation of a literate population are well known. While each individual pursues educational opportunities to better himself or herself and generate private returns, the society as a whole receives additional benefits from an educated populace. Expanding public education can lead to greater productivity and more innovations that can create potentially high social returns—greater than the private returns. Other social benefits include individuals able to knowledgably participate in a democratic polity, individuals able to make informed decisions on the quality of their health care, individuals able to control decisions regarding reproduction and family size, and so on.

Traditional economic analysis has recognized education as providing positive externalities locally (i.e., neighborhood effects). As the argument goes, even a married couple without children can find it in their interests to be surrounded by a literate population with arithmetic and quantitative skills, and thus share in the social benefits of a population with (at a minimum) a basic education. While perhaps seeking to be a "free rider" and not pay, the couple is likely to see it as in their interests for the community to provide a local school system. As society has become increasingly mobile, these external benefits generated by local school systems have been shared nationally, and now with the interconnectedness of the world, increasingly spread globally. Thus, today, education provides positive international externalities.

There is generally greater economic justification for user fees and tuition to be charged the individual for secondary and college education. The individual is the primary beneficiary of this advanced education with significant private returns expected over the individual's lifetime. While primary education also greatly benefits the individual, the social benefits to society as a whole are abundantly clear. Advanced wealthier countries thus provide compulsory and free rudimentary education to all citizens.

The Global Dimension: Education as a Global Public Good

The essence of the human right to education, as defined in international law, is free and compulsory primary education. Primary education in LDCs is critical to the rate at which better fertility and health practices are spread and innovations in agriculture are adopted. Some of the newly industrialized countries, including the Republic of Korea, have gone beyond primary education and successfully closed the gap between themselves and more advanced industrial countries in secondary education, especially in science and technology. The governments in the countries that successfully overcame extreme poverty and industrialized invested heavily in education and made it a public policy priority.

The global benefits to the promotion of a right to education in every country around the world are multiple. Raising the educational standards in the LDCs will have a positive external effect in the world as a whole in the economic, political, and social arenas:

- In the economic realm, a trained and educated workforce in LDCs should lead to an increase in the overall purchasing power of the working class and emerging middle class in these countries. Such an increase should in theory lead to an increase in imports of products from the developed countries and other LDCs, thus stimulating production in the rich and poor countries and increasing world trade.
- In the political realm, the provision of basic education in LDCs should create an informed citizenry able to hold leaders accountable to the norms of basic civil and political rights. An educated citizenry is essential for a democracy to flourish. Many political scientists believe that there is a fundamental link between democracy and world peace as democratic states seem less prone to go to war with other democratic states.
- In the social realm, the provision of basic education globally should greatly facilitate the efforts to combat infectious diseases and global health dangers. An educated person is better able to become informed and able to participate in vaccination campaigns (e.g. polio) and preventive health campaigns (e.g. HIV/AIDS). Numerous studies show women's literacy and education is a significant positive determinant of child participation in inoculation campaigns (e.g., measles) and of child survival rates. Citizens in all nations benefit from the success of these health initiatives. A robust, vibrant global society requires the successful provision of public education throughout the world.

Human Right to a Healthy Environment

Legal Claim:
Right to a clean, ecologically
  sound, and sustainable
  environment

*Economic Justification for
Government Intervention:*
The environment as a common
  resource and a global public good

The Environment as a Public Good

Many components of the environment can be considered pure public goods. Clean air, for example, is nonrivalrous and nonexcludable. An individual's consumption of a unit of clean air does not subtract from any other individual enjoying a similar amount of fresh, healthy air. Protecting the stratospheric ozone layer (which acts as a protective shield for the earth) against harmful ultraviolet radiation also provides a global public good. All of us enjoy, and no one can be excluded from, the benefits of this protection. Likewise, the troposphere (the lower portion of the atmosphere) is a global public good; protecting this realm from an accelerated "greenhouse" effect leading to global warming provides nonrivalrous and nonexcludable benefits to all. In contrast, the dramatic changes in the world's temperature and precipitation from a thermal expansion of the oceans caused by a melting of snow and ice in the Polar Regions would be extremely disruptive to the vast majority of the world's peoples and likely devastating to coastal cities and countries on all continents.[83]

Biodiversity can also be considered a public good in the sense that its conservation offers benefits that are largely nonexcludable and nonrival. The Convention on Biological Diversity defines biodiversity as "the variability among living organisms from all sources including, *inter alia,* terrestrial, marine and other aquatic ecosystems and the ecological complexes of which they are part; this includes diversity within species, between species and of ecosystems."[84] Protecting and preserving biodiversity serves to maintain the information contained in the global gene pool, which according to Charles Perrings and Madhav Gadgil, is a pure public good. In addition, biodiversity sustains the world's ecosystems, the loss of which would cause long-term damage to all people's health and food security.[85]

Unpolluted oceans and transnational lakes, rivers, and seas have also been identified as global public goods. As with air, these bodies of water cross borders and their benefits are nonrivalrous and nonexcludable.

Common Resources

Many components of the environment can be considered common resources, characterized by nonexcludable yet rivalrous use. Over half of the world's surface is outside the national borders of any one state and thus beyond national jurisdiction. Common resource areas, which include the high seas, the sea-bed, Antarctica, and outer space, have been termed the "common heritage of humankind" in international environmental law. Due to the "free-rider" problem, described earlier, there is a strong argument for global government regulation and intervention to protect these common resources. Open access can lead to the "tragedy of the commons" and overexploitation and depletion, as the example of over-fishing so dramatically demonstrates.

Due to ecological interdependence, there are also common resources within the borders of sovereign nations. All of humanity may have a collective interest in actions that take place within a given country. Biodiversity preservation, for example, is of interest to all even though the resources that need protection may be located within a particular national jurisdiction. This high level of ecological interdependence led to the formation of the concept of a "common concern for humankind" in international environmental law. The Biodiversity Convention preamble affirms that "the conservation of biological diversity is a common concern of humankind," even though, as noted by David Hunter, James Salzman, and Durwood Zaelke, most terrestrial biodiversity is found within sovereign states.[86] Global regulation, again through international law, is often needed to protect, restore, and defend these common resources.

Negative and Positive Externalities

The negative environmental externalities caused by industrialization, modern agriculture, and overpopulation are well known. Air pollution from industrial plants, mills, and cars; overfishing and pesticide runoff and other pollution in the oceans, waterways, and underground aquifers; and toxic wastes polluting the lands—all generate such negative effects as illness, chronic health conditions, and even death; high costs to businesses that require clean environmental resources; and the like. The positive externalities from preserving a healthy environment are also well known as the sustainability of human life itself depends upon the protection of the ecosystem. Global regulation and intervention in the economy is therefore necessary to remedy the negative consequences and protect the external benefits that come from a healthy environment.

The Global Dimension: The Environment as a Global Public Good

Environmental scientists point to at least four global environmental problems where the planet may have reached the sustainable limits of human activity—climate change, including global warming; stratospheric ozone depletion; species extinction and the loss of biodiversity; and environmental contamination by hazardous chemicals and wastes. In addition, the alleviation of global poverty and protection of the environment are increasingly recognized as complementary and interdependent goals. As Indira Gandhi reportedly said, "Poverty is the worst polluter." Poverty pushes the poor to unsustainable land use, which in turn, reduces the amount and quality of resources available, perpetuating an environmentally destructive spiral.[87]

The human species is drastically altering the world's natural ecosystems. Human impacts are no longer local or national, but global and can be detected in the most remote reaches of the biosphere. In fact, as human population and industrial activity expands, we have pushed up against the limit of what that biosphere can support. The global ecosystem is a global public good in the sense that it generates benefits that are nonrivalrous and nonexcludable. The creation of a World Environment Organization, outlined in chapter 9, can potentially provide the institutional and legal framework for states to act cooperatively to protect the environment and end unsustainable and ecologically damaging practices.

Human Right to Food and Water

Legal Claim:	*Economic Justification for Government Intervention:*
Essential nutrition = Equal access to adequate and affordable diet; Equal access to clean water	Positive externalities for society as a whole

Food and Water as Public Goods

The Economic Rights Committee declares that the "human right to water entitles everyone to sufficient, safe, acceptable, physically accessible and affordable water for personal and domestic use."[88] The committee also writes that the right to adequate food implies "[t]he availability of food in a quantity and quality sufficient to satisfy the dietary needs of individuals."[89] Upholding the human right to clean water and basic nutrition is central to providing substance to all other legal rights, including education, health, housing, and life itself.

Yet, both food and water are rivalrous and excludable in consumption, and thus don't meet the standard definition in economics of public goods. For example, if someone eats an apple, no one else can eat it. There may be enough food and clean water in the world for all, but consuming each unit of food and clean water is rivalrous. One person's consumption of that unit of food or water means that no one else can consume that unit. In addition, food and water can be excludable. A state, for example, could decide that only those people who pay can have access to a certain water or food supply. While we may wish that these basic goods were nonrivalrous and nonexcludable, in fact they actually are not.

Are there any elements of the conception of public goods that apply to the human right to food and water? Yes. The substantial *benefits to society* of a population with access to an adequate diet and clean water are both nonrivalrous and nonexcludable. Water and food security allow individuals to lead healthy, dignified, and productive lives. When these conditions are not met, individuals face lives of poor health, low productivity, and a disruption of livelihoods. In contrast, the adequate consumption of food and water means that individuals are nourished and well-fed and able to be productive members of society. One country benefiting from the improved economic and social sphere created by a healthy population does not detract from other countries sharing the social benefits generated by this healthy society. In this sense, the benefits from equal access to adequate food and clean water have public good characteristics.

Negative and Positive Externalities

The negative externalities linked to inadequate access to clean water and basic nutrition are shocking. The UNDP noted in 2006 that "the 1.8 million child deaths each year related to unclean water and poor sanitation dwarf the casualties associated with violent conflict. No act of terrorism generates economic devastation on the scale of the crisis in water and sanitation. Yet the issue barely registers on the international agenda."[90] The World Food Program reported that on average there were four million new hungry people a week throughout 2009, with the number of hungry people around the world totaling over one billion.[91] Societies around the world facing inadequate access to clean water and basic nutrition are plagued with malnutrition, ill health, and instability. Such conditions undermine productivity and economic growth and perpetuate conditions of acute poverty and suffering.

The positive externalities of clean water and adequate nutrition are often taken for granted today in the industrialized world. Yet, social progress in the rich countries was historically based upon a social contract between the government and citizens to establish clean water systems, sanitation, and access to adequate food. At the end of the 19th century, the child death rates in London, New York, and Paris were as high then as they are now in much of Sub-Saharan Africa. Clean water, sanitation, and increased food production changed all this. For example, half the mortality reduction in the U.S. in the first third of the 20th century has been attributed to the establishment of water purification systems.[92] As previously noted, due to the "free-riders" dynamic, there is little incentive in a market economy for individual rational actors to provide positive externalities that are socially beneficial for all. As a result, there is a strong case for government intervention in the economy to fulfill the human right to access to food and water.

The Global Dimension: Food and Water as Global Public Goods

Inge Kaul, Isabelle Grunberg, and Marc Stern assert that "a poverty alleviation programme for Sub-Saharan Africa could be a global public good if, by meeting the needs of local populations, it were also to contribute to conflict prevention and international peace, reduce environmental degradation of potentially international consequences and improve global health conditions."[93] A parallel argument can be made for food and water. Programs to create systems for clean water and access to adequate food in regions of Africa (and elsewhere) could also be considered global public goods as they would produce similar positive global outcomes of conflict reduction and improved global health conditions.

Kaul, Grunberg, and Stern define final public goods in relation to "outcomes" rather than "goods." They write that these outcomes "may be tangible (such as the environment or the common heritage of mankind) or intangible (such as peace or financial stability)."[94] It is in this sense that we can also define food and water as global public goods. Clean water and bountiful food production are essential to human development and the growth of stable societies. The tangible outcome of individual governments working to respect, protect, and fulfill the human rights to food and water is an improvement in global health, global conflict prevention, and increased global trade and development.

Human Right to Health

Legal Claim:
Primary health care = Equal
  access to adequate and
  affordable health care and
  sanitation

Economic Justification for
Government Intervention:
Health as a global public good

Health as a Public Good

Globalization has had a profound impact on many aspects of life, including health. The massive movements of people across borders—refugees, immigrants, international travelers—combined with new linkages in trade have created new global health vulnerabilities and increased global health risks; and the revolution in information technology has enabled rapid dissemination and sharing of health information globally. As H1N1 (swine flu), avian flu, HIV/AIDS and smallpox demonstrate, health risks emanating from one country can create threats and dangers to populations around the world.[95]

The human right to health contains characteristics of public goods. For example, the benefits from immunizations against contagious diseases, and the establishment of sewage systems, sanitation, and global epidemiological surveillance are essentially nonrivalrous and nonexcludable. A person can enjoy a sanitary, disease-free environment without infringing upon another person's enjoyment of this clean environment. Everyone can benefit from knowledge about the world's health and awareness of foreign outbreaks of infectious diseases. Upon receiving a health alert, individual nations can then prepare their people to respond and cope with the disease. However, the provision of these goods will fall short of social efficiency without government action. State involvement, for example, is necessary to coordinate and implement society-wide immunization and disease monitoring programs.[96]

Due to the global nature of the new health threats, close international cooperation and coordination is necessary to guarantee the provision of these goods for all. The World Health Organization's (WHO) effort to eradicate smallpox exemplifies the global nature of these public goods. One nation acting alone was unable to defeat smallpox; yet the eradication of smallpox offered benefits to all countries, in the form of reduced health risks and reduced allocation of resources towards smallpox precautions, prevention, and treatment. The WHO's coordination of a worldwide system of disease control, health improvements, and immunizations is essential in our modern world. It is in the interests of all nations to help poor countries succeed in the provision of basic health care and sanitation.[97]

Negative and Positive Externalities

Basic primary health care is essential to the enjoyment of all public and private goods. The negative externalities of inadequate health care and health provisioning are well known and include not only greater risks of contracting contagious sickness and disease but potentially tremendous harmful economic consequences for the society as a whole. Global public "bads," such as malaria, TB, or HIV/AIDS, hurt the rich and the poor countries alike, but especially those individuals whose only asset is their health and physical strength.[98]

The positive externalities that occur with the provision of basic health care are also well-known and include a healthy and motivated workforce and the ability to maintain open trade and cultural relations with the outside world. The international community as a whole benefits from any one nation's reduction of health risks and advances in public health.[99]

The Global Dimension: Health as a Global Public Good

Human health is fragile and susceptible to dangerous infections and diseases. How is a government able to protect its citizens from medical dangers that originate from outside its borders? In an earlier era, nations established rigorous inspections to monitor international travelers at borders for signs of disease. Individuals thought to be infected or sick were quarantined or sent home. Today, however, such policies are considered ineffective. Mark Zacher notes that "since most diseases have common incubation periods of several days to a few weeks, and leave no clearly discernible physical signs, there is no way to detect most infected persons." Instead of bolstering up inspections at the borders, most experts conclude that resources could be better used "to reduce the number of people with diseases in developing countries and to improve the medical capabilities of those countries to care for the ill." In fact, U.S. health policies reflect this thinking, as the staff of the Quarantine Division of the Centers for Disease Control is only a fraction of what it was in the 1960s. As Zacher writes, this change reflects the realization that "in the modern state, diseases cannot be stopped at the borders."[100] The best way to stop the spread of disease in both the North and the South is to work for the realization of the human right to health for all global citizens. The provision of primary health care to all within a country promises benefits that other countries can share, without rivalry or exclusion. Thus, basic health care is a global public good, warranting international attention, coordination, and commitment.

Human Right to Housing

Legal Claim:	*Economic Justification for*
Adequate shelter = Equal access to	*Government Intervention:*
safe, habitable, and affordable	Positive externalities for society as a
homes	whole

Housing as a Public Good

The human rights idea revolves around the principle that an individual can claim certain entitlements simply by being alive. One such human rights claim is a right to adequate housing, which is found in both the UDHR and the Economic Rights Treaty. While property rights remain central in U.S. law, including volumes of law that apply to real estate, the idea of a human right to housing remains undeveloped. Yet, the U.S. came close to accepting the human right to adequate housing in the Housing Act of 1949 which called for "the realization as soon as feasible of a decent home and suitable living environment for every American family." The goal of a decent home for all U.S. citizens was later reaffirmed by the U.S. Congress in 1968, 1974, 1987, and 1990.[101]

Housing, like food, is not a pure public good. Even if a government ensured that all citizens had access to shelter that was habitable and affordable, housing (like food) would remain rivalrous and excludable. Why? Even with an abundance of affordable housing for all, each individual unit of housing remains rivalrous. If someone resides in a house, it is not available for others to reside in; consumption is thus characterized by rivalry. And, there are a variety of ways in which housing can be excludable. Housing can be limited to those with substantial incomes, and exclude the lower working class and poor. If individuals do not pay for housing, they can be easily excluded from this resource with the installation of inexpensive locks, and so on. Thus, housing does not meet the standard definition in economics of a public good.

Yet, the human right to housing does contain elements of a public good. While there may be significant costs in the creation and provision of affordable housing, once established, adequate shelter brings significant benefits to the entire society. Affordable housing, for example, can be created through a variety of governmental actions, including the establishment of rent control and zoning requirements, the construction of public housing and homeless centers, the provision of rent (or income) supplements, and the enactment of laws guaranteeing that people are not subject to arbitrary eviction and harassment. Affordable housing can help individuals lead full and productive lives and contribute to the overall well-being and stability of the community as a whole. The potential social benefits from such stability are numerous, including economic productivity and prosperity, social cohesion, an engaged citizenry, and political solidity. Since other countries can share in these benefits, without rivalry or exclusion, equal access to safe, habitable, and affordable homes has aspects of public goods.

Negative and Positive Externalities

Population growth, urban migration, massive refugee flows, environmental degradation, and global economic contractions have resulted in widespread homelessness and inadequate housing. Global poverty, worsening inequality, and the lack of affordable shelter options have exacerbated these dire conditions. The United Nations estimated in 2005 that there were over 1.6 billion people worldwide inadequately housed and over 100 million who were completely homeless, comprising 20 to 40 million in urban areas and about 60 million in rural areas.[102] In every country in the world, countless men and women (including the very young and the elderly) "squat" in buildings, live on the streets, and sleep on sidewalks and under bridges. The negative externalities of these conditions on society include increases in crime, drug use, prostitution, and infectious diseases. The quality of life for society as a whole is diminished when substantial numbers of citizens have no place to call home.

In addition, crowded, dilapidated, substandard housing also generates negative externalities. Safety, fire, and health risks, including structural collapse and the spread of disease, are associated with dirty, unhealthy living conditions. And finally, substandard housing can lower property values for neighboring property, thus negatively impacting on the community overall.

The positive externalities of ensuring adequate shelter for all are obvious. As individuals gain the security of a place to live, they are able to focus on other dimensions to life. The stability of a home gives each of us the ability to move beyond an hourly struggle to attain basic survival needs and gives us the potential to fully develop our individual capabilities. With a place to live, it becomes easier to take care of our individual health and livelihood, and to then begin to think about the needs and concerns of others. As with education and health care, adequate shelter is essential to the enjoyment of all public and private goods.

The Global Dimension: Housing as a Global Public Good

Miloon Kothari, UN Special Rapporteur on the Right to Adequate Housing, highlighted the global dimensions to the housing crisis. In his 2005 report, Kothari documented the breadth of the homeless problem from the LDCs to the rich countries. For example, in India from November 2004 to February 2005, about 90,000 dwellings were demolished in Mumbai, rendering some additional 400,000 people homeless. At the same time (2005), the report highlighted worsening conditions in Australia, Canada, and the

U.S. For example, in the U.S. in 2005, the UN estimated that there were 840,000 individuals homeless at any given time, and between 2.5 to 3.5 million people homeless over the course of a year, of which about 1.35 million were children. In addition, Kothari reported that globally there was a "culture of silence" regarding women's rights to housing, land, property, and inheritance. This ongoing discrimination against women was a critical factor severely affecting women's right to adequate housing.[103]

The protection of the right to housing in every country around the world will have global benefits. Countries that ensure this human right could experience more rapid economic growth, as individuals with the security of safe and adequate shelter and a healthy living environment are able to lead more productive lives. A secure, healthy, and motivated workforce could help a nation grow its economy and expand its global trade and economic relations. And finally, the security of a home would diminish the number of economic immigrants fleeing insecure conditions in search of economic opportunities abroad. Such developments would benefit other countries, without rivalry or exclusion; and recognizing these effects, housing can be classified as a global public good.

3

The United Nations and Economic and Social Human Rights

How does the UN approach economic and social human rights? How are these rights defined in international law? Is it possible to develop accurate indicators of social development to measure the achievement of economic and social human rights? How does the UN monitor and enforce a state's compliance with international human rights law? Are workers' interests in developed and developing countries furthered by enforcement of international economic and social standards? Is it possible to energize the global implementation and monitoring of these basic human rights and enact effective policies to protect the vulnerable during periods of rapid economic globalization?

As part of my class on International Organization, I travel to Geneva with students approximately every other year to better understand the work of various international organizations, national missions to the UN, and nongovernmental organizations (NGOs). During our meetings, a series of incidents brought into sharp focus the ongoing UN deadlock between the North and the South over economic and social human rights and development.

This impasse was strikingly visible, for example, in the approach to the internationally recognized "right to development."[1] The human rights officer of the Pakistani mission to the UN told us in 1998 and again in 2007 that the right to development was the most important human right. As a priority, his government would fight for the right to development to be included as part of the International Bill of Human Rights.[2] His stress on the critical importance to poor countries of development rights brought back the oft-quoted words of Leopold Senghor, the former president of Senegal: "[H]uman rights begin with breakfast."[3] At subsequent meetings at the U.S. mission to the UN, U.S. human rights officers have consistently declared that the right to development was simply rhetoric and held no real meaning. The U.S. position was that this claimed "right" was impossible to implement and was pushed by the less developed countries (LDCs) to pressure the developed countries into increasing aid levels. The U.S. formal acceptance of the validity of development as a human right at the 1993 Vienna World Conference on Human Rights did not appear to change U.S. policy. After leaving these meetings, it was hard to see how even a dialogue could move forward given these diametrically opposed positions.

Conflicts between the North and the South also surfaced in meetings with the World Trade Organization (WTO), the Office of the U.S. Trade Representative to the WTO, and the World Wide Fund for Nature (WWF). Rulings by the WTO Appellate Body struck down U.S. legal protections for endangered sea turtles. The Eckerd College students I traveled with were environmentally conscious and concerned not only about this ruling, but also about how intertwined trade and environmental policies have become. According to the WWF, sea turtles are an internationally protected species endangered around the world by the loss of their habitat. They became an international trade issue with the advent of mechanized shrimp trawling, which by 1990 had caused some 100,000 adult turtles to drown each year in nets. This loss is easily preventable. A turtle excluder device has proven effective in keeping turtles out of the shrimp nets. The device is inexpensive, easy to install, and standard practice in more than a dozen countries. The United States not only required its domestic shrimp industry to use turtle excluders, but applied identical standards to countries selling shrimp in U.S. markets. In response, Malaysia, Thailand, India, and Pakistan filed a complaint with the WTO claiming that the requirement deprived them of market access guaranteed under most-favored-nation status. The WTO Appellate Body decided in favor of the four Asian countries, expressing concern over the coercive effect of the U.S. measure on the policies of other governments. The United States was required to open its markets to countries whose fishing methods threaten sea turtles.[4]

The WTO representative characterized U.S. policy as imperialistic. She claimed that the United States had no right to impose its environmental standards on the rest of the world. She sided with the shrimp fishermen in Malaysia whose jobs, she claimed, were threatened by turtle excluder devices.[5] The U.S. trade representative referred us to President Bill Clinton's 1998 address to the WTO. President Clinton had declared, "We must do more to harmonize our goal of increasing trade with our goal of improving the environment and working conditions. . . . International trade rules must permit sovereign nations to exercise their right to set protective standards for health, safety, and the environment and biodiversity. Nations have a right to pursue those protections—even when they are stronger than international norms."[6]

A further dramatic example of the clash between the developed and less developed countries over trade and development was the formal collapse of the "Doha" rounds of WTO trade negotiations in July 2008. The objective of the Doha Development Round of trade negotiations was to lower trade barriers and increase global trade specifically to help the less developed nations. These discussions began in Doha, Qatar, in 2001. After seven years of ministerial meetings that stretched from Cancun to Hong Kong to Paris to Potsdam and Geneva, the talks failed to achieve a compromise on agricultural import rules. In particular, there were disagreements between the developed and developing nations over the "special safeguard mechanism," a measure designed to protect poor farmers by allowing LDCs to impose a special tariff on certain agricultural goods in the event of a fall in prices or an import surge.[7]

These differences toward economic rights and development between the developed and less developed countries demonstrate the difficulty of achieving a global understanding of economic and social human rights. The United States not only undermines the right to development, but also refuses to ratify the Economic Rights Treaty (the International Covenant on Economic, Social and Cultural Rights), which is strongly supported by the LDCs. Many LDCs continue to see not only environmental regulations, which are often strongly supported by developed countries, but also trade-labor linkages as impediments to their economic growth. For example, in 1996 developing countries succeeded in derailing the social clause movement—in other words, the attempt to link adherence to basic labor rights with membership in the WTO. The LDCs argued that the social clause would infringe on their sovereignty and deny them a legitimate comparative advantage. This opposition allowed the WTO to declare that it would not pursue the trade-labor linkage any further. Economic and social human rights thus exist within a global framework filled with discord, fragmentation, and dissension. Progress depends on overcoming these different world views which have unfortunately led to a fundamental mistrust between the North and the South.

Human rights claims evolve over time. There is a strong link between the growth of new human rights and social development. As modern global society has matured, accompanied by deep ecological interdependence, new threats to the individual and the group have surfaced. To combat these threats, governments and nongovernmental organizations (NGOs) have raised issues of environmental balance, economic growth, social equality, and disease eradication. Global cooperation between state and nonstate actors is seen as critical to address this perplexing new agenda of world politics. Accordingly, the list of human rights claims keeps growing. Complex social relations give rise to these demands as new claims are made to alleviate suffering. What appears fundamental in one historical era may not be in another. Human rights claims today have no relation to a primitive state of nature where people lived with a few essential needs. As Norberto Bobbio points out, there are no current charters of rights that do not recognize the right to education, which broadens as society develops to include secondary and university as well as primary education. Yet, none of the better-known descriptions of the state of nature mention such a right.[8] International human rights today are a product of this particular historical period.

The International Bill of Human Rights incorporates civil, political, economic, social, and cultural rights. It acknowledges human needs of survival, well-being, identity, and freedom. In the twenty-first century, collective human rights of gender, class, sexuality, and ethnicity/race have been added to this framework. The goal is to create political, civil, and socioeconomic rights that enable all individuals through group membership to develop a valuable, independent life in civil society. We now have the ability to create a world of humane governance informed by these normative priorities. Perhaps in other times such an ambitious agenda was not possible, but there is no question that today with new economic developments, technological breakthroughs, and innovations in communications, we have the ability to protect basic human dignity.

It is now commonly accepted that it is not possible to achieve significant progress on human rights without subsistence needs (food, sanitation, education, and so on) being met. It is also impossible to achieve human rights progress and development in societies controlled by repressive and corrupt regimes. The government can be the main obstacle to achieving either economic or political rights. Most UN scholars and human rights activists promote an interdependence between the two sets of rights (civil/political and economic/social/cultural) and criticize those who make too sharp a distinction between them. As will be demonstrated in this chapter, economic and social rights are complimentary to the human rights principles found within civil and political rights. And, civil and political rights can be fully realized only if everyone has a minimum of economic security, as impoverished peoples often have scant motivations and abilities to fully participate in the civic life of society. The two sets of rights are thus both symbiotic and mutually dependent.

This chapter examines the following key aspects of the UN approach to economic and social human rights:

- defining,
- measuring,
- monitoring and enforcing, and
- strengthening global compliance.

Defining Economic and Social Human Rights

The UN approaches economic and social human rights through a framework of legal positivism—that is, rights are defined by what states have actually agreed to through consent. Consent is most often demonstrated either through written agreement (treaty, convention, and so on) or through customary practice. A legal positivist looks to state treaties, customs, and general principles of international law as the primary sources of international economic and social human rights. These socially constructed legal principles of rights and obligations reflect the bias of the governing elites of global politics. Thus, for the most part the poor and dispossessed do not have a voice in the formation of the international legal rights that are often proclaimed in their name.[9]

Women have also traditionally been left out of the formation of international law (see chapter 6). The distinct needs and rights of women are not reflected in most international legal instruments. The private sphere where women often face both domestic violence and economic exploitation has not been adequately addressed through existing legal norms. The specific needs of women in relation to the biological functions of raising and breast-feeding children have also been inadequately addressed. The issue here is not just equality with men, but the distinct economic and social rights of women.

Conventions on economic and social rights have been developed by the UN-affiliated International Labor Organization (ILO). As of July 2009, the ILO had adopted 188 conventions establishing labor standards on a wide range of issues from the most general (such as freedom of association) to the specific (such as road transport). The ILO has prioritized these standards and established the following basic human rights conventions: freedom of association and collective bargaining, abolition of forced labor, equal remuneration, and nondiscrimination in employment. Virginia Leary points out that these are the most widely ratified ILO conventions and are those to which the ILO devotes most of its attention. To many scholars, the ILO's basic human rights conventions form the corpus of minimum international labor standards or internationally recognized worker rights.[10]

The UN also has a corpus of international treaties addressing economic and social rights. The broad consensus on the content of these two types of rights, and the distinction between them, is generally seen as follows:

- Social rights are those rights necessary for an adequate standard of living (Universal Declaration of Human Rights [UDHR], article 25; Economic Rights Treaty, article 11; and Convention on the Rights of the Child, article 27). Paul Hunt includes rights to food, shelter, health, and education as key social rights.[11] Asbjørn Eide links social rights to "necessary subsistence rights—adequate food and nutrition rights, clothing, housing, and the necessary conditions of care."[12] The right to education affirms free and compulsory primary education and equal access to secondary and higher education. The right to health ensures access to adequate health care, nutrition, sanitation, and to clean water and air. The right to housing provides guarantees against forced eviction and access to a safe, habitable, and affordable home. The right to food requires that states cooperate in the equitable distribution of world food supplies and respect and assure the ability of people to feed themselves.[13]

• Economic rights, on the other hand, refer to the right to property (UDHR, article 17), the right to work (UDHR, article 23; Economic Rights Treaty, article 6), and the right to social security (UDHR, articles 22 and 25; Economic Rights Treaty, article 9; and Convention on the Rights of the Child, article 26). The right to work denotes the opportunity to earn a living wage in a safe environment and embraces the freedom to organize and bargain collectively.[14]

In 1986, a group of distinguished experts in international law, meeting at the University of Limburg (Maastricht, the Netherlands), drafted guidelines on the nature and scope of states' obligations under the Economic Rights Treaty. "The Limburg Principles on the Implementation of the International Covenant on Economic, Social and Cultural Rights" (hereinafter the "Limburg Principles") have been extremely useful to human rights advocates, lawyers, and diplomats attempting to interpret the legal duties of states under this convention.[15] The "Limburg Principles" comprehensively summarized the state of international law in relation to economic and social rights as of 1986.

On the tenth anniversary of the "Limburg Principles," a group of experts again met in Maastricht to elaborate on the nature and scope of violations of economic, social, and cultural rights and appropriate responses and remedies. This 1997 meeting resulted in "The Maastricht Guidelines on Violations of Economic, Social and Cultural Rights" (hereinafter the "Maastricht Guidelines"), which reflect the evolution of international law since 1986 and clearly demonstrate the emerging consensus within the legal community as to state responsibility and accountability under the Economic Rights Treaty.[16]

These principles and guidelines are intended to outline what a state must do to meet the obligations and duties that flow from the economic, social, and cultural rights articulated in the Economic Rights Treaty—that is, the right to work, the right to housing, the right to health care, and so on. The experts were able to draw on the work of many others, including that of the UN Economic Rights Committee and various UN conferences and reports.[17] As a result, the "Maastricht Guidelines" are a very clear summary of the current understanding of economic and social rights in international law.

The following are some key principles found in the "Maastricht Guidelines":

1. The state remains the primary actor responsible for implementing international economic and social rights. The guidelines claim to recognize the global forces at work at the end of the twentieth century weakening the state's ability to control its economic destiny. However, "as a matter of international law, the state remains ultimately responsible for guaranteeing the realization of these rights."[18] The UN's approach is to hold governments accountable for the provision of basic social services, including health care, employment, and education.

2. States have obligations to respect, protect, and fulfill. This three-part approach to explaining economic and social rights was first formulated by Henry Shue.[19] Eide, as special rapporteur on the right to food, further developed these three categories.[20] As stated in the "Maastricht Guidelines":

> The obligation to respect requires States to refrain from interfering with the enjoyment of economic, social and cultural rights. Thus, the right to housing is violated if the State engages in arbitrary forced evictions. The obligation to protect requires States to prevent violations of such rights by third parties. Thus, the failure to ensure that private employers comply with basic labor standards may amount to a violation of the right to work or the right to just and favorable conditions of work. The obligation to fulfill requires States to take appropriate legislative, administrative, budgetary, judicial and other measures toward the full realization of such rights. Thus, the failure of States to provide essential primary health care to those in need may amount to a violation.[21]

3. The guidelines outline violations through acts of commission (direct action by states) and omission (failure of states to act). Acts of commission include the formal removal of legislation and/or funding necessary for the continued enjoyment of an economic or social right, the active denial of such rights to particular individuals or groups, and the reduction of specific public expenditures to protect social welfare resulting in the denial of minimum subsistence rights for everyone. Violations of omission include the failure to enforce legislation designed to implement provisions of the covenant and the failure to utilize the maximum of available resources toward the full realization of the covenant.

4. States are allowed a "margin of discretion in selecting the means for implementing their respective obligations." However, "certain

steps must be taken immediately and others as soon as possible." A state violates the covenant when it fails to satisfy what the Economic Rights Committee refers to as "a minimum core obligation to ensure the satisfaction of, at the very least, minimum essential levels of each of the rights. . . . Thus, for example, a State party in which any significant number of individuals is deprived of essential foodstuffs, of essential primary health care, of basic shelter and housing, or of the most basic forms of education is, prima facie, violating the Covenant." Resource scarcity does not relieve the state of these minimum obligations.[22]

5. States are required to ensure that private entities or individuals, including transnational corporations within their jurisdiction, do not deprive individuals of social or economic rights. "States are responsible for violations of economic, social and cultural rights that result from their failure to exercise due diligence in controlling the behavior of such non-state actors."[23]

6. States are required to eliminate all forms of discrimination against women. "Discrimination against women in relation to the rights recognized in the Covenant, is understood in light of the standard of equality for women under the Convention on the Elimination of All Forms of Discrimination Against Women. That standard requires the elimination of all forms of discrimination against women, including gender discrimination arising out of social, cultural and other structural disadvantages."[24]

The Economic Rights Treaty

The Economic Rights Treaty, which entered into force on 3 January 1976, is divided into five parts. The focus of part one is the right to self-determination; part two defines the general nature of states parties' obligations; part three recognizes specific substantive rights; part four addresses international implementation; and part five states specific legal provisions. Substantive provisions in part three include rights to the following: an adequate standard of living, including food, clothing, and housing; physical and mental health; education; scientific and cultural life; the opportunity to work; just and favorable conditions of work; rest and leisure; social security; special protection for the family, mothers, and children; and the right to form and join trade unions and to strike.

The challenge is to identify approaches to holding nations accountable to fulfill their obligations in the treaty. The Economic Rights Treaty demands that governments take all appropriate means and use the maximum available resources to fulfill these specific rights, but it gives no further guidance. Legislative and judicial remedies are key, but overall economic and social development planning and intervention by the government may be even more important.

Unlike the Political Rights Treaty (the International Covenant on Civil and Political Rights), which has an independent group of experts supervising implementation of the covenant's provisions (the Human Rights Committee), the UN's Economic and Social Council (ECOSOC), a body of governmental representatives, was charged with implementation responsibility of the Economic Rights Treaty. In the late 1970s and into the 1980s, ECOSOC set up a series of sessional working groups of governmental delegates to help with these responsibilities. These working groups were a failure. In 1987, ECOSOC replaced them with a body of human rights experts operating in their personal capacity, the Economic Rights Committee. The Economic Rights Committee thus began from a weaker position than its counterpart, the Human Rights Committee. The Economic Rights Committee's existence depends on the continued support of ECOSOC. Theoretically, if Economic Rights Committee decisions upset the members of ECOSOC, its continued existence could be jeopardized. The Human Rights Committee, on the other hand, exists by legal statute, as it is a part of the Political Rights Treaty.[25]

The Economic Rights Committee is charged with monitoring the compliance of states parties to the Economic Rights Treaty and is the principle UN body concerned with implementation of this treaty. The composition of the Economic Rights Committee is similar to the Human Rights Committee with eighteen independent experts elected by ECOSOC for four-year terms. Membership reflects an equitable geographic representation. States parties to the Economic Rights Treaty must submit an initial report within two years of ratification with subsequent reports required every five years. The reporting procedure involves a dialogue between the state party and the Economic Rights Committee. The Economic Rights Committee's examination of states parties' reports and their adoption of general comments have been useful and innovative.[26]

Political Rights Treaty/Human Rights Committee

As a point of comparison, it is useful to look at the reporting and implementation mechanisms established through the Human Rights Committee. The Human Rights Committee was established as an independent body of human rights experts. Human rights activists hoped that these experts would prove to be more objective and less political in assessing human rights violations than the political appointments made by nation-states to the Human Rights Commission (now the Human Rights Council). The Human Rights Committee conducts public examinations of reports submitted by states parties. Its power was enhanced with the passage of the first optional protocol that allows for communications from individuals whose civil and political rights have been violated.[27]

In July 2009, there were 164 states parties to the Political Rights Treaty and 111 states parties to the First Optional Protocol.[28] The Office of the High Commissioner for Human Rights (OHCHR) reports that by the end of the summer of 2008 the Human Rights Committee had considered some 1,800 complaints submitted under the Protocol and adopted 635 decisions on their merits (while the remainder were either declared inadmissible, discontinued, withdrawn, or not yet concluded). In the 635 decisions, the committee found 503 violations of the Covenant by states parties. The views of the Human Rights Committee interpreting the substance of the Political Rights Treaty can be termed "international human rights jurisprudence." National courts that now refer to the decisions and views of the Human Rights Committee include the Supreme Court of Zimbabwe, the Judicial Committee of the Privy Council in London, and the Constitutional Court of South Africa. This interplay between UN treaty bodies and national juridical organs is a very positive development.[29]

The individual complaint procedures developed through the optional protocol have been refined. According to Mercedes Morales, a human rights officer to the OHCHR in Geneva, after exhausting all domestic remedies individuals may submit complaints directly to the UN. The complaint can be of any length—from one page to hundreds. Once admissibility is determined, a summary of the case is submitted to a special rapporteur. The rapporteur reports to the Human Rights Committee, which ultimately makes all final decisions. If the Human Rights Committee finds that a violation has been committed, implementation of its decision through either compensation or a change in legislation is expected to take place at the national level. Despite the fact that these judgments are not legally binding, Morales estimates that there is around a 40 percent compliance rate with the decisions of the Human Rights Committee. This is significant progress. The Human Rights Committee's annual report lists those countries that do not reply to complaints.[30]

Many states move to implement the views of the Human Rights Committee by releasing political prisoners, awarding compensation to victims of human rights violations, reinstating individuals in the civil service, amending legislation considered incompatible with the provisions of the Political Rights Treaty, or granting other remedies. All of these measures depend on the good will of the states parties. Colombia was the first state to pass enabling legislation, "which elevates the decisions of UN and regional human rights bodies to the level of enforceable judgements at the national level."[31] Yet, states do seem to listen to the Human Rights Committee. The Human Rights Committee and the Committee against Torture have requested hundreds of interim measures of protection, for example, in death penalty, extradition, or deportation cases requesting stays of execution or temporary suspension of extradition. These requests have been respected in all but a few cases.[32]

Economic Rights Treaty/Economic Rights Committee

In contrast to the previous complaint and enforcement system for civil and political rights, the implementation procedures of the Economic Rights Treaty are still being developed. In theory, the 160 nations that had ratified the Economic Rights Treaty as of July 2009 agreed that these economic and social claims had equal status to civil and political rights.[33] In practice, these same nations have failed to take the necessary implementation steps (legislative, administrative, or judicial) to make these claims equal to civil and political rights.

The General Assembly finally approved the Optional Protocol to the Economic Rights Treaty, establishing an individual complaint mechanism, on 10 December 2008. This Protocol will enter into force when ratified by ten parties. Until this is ratified, the Economic Rights Committee may not receive formal complaints from individuals alleging violations of the Economic Rights Treaty. Upon ratification, the Optional Protocol establishes a formal complaints procedure for individuals and groups who feel that their rights under the Economic Rights Treaty have been violated to petition directly to the Economic Rights Committee. The proposals for a Global New Deal (in chapter nine), designed to strengthen global compliance with economic and social human rights law, include a call for states to rapidly move to ratify this important protocol.

Louis Henkin believes that the differences in implementation procedures between the Political Rights Treaty and the Economic Rights Treaty are significant. The Political Rights Treaty calls for full and immediate realization while the Economic Rights Treaty only requires steps "to the maximum of [a state's] available resources" with a view to progressively achieving the full realization of rights. He identifies a "subtle but conscious and pervasive difference in tone and in the terms of legal prescription." The Political Rights Treaty speaks of individual rights: "Every human being has the inherent right to life. . . . No one shall be held in slavery. . . . Everyone shall have the right to hold opinions without interference." The Economic Rights Treaty, on the other hand, addresses state action and obligation, not individual rights: "The states-parties to the present covenant recognize the right to work . . . the states . . . undertake to ensure . . . the right of everyone to form trade unions . . . the states . . . recognize the right of everyone to social security . . . to an adequate standard of living . . . to education."[34]

The Economic Rights Treaty thus reflects the social reality of economic and social human rights claims. These collective human rights depend on national and global planning for their fulfillment. Within this context, the "Limburg Principles" and the "Maastricht Guidelines" provide state and nonstate actors with clear guidelines for meeting their human rights obligations in their economic planning. The Economic Rights Committee works to hold states accountable to these norms and obligations.

The Economic Rights Committee functions to a large degree in a manner similar to the Human Rights Committee described earlier. Regular reports are submitted by states parties, deliberations are held, and general comments are published. The Economic Rights Committee seeks to achieve three principal objectives: "(1) development of the normative content of the rights recognized in the Covenant; (2) acting as a catalyst to state action in developing national benchmarks and devising appropriate mechanisms for establishing accountability, and providing means of vindication to aggrieved individuals and groups at the national level; and (3) holding states accountable at the international level through the examination of reports."[35]

According to Matthew Craven, the largest problem facing the Economic Rights Committee is the substance of the covenant itself. The Economic Rights Treaty suffers from excessive generality and lack of clear responsibility for supervision. It is this void that the Economic Rights Committee has sought to fill. "The breadth of subjects covered by the Covenant, combined with the lack of case law (whether national or international) in certain vital areas such as health and nutrition, mean that significant importance has to be placed upon the committee's 'creative' or 'interpretative' functions." Key in this effort is the drafting of general comments to "develop an understanding of the normative content" of economic and social rights.[36]

The Economic Rights Committee has devoted considerable energy to overcoming and resolving the problems of generality in the definitions of economic, social, and cultural human rights. In particular, through its general comments the committee has provided state and nonstate actors with a clearly defined understanding of the obligations and duties these rights entail. In fact, the General Comments of the Economic Rights Committee (summarized below in appendix 3.1) provide the clearest articulation of the economic, social, and cultural rights affirmed in international law. It is thus no longer credible to argue that economic and social rights are too vague to enforce. The general comments provide clarity and outline the substance of these rights.

Through its general comments, the Economic Rights Committee has clarified and articulated the minimum core content of the Economic Rights Treaty. The general comments spell out the legal duties of states in key areas, including rights to education, food, health care, housing, water, work, and so on. It is now the legal duty of states, regardless of their political and social systems, to respect, protect, and fulfill these core rights for all citizens.

A central debate over economic and social rights relates to their legal validity. Some scholars argue that by their very nature, economic and social rights are not "justiciable," which is to say that they are not capable of being brought to a court of law and applied by a judge and thus the state's obligations under existing treaties on economic and social rights are predominately of a "political," as opposed to a legal, character. Furthermore, judicial remedies, while useful to monitor "obligations of conduct," are not that helpful regarding the "obligations of result" at the core of economic and social rights claims. The level of housing, nutrition, and health care a person is entitled to is thus considered a question to be determined in the political, and not the legal, sphere and sorted out in the democratic process. Critics also raise the issue of the duty bearer. Who is legally responsible when there is an infringement of an individual's economic rights? Is the duty bearer the nation, the corporation, or perhaps a powerful individual?[37]

In international law, the state is legally responsible for implementing international economic and social rights. While global forces may have severely weakened an individual state's ability to control its own economic destiny, the state remains ultimately responsible for guaranteeing the realization of these rights. The approach of the UN's Office of the High Commissioner for Human Rights is thus to hold governments accountable for the provision of basic social services, including health care, employment, and education. Furthermore, the UN does see key economic and social rights claims as "justiciable" (see summary of general comment no. 9 below in appendix 3.1). And, as noted in the "Maastricht Guidelines," states are also required to ensure that private entities, including multinational corporations, within their jurisdiction, do not deprive individuals of social or economic rights.

In fact, economic and social human rights have been clarified and interpreted in specific cases in national and regional courts. National case law, and the case law of regional human rights systems, has demonstrated the ways in which economic and social rights are, in fact, justiciable. For example, the Indian Supreme Court considered the "right to food" within the context of public interest litigation brought in 2001 by the People's Union for Civil Liberties. As a consequence of this legal action, the court devised a range of affordable measures that the government has subsequently implemented.[38]

Democratic Participation in the Implementation of Economic and Social Rights

There is a minimum core content to economic and social human rights that the Economic Rights Committee is valiantly struggling to refine and articulate. The Economic Rights Committee has been able to criticize governments for violations of this core content. All states have the duty to enforce these universal human rights. The 1993 Vienna Declaration of the UN World Conference on Human Rights states, "While the significance of national and regional particularities and various historical, cultural and religious backgrounds must be borne in mind, it is the duty of states, regardless of their political, economic and social systems, to promote and protect all human rights and fundamental freedoms."

However, the move from merely "denouncing" violations to the actual implementation of a strategy to improve the working and living conditions of the most vulnerable sectors must involve democratic participation. The people whose economic and social rights have been violated should be a part of the implementation process. Universal standards must take account of local cultures and adjust to local conditions. This is not an argument for cultural relativism, but an argument for modesty and effectiveness. It is impossible for any outsider to know the best methods for every unique culture and society to implement economic rights progressively. Rather, to be effective these economic approaches and human rights theories must engage in what Abdullahi Ahmed An-Na'im describes as a "cross-cultural dialogue." An-Na'im stresses the need to verify and substantiate the genuine universality of the existing human rights standards through a process of retroactive legitimation. While existing human rights standards should be maintained, they should be respectfully implemented through a cross-cultural dialogue of mutual learning. Those of one cultural tradition "must never even appear to be imposing external values in support of the human rights standards they seek to legitimize within the framework of the other culture."[39]

State action becomes decisive. The state has a duty to open up the space for democratic participation. There is a link here between civil and political rights, and economic, social, and cultural rights. The *African Charter for Popular Participation in Development and Transformation* articulates this well:

> We believe strongly that popular participation is, in essence, the empowerment of the people to effectively involve themselves in creating the structures and in designing policies and programmes that serve the interests of all as well as to effectively contribute to the development process and share equitably in its benefits. Therefore, there must be an opening up of political process to accommodate freedom of opinions, tolerate differences, accept consensus on issues as well as ensure the effective participation of the people and their organizations and associations. This requires action on the part of all, first and foremost of the people themselves. But equally important are the actions of the State and the international community, to create the necessary conditions for such an empowerment and facilitate effective popular participation in societal and economic life. This requires that the political

system evolve to allow for democracy and full participation by all sections of our societies.[40]

Democratic participation and cross-cultural dialogue are essential for the implementation of economic and social human rights. The enactment of measures to enable people to exercise economic and social rights is vital. A legal positivist human rights approach has promise if it is combined with a strategy of democratic participation. Universalism and localism need not be seen in opposition. Effective implementation of international economic and social human rights law depends on its adaptation and acceptance by local communities.

Despite the shrinking nature of our global community, the state is still central in the creation of the proper environment for the fulfillment of these rights. The state can enact measures to respect, protect, and fulfill basic human rights. The state can open up the political space so that democratic participation can become a reality. And the state can regulate the activities of other transnational economic actors whose practices violate basic human rights protections.

Without the participation and involvement of the working class and vulnerable sectors of the South, attempts by the North to impose labor and environmental regulations will continue to be viewed with suspicion. This mistrust can be conquered. Workers in both the developed and developing countries have an objective interest in seeing the fulfillment of the UN's right to development and the full implementation of the ILO's basic human rights conventions. Perhaps through a cross-cultural dialogue on universal human rights standards, the historical legacy of mistrust between the North and South can be overcome.

Measuring Economic and Social Human Rights

The UN Development Program (UNDP) has played a leadership role in the development of indices and measurements of basic economic and social human rights. The yearly UNDP *Human Development Report* consistently refines its approach and generates sophisticated and functional statistics and analyses on poverty and human capabilities. These thoughtful reports provide all economic actors—states, IFIs, TNCs, and so on—with the critical information central to the development of public policy to achieve economic and social human rights.

The human development approach draws on three different perspectives of poverty: income, basic needs, and capabilities. The income perspective asserts that a person is poor if his or her income level is below a defined poverty line, which some have determined by the amount necessary for a specified amount of food in LDCs. The basic needs

---

PIVOTAL NGOs WORKING ON
ECONOMIC AND SOCIAL HUMAN RIGHTS:
BUILDING DEMOCRATIC PARTICIPATION

Numerous Non-Governmental Organizations (NGOs) are active in organizing for economic and social human rights fulfillment around the world. The following three organizations demonstrate the vitality and resourcefulness of these critical new players in international politics.

Center for Economic and Social Rights (CESR)
162 Montague St., 2nd Floor, Brooklyn, NY 11201
Tel: (718) 237–9145; Fax: (718) 237-9147
E-mail: rights@cesr.org; Web: www.cesr.org

"The Center for Economic and Social Rights (CESR) was established in 1993 to promote social justice through human rights. CESR works with social scientists and local partners in affected communities to document rights violations, advocate for changes in policies that impoverish and exploit people, and mobilize grassroots pressure for social change. As one of the first organizations to challenge economic injustice as a violation of international human rights law, CESR believes that economic and social rights—legally binding on all nations—can provide a universally accepted framework for strengthening social justice activism." (www.cesr.org/about2.htm)

---

perspective argues that poverty is the result of the lack of the resources for the fulfillment of basic human needs, including food. This approach goes beyond the lack of private income and includes the need for basic health, education, and essential services to be provided by the community to prevent individuals from falling into poverty. In the capabilities perspective, poverty is the absence of the opportunity to achieve some basic capabilities to function. As we saw in the discussion of Sen's analysis in chapter 2, capability functions include being well-nourished, adequately clothed and sheltered, able to avoid preventable morbidity, and able to partake in the life of the community. Poverty clearly cannot be reduced to a single dimension. The capabilities approach most fully captures this total picture.[41]

The 1996 UNDP *Human Development Report* introduced a new, multidimensional measure of human deprivation: the capability poverty

Social Watch
Casilla de Correo 1539
Montevideo 1100, Uruguay
Tel: 598 2 419 6192; Fax: 598 2 411 9222
E-mail: socwatch@socialwatch.org; Web: www.socialwatch.org

"Social Watch is an international network informed by national citizens' groups aiming at following up the fulfilment of internationally agreed commitments on poverty eradication and equality. These national groups report, through the national Social Watch report, on the progress—or regression—towards these commitments and goals." (http://www.socialwatch.org/en/acercaDe/index.htm)

Foodfirst Information and Action Network (FIAN)
PO Box 102243, D-69012 Heidelberg, Germany
Tel: 49 6221 830 620; Fax: 49 6221 830 545
E-mail: fian@fian.org; Web: www.fian.org

"Our mission is to realize the human right to adequate food through concrete action. FIAN is a non-partisan human rights organization. It has a consultative status with the United Nations. FIAN acts when, for example, the pollution of fishing-grounds, land evictions or the non-respect of minimum wages threaten the livelihoods of the poor and their right to feed themselves is violated. We support the victims in their struggle for justice by campaigning for an end to the violation." (www.fian.org)

measure (CPM). To a considerable extent, this device incorporated Sen's model and attempted to assess the capability to function and realize the freedom to achieve. The CPM calculated the percentage of people who lack basic, or minimally essential, human capabilities in health, nourishment, and education.[42]

The CPM provided a vehicle to measure the capability to achieve adequate functioning. It gave a more accurate assessment of deprivation and poverty than estimations based on levels of national income poverty alone. For example, the World Bank estimated in 1996 that approximately 900 million people in the developing world, 21 percent of the total, were income poor and lived below the poverty line. The corresponding figure for capability poverty was 1.6 billion, or 37 percent of the people in the developing countries. In Pakistan, for example, only one-third of the population were income poor, but more than three-fifths were capability poor. In Bangladesh, 55 million people were income poor, but 89 million were capability poor.[43]

In 1997, the *Human Development Report* developed these ideas further and introduced the Human Poverty Index (HPI), which refined and replaced the CPM. The HPI compiles in one index the deprivation in four basic dimensions of human life: a long and healthy life, knowledge, economic provisioning, and social exclusion. The indicators to measure these deprivations differ between developing and industrialized countries.[44]

HPI-1 brings together in one index the first three deprivations in developing countries. The deprivation of a long and healthy life is measured by the percentage of people not expected to survive to age forty. The deprivation of knowledge is measured by adult illiteracy rates. The deprivation of economic provisioning is measured by the percentage of people without access to safe water and health services and the percentage of children under five who are moderately or severely underweight.[45] Due to a lack of data and the absence of suitable indicators, HPI-1 does not reflect deprivations in social inclusion in developing countries.

HPI-2 brings together in one index these deprivations in industrialized countries. The deprivation of a long and healthy life is measured by the percentage of people not expected to survive to age sixty. The deprivation of knowledge is measured by the adult functional illiteracy rate. The deprivation of economic provisioning is determined by the percentage of people living below the income poverty line. And the deprivation of social inclusion is determined by the long-term unemployment rate of twelve months or more.[46]

HPI-1 and HPI-2 thus focus on different variables to identify human poverty in developing versus industrialized countries. First, in developing countries public provisioning is more important than private income in the determination of a decent standard of living. For example, the UNDP estimated in 2000 that more than four-fifths of private income in developing countries was spent on food. Private income alone does not capture the total deprivation in economic provisioning. Lack of access to health services and safe water and the level of malnutrition provide a better description of real conditions of poverty. In industrialized countries, on the other hand, private income is the most important source of economic provisioning.[47]

Some of the conclusions in the human development and human poverty indexes published in the UNDP's Human Development Reports are the following:

- People in many developing countries face conditions of extreme, desparate human poverty. Statistics from the 2007/2008 report reveal that HPI-1 exceeded 50 percent in Burkina Faso, Chad, Ethiopia, Mali, Mozambique, Niger, and Sierra Leone. In close to a third of all developing countries where the HPI-1 rate was calculated, it exceeded 33 percent, indicating that at least a third of the people in each country suffer from extreme poverty.[48]

- In 2003, the UNDP reported that over the previous 30 years, life expectancy overall increased by eight years in the developing world and illiteracy was cut nearly in half. Yet for many LDCs the last decade of the 20th century was filled with despair. By 2003, some 54 countries were poorer than in 1990; 21 had a larger proportion of people going hungry; 14 had more children dying before the age of five; 12 had primary school enrollments shrink; and 34 had life expectancy rates fall. These were startling statistics, as such reversals in human development had been rare. Overall, 21 countries registered a decline in the human development index, which was also rare as, according to the UNDP, "capabilities captured by the HDI are not easily lost."[49]

- Public policy can make a significant difference in lowering the poverty rate in developing countries. For example, the UNDP compared Mexico and Trinidad and Tobago in the 2000 report. Mexico has a higher gross domestic product (GDP) per capita ($7,704) than Trinidad and Tobago ($7,485). The two countries score a similar rate on the Human Development Index, with Trinidad and Tobago ahead by only 0.009 percent. But Mexico has twice the level of poverty (HPI-1 rate) compared to Trinidad and Tobago. Clearly, the public policies to address the economic provisioning of basic services have been more successful in Trinidad and Tobago than in Mexico.[50]

- A similar outcome was seen in comparing Guatemala to Tanzania in the 2000 report. Both suffered terrible conditions of human poverty with HPI-1 rates between 29 and 30 percent. Guatemala and Tanzania ranked next to each other, forty-ninth and fiftieth, respectively, in the HPI-1 overall rankings; 32 to 34 percent of the populations of both countries did not have access to safe drinking water; and 13 to 14 percent of the populations of both countries did not have access to adequate sanitation. In both countries, 27 percent of all children under the age of five were underweight. Yet, Tanzania faced conditions of low human development and a GDP per capita of only $480. Guatemala, on the other hand, had conditions of medium human development and a GDP per capita of $3,505. Guatemala unquestionably had the economic wealth and financial ability to implement public policies to alleviate the human suffering these poverty figures expose. Neither economic equality nor the protection of public goods was a priority in Guatemala. In that country, the richest 20 percent consumed 63 percent of the national income while the poorest 20 percent struggled to survive with only 2.1 percent.[51]

- HPI-2 reveals that poverty is not confined to developing countries. The 2007/2008 report documented that among the developed countries, Italy had the highest levels of human poverty (29.8 percent), followed by Ireland (16 percent), the United States (15.4 percent) and the United Kingdom (14.8 percent). It is startling to learn that in Italy, Ireland, the United States, and the United Kingdom more than one in five adults are functionally illiterate. More than 17 percent of people in the United States are income poor, with the income poverty line set at 50 percent of the median disposable household income.[52]
- The UNDP also tracks the disparities within countries—between rural and urban areas, between regions and districts, and between ethnic and language groups. For example, according to the 2000 report, in South Africa the unemployment rate among African males at 29 percent was more than seven times that among white males at 4 percent. And in India, the illiteracy rate among ethnic tribes was 70 percent, compared with 48 percent for the country as a whole.[53]

The HPI is a superb step forward in the evaluation of the true depths of global poverty. These data are central to the articulation of plans for the alleviation of needless human suffering. UNDP analysis of these figures demonstrates the importance of public action to protect economic and social human rights. It is encouraging to note that even countries with low GDP rates have successfully provided programs to meet basic needs in sanitation, nutrition, education, and health care.

In this era of economic interdependence, how are states and other economic actors held accountable to international economic and social human rights standards? As outlined in the first part of this chapter, the obligation to respect, protect, and fulfill economic and social human rights is clearly articulated in international law. Through the HPI tracking of poverty, the UNDP not only identifies the ways in which these rights are being violated, but also clearly points to policy directions for the provision of these rights. Can global governance evolve in a way that prioritizes the economic and social rights of the most vulnerable?

Monitoring and Implementing
Economic and Social Human Rights

Virginia Dandan, the former chair of the Economic Rights Committee, believes that economic and social rights are so interrelated that it is totally arbitrary to draw a line between them. In my interview with her in 2000, she noted that these distinctions were made decades ago when there was a less clear understanding of the nature of rights. The reality is that economic rights have a social basis and social rights have an economic basis.

Both classifications of rights are of equal importance and interdependent. But Chairperson Dandan recognized that the categories of "social" and "economic" have become the traditional terms to refer to these rights, and it is the way they are described in the Economic Rights Treaty. If these original definitions make things clear to the public and to states, then the division perhaps does serve a purpose. There is also no better term at the moment, so as a matter of convenience the Economic Rights Committee continues with this conceptualization. But Chairperson Dandan stressed the importance of understanding economic and social rights in their totality and not as separate items.[54]

Chairperson Dandan believes that, overall, states parties are taking the Economic Rights Committee increasingly seriously. States are concerned about their reputations, and they respond to committee requests. The Economic Rights Committee does utilize the three-part approach to economic and social human rights to respect, protect, and fulfill. Of particular importance to the committee is the issue of respect, which implies an obligation of an immediate nature. No matter what the economic condition of a state, if it has ratified the Economic Rights Treaty, it must respect the economic and social rights of its citizens. A state may not use resource scarcity as an excuse to avoid its obligations. The Economic Rights Treaty is clear: Each state must achieve the realization of economic and social human rights to the maximum of its available resources. Chairperson Dandan noted that it takes no money to desist from violations (the duty to respect). It also takes little money to review legislation to make sure that a state's laws are in conformity with the Economic Rights Treaty. And furthermore, the convention calls for progressive compliance with demonstrable progress. The Economic Rights Committee thus looks for steady improvement and does not accept a nation standing still or going backward.[55]

The Economic Rights Committee applies a single standard for rich and poor countries. The standard applied is the "maximum of its available resources." For example, the United States may have a resource base of eight while the Democratic Republic of the Congo's resource base is two. The issue for the Economic Rights Treaty is how each country is applying its specific resource base to the achievement of economic and social human rights. More resources can be applied in one case, but each must apply the maximum available.

Despite progress, the Economic Rights Committee still faces major problems in state reporting. Many states don't bother to report at all, while others' reports are inexcusably late. When a state does not report on time, the committee writes to the state's representative to inform him or her that its case will be heard with or without the state reporting. The committee again invites the state representative to submit a report. If a state claims that it does not have the resources to pull together such a detailed report, the OHCHR will help by providing technical assistance. Dandan noted, for example, that the UN provided such assistance to the Solomon Islands in the preparation of its report. There is therefore absolutely no excuse for countries not to meet their reporting obligations.[56]

But, with or without the state report, the committee will eventually go ahead with the hearing. The state is invited to take part in the hearing even if it does not submit a report (e.g., the Democratic Republic of the Congo, Dandan noted, sent a delegation to the hearing after not submitting the required report). Information on the state's compliance with the Economic Rights Treaty is gathered from a variety of sources beyond the state, including other UN agencies (ILO, UNDP, UN Environment Program, World Health Organization, Food and Agriculture Organization, and so on), and expanded NGO participation and reporting. A special rapporteur is often assigned to conduct an independent country investigation and to submit a draft of preliminary observations to the committee. The final step is a three-hour hearing by the Economic Rights Committee on the state's compliance with the Economic Rights Treaty. The Economic Rights Committee will adopt either preliminary observations or concluding observations. Concluding observations are contingent on state submission of the required report.[57]

Unfortunately, many states parties view the process as an unwarranted intrusion and burden and try to fill the reporting requirement as superficially as possible. Many of the reports submitted are of poor quality and do not follow the reporting guidelines established by the committee. More detailed and comprehensive NGO alternative reports (also called shadow reports) have proved of enormous importance in providing the information missing from these states' reports. These alternative reports highlight inaccuracies and distortions in a government report and provide new information and ideas for appropriate policy. Scott Leckie reports that these alternative reports have also acted as a catalyst in the emergence of new coalitions and movements between previously unconnected groups in the Dominican Republic, Panama, the Philippines, Israel, and elsewhere. International human rights law, and in particular the Economic Rights Treaty, is being used by these NGO coalitions as a basis for demands on states, giving new importance to international legal documents.[58]

These NGO coalitions are one example of the impact of the work of the Economic Rights Committee on the national level. "Success," of course, is difficult to measure. Human rights officers at the OHCHR assessed in 2000 that the concluding observations on Canada, the Democratic Republic of the Congo, the Dominican Republic, Hong Kong, Israel, the Philippines, and the Solomon Islands have had a positive impact on government policies and actions. In a number of these cases, the Economic Rights Committee and the UN provided technical assistance so these countries could correct policies and remedy violations. In the Dominican Republic and Panama, for example, such assistance was provided in the area of housing.[59]

The Economic Rights Committee takes into account the many difficulties that governments face, such as population growth, inflation, and special circumstances like weather calamities, and tries to help states define policies to meet their human rights obligations. As a result of constantly changing conditions, every state is probably out of compliance somewhere. Yet, despite these conditions every state has a duty to keep striving for 100 percent compliance. The Economic Rights Committee sees its role as helping states define policies to progressively meet their economic, social, and cultural rights obligations.[60]

Actions recommended by the Economic Rights Committee include the adoption of new legislation, the repeal of existing legislation, the implementation of existing legislation, the encouragement of preventive actions, and the implementation of NGO-devised plans and other specific policy measures. For example, the Philippines government was urged by the committee in 1995 to give "consideration . . . to the repeal of Presidential Decrees 772 and 1818 and [the committee] recommends that all existing legislation relevant to the practice of forced evictions should be reviewed so as to ensure its compatibility with the provisions of the covenant." Belgium, on the other hand, was encouraged to implement its current legislation. In 1994, the committee expressed to Belgium "concern at the adequacy of the measures taken to actually enforce that [housing rights] constitutional provision. The committee urges the Government to more intensively apply existing laws allowing the government to requisition properties and housing left unoccupied by owners."[61]

The Economic Rights Committee recognizes that other powerful international actors besides states are also responsible for the impact of their policies on the most vulnerable. In its 1998 statement on globalization, the committee emphasized that the realms of trade, finance, and investment are in no way exempt from human rights principles and that "the international organizations with specific responsibilities in those areas should play a positive and constructive role in relation to human rights."[62] The Economic Rights Committee directly addressed these issues in its statement to the Third Ministerial Conference of the WTO in Seattle in 1999, stating:

> Human rights norms must shape the process of international economic policy formulation so that the benefits for human development of the evolving international trading regime will be shared equitably by all, in particular the most vulnerable sectors. The Committee recognizes the wealth-generating potential of trade liberalization, but it is also aware that liberalization in trade, investment and finance does not necessarily create and lead to a favourable environment for the realization of economic, social and cultural

rights. Trade liberalization must be understood as a means, not an end. The end which trade liberalization should serve is the objective of human well-being to which the international human rights instruments give legal expression.[63]

The Economic Rights Committee is thus clearly aware of the profound impact of the policies and decisions of global trade organizations, IFIs, and TNCs on the economic well-being of citizens in most states. Yet, Chairperson Dandan insisted that this changing role of the state does not relieve it of its human rights obligations. A state cannot argue that the WTO or the IMF made it do X, nor can it claim that a TNC forced it to do Y. It is the state's responsibility to protect the resources that are critical to the livelihood and environmental balance of its territory. The Economic Rights Committee asks states to take their obligations for meeting economic and social human rights into their negotiations with trade organizations, IFIs, and TNCs. The state must make sure that its obligations are not compromised by the conditions of external aid and foreign investment.[64]

However, this attempt to link human rights to the work of trade organizations, IFIs, and TNCs has so far failed to produce significant results. On the one hand, it has proven to be very difficult to get these international organizations to engage with the Economic Rights Committee or to define their work in human rights terms. The World Bank has been the most human rights sensitized—attending more meetings of the Economic Rights Committee than other powerful international trade and finance organizations and demonstrating a greater willingness to define its message in human rights terms. For example, the World Bank publication *World Development Report 2000/2001: Attacking Poverty* presented a "poverty reduction agenda" that focused not only on income deprivation, but also on low achievements in education and health—that is, social human rights.[65] The IMF, on the other hand, remains distant and attends few meetings. And there has been little cooperation between the WTO and the Economic Rights Committee. To many observers, the WTO has ignored the invitation of the Economic Rights Committee to "collaborate . . . on these matters and thereby be active partners toward the realization of all the rights set forth in the Economic Rights Treaty."[66] Overall, international trade organizations and IFIs continue to fail to link their work to the UN's approach to economic and social human rights fulfillment. And, unfortunately, structural adjustment programs and debt payment plans often deepen poverty and worsen social conditions for the poor, in particular for women and children in the LDCs.

On the other hand, the LDCs themselves are often hesitant to bring their legal obligations under the Economic Rights Treaty into their negotiations with trade organizations, IFIs, and TNCs. Some of these states fear the creation of new social conditionalities on aid and loans needed for development. Some fear losing a competitive advantage in global wage rates. For these reasons it is hard to convince LDCs to link economic and social rights to relations with trade organizations, IFIs, and TNCs.[67] And it is up to the states to take this action. Legally, the Economic Rights Committee has little influence and no actual power to force trade organizations, IFIs, or MNCs to take these rights seriously. States, however, command this authority, and state pressure could make a difference.[68]

There is, of course, plenty of opposition to the Economic Rights Committee expanding its focus to include actors beyond states. Yet, Chairperson Dandan argued that there are "many ways to skin a cat." She believed that if we keep "chipping away at the tall wall," with persistence and patience, eventually it will not be possible to ignore the links between global trade and financial policies and human rights fulfillment. All efforts in this direction—from the Economic Rights Committee statement to the WTO meeting in Seattle to the work of NGOs—help focus the global community on these issues and the plight of the voiceless.[69]

Incorporating Economic and Social Rights into UN Development Programs

In the late 1990s, former UN Secretary General Kofi Annan initiated a process of mainstreaming human rights into all UN activities, including its development programs. In support of this framework, the Economic Rights Committee asserted that development activities that do not contribute to respect for human rights are not worthy of the name. Mary Robinson, the former UN high commissioner for human rights, endorsed this approach when she suggested that decisions as to appropriate priorities in the quest for development "can be made easier by using the language and standards of human rights and placing the decision-making process firmly in the context of the government's international human rights obligations. These obligations stretch also to international organizations."[70]

The integration of human rights into the UN's development programs can be seen in the work of the UN Development Assistance Framework (UNDAF), Common Country Assessments (CCA), and the Human Rights Strengthening (HURIST) project. These programs are part of the overall effort to enhance the UN's capacity to implement a rights-based development mandate. The initial evaluations of the effectiveness of these initiatives is positive. These programs appear to be providing clear mechanisms and solid support for individual countries to base development policy on the achievement of economic and social human rights.

The UNDAF attempts to bring greater coherence to the UN's assistance programs at the country level. It establishes a planning framework for the development operations of the UN system. The CCA is viewed as the first step in the preparation of the UNDAF. It articulates a common understanding of the causes of the development problems, needs, and priorities of a country. The CCA process includes the participation of UN agencies (UNDP, OHCHR, and so on), the national government, civil society (NGOs, research institutes, and so on), the private sector (companies, business associations, and so on), the donor community, and the Bretton Woods Institutions (World Bank and IMF). These partners in the development of the CCA work together to develop a consensus on the development problems, priorities, and needs of the country requesting assistance. The common understanding, agreed to by these development partners, becomes the key document used to define the overall purpose and strategy of UN system support to the country.[71]

The UNDAF–CCA helps the UN establish a unified voice in its development work. It is moving the UN away from a top-down process to a country-led and country-managed approach to development. It builds partnerships within the UN system and with national authorities, civil society, the private sector, and so on. And most significantly, human rights criteria form the base of its indicators for development.

The UNDAF–CCA process provides an entry point for a human rights–based approach to development assistance for the UN system as a whole. UN agencies have for years worked in the areas of education, housing, poverty eradication, and health. This work "for the promotion of the economic and social advancement of all peoples," as stated in the UN Charter, continues. But the UNDAF–CCA strategy represents a shift to a rights-based approach.[72]

An advantage of a rights-based approach to development is that it equips the UN with a whole range of legal instruments to utilize in negotiations and discussions with state and nonstate actors. The international human rights law impacts on the development area with rules covering nondiscrimination, education, social security, health, participation, and an adequate standard of living, which minimally entails access to food, water, and housing. As documented above, many of the human rights agreements are binding on states and thus require compliance. Through this linkage of international law to development planning, the UN is trying to move beyond the human rights standard setting and into human rights implementation and monitoring. This program represents a significant maturation and advancement in the understanding and approach to human rights fulfillment at the UN.

UNDAF–CCA guidelines include references to human rights and guide country teams to learn where to find information on human rights in general and on the human rights situation in a given country. Development is assessed through the CCA Indicator Framework, which embraces a human rights core. Framework indicators for economic and social human rights include income poverty, food security and nutrition, health and mortality, reproductive health, child health and welfare, education, gender equality and women's empowerment, employment and sustainable livelihood, housing and basic household amenities and facilities, the environment, and drug control and crime prevention. Framework indicators for civil and political human rights include ratification of international human rights instruments, democracy and participation, administration of justice, and liberty and security of person.[73]

Through the CCA Indicator Framework, states are able to establish specific benchmarks to measure their own performance in the realization of economic, social, and cultural rights. The UN system can respond with technical assistance and aid in an integrated and holistic manner.

The OHCHR, in particular, helps countries adopt a human rights approach to development programming. The OHCHR helps translate development issues into human rights terms. This places these development issues within the framework of internationally agreed on and binding human rights law. The OHCHR links development issues to their "human rights substance" in terms of content, minimum standards, and benchmarks according to the various human rights instruments (including the Economic Rights Treaty). Through this adoption of a human rights–based approach, the UN is able to identify progress in the enjoyment of human rights and identify areas where work remains to be done.[74]

For example, after reviewing the progress in the enjoyment of key economic and social human rights in areas of health, education, water and sanitation, standard of living, food, and gender, the OHCHR can point to remaining obstacles to the enjoyment of these rights by vulnerable populations. Public policy can then be identified for action to overcome these obstacles. Examples of such successful policy identified in an internal review conducted by the OHCHR of the UNDAF-CCA included (1) establishing community monitoring systems to ensure that resources meant for development are used effectively and efficiently; (2) developing local area planning systems to reflect the demands and priorities of the poor; (3) expanding the economic opportunities of women; (4) addressing the much-neglected area of violence against women and children; and (5) promoting education programs to alter mindsets that perpetuate antifemale biases.[75]

Sylvie Saddier, a human rights officer at the OHCHR, noted the many obstacles that occur at the country level in implementing the CCA. Most governments are not familiar with human rights indicators and do not know how to integrate this approach into development planning. Some states are openly hostile to the ideas and object to even using the words "human rights." The OHCHR has shared with country teams various concrete experiences that demonstrate not only the successful implementation of this approach, but also that there is not only one way to integrate human rights into development. The process must be sensitive to the specifics of a given culture and country. Despite these hurdles, the UNDAF–CCA rights-based approach to development programs has successfully helped to integrate human rights into the UN's development programs.[76]

HURIST is a joint program of the UNDP and the OHCHR designed to support the implementation of the UNDP's policy on human rights presented in the 1998 document Integrating Human Rights with Sustainable Development. The purposes of HURIST are to help in the development of national capacities for the promotion and protection of human rights and the application of a human rights approach to development programming. It supports government requests for assistance in the field of human rights by helping to develop action plans at the country level. The goal is to link development and human rights in practice through the integration of human rights into the work of the UNDP.

The UNDP has identified four focus areas for its programming in sustainable human development: the eradication of poverty, the creation of jobs and sustainable livelihoods, the advancement of women and gender equity, and the protection and regeneration of the environment. The importance of an enabling environment for the enhancement of the well-being of people, including the rule of law, the maintenance of peace, security and political stability, and a stable legal and political framework, is also recognized as a key to sustainable human development. Participatory approaches to development, good governance, and human rights are also UNDP priorities.[77]

The HURIST project was initially divided into two phases (1999–2002; 2002–2005), with a "midterm review" occuring in 2004. HURIST has initiatied cooperation for the development of national human rights plans and the development of human rights capacity in institutions of governance in twenty-three countries, seven in Africa, five in Asia and the Pacific, four in the Arab Region, three in Latin America and the Caribbean and three in Eastern Europe and the Former Soviet Union. A primary purpose of HURIST is to promote national capacity for the protection and promotion of human rights and the integration of human rights into national development planning. HURIST advanced human rights guidelines in a vareity of development areas including poverty, gender, environment, water, and sustainable livelihood. A "midterm review" of HURIST activities concluded that the program was "highly relevant in the context of UN reforms and UNDP's policy to integrate human rights with sustainable development." While HURIST was clearly "making its mark," the internal review also concluded that "human rights mainstreaming in development is far more demanding than was originally anticipated." The reviewers went on to note that HURIST was "operating with slender and overworked resources, funding uncertainties, and short time horizons." Future success will depend on an enlarged commitment by the UNDP to this project.[78]

As with the UNDAF–CCA, HURIST also represents a positive step toward a more thorough integration of human rights into the UN development programs. HURIST articulation of a rights-based development model is hopefully useful for individual states to achieve economic and social human rights for all citizens.

This integration of human rights into UN development programs has greatly enhanced the importance and stature of the OHCHR. Under the leadership of Annan and Robinson, the OHCHR became the lead human rights agency within the UN system. The office was formerly seen as having a narrow mandate to solely serve the UN's Human Rights Commission. The expertise of the staff of the OHCHR is now seen as central to the success of the UN's rights-based framework for human development. Unfortunately, the budget and staffing of the OHCHR does not match its new prominence. The dedicated OHCHR staff works valiantly with limited resources. Without more support from the states of the UN, the promising rights-based development framework, and the other critical work of the OHCHR, will not be realized.[79]

Strengthening Global Compliance with Economic and Social Human Rights

As can be seen, the OHCHR and the Economic Rights Committee effectively encourage states to adopt and enforce economic and social human rights, which have been clearly defined and articulated in international law. Complimenting moral obligations, states now have legal duties to respect, protect and fulfill economic and social human rights. This system, however, relies on states to voluntarily comply with the law and fulfill these obligations. Many states, unfortunately, ignore this human rights framework and resist UN efforts to broaden human rights compliance. As a result, scholars and diplomats have developed proposals and measures to strengthen global compliance with economic and social human rights. This section critiques two such proposals to enhance the implementation and compliance with these rights: an optional protocol to the Economic Rights Treaty and a social clause to the WTO.

Optional Protocol

As noted earlier, it wasn't until 10 December 2008 that the UN General Assemby finally adopted the Protocol to the Economic Rights Treaty which gives individuals and groups, who feel that their rights under the Treaty have been violated, a mechanism to submit formal complaints to the committee. The absence of this procedure until now has effectedly denied victims of abuse a recognized, workable vehicle for achieving international and national redress. Its absence further constrained the ability of the Economic Rights Committee to develop jurisprudence and case law in economic, social, and cultural rights. Fortunately, the General Assembly recognized the compelling arguments in favor of the optional protocol: a strengthening of international accountability of states parties; increased congruence in the legal standing accorded to both principal international human rights treaties (since, as outlined earlier, the Political Rights Treaty already has an optional protocol); a refinement of the rights and duties emerging from the Economic Rights Treaty; and, overall, a strengthening of international accountability of states parties.[80]

The 1993 World Conference on Human Rights in the Vienna Declaration and Programme of Action "encourage[d] the Commission on Human Rights, in cooperation with the Committee on Economic, Social and Cultural Rights, to continue the examination of optional protocols to the Covenant on Economic, Social and Cultural Rights."[81] After in-depth discussions and broad consultation, the Economic Rights Committee at its fifteenth session in 1996 adopted a draft optional protocol for submission to the Human Rights Commission. In its work, the Economic Rights Committee took careful note of the oral and written submissions of the ILO, the UN Division for the Advancement of Women, representatives of various NGOs, and the work of an expert meeting convened in Utrecht by the Netherlands Institute for Human Rights in January 1995.[82]

The report of the Economic Rights Committee to the Human Rights Commission emphasized a number of key aspects to the optional protocol. First, the protocol is strictly optional and thus applicable only to those states parties who agree to it by way of ratification or accession. Second, this procedure is in no way new nor especially innovative. In addition to the First Optional Protocol to the Political Rights Treaty, similar precedents exist within the Minority Rights Treaty; Women's Rights Treaty; Convention against Torture; ILO; UN Educational, Scientific, and Cultural Organization; the American Convention on Human Rights in the Area of Economic, Social and Cultural Rights (the Protocol of San Salvador of 1988); and the Council of Europe. Third, the experiences to date with these existing individual petition procedures indicate that there is no basis to fear that an optional protocol would result in large numbers of complaints. Individuals must first exhaust all domestic remedies before appealing to the regional and international bodies. And fourth, the state party concerned retains the final decision as to what will be done in response to any views adopted by the Economic Rights Committee in response to individual complaints.[83]

The new optional protocol providing an individual complaints procedure will hopefully improve the effectiveness of UN supervisory mechanisms by adding additional pressure on states parties to comply with international economic, social, and cultural rights standards. This approach makes it clear to states that economic and social rights are justiciable—that is, that these are real legal rights, appropriate for court trial, and not mere "wishes." States parties have legal obligations to respect, protect, and fulfill these rights and individuals have legal recourse to hold their individual state accountable. If an individual has exhausted all recourse for remedy within the state, he or she can then appeal through the optional protocol for redress through the Economic Rights Committee. The existence of this process alone should pressure states parties to be more attentive to their legal obligations in regard to these issues.

The success of the optional protocol to the Political Rights Treaty is strong evidence that a similar procedure attached to the Economic Rights Treaty would also be beneficial. The recommendations and suggestions from the Political Rights Treaty have been followed up by the affected states parties. National legislation has been modified and amended following Political Rights Treaty decisions. These decisions also give NGOs in civil society additional tools to pressure governments to change policy. The optional protocol represents a realistic strengthening of the UN system for monitoring and implementing international economic and social human rights.

Unfortunately, in the past this thoughtful proposal became overly politicized, resulting in a dampening of enthusiasm for it by states. Some developed countries often opposed the adoption of this optional protocol due to the potential financial commitments involved. Some of these states have also expressed concerns about the difficulty of measuring progress in state fulfillment of economic and social rights obligations. Many LDCs, on the other hand, generally supported this effort, even though these states may be the most affected. It is likely that there would be more individual complaints from citizens in the LDCs than from elsewhere. The LDCs, however, may welcome this attention to their economic plight. It could provide a way to dramatize requests for aid and reform of international economic structures that contribute to perpetuating these unacceptable conditions. Due to these differing perspectives, the optional protocol is still a contentious issue and still has a long way to go to achieve a significant number of ratifications by states parties to the Economic Rights Treaty.[84]

It is necessary to break through these divisions and ratify this mechanism for individual and group complaints to be adjudicated at the international level. The Global New Deal (outlined in chapter 9) picks up on these ideas and embraces the optional protocol as one mechanism for respecting, protecting, and fulfilling economic and social human rights in a globalized economy.

Social Clause

A second device designed to hold states accountable to international economic and social human rights standards is a proposed social clause to the rules of the WTO. Economic globalization has seriously impacted the autonomy of the state and has made it more difficult for governments to protect their citizens' public goods (see chapter 2). The goal of the social clause is to link trading privilges with compliance to economic and social human rights law. WTO membership and benefits would be contingent on ratification and implementation of the social clause. The objective of this linkage is to halt the deteriorating working and living standards for the poor that has accompanied economic globalization and liberalized trade.

Some economists, however, fear that any linkage between WTO benefits and adherence to human rights law would damage "free trade" by undermining access to inexpensive labor markets. Some argue further that attempts to establish fixed labor standards are really nothing more than protectionism by the North. Establishing minimum wages, these economists maintain, is an attempt to equalize differences in the costs of production between a domestic article and a similar foreign article. Such equalizing of labor costs, while perhaps protecting jobs in the North, would take away incentives for corporations to invest in the LDCs and potentially take away jobs in the South. The resulting lack of employment opportunities could thus cause great hardship for the working class and the poor in LDCs.

Critics of the current economic globalization model, on the other hand, argue for "fair trade" and criticize current international economic structures that pressure countries to lower their labor standards and practice what has pejoratively been labelled "social dumping." Membership in the WTO requires that a country abolish the practice of "dumping"—that is, actions by governments, such as subsidies and tax breaks, designed to artificially lower the price of an export commodity in order to undercut a comparable product abroad. By "dumping" cheaper export products into the market, the exporting country hopes to drive competitors out of business and capture the market. "Social dumping" is a similar phenomena. A state utilizes unacceptable labor practices to lower the price of production and undercut competitors. Labor and social activists contend that these practices should also be banned under the existing rules of the WTO.

Erika de Wet argues that a social clause does not necessarily imply either protectionism or cost equalization. She uses the example of ILO Convention no. 131 on Minimum Wage Fixing to demonstrate how global standards work. This ILO convention is not an attempt to establish a uniform minimum wage across countries. Its intent is to establish the universal principle of a minimum wage. The ILO recognizes that it is unrealistic to expect comparable wages to be paid in the highly industrialized countries and LDCs. The point of Convention no. 131, however, is to require every country to establish at least a minimum wage in their nation. This bare minimum demand clearly will not create cost equalization across borders, nor will it eliminate the competitive advantage of low wages and large labor pools in many LDCs. However, the hope is that it would prevent a country from implementing a strategy to create competitive advantage by suppressing wages.[85]

A pivotal hurdle holding up progress toward implementing a social clause has been disagreement over which economic and social standards should be included. The standards advocated by the International Confederation of Free Trade Unions (ICFTU), the World Confederation of Labor, and the European Trade Union Confederation include rights to freedom of association and collective bargaining (ILO Conventions nos. 87 and 98), the prevention of forced labor (ILO Conventions nos. 29 and 105), prohibition of discrimination (ILO Conventions nos. 100 and 111), and the introduction of a minimum work age (ILO Convention no. 138). Other advocates add standards on occupational safety and health (ILO Convention no. 155) and minimum wage fixing (ILO Convention no. 131).[86]

Christian Barry and Sanjay Reddy go beyond a "social clause" to the WTO and instead propose the creation of an international institution to promote global trade and improve labor standards, the "Agency for Trade and Labor Standards" (ATLAS). Their proposal envisions ATLAS being jointly administered by the WTO and the ILO. Through ATLAS trade privileges would be conditional on the promotion of specific labor standards. Barry and Reddy argue that this would not be a "top down" imposition, but rather these conditions would arise out of a process of fair negotiation and be *"unimposed, transparent, and rule-based; involve adequate burden sharing; incorporate measures that ensure appropriate account is taken of viewpoints within states; and applied in a context-sensitive manner"* (italics in original). Such a proposal has great merit in that it attempts to create incentives for cooperation rather than threatening sanctions. LDCs would have access to Northern markets in exchange for adhering to economic and social human rights and improving local labor standards. Technical assistance and resource transfers to LDCs could help these countries absorb the costs of improving labor standards. ATLAS would "help countries identify and execute measures that promote adherence to labor standards," and it would "determine whether serious neglect of labor standards had occurred."[87]

The idea of enforcing these labor standards through either new global institutions (like ATLAS) or through universal or regional trading agreements has not moved forward. Developing countries, in particular, have opposed the social clause in the WTO. Some LDCs see this list of labor standards as disguised protectionism and an attempt to undermine their competitive advantage in lower labor costs. Furthermore, some LDCs argue that these universal standards are not sensitive to the specific cultural environment of a poor nation.

Examine, for example, the issue of child labor. A number of these labor standards attempt to end the exploitation of children through the elimination of child labor. Yet, in some cases working outside the home may be an attractive alternative, in particular to young girls. A 1998 report by Population Council researchers suggests that in some cultures child labor for young girls may actually prolong their adolescence. Working outside the home delays the birth of their first child, gives their reproductive systems time to mature, and gives them some independence and self-esteem.

However, the use of child labor often involves brutal exploitation. At the beginning of the 21st century, for example, garment factory work in Bangladesh remains low paying and grueling. Some 90 percent of the factory workers are female and they range in age from ten to nineteen. A typical monthly wage for the youngest and most inexperienced is $15. Yet, the researchers conclude that despite this exploitation, female factory workers live better, more emancipated lives than their sisters who stayed behind in the villages. The girls working in the factory were able to not only support themselves, but also to learn complex machinery, work alongside men, and challenge authority by demanding higher wages. They were able to put off marriage and childbirth and overcome naivete and ignorance. They were thus liberated as well as exploited.[88]

International human rights law has been attentive to the issue of child labor. The ILO Convention on Child Labor establishes that "the minimum age . . . should not be less than the age of compulsory schooling and, in any case, shall not be less than 15 years. . . . [C]ountries whose economy and educational facilities are insufficiently developed [are allowed] to initially specify a minimum age of 14 years and reduce from 13 years to 12 years the minimum age for light work." It is critical to advocate this minimal standard as the abuse of child labor takes many forms including poor wages, long workdays, unhealthy working conditions, abuse, and the lack of education. According to the ILO, at the beginninig of the 21st century, 95 percent of the approximately 200 million child workers around the world are in the LDCs. Clearly, the exploitation of children must end.[89]

However, in a situation where children contribute needed income to their households, face increased poverty if they leave their factory job, and gain valuable vocational skills, the course of action becomes complex. Ending child labor must be combined with an overall program to provide further options and opportunities to these children. If ending child labor means eliminating the primary vehicle through which literally tens of thousands of families avoid poverty, then an alternative road to paid work must be created. Accompanying the elimination of child labor must be a commitment to education, health care, and job creation (for adults) so that these families have alternatives. All of this testifies to the importance of democratic participation in this process. A top-down directive from the Economic Rights Committee to the LDCs to abolish child labor will go nowhere. A grassroots effort in the community to alter exploitative practices, on the other hand, has a chance of success. The ICFTU stated it most clearly: "We seek a commitment to the progressive elimination of child labour as poverty is reduced and education expanded and prosperity rises."[90]

Stephen Herzenberg notes that the fight for minimum labor standards in the United States did not simply revolve around an effort to abolish child labor, but around eliminating the sweatshop as a way of doing business. The overall strategy was to push business away from a reliance on low wages, high levels of physical effort, and worker vulnerability. The strategy incorporated "promotive, preventive, and participative" standards, with the abolition of child labor as a key component.[91]

As with child labor, the issue of night work for women also exposes regional differences in approach and understanding of universal rights. Examine the different understanding of women's human rights in Europe and East Asia in relation to this issue. The European Court of Human Rights ruled that the ban on night work for women violated the regulations guaranteeing equality of women. European governments were compelled to redraft laws forbidding such night work and distance themselves from the ILO convention on this subject. Compare this decision to conditions in East Asia, where upholding the ban on night work for women is seen as a victory for the rights of women workers. In East Asia, the ban is an affirmation of the human right to decent working conditions for women. In Europe, the ban is seen as a denial of a woman's right to access to the same jobs as men. The objective real differences in the lives of working women in Asia and Europe result in differing attitudes toward night work for women. It is clearly not easy to draw up a list of universal social and economic rights.[92]

The examples of child labor and night work for women point to difficulties in implementing the social clause proposal. A social clause imposed through international law and international organization is fundamentally problematic as it does not incorporate enough local involvement or democratic participation. Furthermore, such action is often not responsive to the local context and the ways in which rights are prioritized by victimized groups to address the most acute forms of human suffering. To be effective, the implementation of economic and social rights must incorporate local perspectives and strategies, as dramatically demonstrated in the campaign to abolish child labor. For many of these reasons, strong opposition to a social clause has emerged from governments of developing countries and many civil society groups.[93]

The Global New Deal and the United Nations

Summary Observations

The UN has been remarkably effective in defining the core content of economic and social human rights. As documented in this chapter, the General Comments of the Economic Rights Committee (see appendix 3.1) provide the most developed enunciation of economic, social, and cultural rights codified in international law. It is thus impossible to maintain that these rights are too vague to enforce. The Economic Rights Committee provides us with the clarity and substance of these rights. Economic and social rights claims are not pleas for charity or "alms for the poor," but are legal obligations which all states have a duty to uphold. The Economic Rights Committee has, in addition, established key criteria to monitor states' compliance with international human rights law. Powerful new global economic actors, including global trade organizations, IFIs, and TNCs, are beginning to be held accountable to economic and social human rights law. Accurate indicators of social development to measure the achievement of economic and social human rights are being refined at the UNDP. Furthermore, the UN has incorporated human rights into its development programs, including the UNDAF, CCA, and HURIST projects.

However, in both the North and the South, states have been hesitant to fully implement and monitor

Global New Deal Proposals

The Global New Deal attempts to build a bridge and be responsive to both the concerns of the developed and less developed countries. It calls for enhancing the powers of the Economic Rights Committee. It seeks to provide a place in international organizations for the voices of the victims denied economic and social human rights to be heard. Ratification of the Optional Protocol to the Economic Rights Treaty outlined in chapter 9 could be critical to the successful adjudication of violations of economic and social human rights.

The Optional Protocol approved by the UN General Assembly provides the basic framework for a workable system. It gives legal standing to the victims of abuse and those organizing for social change. The voices of those individuals denied economic and social human rights can be heard through these proposed procedures. The legal cases of the vulnerable deserve adjudication. This approach is respectful of the need for democratic participation and a cross-cultural dialogue in the implementation of economic and social human rights. As discussed above, effective implementation of economic and social human rights law depends on its adaptation and acceptance by local communities. The Optional Protocol creates a vehicle for such local participation and the uniting of universal human rights with local cultures.

economic and social human rights. Global compliance with this corpus of international law is thus too weak or, in some cases, nonexistent. Thus, new mechanisms have been drafted to strengthen enforcement, including an optional protocol to the Economic Rights Treaty and a social clause to link human rights protection to the rules of international trade.

The global community seems divided on these two reform proposals. On one side, some developed states often oppose the optional protocol, while giving some support for a social clause and the linking of trade and workers' rights. On the other side, many LDCs tend to oppose the social clause and any trade–rights linkage, while stating support for the optional protocol. Is there a way to span this divide?

In addition, the Protocol provides the Economic Rights Committee with the authority to examine the work of global trade organizations, IFIs, and TNCs. Individuals and groups will be able to point to violations of economic and social human rights by these powerful international actors as well as states. Thus, instead of a social clause, the Global New Deal calls for the ratification of the Optional Protocol which will enhance the power of the Economic Rights Committee to be able to hear individual complaints and hold states and global economic actors accountable to human rights law.

* * *

Appendix 3.1 General Comments of the Economic Rights Committee

The General Comments of the Economic Rights Committee cover the following subjects:

#1 (1989), "Reporting by States Parties"
#2 (1990), "International Technical Assistance Matters"
#3 (1990), "The Nature of States Parties' Obligations"
#4 (1991), "The Right to Adequate Housing"
#5 (1994), "Persons with Disabilities"
#6 (1995), "Rights of Older Persons"
#7 (1997), "Housing and Forced Evictions"
#8 (1997), "Economic Sanctions"
#9 (1998), "The Domestic Application of the Covenant"
#10 (1998), "The Role of National Human Rights Institutions"
#11 (1999), "Plans of Action for Primary Education"

#12 (1999),"The Right to Adequate Food"
#13 (1999), "The Right to Education"
#14 (2000), "The Right to the Highest Attainable Standard of Health"
#15 (2002), "The Right to Water"
#16 (2005), "The Equal Right of Men and Women"
#17 (2005), "Scientific, Literary or Artistic Production"
#18 (2005), "The Right to Work"
#19 (2007), "The Right to Social Security"
#20 (2009), "Non-Discrimination"

General Comments nos. 1–3 (1989–1990): On Refining and Clarifying the State Reporting System

The Economic Rights Committee notes in the first three general comments that the Economic Rights Treaty imposes two immediate obligations on states parties: the undertaking to guarantee that relevant rights "will be exercised without discrimination" and the commitment "to take steps" within a reasonably short time after the covenant's entry into force to meet the recognized obligations.[94] The Economic Rights Committee continues:

> [T]he Committee is of the view that a minimum core obligation to ensure the satisfaction of, at the very least, minimum essential levels of each of the rights is incumbent upon every State party. Thus, for example, a State party in which any significant number of individuals is deprived of essential foodstuffs, of essential primary health care, of basic shelter and housing, or of the most basic forms of education is, prima facie, failing to discharge its obligations under the Covenant.[95]

The Economic Rights Committee's attempt to establish a "minimum threshold" that should be achieved by all states at the earliest possible moment irrespective of their economic situation has appeal. It is then possible "to speak of the widespread violation of economic, social and cultural rights in a technical legal sense instead of merely as a moral injunction."[96] The burden of proof shifts to the state. It must prove that existing poverty, hopelessness, and hunger are due to factors beyond its control and that it has mobilized its resources to meet the needs of the most vulnerable. The Economic Rights Committee thus works to establish universal criteria through which states can be held accountable.

However, this approach is not without its problems. It is exceedingly difficult to establish minimum thresholds and standards for economic and social rights at the international level. Are different criteria to be applied to resource-poor as opposed to resource-rich countries? Should the minimum level be raised in those countries that have the ability to meet a higher level of demand? Or will the Economic Rights Committee only focus its attention on the basic needs of the developing states and ignore the developed states?

Furthermore, the Economic Rights Committee will have to address the issue of responsibility. In a globalized economy, the impact of transnational actors (e.g., global corporations and banks, international financial institutions [IFIs], and powerful individuals like George Soros and Carlos Slim) often have a direct impact on the well-being and/or destitution of a population. Mechanisms must be created to hold these state and nonstate actors accountable to international human rights law.[97]

Sigrun I. Skogly notes the ways in which the Economic Rights Committee has deliberated on the impact of IFIs on economic and social human rights. Reporting states are asked whether they consider the human rights implications of proposed World Bank and International Monetary Fund (IMF) projects and programs. These states are also systematically asked whether they consider the human rights implications of their own voting behavior inside the World Bank and the IMF. The Economic Rights Committee has also attempted to draw the World Bank and IMF into its deliberations. The committee requests the assistance of these specialized agencies to help provide information on nonreporting states—that is, states that have not submitted required reports and failed to comply with their obligations under the treaty.[98]

The Economic Rights Committee has been clear about state responsibility. Through either legislation, judicial remedy, or public policy, governments are required to take immediate and targeted steps toward the realization of economic and social rights. Governments have discretion to decide what steps to take but are required, at the very least, to ensure minimum levels of basic rights to their citizens.

General Comment no. 4 (1991): On the Right to Adequate Housing

The Economic Rights Committee affirms that the right to adequate housing applies to everyone and should "be seen as the right to live somewhere in security, peace and dignity." The Economic Rights Committee identifies certain aspects of this right that must be taken into account: legal security of tenure; availability of services, materials, facilities, and infrastructure; affordability; habitability; accessibility; location; and cultural adequacy. It states: "Regardless of the state of development of any country, there are certain steps which must be taken immediately." The Economic Rights Committee notes that certain actions require an abstention of the government from certain practices, while other actions require that priority be given to social groups living in unfavorable conditions.

> While appropriate means of achieving the full realization of the right to adequate housing will inevitably vary significantly from one State party to

another, the Covenant clearly requires that each State party take whatever steps are necessary for that purpose. This will almost invariably require the adoption of a national housing strategy. . . . Effective monitoring of the situation with respect to housing is another obligation of immediate effect. . . . Measures designed to satisfy a State party's obligations in respect of the right to adequate housing may reflect whatever mix of public and private sector measures is considered appropriate.[99]

The Economic Rights Committee also considers that "instances of forced eviction are prima facie incompatible with the requirements of the covenant and can only be justified in the most exceptional circumstances, and in accordance with the relevant principles of international law." And finally, the last paragraph of this general comment addresses the impact of international finance on housing by calling for international housing assistance to be targeted to the housing needs of disadvantaged groups and stating that IFIs' structural adjustment "should ensure that such measures do not compromise the enjoyment of the right to adequate housing."[100]

The state clearly has a primary role in creating conditions whereby the right to housing becomes a reality. But the Economic Rights Committee is clear that this role includes enabling strategies through which local community-based organizations and private citizens are encouraged to build houses themselves; the government must take positive steps to encourage private housing construction. "[P]rivate individuals and groups should be able to construct housing themselves without excessive conditions being placed upon them."[101] But, as Craven notes, this does not absolve states from responsibility for the provision of housing. For example, the Economic Rights Committee criticized Chile following a sharp reduction in government low-cost housing projects. By placing the housing problem entirely in the hands of the private sector, one member commented that Chile was ignoring the position of the poor. The Economic Rights Committee has directed similar criticisms toward Italy's shortage of low-income housing.[102]

General Comment no. 5 (1994): On Persons with Disabilities

The Economic Rights Committee notes that in its experience to date, states parties have devoted very little attention to persons with disabilities. States parties are called on "to take appropriate measures, to the maximum extent of their available resources, to enable such persons to seek to overcome any disadvantages, in terms of the enjoyment of the rights specified in the covenant, flowing from their disability." States must do more than merely abstain from taking measures that might have a negative impact on persons with disabilities. "The obligation in the case of such a vulnerable and disadvantaged group is to take positive action to reduce structural disadvantages and to give appropriate preferential treatment to people with disabilities."[103]

Of particular interest is the attention that the Economic Rights Committee pays to the impact of market-based policies on the disabled. The Economic Rights Committee calls for regulation of the private sphere to

> ensure equitable treatment of persons with disabilities. In a context in which arrangements for the provision of public services are increasingly being privatized and in which the free market is being relied on to an ever greater extent, it is essential that private employers, private suppliers of goods and services, and other non-public entities are subject to both nondiscrimination and equality norms in relation to persons with disabilities. . . . In the absence of government intervention there will always be instances in which the operation of the free market will produce unsatisfactory results for persons with disabilities, either individually or as a group, and in such circumstances it is incumbent on Governments to step in and take appropriate measures to temper, complement, compensate for, or override the results produced by market forces.[104]

The Economic Rights Committee also notes the ways in which persons with disabilities are treated as "genderless human beings," and the double discrimination faced by women with disabilities. "Women with disabilities also have the right to protection and support in relation to motherhood and pregnancy."[105]

General Comment no. 6 (1995): On the Rights of Older Persons

The Economic Rights Treaty does not specify precise rights for older persons, although article 9 does recognize the right to old-age benefits by declaring "the right of everyone to social security, including social insurance." The Economic Rights Committee "notes that the great majority of States parties reports continue to make little reference to this important issue. It therefore wishes to indicate that, in the future, it will insist that the situation of older persons in relation to each of the rights recognized in the Covenant should be adequately addressed in all reports." General Comment no. 6 develops rights relating to work, social security, the protection of the family, an adequate standard of living, education, and culture as they relate to older persons.[106]

In accordance with article 3 of the covenant, the Economic Rights Committee calls on states parties to

> pay particular attention to older women who, because they have spent all or part of their lives caring for their families without engaging in a remunerated activity entitling them to an old-age pension, and who are also not entitled to a widow's pension, are often in critical situations . . . states parties should institute non-contributory old-age benefits or other assistance for all persons,

regardless of their sex, who find themselves without resources on attaining an age specified in national legislation. Given their greater life expectancy and the fact that it is more often they who have no contributory pensions, women would be the principal beneficiaries.[107]

General Comment no. 7 (1997): On Housing and Forced Evictions

The Economic Rights Committee articulates the circumstances under which forced evictions are permissible and spells out the types of protection required under the covenant: "The State itself must refrain from forced evictions and ensure that the law is enforced against its agents or third parties who carry out forced evictions." Furthermore, the Economic Rights Committee calls on states to enact legislative measures against forced evictions that provide the greatest possible security of tenure to occupiers of houses and land and designate the circumstances under which evictions may be carried out. These measures must apply to forced evictions carried out by private persons or bodies as well as governmental actions.[108]

Where forced evictions are justified, as in the case of persistent nonpayment of rent, the relevant authorities must "ensure that those evictions are carried out in a manner warranted by a law which is compatible with the Covenant. . . . Evictions should not result in rendering individuals homeless or vulnerable to the violation of other human rights."[109]

General Comment no. 8 (1997): On Economic Sanctions

The Economic Rights Committee notes the increasing frequency with which economic sanctions are being imposed internationally, regionally, and unilaterally. These sanctions have a direct impact on the rights recognized in the Economic Rights Treaty by, for example, disrupting the distribution of food and sanitation supplies. Since insufficient attention has been paid to the impact of these acts on vulnerable groups, the Economic Rights Committee sees the need to "inject a human rights dimension into deliberations on this issue."[110]

The Economic Rights Committee outlines two sets of obligations. The first set relates to the affected state, which still "must take steps 'to the maximum of its available resources' to provide the greatest protection for the economic, social and cultural rights of each individual living within its jurisdiction." The second set relates to the party or parties responsible for the imposition of sanctions. These parties must take into account the impact of their actions on the economic, social, and cultural rights of the most vulnerable sectors of the population. Effective monitoring of the suffering caused by the sanctions must be implemented. Furthermore, action must be taken "to respond to any disproportionate suffering experienced by vulnerable groups within the targeted country."[111]

General Comment no. 9 (1998): On Domestic Application

The Economic Rights Committee notes that the Vienna Convention on the Law of Treaties obligates each state party to modify its domestic legal order to give effect to its treaty obligations. Legally binding human rights standards should operate "directly and immediately within the domestic legal system of each State party, thereby enabling individuals to seek enforcement of their rights before national courts and tribunals." It is unfortunate that the assumption is often made that there are no judicial remedies for violations of economic and social rights. The Economic Rights Committee asserts that "there is no Covenant right which could not, in the great majority of systems, be considered to possess at least some significant justiciable dimensions." The courts' capacity to protect the rights of the most vulnerable and disadvantaged groups in society should not be curtailed.[112]

General Comment no. 10 (1998): On the Role of National Human Rights Institutions

In 1998, the Economic Rights Committee issued a short statement on the role of national human rights institutions in the protection of economic, social, and cultural rights. These national institutions—from national human rights commissions to human rights advocates—can play an important role in the implementation of human rights by promoting educational programs, scrutinizing existing laws, providing technical advice, monitoring compliance with specific rights, and so on. The Economic Rights Committee urges states to ensure that the mandates accorded all national human rights institutions include appropriate attention to economic, social, and cultural rights.[113]

General Comments nos. 11 and 13 (1999): On the Right to Education

In these two general comments, the Economic Rights Committee argues that education at all levels should exhibit four essential features: availability, accessibility, acceptability, and adaptability. These concepts clarify state obligations under international law in relation to the right to education. The committee writes:

> States have obligations to respect, protect and fulfill each of the "essential features" (availability, accessibility, acceptability, adaptability) of the right to education. By way of illustration, a State must respect the availability of education by not closing private schools; protect the accessibility of education by ensuring that third parties, including parents and employers, do not stop girls from going to school; fulfill (facilitate) the acceptability of

education by taking positive measures to ensure that education is culturally appropriate for minorities and indigenous peoples, and of good quality for all; fulfill (provide) the adaptability of education by designing and providing resources for curricula which reflect the contemporary needs of students in a changing world; and fulfill (provide) the availability of education by actively developing a system of schools, including building classrooms, delivering programmes, providing teaching materials, training teachers and paying them domestically competitive salaries.[114]

Under international law, primary education is to be "compulsory" and "available free to all." Secondary education is to "be made generally available and accessible to all by every appropriate means, and in particular by the progressive introduction of free education." And higher education "shall be made equally accessible to all, on the basis of capacity."[115]

General Comment no. 11 focuses on plans of action for primary education. "[N]either parents, guardians, nor the State are entitled to treat as optional the decision as to whether the child should have access to primary education." Primary education should be available without charge to the child, parents, or guardians. Financial difficulties arising from either the debt crisis or the impact of structural adjustment programs do not relieve a state from its obligation to adopt a plan of action for primary education. "This obligation needs to be scrupulously observed in view of the fact that in developing countries, 130 million children of school age are currently estimated to be without access to primary education, of whom about two-thirds are girls."[116]

General Comment no. 12 (1999): On the Right to Adequate Food

The committee writes that the core content of the right to adequate food implies: "The availability of food in a quantity and quality sufficient to satisfy the dietary needs of individuals, free from adverse substances, and acceptable within a given culture; the accessibility of such food in ways that are sustainable and that do not interfere with the enjoyment of other human rights."[117]

Like other human rights, the right to adequate food imposes obligations to respect, protect, and fulfill.

The obligation to respect existing access to adequate food requires States parties not to take any measures that result in preventing such access. The obligation to protect requires measures by the State to ensure that enterprises or individuals do not deprive individuals of their access to adequate food. The obligation to fulfill (facilitate) means that the State must proactively engage in activities intended to strengthen people's access to and utilization of resources and means to ensure their livelihood, including food security. Finally, whenever an individual or group is unable, for reasons beyond their control, to enjoy the right to adequate food by the means at their disposal,

States have the obligation to fulfill (provide) that right directly. This obligation also applies for persons who are victims of natural or other disasters.[118]

General Comment no. 12 illuminates clear violations of the right to food, such as

> the formal repeal or suspension of legislation necessary for the continued enjoyment of the right to food; denial of access to food to particular individuals or groups, whether the discrimination is based on legislation or is proactive; the prevention of access to humanitarian food aid in internal conflicts or other emergency situations; adopting legislation or policies which are manifestly incompatible with pre-existing legal obligations relating to the right to food; and failure to regulate activities of individuals or groups so as to prevent them from violating the right to food of others, or the failure of a State to take into account its international legal obligations regarding the right to food when entering into agreements with other States or with international organizations.[119]

Large segments of the world's population face food insecurity due to a lack of access to available food. The right to food rests on the fact that hunger and malnutrition is not a product of a lack of food, but a result of crippling poverty limiting access to these abundant food supplies. The Economic Rights Committee noted in 1999 that more than 840 million people throughout the world are chronically hungry. While problems of hunger and malnutrition are particularly acute in developing countries, undernutrition and other problems related to the lack of access to adequate food exist in some of the most economically developed countries. Each state party is required to "take whatever steps necessary to ensure that everyone is free from hunger and as soon as possible can enjoy the right to adequate food. This will require the adoption of a national strategy to ensure food and nutrition security for all."[120]

General Comment no. 14 (2000): On the Right to Health

Article 12.1 of the Economic Rights Treaty recognizes "the right of everyone to the enjoyment of the highest attainable standard of physical and mental health," while article 12.2 enumerates a number of "steps to be taken by the States parties . . . to achieve the full realization of this right." The Economic Rights Committee acknowledges that for millions of people throughout the world, the full enjoyment of the right to health remains a distant goal.[121]

As with education, the Economic Rights Committee again stresses availability and accessibility. Functioning public health and health care facilities, goods and services, and programs have to be available in sufficient quantity. These will include safe and potable drinking water and adequate sanitation facilities, hospitals, clinics and other health-related buildings, trained medical and professional personnel receiving domestically competitive salaries, and essential drugs. These health facilities and goods and services have to be accessible to everyone without discrimination and within the jurisdiction of the state. Accessibility has four overlapping dimensions: nondiscrimination, physical accessibility, economic accessibility (affordability), and information accessibility.[122]

General Comment no. 14 describes in detail states parties' obligations to respect, protect, and fulfill the right to health. Violations of the obligation to respect are those state actions, policies, or laws that are likely to result in bodily harm, unnecessary morbidity, and preventable mortality. "Examples include the denial of access to health facilities, goods and services to particular individuals or groups as a result of de jure or de facto discrimination [and] . . . the suspension of legislation or the adoption of laws or policies that interfere with the enjoyment of any of the components of the right to health."[123]

Violations of the obligation to protect arise from a state's refusal or failure to safeguard persons within their jurisdiction from infringements of the right to health by third parties. This includes such omissions as

> the failure to protect consumers and workers from practices detrimental to health, e.g. by employers and manufacturers of medicines or food; the failure to discourage production, marketing and consumption of tobacco, narcotics and other harmful substances; the failure to protect women against violence or to prosecute perpetrators . . . and the failure to enact or enforce laws to prevent the pollution of water, air and soil by extractive and manufacturing industries.[124]

Violations of the obligation to fulfill are the result of states parties' failure to take all necessary steps to ensure the realization of the right to health.

> Examples include the failure to adopt or implement a national health policy designed to ensure the right to health for everyone; insufficient expenditure or misallocation of public resources which results in the non-enjoyment of the right to health by individuals or groups, particularly the vulnerable or marginalized; the failure to monitor the realization of the right to health at the national level, for example by identifying right to health indicators and benchmarks; the failure to take measures to reduce the inequitable distribution of health facilities, goods and services; the failure to adopt a gender-sensitive approach to health; and the failure to reduce infant and maternal mortality rates.[125]

General Comment no. 15 (2002): On the Right to Water

The Economic Rights Committee notes that the "human right to water is indispensable for leading a life in human dignity. It is a prerequisite for the realization of other human rights." Yet, the World Health Organization reported in 2002 that over 1.1 billion people lacked access to a basic water supply. A further 2.3 billion people suffered from diseases linked to water as a result of inadequate sanitation leading to water contamination. This situation creates profound suffering and exacerbates existing poverty. The committee thus calls on states parties to "adopt effective measures to realize, without discrimination, the right to water."[126]

After establishing the legal basis to the right to water, the Economic Rights Committee outlines the legal obligations of states to respect, protect, and fulfil this right. The obligation to respect requires that states parties "refrain from interfering directly or indirectly with the enjoyment of the right to water." The committee provides the following examples of this obligation: "refraining from engaging in any practice or activity that denies or limits equal access to adequate water; arbitrarily interfering with customary or traditional arrangements for water allocation; unlawfully diminishing or polluting water, for example through waste from State-owned facilities or through use and testing of weapons; and limiting access to, or destroying, water services and infrastructure as a punitive measure, for example, during armed conflicts in violation of international humanitarian law."[127]

The obligation to protect obligates states parties

to prevent third parties from interfering in any way with the enjoyment of the right to water. Third parties include individuals, groups, corporations and other entities as well as agents acting under their authority. The obligation includes, inter alia, adopting the necessary and effective legislative and other measures to restrain, for example, third parties from denying equal access to adequate water; and polluting and inequitably extracting from water resources, including natural sources, wells and other water distribution systems.[128]

And finally, the Economic Rights Committee maintains that the three components to the obligation to fulfill encompass duties to facilitate, promote, and provide.

The obligation to facilitate requires the State to take positive measures to assist individuals and communities to enjoy the right. The obligation to promote obliges the State party to take steps to ensure that there is appropriate education concerning the hygienic use of water, protection of water sources and methods to minimize water wastage. States parties are also obliged to fulfil (provide) the right when individuals or a group are unable, for reasons beyond their control, to realize that right themselves by the means at their disposal.[129]

The committee further calls on states parties to ensure that "their actions as members of international organizations take due account of the right to water." Members of IFIs (in particular the IMF and World Bank) are thus required to "take steps to ensure that the right to water is taken into account in the lending policies, credit agreements and other international measures."[130]

This General Comment provides detailed information for states to utilize to formulate national plans to meet their obligations to respect, protect, and fulfill the right to water.

General Comment no. 16 (2005): On the Equal Right of Men and Women

The economic and social rights established in the Economic Rights Treaty are to be enjoyed by men and women equally. The Economic Rights Committee acknowledges the many ways in which women have been often denied their human rights by virtue of a lesser status ascribed to them by tradition and custom and by overt and covert discrimination. General Comment 16 explores the ways in which states parties can act to guarantee both non-discrimination on the basis of sex and the equal enjoyment of rights by men and women.

After outlining the states' responsibilities to respect and protect, the Economic Rights Committee provides detailed steps to ensure that states meet their obligations to fulfill gender equality. For example, three recommended steps are:

- To make available and accessible remedies, such as compensation, reparation, restitution, rehabilitation, guarantees of non-repetition, declarations, public apologies, educational programs and prevention programs.
- To design and implement policies and programs to give long-term effect to the economic, social and cultural rights of both men and women on the basis of equality. These may include the adoption of temporary special measures to accelerate women's equal enjoyment of their rights, gender audits, and gender-specific allocation of resources.
- To integrate, in formal and non-formal education, the principle of the equal right of men and women to the enjoyment of economic, social and cultural rights, and to promote equal participation of men and women, boys and girls, in schools and other education programs.[131]

General Comment no. 17 (2005): On Scientific, Literary, or Artistic Production

The right of everyone to benefit from the protection of the moral and material interests resulting from any scientific, literary, or artistic production of which he or she is a member is recognized (article 15, paragraph 1 (c), of the Covenant).

The Economic Rights Committee makes an important distinction in this General Comment between intellectual property rights and the human right of everyone to benefit from his or her scientific, literary or artistic work. "Human rights are fundamental as they are inherent to the human person as such, whereas intellectual property rights are first and foremost means by which States seek to provide incentives for inventiveness and creativity, encourage the dissemination of creative and innovative productions, as well as the development of cultural identities, and preserve the integrity of scientific, literary and artistic productions for the benefit of society as a whole."[132]

The core obligations of states under General Comment no. 17 are

(a) To take legislative and other necessary steps to ensure the effective protection of the moral and material interests of authors; (b) To protect the rights of authors to be recognized as the creators of their scientific, literary and artistic productions and to object to any distortion, mutilation or other modification of, or other derogatory action in relation to, their productions that would be prejudicial to their honour or reputation; (c) To respect and protect the basic material interests of authors resulting from their scientific, literary or artistic productions, which are necessary to enable those authors to enjoy adequate standard of living; (d) To ensure equal access, particularly for authors belonging to disadvantaged and marginalized groups, to administrative, judicial or other appropriate remedies enabling authors to seek and obtain redress in case their moral and material interests have been infringed; (e) To strike an adequate balance between the effective protection of the moral and material interests of authors and States parties' obligations in relation to the rights to food, health and education, as well as the rights to take part in cultural life and to enjoy the benefits of scientific progress and its applications, or any other right recognized in the Covenant.[133]

General Comment no. 18 (2005): On the Right to Work

The Economic Rights Committee states that the right to work

affirms the obligation of States parties to assure individuals their right to freely chosen or accepted work, including the right not to be deprived of work unfairly . . . The right to work is an individual right that belongs to each person and is at the same time a collective right. It encompasses all forms of work, whether independent work or dependent wage-paid work. The right to work should not be understood as an absolute and unconditional right to obtain employment . . . the right of every human being to decide freely to accept or choose work. This implies not being forced in any way whatsoever to exercise or engage in employment and the right of access to a system of protection guaranteeing each worker access to employment. It also implies the right not to be unfairly deprived of employment.[134]

General Comment no. 18 defines specific state obligations in regard to the right to work and women, young persons, child labor, older persons, persons with disabilities, and migrant workers. The principle obligation of states is to ensure the progressive realization of the right to work by adopting, as quickly as possible, measures aimed at achieving full employment. States are under obligations to respect the right to work by "prohibiting forced or compulsory labor and refraining from denying or limiting equal access to decent work for all persons." Obligations to protect the right to work include "the duties of States parties to adopt legislation or to take other measures ensuring equal access to work and training and to ensure that privatization measures do not undermine workers' rights." And finally, states are obligated to fulfill the right to work "when individuals or groups are unable, for reasons beyond their control, to realize that right themselves by the means at their disposal." This means that states must formulate and implement a national employment policy with a view to "stimulating economic growth and development, raising levels of living, meeting manpower requirements and overcoming unemployment and underemployment."[135]

General Comment no. 19 (2007): On the Right to Social Security

Article 9 of the Economic Rights Treaty declares, "The States Parties to the present Covenant recognize the right of everyone to social security." In this General Comment, the committee clarifies that the right to social security "encompasses the right to access and maintain benefits, whether in cash or in kind, without discrimination in order to secure protection, inter alia, from (a) lack of work-related income caused by sickness, disability, maternity, employment injury, unemployment, old age, or death of a family member; (b) unaffordable access to health care; (c) insufficient family support, particularly for children and adult dependents."[136]

Around the world, there is tragically a very low level of access to this human right with about 80 percent of the global population lacking any form of formal social security protection. States parties have an obligation to address the elements of the right to social security, which include the following nine principle branches: adequate health services, disability benefits, old age benefits, unemployment benefits, employment injury insurance, family and child support, maternity benefits, disability protections, and provisions for survivors and orphans.

As with all economic and social human rights, the right to social security imposes obligations to respect, protect, and fulfill. General Comment 19 clearly outlines these state obligations. For example, the obligation to fulfill

> requires States parties to adopt the necessary measures, including the implementation of a social security scheme . . . [and] can be subdivided into obligations to facilitate, promote and provide. The obligation to facilitate requires States parties to take positive measures to assist individuals and communities to enjoy the right to social security . . . according sufficient recognition of

this right within the national political and legal systems, preferably by way of legislative implementation; adopting a national social security strategy . . . ensuring that the social security system will be adequate, accessible for everyone and will cover social risks and contingencies.[137]

General Comment no. 20 (2009): On Non-Discrimination in Economic, Social and Cultural Rights

Non-discrimination is recognized throughout the Economic Rights Treaty. The committee notes that "discrimination constitutes any distinction, exclusion, restriction or preference or other differential treatment that is directly or indirectly based on the prohibited grounds of discrimination and which has the intention or effect of nullifying or impairing the recognition, enjoyment or exercise, on an equal footing, of Covenant rights. Discrimination also includes incitement to discriminate and harassment." This General Comment notes the many different types of discrimination: formal and substantive; direct and indirect. Such discrimination can occur in the public and private spheres and is often pervasive, systemic and deeply entrenched.[138]

The Economic Rights Committee interprets the treaty as prohibiting all discrimination on the basis of race or colour, sex, language, religion, political opinion, national or social origin, property status, birth status, disability, age, nationality, marital and family status, sexual orientation and gender identity, health status, place of residence, and economic and social situation. States parties are required to take "concrete, deliberate and targeted measures to ensure that discrimination in the exercise of Covenant rights is eliminated."[139]

4

The Environment and
Economic and Social Human Rights

Is there a human right to a healthy environment? What are environmental rights? What are the links between international human rights law and international environmental law? Is a rights-based approach a reasonable path to work for ecological balance? Does international human rights law provide mechanisms to push states and all economic actors to account for environmental costs and correct harmful practices? Does a human rights approach provide a useful means to bridge the perceived gap between economic development and ecological balance? How do the UN Environment Program (UNEP), the Commission on Sustainable Development (CSD), and the Global Environment Facility (GEF) approach these issues? What public policy successfully links ecological balance to economic and social human rights?

The late twentieth and the beginning of the twenty-first centuries brought new awareness of the ecological fragility of our planet. Following the 1972 UN Conference on the Human Environment in Stockholm (hereafter the Stockholm Conference), the international community enacted multiple measures in international law designed to protect the environment. Further action was formulated in 1992 at the UN Conference on the Environment and Development in Rio de Janeiro (hereafter the Rio Conference) and in 2002 at the World Summit on Sustainable Development in Johannesburg (hereafter the Johannesburg Conference). It is estimated that there are well over 300 multilateral treaties and more than 900 bilateral treaties dealing with the protection and conservation of the biosphere.[1] There are at least ten significant global environmental agreements in force, including the Convention on Biodiversity, the Convention on International Trade in Endangered Species (CITES), the Basel Convention (on hazardous wastes), the Montreal Protocol (on ozone depletion), the UN Framework Convention on Climate Change, the Kyoto Protocol (on climate change), the Desertification Convention, the Ramsar Convention (on wetlands protection), the UNESCO Heritage Convention, and the Law of the Seas Convention. All of these global environment agreements can now boast more than 150 countries as parties.[2]

Yet, despite this action the global environment continues to be under siege. This progress in international environmental law has unfortunately not been adequate to protect our biosphere. Examine, for example, just one critical issue confronting the global community: climate change. In 1988, the UN created the Intergovernmental Panel on Climate Change (IPCC), an organization made up of hundreds of the world's leading scientists, to assess the scientific evidence for global warming. The IPCC has produced a series of scientific reports on human-induced global climate change. For example, in 2001 the IPCC reported that fossil fuel combustion was estimated to have raised atmospheric concentrations of carbon dioxide to their highest levels on record. This scientific body stated that societies' release of carbon dioxide and other greenhouse gases "contributed substantially to the observed warming over the last 50 years." The warming in the twentieth century was likely to have been the greatest of any century in the last 1,000 years for the Northern Hemisphere. The 1990s was the warmest decade of the last millennium. Snow cover since the 1960s had been cut by 10 percent. The sea level rose at a rate ten times faster than the average rate over the last 3,000 years. The IPCC concluded that by the end of the twenty-first century temperatures would likely be approximately eleven degrees higher than in 1990. This increase would be greater than the change in temperature between the last Ice Age and today.[3]

The 2007 IPCC scientific report was even more stark and alarming. "Warming of the climate system is unequivocal, as is now evident from observations of increases in global average air and ocean temperatures, widespread melting of snow and ice and rising global average sea level. Eleven of the last twelve years (1995–2006) rank among the twelve warmest years in the instrumental record of global surface temperature (since 1850)." The world's scientists continued: "Most of the observed increase in global average temperature since the mid-20th century is *very likely* due to the observed increase in anthropogenic GHG [green house gas] concentrations. It is *likely* that there has been significant anthropogenic warming over the past 50 years averaged over each continent (except Antarctica)." "Altered frequencies and intensities of extreme weather, together with sea level rise, are expected to have mostly adverse effects on natural and human systems." Additional scientific documentation demonstrated that "[a]verage Arctic temperatures increased at almost twice the global average rate in the past 100 years." The IPCC Synthesis Report concluded that "anthropogenic warming could lead to some impacts that are abrupt or irreversible, depending upon the rate and magnitude of the climate change. Partial loss of ice sheets on polar land could imply metres of sea level rise, major changes in coastlines and inundation of low-lying areas, with greatest effects in river deltas and low-lying islands . . . Climate change is *likely* to lead to some irreversible impacts" (emphasis in original).[4]

Despite this evidence, the global community from 1990 to 2010 has been unable to come to agreement on a binding treaty to limit the production of greenhouse gases. The Kyoto Protocol, for example, would have required countries to reduce greenhouse gas emissions, primarily coal and oil, to 7 percent below 1990 levels. While many European states agreed to these targets, the U.S. resisted and instead attempted voluntary measures, which failed. For example, according to the U.S. Energy Department, Americans produced 12 percent more carbon dioxide annually during the last decade of the twentieth century than they did when President Bill Clinton took office (1992). The Kyoto Protocol would have at least forced participating countries to slow these harmful trends.[5]

At a G-8 meeting in July 2009, the leaders of the U.S., Britain, France, Germany, Italy, Japan, Canada, and Russia agreed to an aspirational target of reducing their carbon emissions by 80 percent by the year 2050. This was a big improvement over the 50 percent agreement agreed to the previous year. Yet with no binding commitment established, it is hard to see this declaration having a direct impact on economic growth policies. In addition, the LDCs have been unwilling to even establish such a goal over concern that such environmental actions might interfere with economic growth and poverty alleviation. Thus, while all of the nations could agree that the Earth's average temperature should not rise more than 3.6 degrees Fahrenheit (2 degrees Celsius) above preindustrial levels, it remained unclear how that goal would be achieved. And, neither the wealthy nor the LDCs felt the other side was doing enough. While the international community slowly slogs ahead in these negotiations, the atmosphere continues to warm. According to Nobel Prize Laureate Rajendra Pachauri, chair of the IPCC, we have "a very short window of time" if we want to avoid some of the increasingly likely scenarios which include, for example, a 20 foot sea-level rise. Yet, despite these scientific warnings, global action still does not seem imminent.[6]

Our oceans, wildlife, and entire biosphere face severe threats from industrialization, modernization, and globalization. For example, the 2008 International Union for Conservation of Nature and Natural Resources (IUCN) Red List contains 16,928 species threatened with extinction, including 12 percent of all birds, 21 percent of all mammals, and 30 percent of all amphibians. Fish populations are in the most extreme danger, with

37 percent of the world's fish species already threatened with extinction.[7] In areas like species preservation, biodiversity, and global warming, some scientists believe that it may already be too late. We may have set forces in motion that we cannot now control. Despite the scientific certainty of the depths of our environmental problems, few leaders seem willing or able to implement workable policies to curb destructive human behavior.

Tragically, economic development and modern living have often conflicted with environmental protection. On the one hand, developed countries have shown an unwillingness to limit ingrained patterns of nonsustainable consumption. The U.S. economy and society, for example, are structured around the heavy consumption of fossil fuels, which significantly contribute to global warming. Limiting these emmissions may require fundamental changes in both economic planning and the U.S. lifestyle. On the other hand, underdeveloped countries, facing massive problems of poverty and destitution, have had difficulty prioritizing ecological balance. The priority for the poor is often seen as economic development and growth based on an industrialization model that is environmentally destructive. Thus, both the developed and underdeveloped nations have demonstrated insufficient motivation to mobilize either international law or international organization for environmental protection and ecological renewal.

This chapter explores the links between economic and social human rights and environmental rights in the following sections:

- human rights and the environment,
- the UN Environment Program,
- the UN Commission on Sustainable Development,
- the Global Environment Facility, and
- the marriage of economic and environmental health.

Human Rights and the Environment

Environmental and human rights issues converge in a myriad of ways. Environmental degradation carries a high human cost. Unfair distribution of the costs of ecological damage, often referred to as "environmental racism" or "environmental injustice," raise human rights issues of equality and discrimination. Environmental organizations in civil society depend on such human rights as the right to associate and freedom of speech to lead successful environmental movements. In countries where civil and political rights are weak, such as Russia, ecological damage is often high.

The links between human rights and the environment were vividly brought to the public's awareness in the 1980s and 1990s with the brutal killings of Chico Mendes in Brazil and Ken Saro Wiwa in Nigeria. Mendes was murdered by ranchers with close ties to government officials because of his efforts to protect the rain forests of Brazil from deforestation. Mendes saw that the livelihood and economic human rights of the Brazilian rubber tappers was linked to the preservation of the natural ecosystem. To silence Saro Wiwa, the former Nigerian dictatorship had him hung. His crime was protesting the oil development in his native Ogoni lands. In these and other cases, the international human rights movement has organized and protested against these acts of internal repression.[8]

Both human rights and environmental law seek the modification of human activity through norms that trump all other considerations. The importance of protecting human rights and the environment is clearly a common concern of all of humanity. Yet, despite the growing awareness of the links between their work, tensions remain between human rights and environmental activists. The priority of the human rights movement is the protection and development of the human species. The priority of the environmental movement is the protection and survival of all species and all natural ecosystems. Although the perception may be that these priorities collide, in fact they can support each other.

On one side, some environmentalists fear that the anthropocentric focus of human rights law will lead to environmental destruction. Human rights law privileges the life, health, standard of living, and overall welfare of human beings. A likely consequence of economic development focused on growth and increasing human consumption is the rapid depletion of natural resources. Fulfilling the economic needs of a global population of over 6 billion people could have devastating repercussions on the environment. A response to these concerns, however, is to see human rights protection as a vehicle for the realization of environmental protection. The protection of civil and political rights creates the political space for organizing and speaking out for environmental protection. A human right to a satisfactory environment, and the creation of the legal means to support this right, could provide tools to advance a sustainable development agenda.

On the other side, some human rights activists fear that the urgency of ending existing human suffering becomes muted and displaced when the priority becomes long-term ecological balance and the rights of future generations. The environmental movement is seen as neglecting pressing human needs while privileging the rights of other species and the protection of the natural global ecosystem. The economic rights of the sick and hungry are seen as a human rights priority that environmentalists often ignore. A response to these concerns, however, is to see environmental protection as a vehicle for the fulfillment of human rights. Human rights to health and life cannot be achieved in a degraded physical environment. Acts leading to a degraded environment (deforestation, oil spills, toxic dumps, and so on) can be a violation of internationally recognized human rights. Such acts can literally deprive local populations of the ability to survive. Environmental law is thus of assistance not just to future generations, but also to those who depend on natural resources for their survival, including indigenous groups.[9]

The Right to a Healthy Environment in International Law

Although most human rights treaties do not explicitly mention a general right to a healthy environment, a case can be made that such a right exists in international law. International law includes both "hard law" and "soft law." Hard law refers to treaties, customary law, and general principles of international law (as defined by article 38 of the Statute of the International Court of Justice). Hard law is considered binding on states and is often incorporated into national jurisprudence. Soft law refers to actions by state and nonstate actors that fall between law in this strict sense and a mere political statement with no consequences. Soft law can take many forms including recommendations, declarations, clarifications, directives, standards, and so on. In both hard and soft law, the international community has endorsed the human right to a healthy environment.

Hard Law

The following two agreements specifically call for a right to a healthy environment: the African Charter on Human and Peoples' Rights (African Charter) and the San Salvador Additional Protocol to the American Convention on Human Rights in the Area of Economic, Social and Cultural Rights (San Salvador Protocol). In addition, the linkage between fundamental human rights, such as the right to life and the right to health, and a healthy environment can be drawn directly from the International Bill of Human Rights,[10] international humanitarian law, and other human rights treaties. And finally, individual nations have expressed a concern for the protection of the environment in their national laws and constitutions.

Article 24 of the African Charter states: "All peoples shall have the right to a general satisfactory environment favourable to their development."[11]

Scholars often situate the claims that the African Charter defines as peoples' rights within third-generation rights. First-generation rights are seen as civil and political rights, whereas economic, social, and cultural rights are classified as second-generation rights. Third-generation rights are frequently called "solidarity rights" as they are based on norms of fraternity. These rights include the right of peoples to self-determination, full sovereignty over their natural resources, development, and a general satisfactory environment.

As seen in article 24, the African Charter links a satisfactory environment to development. The implications of this linkage are not clear. In a conflict between conservation and development, for example, which would prevail? There is also no clear definition of a "general satisfactory environment." Overall, the African Charter focuses much more on issues of development than on the environment. The preamble calls on states to "pay . . . particular attention to the right to development." And, article 22(1) states: "All peoples shall have the right to their economic, social and cultural development with due regard to their freedom and identity and in the equal enjoyment of the common heritage of mankind." Ecological balance is not on equal footing with the "right to development" in the charter.

In 1989, the African Commission on Human and Peoples' Rights noted that the main purpose of article 24 "is to protect the environment and keep it favourable for development." The commission suggested that states parties should "establish a system to monitor effective disposal of waste in order to prevent pollution." The commission urged states to report on legislation and other measures taken to prohibit pollution on land, in water, and in the air, to prevent the international dumping of toxic wastes, and to curb wastes generally. Critics have noted that the commission took a narrow, largely anthropocentric, view of what is meant by a "satisfactory environment," since there was no reference to the conservation of species or habitats, global climate change, and so on.[12]

Article 11 of the San Salvador Protocol recognizes:

1. Everyone shall have the right to live in a healthy environment and to have access to basic public services.
2. The states parties shall promote the protection, preservation, and improvement of the environment.[13]

The San Salvador Protocol, which entered into force on 16 November 1999,[14] does not define a "healthy environment." Article 1 maintains that the parties "undertake to adopt the necessary measures, both domestically and through cooperation, especially economic and technical, to the extent allowed by their available resources, and taking into account their degree of development, for the purpose of achieving progressively and pursuant to their internal legislations, the full observance of the rights recognized in the Protocol." This implies that states parties should do what they can to promote a healthy environment only as far as their resources allow. They need do nothing if they lack the resources. But if they have the resources, they must take some measures to protect the human environment. Article 11 thus represents a weak environmental right. States parties essentially must do no more than they feel able to do to promote a healthy environment. Given the extensive poverty and poor economic conditions prevailing throughout Latin America, it is hard to see nations transferring scarce resources to environmental protection.[15]

Environmental protection can also be found in the International Bill of Human Rights and other human rights conventions in calls for the right to life, the right to good health, the right to healthy working conditions, and the right to adequate living standards. There is a direct link between these concerns (life, health, and adequate working and living conditions) and a healthy environment. This connection is made clear, for example, in article 24 of the 1989 "Convention on the Rights of the Child." Children have the right to enjoy the highest attainable standard of health, and states are to take measures to "combat disease and malnutrition . . . through . . . the provision of adequate nutritious foods and clean drinking water, taking into consideration the danger and the risks of environmental pollution."[16] These human rights treaties thus bind states to address environmental protection in their development policies.

In regard to international humanitarian law, concern for the protection of the environment is found in articles 35(3) and 55 of the 1977 Additional Protocol I to the 1949 Geneva Conventions (prohibition of methods or means of warfare severely damaging the environment) and the 1977 UN Convention on the Prohibition of Military or Any Other Hostile Use of Environmental Modification Techniques.[17]

The right to a healthy environment has thus been clearly recognized in positivist international law. It has also been recognized in national legislation and national constitutional provisions. Clauses related to environmental protection—either as a duty of the state or as an individual right or both—are found in at least forty-four national constitutions. The constitution of Brazil, for example, states: "Everyone has the right to an ecologically balanced environment, an asset for the common use of the people and essential to the wholesome quality of life. This imposes upon the Public Authorities and the community the obligation to defend and preserve it for present and future generations."[18] The South African Constitution gurantees the right to a healthy environment as follows: "Everyone has the right (a) to an environment that is not harmful to their health or well being; and (b) to have the environment protected, for the benefit of present and future generations, through reasonable legislative and other measures that (i) prevent pollution and ecological degradation; (ii) promote conservation; and (iii) secure ecologically sustainable development and use of natural resources while promoting justifiable economic and social development."[19]

Soft Law

Since the 1972 Stockholm Conference, there have been numerous instruments of soft law (resolutions, declarations, and so on) embracing a human right to a healthy environment. Principle 1 of the "Stockholm Declaration of the United Nations Conference on the Human Environment" declares: "Man has the fundamental right to freedom, equality, and adequate conditions of life, in an environment of a quality that permits a life of dignity and well-being, and he bears a solemn responsibility to protect and improve the environment for present and future generations."[20]

In 1974, the UN Charter of Economic Rights and Duties of States declared in article 30 that the "protection, preservation and enhancement of the environment for the present and future generations is the responsibility of all States. . . . All States have the responsibility to ensure that activities within their jurisdiction or control do not cause damage to the environment of other States or of areas beyond the limits of national jurisdiction."[21]

The 1982 World Charter for Nature reaffirms that humanity must "acquire the knowledge and enhance [its] ability to use natural resources in a manner which ensures the preservation of the species and ecosystems for the benefit of present and future generations."[22]

In 1989, the UN General Assembly, in its call for the convening of the Rio Conference, recognized the global character of environmental problems, and affirmed that the protection and enhancement of the environment were major issues that affected the well-being of peoples everywhere.[23]

In 1992, the Rio Conference adopted "Agenda 21," an 800-page detailed blueprint for launching an ambitious "global partnership for sustainable development." "Agenda 21" refers directly to two human rights instruments—the Universal Declaration of Human Rights (UDHR) and the UN Covenant on Economic, Social and Cultural Rights (Economic Rights Treaty).[24] In addition, Principle 1 of the "Rio Declaration" states: "Human beings are at the center of concerns for sustainable development. They are entitled to a healthy and productive life in harmony with nature."[25]

In 1993, the World Conference on Human Rights adopted the "Vienna Declaration and Programme of Action," which establishes in point eleven that: "The right to development should be fulfilled so as to meet equitably the developmental and environmental needs of present and future generations." The declaration further declares that the "illicit dumping of toxic and dangerous substances and waste potentially constitutes a serious threat to the human rights to life and health of everyone."[26]

In July 1994, Fatma Zohra Ksentini, the UN's special rapporteur on human rights and the environment, released her final report. "Human Rights and the Environment" (hereafter the Ksentini Report) argues that there has been "a shift from environmental law to the right to a healthy and decent environment."[27] The Ksentini Report proposes a set of "Draft Principles on Human Rights and the Environment."[28] Part one of the draft principles declares the following:

1. Human rights, an ecologically sound environment, sustainable development and peace are interdependent and indivisible

2. All persons have the right to a secure, healthy, and ecologically sound environment
3. All persons shall be free from any form of discrimination in regard to actions and decisions that affect the environment
4. All persons have the right to an environment adequate to meet equitably the needs of present generations and that does not impair the rights of future generations to meet equitably their needs.

The draft principles conclude by calling on all states to "adopt administrative, legislative and other measures necessary to effectively implement the rights in this Declaration." Such measures shall include the

• collection and dissemination of information concerning the environment
• regulation or prohibition of activities and substances potentially harmful to the environment
• public participation in environmental decision making
• monitoring, management and equitable sharing of natural resources
• measures to reduce wasteful processes of production and patterns of consumption
• measures aimed at ensuring that transnational corporations, wherever they operate, carry out their duties of environmental protection, sustainable development, and respect for human rights.[29]

In 2002, leaders from around the world adopted the "Johannesburg Declaration on Sustainable Development." Article 2 of the declaration states: "We commit ourselves to building a humane, equitable and caring global society, cognizant of the need for human dignity for all." The declaration concludes with article 37: "From the African continent, the cradle of humankind, we solemnly pledge to the peoples of the world and the generations that will surely inherit this Earth that we are determined to ensure that our collective hope for sustainable development is realized."[30]

In 2005, the UN held the World Summit in New York to coincide with the 60th Session of the UN General Assembly. At this high-level plenary meeting, the UN member states affirmed their commitment to achieve sustainable development through the implementation of Agenda 21 and the Johannesburg Plan of Implementation. The General Assembly Resolution summarizing the World Summit Outcome stated: "Poverty eradication, changing unsustainable patterns of production and consumption and social development are overarching objectives of and essential requirements for sustainable development."[31]

The combined impact of these soft law environmental instruments (resolutions, declarations, and so on) should not be underestimated. Soft law is important in providing a means for articulating a new normative international program. As soft law norms evolve, it becomes increasingly difficult for international actors to ignore internationally accepted ethical guidelines and human rights principles. The soft law case for a human right to a healthy environment is potent and persuasive.

These rights claims can be potentially effective in the struggle for ecological balance. They establish a standard from which to judge the behavior of not only states, but all economic organizations and actors. This human rights approach is useful for clarifying definitive claims that should not be violated. They provide a link to the UN international legal framework of reporting and accountability. Existing environmental treaties have already established supervisory institutions (e.g., the Convention on International Trade in Endangered Species [CITES] and the Convention on Biological Diversity). As documented in chapter three, the human rights treaty monitoring bodies also play a significant role in supervising state adherence to international norms. Environmental protection and human rights protection are linked, as both strive to guarantee basic human survival. A human right to a healthy environment embraces claims to sustain life over generations for all individuals and groups. It pertains to biological necessities (i.e., rights claims to access to food, water, and shelter) and the management of ecosystems (i.e., rights claims to environmental sustainability).

The United Nations and Ecological Balance

Institutions are needed for the development and implementation of human rights. At the local level, for example, huge state bureaucracies exist to enforce civil and political human rights. State welfare agencies are often committed to the protection of basic economic and social human rights. At the international level, the UN Human Rights Council and the UN Human Rights Committee primarily attend to state violations of civil and political rights. The work of the UN Economic Rights Committee to monitor state actions of omission and/or commission that may violate the Economic Rights Treaty was reviewed in chapter 3.

Global institutions are particularly relevant to the achievement of ecological balance. Pollution readily crosses borders with impunity. Acting after the environmental damage has been done is often of little help. The protection of the oceans, seas, land, forests, and atmosphere involves managing the affairs between state and nonstate actors. Public and private international organizations, both in and outside of the UN system, are key to increasing the cooperation and coordination among all these stakeholders. Creating global environmental management through international organization is central to achieving a healthy environment.

There exists no single institution in control of the management of global environmental affairs. Yet, international organizations committed to the development and implementation of the right to a healthy environment have grown in strength and scope since the 1972 Stockholm Conference. The chief international environmental organization is UNEP, initially created at Stockholm. Twenty years later at the 1992 Rio Conference, the CSD was born. Also in the 1990s, GEF was established. There are a myriad of other intergovernmental organizations (IGOs) and nongovernmental organizations (NGOs) working globally on environmental protection. In addition, bodies have been created under specific international environmental treaties to monitor states parties' compliance with the agreed-on global environmental rules and norms. Due to their overall importance, this section focuses on the work of UNEP, the CSD, and GEF.

UN Environment Program

UN General Assembly Resolution 2997 created UNEP in 1972 as the first UN agency with a specific environmental agenda. The following functions and responsibilities for UNEP were articulated by the General Assembly:

- To promote international co-operation in the field of the environment
- To provide general policy guidance for . . . environmental programmes within the UN system
- To keep under review the world environmental situation in order to ensure that emerging environmental problems of wide international significance receive appropriate and adequate consideration by Governments
- To promote the . . . acquisition and exchange of environmental knowledge and information
- To maintain under continuing review the impact of national and international environmental policies on developing countries.[32]

UNEP was established as a coordinating body acting to encourage environmental cooperation between member states.

UNEP was also intended to be a catalyst for environmental activities throughout the UN system. It was meant to spur the larger UN specialized agencies, such as the UNDP and the Food and Agriculture Organization, to incorporate environmental protection and planning into their projects. To accomplish these objectives, UNEP was given a modest staff and small budget. Governments promised an "environment fund" for UNEP to utilize in promoting environmental action throughout the UN. Unfortunately, the environment fund was never given significant revenues, and UNEP's total resources over its first twenty years amounted to only $1 billion. Its resources are anemic compared to the programs of the World Bank or the International Monetary Fund (IMF). (In 1998, for example, total World Bank expenditures totaled over $28 billion and IMF expenditures surpassed $27 billion.)[33]

UNEP has consistently faced financial difficulties. Only around 4–6 percent of all UNEP funds now comes from the regular UN budget. Voluntary contributions thus make up over 90 percent of the organization's budget. States often reduce their voluntary contributions to express displeasure with the direction of the organization. For example, the U.S., which strongly supported UNEP in 1993 with $21 million in voluntary donations, gave less than $6 million in 2004. As a result of this situation, UNEP's senior management are constantly traveling the world to try to raise funds. This has led overall to more money for specific programs, and not enough for basic, core administrative needs. This fundraising succeeded in raising the 2006–2007 UNEP budget to over $300 million.[34] But, in a critique of UNEP, NGOs issued a "Global Civil Society Statement" which asserted that the UNEP budget for 2006–2007 was simply too low for the organization to adequately respond to the increasingly complex and growing list of environmental challenges. The NGOs pointed out that global military expenditures were then approaching a trillion dollars a year. "If only Governments would set aside a fraction of their military expenditures as called for in Agenda 21, chapter 33, paragraph 16, there would be ample financial resources to solve many of the most pressing and sustainability challenges we face." Larger and more secure funding is clearly needed to fully support the pressing environmental priorities of UNEP.[35]

Despite its limited budget—smaller than many private environmental organizations—and small staff, UNEP is credited with some significant accomplishments. For example, UNEP's Division of Programs includes a specific unit dedicated to promoting international environmental law. The work of this unit has to be judged a success. Once a draft legal instrument is agreed on by the working group, UNEP may then convene a diplomatic conference to consider adoption. The Vienna Convention for the Protection of the Ozone Layer (Vienna Convention) and the Montreal Protocol on Substances that Deplete the Ozone Layer (Montreal Protocol) were both adopted through this technique. In fact, more than forty multilateral environmental treaties have been negotiated under UNEP's leadership, including the Basel Convention on the Control of Transboundary Movements of Hazardous Waste and Their Disposal (Basel Convention), the UN Convention to Combat Desertification, and CITES.[36]

In the area of soft law, UNEP has developed some important agreements, including the World Charter for Nature[37] and the Declaration of Environmental Policies and Procedures Relating to Economic Development.[38] This latter declaration was signed by the World Bank, the UNDP, UNEP, the Organization of American States, and six other development assistance agencies. UNEP played a central catalytic role in bringing these IGOs together to coordinate environmental action. By signing the declaration, the participating organizations agreed to submit all development activities to systematic environmental assessment and evaluation.

In addition, these organizations agreed to support projects that enhanced the environment of developing nations. These IGOs then established the Committee of International Development Institutions on the Environment to regularly review the implementation of the declaration.[39]

UNEP also plays a significant role in monitoring, gathering, assessing, and disseminating data regarding the earth's environment. For example, the Global Environmental Monitoring System (GEMS), part of UNEP's Earthwatch system, enlists thousands of scientists around the world to assess the health of the world's ecosystems. Additionally, UNEP established INFOTERRA as a global environmental information exchange system. The Global Resource Information Database was organized to disseminate environmental information to assist the African, Mediterranean, and West Asia Environment Research and Information Networks. UNEP maintains a global chemicals information clearinghouse, including an International Register of Potentially Toxic Chemicals, designed to increase awareness about the hazards of chemical production.[40]

Despite this progress, the UN system as a whole did not keep up with the serious environmental threats confronting the planet at the end of the twentieth and in the first decade of the twenty-first century. Scholars have documented the ways in which UNEP failed to keep pace with the dramatic changes in international environmental policy making. When UNEP was created in the 1970s, there were few other international actors trying to influence the environmental agenda. As noted earlier, since the Stockholm Conference hundreds of bilateral, multilateral, and global environmental treaties have been negotiated, establishing implementation mechanisms and state obligations to protect biodiversity and the ozone layer, to combat desertification, and so on. Due to its limited budget and size, UNEP has been unable to manage and direct this widening scope of global environmental politics. This, of course, has produced disappointment with the organization among some environmentalists.[41]

As the management of global environmental affairs has grown, UNEP's mission has remained broad and unfocused. For a financially constrained organization, UNEP is criticized for taking on too many tasks. For example, the UNEP's Governing Council reported to the June 1997 Earth Summit Plus Five special session of the General Assembly on significant activities relevant to every single chapter of "Agenda 21."[42] Former UNEP executive director Elizabeth Dowdeswell acknowledged UNEP's lack of clear priorities: "A rigorous review of current activities reveals a number that are no longer on the leading edge or represent sufficient added value given the scarce resources of UNEP. Others are self-perpetuating, continuing long after 'catalysis' should have been completed. Furthermore, activities once undertaken by UNEP, such as certain types of coordination, may now be better accomplished by others."[43]

UNEP has been a clear success in (1) negotiation management of international environmental law and (2) gathering, disseminating, and assessing environmental information. UNEP can build on the past strengths it has demonstrated in both of these areas. These two functions could provide the future focus for a streamlined, directed UNEP with a clear mission. With adequate staff and resources, UNEP could fulfill both of these tasks more effectively. As David L. Downie and Marc A. Levy write: "Doing so would meet all the relevant criteria for what a streamlined UNEP ought to focus on—UNEP is good at it, the world needs it, and no one else is doing it."[44] UNEP could continue to carry out these two critical functions as a division within the new environmental IGO, the World Environment Organization, proposed in chapter 9 as part of the Global New Deal.

In partial recognition of the limitations of UNEP, the Rio Conference in 1992 called for the creation of the CSD.

Commission on Sustainable Development

Chapter 38 of "Agenda 21," adopted at the Rio Conference, recommended the establishment of the CSD, a high-level, intergovernmental forum to oversee the implementation of the promises made at Rio and to pursue avenues toward sustainable development. Rio Conference delegates felt the need to improve the institutional arrangements at the international level to be able to more effectively address sustainable development. "Agenda 21" strives to integrate environmental and development goals and thus requires extensive coordination between various UN agencies and other international bodies. The CSD was designed to provide the institutional framework for this coordination to take place. Additionally, the CSD was envisioned as providing a forum for the continued debate on sustainable development and solutions to problems of the environment and development.[45]

In response to these recommendations from the Rio Conference, the UN General Assembly created the CSD in January 1993. The General Assembly empowered the CSD with the expansive functions recommended in "Agenda 21." The CSD is charged with monitoring progress in implementing "Agenda 21" both within the UN system and by states parties through a review of their national reports regarding activities undertaken to implement "Agenda 21." Through the power of publicity and peer pressure, the CSD can encourage states parties to implement "Agenda 21" and other Rio agreements. This approach is modeled, of course, on the UN Human Rights Treaty Bodies (Economic Rights Committee, Women's Rights Committee, Human Rights Committee, and so on), which, although lacking formal enforcement powers, have been able to expose violations and work with countries to change unacceptable human rights practices. The CSD approach is similar and focuses on positive recommendations and reinforcements as opposed to censure. UN Resolution 47/191 gave three broad responsibilities to the CSD:[46]

- To review progress toward the implementation of the recommendations and commitments contained in the final documents of the Rio Conference, including "Agenda 21," the "Rio de Janeiro Declaration on Environment and Development," and the Forest Principles
- To develop policy options to follow up on the Rio Conference and achieve sustainable development
- To build partnerships for sustainable development with governments, IGOs, NGOs, and others with a major role in the transition to sustainability (including women, indigenous peoples, the scientific community, farmers, and so on).[47]

The implementation of "Agenda 21" was reviewed by delegates to the Earth Summit Plus Five Conference held in New York in 1997. This follow-up conference adopted a "Programme for the Further Implementation of Agenda 21" that called on the CSD not only to continue with the three broad responsibilities previously outlined, but also to provide a forum for the exchange of experiences on national, regional, and subregional initiatives and collaborations for sustainable development. In addition, the Earth Summit Plus Five delegates called on the CSD to strive to attract the greater involvement of ministers and high-level national policy makers in their work and to establish closer interaction with international financial, development, and trade institutions.[48]

The CSD must mediate divergent views on the relationship between the environment and development. There remain, for example, strong disagreements on these issues between the developed North and the underdeveloped South. Although all can agree that the environment should be protected, significant divergences exist on appropriate solutions. The North has argued that by protecting the environment development can be enhanced as environmental degradation contributes to poverty and underdevelopment. The South, on the other hand, has maintained that the first priority should be economic development and the alleviation of poverty. The challenge before the CSD is to reconcile these views.[49]

The CSD is made up of fifty-three member states elected on a carefully balanced political and geographical quota system for three-year terms with one-third elected annually. Although only members may vote, other states, UN organizations, and accredited IGOs and NGOs may attend the sessions as observers.

The CSD was given modest resources to achieve its ambitious agenda of working with states to reconcile the environment and development. It has no resources of its own and depends on funding from the shrinking UN budget. It has no regulatory power and is unable to force change at the national or local level. Its mandate is so broad it is difficult to distinguish clear priorities. And finally, the CSD relies on voluntary self-reports of states parties. According to Hilary French from the Worldwatch Institute, when they do reply, the tendency has been for governments "to deliver documents that are long on self-congratulations and short on substantive analysis of remaining challenges." French argues that these structural defects in the formation and operations of the CSD greatly impede substantive progress on environmental protection.[50]

National governments have used the CSD to share information on the implementation of the Rio agreements. "Agenda 21" called on all nations to formulate national sustainable development policies and programs. At least 140 nations have created national organizations or governmental units with the responsibility of implementing "Agenda 21." Governments have been able to use the CSD to exchange views on difficult issues, including trade, unsustainable production, and consumption patterns. In addition, CSD sessions now attract environmental activists and organizations from around the world with hundreds of NGOs actively participating.[51]

In a review of the work of the CSD, Pamela S. Chasek found a mixed record in relation to the three major goals of its mission. First, in relation to reviewing the progress of the implementation of "Agenda 21," national reporting has been problematic. Although the CSD did adopt overall reporting guidelines, it is up to individual governments to decide on the degree of detail and the regularity of their reports to the CSD. Submitted self-reports are often vague, difficult to compare, and hard to verify.[52]

Second, the CSD has a mixed record in the area of policy guidance and options for future activities. Two CSD successes were the establishment of the Intergovernmental Panel on Forests (IPF) and the Comprehensive Freshwater Assessment (CFA). The IPF helped focus an international dialogue on forests that successfully led to an international consensus on approaches for action.[53] The CFA's comprehensive overview of major water quantity and quality problems helped clarify the nature of the water problem facing various regions of the world and the implications of not dealing with these problems. The UN assessment study showed that two-thirds of humanity will suffer from shortages of clean, fresh water by approximately 2035 unless action was taken.[54] Yet, most CSD debates do not result in mobilizing action that could achieve such results. Too often, the discussion does not reach real policy makers at the national level and only remains in the halls of the UN itself.

Third, according to Chasek, the CSD has accomplished the most in its goal of promoting dialogue and building partnerships for sustainable development. The CSD has brought together governments, IGOs, NGOs, and other major stakeholders into dialogue sessions on sustainable development. The CSD has become one of the central UN bodies to incorporate civil society into its deliberation in an effective manner. NGOs dissatisfied with the position of their government's representatives can put on pressure at home. As a result, governments are paying more attention to CSD issues to hold off a potential domestic political backlash. Many governments, of course, are not listening, and some do not have NGOs to worry about. But these dialogue sessions do bring a sense of urgency into the CSD.[55]

Yet, the split between the developed and underdeveloped nations over environmental priorities is unresolved and hampers bold CSD action. This division is perhaps most sharp over the question of who should do what about global warming. At a 2007 lunch meeting of environment ministers and other dignitaries gathered at the UN for the 15th session of the CSD, the guest of honor Gro Harlem Brundtland, former Norwegian prime minister and lead author of the seminal UN 1987 report titled *Our Common Future*, stated that all nations, rich and poor, needed to restrict emissions of carbon dioxide and other gases linked to global warming. But, she noted, that this would only happen if the nations on the opposite sides of the climate change debate learned to trust each other more. Onkokame Kitso Modaila, the minister of environment, wildlife, and tourism of Botswana responded on the reasons for the lack of trust: "Because we are aspiring to get where you are. Because we have many competing needs in our own countries. I feel that the first world, developed countries, want to first use us as guinea pigs. I'm sorry I put it that way. I'm not from the diplomatic school. You have a greater expectation of us while ignoring our competing needs to provide health, water, infrastructure, electricity for our own people . . . Yes, we don't trust each other." Graciano Francisco Domingos, the deputy environment minister of Angola, then described how the situation in Angola demonstrated the differing environmental priorities between the South and the North. In 1975, the capital of Angola, Luanda, held just 500,000 people while in 2007 there were over five million in the city. The environmental priorities for him were vast flows of sewage and waste, not a global buildup of greenhouse gases. It is clear that the CSD will have to pay more attention to the link between the environment and development and work to resolve these global tensions.[56]

Global Environment Facility

International environmental legal agreements are to be implemented at the national level by the ratifying states. As reviewed earlier, UNEP helps facilitate the bargaining process among sovereign states critical to the achievement of agreement on these hard and soft law instruments. The CSD receives self-reports from the states parties on the implementation of international environmental law. This process clearly gives a lot of flexibility to states. They can agree on relatively weak international treaties (e.g., the 1992 Framework Convention on Climate Change) and later strengthen the covenants after building domestic political support. The success of this process has led to the creation of a large body of international environmental law.

However, problems have emerged. For example, LDCs often do not have the resources or capacity to implement the profusion of environmental agreements. This inability to implement international environmental law has been called "treaty congestion." The solution to this dilemma may lie in mobilizing significant international financial resources to help developing countries implement the agreements. Yet, most environmental treaties make no such arrangements and only establish small budgets for administrative expenses. Implementation then depends solely on national wealth. Developed countries with adequate resources are able to implement international environmental law, while poor countries have trouble moving this agenda forward.

GEF was created to assist developing countries in tackling these global environmental problems. In its organization and mandate, GEF is a unique IGO that may serve as a model for strengthening international environmental governance. First, the facility is designed to serve existing international treaties, such as the Conventions on Climate Change and Biodiversity negotiated at the Rio Conference. Its mandate is to financially help the underdeveloped countries implement these instruments. This focus of providing funds for global, as distinct from national, priorities is indeed novel. Everyone on the planet would ultimately benefit from these actions. Second, the facility is structured to integrate global action on environmental problems. It brings together three key organizations—UNEP, the UNDP, and the World Bank—to work collaboratively on these environmental issues. The organization seeks to transform the words of the environmental law treaties into action programs at the national and local levels. GEF creates a bridge between the World Bank and UN agencies where historical distrust on both sides has often prevented previous cooperation.[57]

There is a clear division of labor between the three implementing agencies. The UNDP is to provide technical assistance and to ensure the development and management of capacity-building programs drawing on its broad network of representatives within recipient countries. UNEP is to ensure that GEF's actions are consistent with other international environmental agreements and to provide scientific and technical expertise. UNEP is also to promote environmental management in GEF-financed activities. The World Bank is to review and monitor all investment projects of GEF and is the trustee of the GEF Trust Fund. The World Bank is to ensure the development and management of all GEF projects and to mobilize private-sector resources for projects consistent with GEF objectives.[58]

GEF has become the largest multilateral source of grant funds available for environmental protection. It provides "new and additional grant and concessional funding to meet the agreed full incremental costs of measures to achieve agreed global environmental benefits in the following four focal areas: (a) climate change, (b) biological diversity, (c) international waters, and (d) ozone layer depletion." In addition, the "agreed incremental costs of activities concerning land degradation, primarily desertification and deforestation, as they relate to the four focal areas shall be eligible for funding."[59] This means that GEF covers the difference between the costs of a project undertaken with these global environmental objectives in mind, and the costs of an alternative domestic project that the country would have implemented in any case.

In the negotiations on the creation of GEF, the developing countries fought for the concept of "additionality"; they argued that funds for the environment should be in addition to development assistance. These countries did not want limited development aid suddenly diverted away from other national priorities and funneled to these global environmental concerns. They argued GEF should also not replace national environmental planning nor create an excuse for not improving environmental practices generally; rather, the facility should finance the incremental cost to help projects achieve global environmental benefits.[60]

At the Rio Conference, countries from the South had proposed a large green fund to finance the activities of "Agenda 21." The developed countries offered GEF as the vehicle for additional funding for global environmental problems. NGOs and others were very concerned about the link between GEF and the World Bank. Critics charged the World Bank with a history of supporting environmentally destructive projects and unsustainable development plans. Speaking for the South, the Group of 77 joined with the NGO network in expressing disapproval of the World Bank's initial dominance of GEF. The negotiations that ensued led to a GEF more independent from the World Bank than it was in its pilot phase.

The structure of GEF emerged as a result of compromise and balance between the interests of the North and South. The South, arguing for legitimacy, favored a UN-style system on the basis that it was more democratic. The North, arguing for efficiency, endorsed the decision-making system of the IMF and World Bank, where votes are weighted according to contribution. The negotiations resulted in an assembly, a governing council, and a secretariat. The GEF Assembly is composed of all affiliating countries and meets every three years to review the all-encompassing policies. The GEF Governing Council is responsible for operational policies and programs. The thirty-two seats on the council are divided as follows: sixteen for developing countries, fourteen for developed countries, and two for "transitional economies." The council normally will arrive at decisions by consensus. However, if this proves impossible and a vote is required, decisions are made on a double-majority basis. Sixty percent of the votes of all countries (UN system / one nation = one vote) and 60 percent of the votes of the contributors (IMF / World Bank system / one dollar = one vote) must be obtained. The chair of the council's meetings also rotates between a government representative elected by the participants (UN system) and the chief executive officer of GEF (IMF/World Bank).[61]

If this hybrid system works, it may be a model for future international organizations to accommodate the perspectives of the North and the South. Compared to the traditional composition and decision making of the Bretton Woods institutions (IMF/World Bank), the final GEF structure gives much more voice to the South. A clear test of this system will be the degree to which the donor nations continue to fund and support this amalgam. Although funding has grown, it is not close to the level of the amounts entrusted to the Bretton Woods system.

The first full assembly of GEF members took place in New Delhi in April 1998 with 119 member governments, 16 IGOs, and 185 NGOs participating. An independent team of consultants presented to the assembly a report on the fund's overall effectiveness. The report highlighted the limited ability of GEF to leverage its modest resources in support of environmentally sound development strategies. As mentioned earlier, the facility is mandated to finance only the "incremental" costs of investment projects for global benefits in the four areas of focus: biodiversity, climate change, ozone depletion, and the seas and waters. GEF is not to finance the costs that nations would normally expect to encounter in their national projects. This is problematic in two regards. First, the developing countries see this as a tendency of the donor states to care more about global as opposed to national environmental threats. Second, it seems to serve as a disincentive for countries to invest in projects that offer global and local benefits at the same time (e.g., biological diversity). The expectation would be that GEF would fund such priorities. The consultants' report also noted that the mere existence of GEF could serve to reduce the pressure on other UN agencies and the World Bank to integrate environmental issues overall in their programs. The report, for example, noted that the World Bank spent more in one year on carbon-emitting fossil fuel projects ($2.3 billion) than GEF's entire replenishment funding for 1994–1998.[62]

The participating governments agreed in March 1994 to make GEF permanent and to provide $2 billion in new resources. In 1998, donor countries agreed to another $2.8 billion to continue funding into the twenty-first century.[63] In 2007 the GEF fund stood at $3.13 billion, supported and maintained by 32 donor countries.[64]

Between 1991 and 2007 the fund provided a total of $6.8 billion in grants and helped secure $24 billion in co-financing for over 1,900 projects in more than 160 countries. [65] This GEF funding included (but was

not limited to) $2 billion for biodiversity conservation, $1.75 billion for
climate change, $767 million for international waters, $177 million for
ozone depletion, $72 million for land degradation, and $141 million for
persistent organic pollutants. Examples of GEF funding include (1) A
$3.3 million grant to Cost Rica to install wind turbines to generate power.
Since this power would have otherwise been provided by thermal plants,
it was classified as a climate-change grant. (2) And, $2.3 million to support
five NGOs in the Patagonian Coastal Zone Management Plan classified as
an international waterways project.[66]

The GEF chief executive, Monique Barbut, has been credited with
streamlining the organizational bureaucracy to more effectively serve
the LDCs. Barbut clearly understands the importance of global environmental issues to the poor countries. She noted, for example, that
the IPCC has predicted that the bulk of suffering from global warming
will be borne by the developing world. "Sub-Saharan Africa, which has
done nothing to cause climate change, could lose all its agriculture,"
Barbut said. "We have to help. There is no way they can deal with it
themselves."[67]

GEF remains a promising international funding agency. The model of
breaking down the top-heavy decision making of the World Bank and
IMF has merit. The voice of the less developed countries can at least be
heard within the GEF. Global environmental priorities can hopefully be
negotiated and acted upon. However, funding will have to be increased.
At the Rio Conference, the total estimated costs for implementing
"Agenda 21" in the developing countries was over $600 billion annually
to the year 2000.[68] The current level of GEF funding is obviously insufficient.

Assessing Environmental Governance at the UN

This review of a human right to a healthy environment and the activities of UNEP, the CSD, and GEF reveal the strengths and weaknesses of
the UN system of international environmental governance. The strengths
of this environmental regime can be seen in the following areas:

1. The successful establishment of a global human rights framework
   that includes a right to a healthy environment. This right is found
   in both hard law (e.g., the African Charter) and soft law (e.g., the
   Ksentini Report).
2. The successful negotiation of global agreements and treaties to preserve and protect the environment. These norms and rules are extensive and range from "soft" principles (e.g., the World Charter for
   Nature and the Common-Heritage Principles) to "hard" rules (e.g.,
   the Montreal Protocol and the Basel Convention). UNEP, in particu-

lar, has been a key catalyst and critical organizer in the creation of this body of international environmental law.

3. The accumulation, interpretation, and distribution of critical data on the global environment (e.g., GEMS and INFOTERRA). Scientists and environmentalists on all continents are able to share information and results.

4. The establishment of certain inspection and compliance regimes to monitor adherence to international environmental treaties (e.g., the compliance procedures of the Montreal Protocol and the liability scheme for environmental damages established by the Law of the Sea Convention).

5. The incorporation of the concept of a "global civil society" into the dialogue within international organizations on environmental governance. Around 7,000 NGOs and between 15,000 to 20,000 citizens from around the world participated in the NGO forums at the Rio Conference. Environmental organizations have played the vital role of pressuring governments, providing information, and mobilizing public opinion on critical environmental issues. Thousands of NGOs work on environmental issues on an ongoing basis. Some NGOs, like Greenpeace, have thousands of members around the world and a budget that surpasses that of UNEP.[69]

The weaknesses of the UN system of global environmental governance are also very clear:

1. There is no global institution with adequate authority to mobilize the financial resources to protect the global commons. Such actions could include the creation of financial incentives for responsible environmental behavior and fines and taxes for irresponsible behavior.

2. There is no independently powerful global authority able to operate with impartiality and even-handedness and to name and publicize nation-states in violation of the norms and rules codified in international environmental law.

3. There is no global authority in charge of coordinating and integrating all the programs and agencies engaged in global environmental governance.

4. There is a lack of integration of environmental and development concerns in policy planning at the global level. The most powerful states, the less developed states, and the leading international economic entities (World Bank/IMF) have consistently prioritized the economic globalization agenda, including the expansion of global trade and finance, over environmental concerns. The environmental IGOs and NGOs lack the resources and power to balance the development agenda. A full integration must become a priority.

The Marriage of Economic and Environmental Health

"Sustainable development" has emerged as the expression to encom-pass the integration of environmental concerns with economic planning. The most popular and perhaps widely accepted definition for the term "sustainable development" is in *Our Common Future*, the report of the UN-sponsored 1987 World Commission on Environment and Develop-ment (WCED). The WCED was chaired by Gro Harlem Brundtland and the report is known as the Brundtland Report. The Brundtland Report defines sustainable development as "development that meets the needs of the present without compromising the ability of future generations to meet their own needs."[70] Sustainability is thus the ability of a process or practice to be carried on indefinitely without undermining current or future environmental quality.

Yet, the term "sustainable development" is controversial and means different things to different constituencies. There are now over 300 defini-tions of the term.[71] Many believe that the phrase is an oxymoron. Skeptics view the term as nothing more than development with an adjective in front of it, a dangerous magical two-word slogan. Anthony D'Amato, for example, writes:

> What the executive board came up with in Rio was an ultimate reduction of all ideas and themes and reports into a magical two-word slogan. If someday the human race is wiped out because there is no oxygen left in the atmosphere, or fried to death due to the depletion of the ozone layer, God might look down and draw a little cartoon about the folly of planet earth. The cartoon should show a now-gray little planet with a tombstone sticking out of it. On the tombstone is emblazoned the two-word slogan of the Rio conference: SUSTAINABLE DEVELOPMENT, R.I.P.[72]

Sustainable development has been too often viewed as "a 'metafix' that will unite everybody from the profit-minded industrialist and risk-minimizing subsistence farmer to the equity-seeking social worker, the pollution-concerned or wildlife-loving First Worlder, the growth-maxi-mizing policy maker, the goal-orientated bureaucrat, and therefore, the vote-counting politician."[73] But is it really possible to synthesize all these different views into a simple "metafix" that successfully links economic growth with ecological balance?

Numerous disturbing questions confront policy makers, including: Will the sustainable development of capitalism safeguard ecological diversity? How does one guarantee that the pursuit of profit will not trample on social equity and environmental health? Is unlimited economic growth compatible with the preservation of the biosphere? Can economic growth and environmental protection go hand in hand?

On the one hand, some environmentalists believe that the answer is no; economic growth, as currently practiced, is not ecologically sustainable. These environmentalists fear that development will be privileged over sustainability, resulting in business as usual. In fact, some argue that the idea of sustainable development has led the environmental movement astray. It offers current industrial and technical developers a new lease on life without changing the life-destroying economic arrangements supporting "growth" models. No one has to reconsider basic capitalist assumptions and operating procedures of efficiency and profit. Rather, the major institutions and corporations would suddenly adopt a more "environment friendly" way of operating. Yet, these critics argue that the ecological crisis in essence is a result of capitalism's insatiable drive for economic growth and new markets. The global environment is under assault from this economic model. Any honest program of sustainability must at least acknowledge the environmental harm created and perpetuated by an economic system based on the unlimited pursuit of growth and profit.[74]

On the other hand, both former presidents Bill Clinton and George W. Bush believe that economic growth and environmental protection go hand in hand; and thus it is appropriate to prioritize economic growth above all else. President Clinton explicitly defined sustainable development as a form of economic growth in his 1993 executive order (no. 12852) setting up the President's Council on Sustainable Development. The council stated that "[t]he issue is not whether the economy needs to grow but how and in what way."[75] The hope that economic growth will alleviate poverty and suffering also leads many social activists concerned about equity and the welfare of the poor to support industrial models of development based on incremental growth. They believe arguing against economic growth to protect the environment works against the interests of the poor.

Environmental activists respond, however, that the drive for economic growth and unrestricted free trade has led to unsustainable consumption patterns in the North and a spreading gap between the world's rich and poor. All of these trends militate against environmental protection and sustainability. In practice, they believe, economic growth has worked against ecological balance.[76]

Economist Herman Daly argues that the pursuit of growth masks an unwillingness to address social and economic inequities. Daly writes:

Our system is hooked on growth per se, and does not see growth as a temporary means of attaining some optimum level of stocks, but as an end in itself. Why? Perhaps because, as one prominent economist so bluntly put it in defending growth: Growth is a substitute for equality of income. So long as there is growth there is hope, and that makes large income differentials tolerable. We are addicted to growth because we are addicted to large inequalities in income and wealth. To paraphrase Marie Antoinette: Let them eat growth. Better yet, let the poor hope to eat growth in the future.[77]

Perhaps if we focus economic policy on the protection of life, rather than growth, it is possible to recognize the fundamental interdependence of environmental and development issues. The natural environment is composed of all life, including human life. Environmental sustainability must therefore also include the protection of human life—which requires economic development. Environmentalists too often ignore these connections. John Nichols, author of *The Milagro Beanfield War*, addresses these issues:

> The tragedy in "environmental action" is often seen only as an effort to save the spotted owl . . . without giving a hoot about the ghettos of Houston, Cleveland, North Philadelphia and the situation of the people on this globe, which is atrocious. Until environment is seen as the entire picture, both natural and human, we're going to have a real problem. . . . [I]f you're a member of National Wildlife Federation you should also be worried about the total destruction of our inner cities and the fact that unemployment among black children between 15 and 24 is 80 to 90 percent. Otherwise, it becomes irrelevant to worry about sea turtles. The clue to any kind of survival of the planet is training people to the macroscopic overview, to understand how their lives are connected to everything else, to understand that if you kill one species you're endangering all others.[78]

Leslie Paul Thiele writes of the "threefold nature of interdependence," across space, species, and time. Interdependence across space is connected to Nichols's plea for environmentalists to relate their efforts to the well-being of all human and natural life, a concern for environmental justice. The benefits to be derived from our biologically rich, life-supporting planet should be equitably shared. Everyone has obligations to his or her neighbor, regardless of nationality, class, gender, race, or sexuality, and to the development of lives and livelihoods that can be environmentally sustained. Interdependence across species refers to the obligation of the human species to integrate ourselves harmoniously with other life-forms on our planet, a concern for ecological justice—that is, to respect our ecological connectedness and the web of ecological relationships that sustain us. Interdependence across time refers to the rights and duties of the present generation to future (and past) generations. The concern here is for intergenerational justice.[79]

The ideas of intergenerational justice were powerfully developed by Edith Brown Weiss in her call for the incorporation of "intergenerational equity" into international law. Weiss writes:

> [E]ach generation receives a natural and cultural legacy in trust from previous generations and holds it in trust for future generations. This relationship

imposes upon each generation certain planetary obligations to conserve the natural and cultural resource base for future generations and also gives each generation certain planetary rights as beneficiaries of the trust to benefit from the legacy of their ancestors. These planetary obligations and planetary rights form the corpus of a proposed doctrine of intergenerational equity, or justice between generations. For these obligations and rights to be enforceable, they must become part of international law, and of national and subnational legal systems.[80]

Sustainable development must incorporate the rights and duties that flow from these norms of environmental justice, ecological justice, and intergenerational justice. As we saw in chapter 2, development is not solely synonymous with economic growth. Development refers to the improvement of human well-being as measured by a healthy environment, increasing life expectancy, food security, education opportunities, health care provisions, and so on. Globalization, economic growth, and an increase in per capita income can either contribute to or subtract from human development. Sustainable development requires that improvements to human well-being are ecologically renewable.

David Reed of the World Wide Fund for Nature elaborates workable public policy guidelines for sustainable development. Reed divides sustainable development into three components—economic, social, and environmental—and articulates viable national and international policy in all three areas.[81]

Policies to address the economic component include poverty-alleviating growth, such as labor-intensive economic policies that maximize employment opportunities for the poor; strengthening domestic food security; state action to defend and protect welfare and social security; and the elimination of distortions in existing pricing structures to include environmental and social costs.

Policies to address the social component include institutionalizing mechanisms to ensure that the poor have access to jobs (or other income-generating activities); improving social services, including education and health care; providing gender equity in the public and private spheres; and providing family planning services.

Policies to address the environmental component include limiting the consumption of renewable natural resources to regenerative rates; ensuring nonrenewable resource consumption rates; decreasing the discharge of atmospheric contaminants, water pollutants, and toxic wastes to not exceed the environment's absorptive capacity; enforcing the "precautionary principle"—that is, refraining from pursuing activities whose potentially irreversible impacts are not fully known; and establishing clear, enforceable legal and regulatory standards for the private sector to protect the environment.

One approach to sustainable development is the call for full-cost accounting and full-cost pricing. The idea is that the price paid for goods and services should include their long-term social and ecological costs (what economists often call "externalities"). Thus, the expenses for pollution prevention, natural resource preservation, and waste disposal would all be incorporated into actual production costs. The air, water, and land are not "free" to be either spoiled or used up by development. Businesses using full-cost accounting would pay social and ecological costs up front, and, of course, pass these expenses on to the consumer. Large majorities of citizens in developed countries have consistently expressed a willingness to pay higher prices for electricity and gasoline to protect the environment.[82]

The internalization of environmental costs through full-cost pricing reform and environmental tax policy are perhaps the most important environmental measure governments can enact. It is unfortunate that former President G.W. Bush made light of Al Gore's attention to photovoltaic cell-derived solar electricity in the 2000 election campaign. Solar energy, as an alternative to fossil fuel-based energy sources, is a way to combat the threat of global warming. A tax on carbon dioxide emissions combined with increasing the price of coal-based electricity would give photovoltaic solar electricity a chance of being competitive domestically and internationally. Tax policy can thus help the transition to new energy sources and help prevent global warming.

Paul Hawken, Amory Lovins, and L. Hunter Lovins call critical environmental resources "natural capital." Natural capital includes not just familiar resources like water, minerals, oil, trees, fish, air, and so on, but also encompasses living systems, including grasslands, wetlands, oceans, coral reefs, and rainforests. It is these living systems that are deteriorating at an alarming, unprecedented rate. Inside these threatened living systems live the ecological communities that make life possible, including amphibians, bacteria, insects, mammals, ponds, fungi, and flowers. Prosperity and industrial growth have put enormous strains on these living systems that support all forms of life.[83]

Hawken, Lovins, and Lovins argue that an economy needs "four types of capital to function properly:

- human capital, in the form of labor and intelligence, culture, and organization,
- financial capital, consisting of cash, investments, and monetary instruments,
- manufactured capital, including infrastructure, machines, tools, and factories, and
- natural capital, made up of resources, living systems, and ecosystem services.

The industrial system uses the first three forms of capital to transform natural capital into the stuff of our daily lives: cars, highways, cities, bridges, houses, food, medicine, hospitals, and schools."[84]

Traditional market economics ignores natural capital; thus, this paradigm has created a nonsustainable form of economic development. The argument here should be made very clear. Hawken, Lovins, and Lovins are not claiming that the world is running out of commodities and raw materials. Supplies for most raw materials are abundant and prices are relatively cheap as a result of the

> globalization of trade, cheaper transport costs, imbalances in market power that enable commodity traders and middlemen to squeeze producers, and in large measure the success of powerful new extractive technologies, whose correspondingly extensive damage to ecosystems is seldom given a monetary value. After richer ores are exhausted, skilled mining companies can now level and grind up whole mountains of poorer-quality ores to extract the metals desired. But while technology keeps ahead of depletion, providing what appear to be ever-cheaper metals, they only appear cheap, because the stripped rainforest and the mountain of toxic tailings spilling into rivers, the impoverished villages and eroded indigenous cultures—all the consequences they leave in their wake—are not factored into the cost of production.[85]

Ignoring the rates at which natural capital is being consumed has brought us to the precipice. There is no longer any scientific dispute about the decline of every living system in the world. One-third of the planet's resources, its natural wealth, were consumed over the last three decades of the twentieth century. The ongoing destruction rates are staggering: If current trends continue, according to Hawkins, Lovins, and Lovins, 70 percent of the world's coral reefs, host to 25 percent of all marine life, face extinction in our lifetimes, freshwater ecosystems are disappearing at the rate of 6 percent a year, and marine ecosystems by 4 percent a year. The capacity of the natural system to recycle carbon dioxide has been exceeded and it is building up in our atmosphere.[86]

Generally Accepted Accounting Practices should clearly include natural capital as an exhaustible resource and a valuable factor of production. Businesses could start to operate as if such principles were in force. Assigning a monetary value to natural capital deserves further consideration as a means to account for and hopefully slow the destruction of our living systems.

Other proposals advanced by Hawkins, Lovins, and Lovins to protect natural capital include increasing resource productivity to slow resource depletion, redesigning industrial systems to eliminate waste, and shifting economic planning to sustainable human services instead of unsustainable goods. All of these proposals have merit and are doable.[87] Yet, such changes would have to be enacted globally so that no nation became disadvantaged in global markets as a result of environmental cost internalization measures—which leads to the Global New Deal proposal for a World Environment Organization (WEO).

A World Environment Organization

The proposal for a WEO (outlined in chapter 9) is to create a strong international organization able to facilitate global cooperation to protect the global environment. The protection and renewal of natural capital is central to the Global New Deal and would be a dominant focus of the proposed WEO. The WEO would be committed to sustaining and restoring natural capital. It would be interested in protecting the biosphere and act on the shared goal of species preservation for all of humanity.

As previously documented, states have a legal obligation under current international law not to degrade the environment and a responsibility for environmental damage. Other duties of states in international environmental law include: "the duty to notify and consult, the need to obtain prior consent of other states for given activities, state responsibility for given activities of private operators, and development of early-warning mechanisms and environmental-impact assessments."[88] The fundamental principle embodied in the maxim sic utere tuo ut alienum non laedas (use your own property so as not to injure the property of another) is central to the work of the International Law Commission, international regimes to protect the environment, and the settlement of international environmental disputes.[89]

Effective enforcement of international environmental law, however, is often difficult. There is no central authority to administer and execute either criminal sanctions and fines, or disincentives and incentives. A WEO could be a critical step in the enhancement of the effectiveness of international environmental standards and regulations. States have voluntarily signed significant global legislation to protect the environment. Their ratification indicates that these states see the enforcement of these treaties in their individual national interest. It is thus not unrealistic to expect governments to understand the need for a strong and effective WEO.

The precautionary principle, in particular, could provide a clear and viable focus to launch the new WEO. First promoted by Greenpeace, the precautionary principle is now a fundamental principle of international environmental law. The precautionary principle, as previously mentioned, shifts the burden of proof to the institution or individual engaged in a potentially dangerous activity. Such activity could not be undertaken until the public is guaranteed that it is harmless. This idea is found in principle 15 of the "Rio Declaration," which declares that "[i]n order to protect the environment, the precautionary approach shall be widely applied by States according to their capabilities. Where there are threats of serious or irreversible damage, lack of full scientific certainty should not be used as a reason for postponing cost-effective measures to prevent environmental degradation."[90] A World Bank paper on global warming states: "When confronted with risks which could be menacing and irreversible, uncertainty argues strongly in favor of prudent action and against complacency."[91] The Kyoto Protocol on climate change in 1997 also adopted the precautionary perspective.[92]

The WEO could begin with a focus on helping nations implement and comply with international environmental law. The organization could facilitate the implementation of the precautionary principle and other global environmental norms and standards into development plans. The WEO could thus play a significant role in the strengthening and enforcement of international environmental law.

The Global New Deal and the Environment

Summary Observations

While innovative thinking on possible solutions to environmental problems did not stop after the 1992 Rio Conference, cooperative international environmental action certainly slowed down, and, in some cases, ceased altogether at the beginning of the 21st century. Environmental activist Vandana Shiva argues that during the 1990s the "Rio process and the sustainability agenda were subverted by the free-trade agenda." Following the Earth Summit, the Uruguay Round of the General Agreement on Tariffs and Trade was completed in 1993. In 1995, the WTO was established and the "rule of trade" overtook the normative political commitment to sustainability proclaimed at Rio. Globalization and liberalized trade and investment create growth, Shiva argues, by destroy-

Global New Deal Proposals

There is a clear need for high-level coordination of global environmental programs and the integration of development and environment decision making within the UN system. There is an urgent need to resolve the fundamental financial needs necessary to address environmental protection and ecological balance. Numerous proposals have been made to reform the UN system to address these concerns. The Global New Deal calls for ecological balance and economic human rights to be linked through the creation of a WEO. The proposed WEO, described in chapter 9, could strengthen the enforcement mechanisms of international environmental law and facilitate the integration of economic and environmental priorities into development planning.

ing the environment and local, sustainable livelihoods. "The new globalization policies have accelerated and expanded environmental destruction and displaced millions of people from their homes and their sustenance base."[93]

Shiva points to an absolute truth about the 1990s and the first decade of the new century. Environmentally destructive economic growth models and corporate globalization were presented as "the only game in town." The free trade agenda did usurp the sustainability agenda of the Rio Conference. Policy to enhance free trade—from NAFTA to the Association of the Southeast Asian Nations to the EU to the WTO—dominated global politics and international relations at the beginning of the new century. Our challenge now is to reinvigorate international organizations with environmental priorities and to link ecological balance with economic human rights and overcome the perceived distance between these two priorities.

The evaluation of the work of UNEP, the CSD, and GEF demonstrates clear programmatic successes, but also significant limitations. Nations need a central organization to address transboundary environmental externalities and other environmental problems accompanying globalization. A central WEO could consolidate research and information sharing. A WEO could help nations bring national policies in balance with other countries and in compliance with international standards. Just as the World Health Organization helps nations eradicate infectious diseases, and just as the International Labor Organization helps nations implement programs that protect workers' rights, so too could a WEO help nations implement cooperative programs for sustainable development and ecological balance.

5

Race and Economic and Social Human Rights

Why are most of the people in the world who experience a life of severe destitution people of color? What political and economic structures perpetuate racial bias in economic outcomes? How is it possible to overcome and reverse the historical record of racial bias? What policies can be implemented at the national and international level to create real economic opportunity for all races? How has the UN Committee on the Elimination of All Forms of Racial Discrimination (Minority Rights Committee) approached these issues of the economic and social rights of minorities?

Simplified racial categories can be misleading and dangerous since individuals are not only members of a race, but also of a class, a gender, and a sexuality. Thus, broad generalizations about race can be deceptive and groundless in individual cases. In the real world, a person does not exist only as a racial category.[1]

According to the Minority Rights Treaty,[2] race encompasses color, descent, and national or ethnic origin. "Descent" suggests social origin: heritage, lineage, and/or parentage. "National or ethnic origin" denotes linguistic, cultural, and historical roots. This broad concept of race is clearly not limited to objective, mainly physical elements, but also includes subjective and social components. The ingredients considered central to a person's race may, in fact, vary from place to place. Some may emphasize linguistic and cultural factors while others emphasize social determinants. Certain castes, for example, are discriminated against for social and not ethnic reasons. Furthermore, nothing is permanent about any of these aspects of race. Anthropologists have shown that environmental influences can profoundly change even the physical appearance of a human being in a relatively short time.[3]

Scientific research on the human genome—the aggregate of genetic material encased in the heart of almost every cell of the body—has confirmed that the racial categories recognized by society are not reflected on the genetic level. Scientists studying the human genome are convinced that the standard labels used to distinguish people by race have little or no biological meaning. The human species does not divide itself into separate biological groups or races. J. Craig Venter, the head of the Celera Genomics Corporation, concludes: "Race is a social concept, not a scientific one. We all evolved in the last 100,000 years from the same small number of tribes that migrated out of Africa and colonized the world." Harold P. Freeman, the chief executive, president, and director of surgery at North General Hospital in Manhattan, who has studied the issue of biology and race, states: "If you ask what percentage of your genes is reflected in your external appearance, the basis by which we talk about race, the answer seems to be in the range of .01 percent. This is a very, very minimal reflection of your genetic makeup."[4]

Therefore, race, most certainly, cannot be understood simply in terms of skin color. Racial classifications, racist bigotry, and racial hatred have often not relied on skin color. Historical examples abound. The German Nazis' belief that the Russians (as white as the Germans) were subhuman led to a massacre of millions of Russian citizens. The white Irish farmers looked like the white British landlords in Ireland in the 1840s; yet the white British elite exported food and gave no concessions to the white Irish farmers and laborers after crop failures in 1846–1847, and thus, "imposed" the Irish potato famine. The issue here was not skin color, but political power and religion. The white Irish farmers had no political or economic power. The powerful white British elite exported the food that could have saved hundreds of thousands of Irish lives. It was easier for the British to justify these policies by classifying the Irish as a backward and inferior people.[5]

The genocide in Rwanda in the mid-1990s was led by black Hutus against black Tutsis. In fact, ethnographers have come to agree that Hutus and Tutsis cannot properly be called distinct ethnic groups. The two groups speak the same language, follow the same religion, intermarry, and share the same social and political culture. Rwanda is one of the few nations that shares one language, one faith, and one law. Yet, the leaders of "Hutu power" mobilized their people around the idea that the Tutsi were "scum" and "cockroaches" and had to be destroyed. Hutu power attempted the organized extermination of an entire people and succeeded in killing between 800,000 and 1 million Tutsi. The program of massacres that decimated the Tutsi of Rwanda in 1994 cannot be understood through a lens of skin color or ethnicity.[6]

A definition and understanding of race and racial discrimination analysis should, therefore, include more than a mere difference of skin color. Race is also tied to power differentials, social status, and other distinctions. Differences in power give one group the ability to declare the less powerful group "inferior." In fact, those in power may share the same skin color and ethnic characteristics as those they oppress, yet use "race" and "ethnic" differences to consolidate their rule.[7]

Those most vulnerable to economic and social deprivations (hunger, illiteracy, disease, and so on) are those groups without wealth and political power, the majority of whom are women and children. Skin color alone will not tell you who will suffer. For example, the numerical majority of U.S. citizens living in poverty are white, the color of most U.S. policy makers.

Yet, most of the people in the world who experience a life of severe destitution are people of color. Suffering continues to be related to the politics of race. According to the administrator of the UN Development Program (UNDP), among the 4.4 billion people in developing countries around the world at the end of the twentieth century, three-fifths lived in communities lacking basic sanitation, one-third went without safe drinking water, one-quarter lacked adequate housing, and one-fifth were undernourished. In addition, nearly one-third of the people in the poorest countries, mostly in sub-Saharan Africa, could expect to die by age forty.[8] And, as documented earlier, in 2005 half of the world's over 6 billion people, 3.1 billion, lived on less than $2.50 a day, and 1.4 billion on less than $1.25 a day.[9] Overwhelmingly, these impoverished people are people of color. A glance at a map of global hunger, for example, graphically shows that the preponderance of the chronically undernourished are peoples in Africa, Asia, and parts of Latin America and the Caribbean. The UN World Food Program and the CIA both publish maps that call attention to "hot spots" where hunger is most severe in the first decade of the twenty-first century. The maps identify huge areas in Asia and sub-Saharan Africa where tens of millions of people of color, most of them women and children, cannot get enough to eat. And, as previously noted, the UN estimated in 2009 that over 1 billion people were hungry and faced food insecurity.[10]

Racial minorities inside the United States also continue to suffer a lack of economic security compared to their white counterparts, both during the "booming" economy of the 1990s and later during the recession of the first decade of the twenty-first century. The following statistics from the 1990s reveal the economic divide between black and white Americans: According to Census Bureau statistics, there was a stark $14,000 per household income gap between blacks and whites (stated in 1997 dollars).[11] The unemployment rate for young black men at all education levels was more than twice that for young white men. In addition, twice the number of young black men between the ages of sixteen and twenty-four were not in school or working.[12] One out of every three black men in their twenties was under the supervision of the criminal justice system, either imprisoned or on probation or parole.[13] Blacks in the United States were six times more likely than whites to be held in jail.[14]

This vast disparity in economic opportunity between blacks and whites in the United States continues in the twenty-first century. The 2008–2009 *American Human Development Report* reveals the following: African American babies were two and a half times more likely to die before age one than white babies. While life expectancy at birth for whites was 78.2 years, for blacks it was 73 years. Over 89 percent of whites will graduate from high school, while only 79.9 percent of blacks will obtain a high school diploma. And finally, while the median earnings for whites was $30,485, for African Americans it was only $23,025.[15]

A similar disparity in economic security exists between whites and Hispanic Americans. The National Council of La Raza reports that Hispanic workers were disproportionately concentrated in low-wage jobs that offered few benefits throughout the 1990s. As a result, married Hispanics with children continued to have higher poverty rates compared to black and white families. In 1997, for example, 21 percent of Hispanic married couples with children were poor, compared with 6 percent of white and 9 percent of black families. That same year only 55 percent of Hispanics twenty-five and older had graduated from high school, and 7.4 percent had graduated from college.[16] As a result of all of these factors, by 2008 Hispanics had the lowest median earnings of any racial/ethinic group, $20,255. American Indians were next with a median income of $21,037.[17]

Any serious program for the protection of economic and social rights must address this reality. These conditions are the result of history, especially the heritage of four major historical processes: conquest, state building, migration, and economic development. Modern states have been built by powerful groups at the expense of the less powerful, with racial prejudice often unfortunately underlying the entire process. For those concerned with economic justice, these issues must be confronted. The Global New Deal in chapter 9 recommends steps for the Minority Rights Committee to incorporate Amartya Sen's capabilities approach into its work to more effectively combat racial injustice in the economic and social realm.

This chapter examines the UN approach to race and economic and social human rights in the following sections:

- the Minority Rights Treaty,
- the Minority Rights Committee, and
- strengthening the UN's approach to minority rights.

The Minority Rights Treaty and
Economic and Social Human Rights

A committee of experts was established under the Minority Rights Treaty, which entered into force on 4 January 1969. Article 8 of the Minority Rights Treaty calls for the committee to consist of eighteen "experts of high moral standing and acknowledged impartiality elected by States Parties from among their nationals." Members of the Minority Rights Committee are not representatives of the states whose nationality they bear. They are elected by secret ballot of the states parties to the convention, and they serve in their personal capacity.

Despite its growth by 2009 to 173 states parties,[18] the Minority Rights Committee continues to meet for just two sessions a year, each three weeks long. With two three-hour meetings each day, there are thirty meetings possible in one session. As much as possible, the Minority Rights Committee divides up these thirty sessions as follows: twenty-two for the consideration of new state reports; two for the review of the implementation of the convention in states whose reports are overdue by five years or more; two to review urgent and early warning procedures regarding the prevention of racial discrimination; and four for other business, including individual communications.[19]

Economic and social rights are covered extensively in the Minority Rights Treaty. Article 1(1) considers bigotry to be a form of racial discrimination, indicating the power of bigotry to nullify economic and social human rights. The Minority Rights Committee asks governments to report on legislative, judicial, administrative, and other measures that give effect to article 5(e). This article of the Minority Rights Treaty obliges states parties "to prohibit and to eliminate racial discrimination in all its forms and to guarantee the right of everyone" to economic and social rights, including the following:

- The right to work
- Free choice of employment
- Just and favorable conditions of work
- Protection against unemployment
- Equal pay for equal work
- The right to housing
- The right to public health
- Medical care, social security, and social services
- The right to education and training

Thus, the Minority Rights Treaty does not oblige a state party to protect these rights, but to make sure that discrimination with respect to the enjoyment of these rights does not occur.[20]

Hence, the Minority Rights Committee is concerned with discriminatory practices only, and not with the absence of economic or social rights in general terms. Therefore, the absence of an economic or social right in the country as a whole is not a focus of the Minority Rights Committee. The Minority Rights Committee is troubled, however, if these rights are given to one racial group as opposed to another—if, for example, the majority racial/ethnic group receives higher health care benefits compared to the minority group.[21]

In fact, Karl Josef Partsch asserts that the Minority Rights Committee has been very cautious in its application of article 5. The Minority Rights Committee has asked "reporting States whether the rights listed in the article are guaranteed by their national legal systems, but it has not indicated that the absence of such guarantees constitutes a failure to comply with the Convention." The Minority Rights Committee thus seeks to establish whether minority rights are protected in the state's legal order.[22]

The Minority Rights Treaty, however, does not stop there. It also advocates state action in order to eliminate disparities and secure de facto equality.[23] Such affirmative action programs are authorized in both articles 1 and 2(2) of the Minority Rights Treaty. Article 2(2) states:

> States Parties shall, when the circumstances so warrant, take, in the social, economic, cultural and other fields, special and concrete measures to ensure the adequate development and protection of certain racial groups or individuals belonging to them, for the purpose of guaranteeing them the full and equal enjoyment of human rights and fundamental freedoms. These measures shall in no case entail as a consequence the maintenance of unequal or separate rights for different racial groups after the objectives for which they were taken have been achieved.

However, as with the International Convention on the Elimination of All Forms of Discrimination against Women (Women's Rights Treaty), there is a tension here between equal treatment (obligation of means) and equal outcome (obligation of result). According to Theodor Meron, the Minority Rights Committee regards equality of result as the principal objective of the convention. In a major policy statement, the Minority Rights Committee states that the Minority Rights Treaty aims "at guaranteeing the right of everyone to equality before the law in the enjoyment of fundamental human rights, without distinction as to race, colour, descent or national or ethnic origin, and at ensuring that the equality is actually enjoyed in practice."[24]

The Minority Rights Treaty intends to address de facto as well as de jure equality. Legal equality is only the first step toward authentic social equality. The preamble refers to the enjoyment of human rights "without distinction of any kind"; article 5 demands the right to equality before the law; article 1(4) allows for distinction for the purpose of affirmative action "to ensure . . . groups or individuals equal enjoyment or exercise of human rights." Combined with the article 2(2) endorsement of affirmative action, this demonstrates that the Minority Rights Treaty promotes not just de jure but de facto equality, which is to say racial equality in fact and not just in law. States are required in article 2(1) to take policy measures to eliminate any laws or regulations that have the effect of creating or perpetuating racial discrimination. Economic and social policies that have the effect of sustaining the disadvantaged position of certain racial groups must be remedied. The costliness or burdensome nature of such actions cannot be used as excuses for inaction. The goal is the equal development of all citizens.[25]

Individual Complaints System

Article 14 of the Minority Rights Treaty establishes an individual complaints system. However, by July 2009, out of the 173 parties to the Minority Rights Treaty, only 53 states had accepted this complaints system.[26] Cecilia Möller, a human rights officer with the Minority Rights Committee, notes that states are hesitant to endorse the complaint system because of the perceived vagueness of the issues. Racial discrimination is not as clear-cut as torture. Discrimination is often hard to define and the issues frequently hard to prove. For example, proving employment discrimination in the interview process or verifying a bank's discrimination in the denial of a loan are both very difficult. Additionally, Möller notes that the Minority Rights Committee had received a relatively small number of individual complaints since the system has been in operation. The low number is partially the result of the fact that individuals must first exhaust all local procedures before submitting a complaint to the Minority Rights Committee. The low rate of ratification of the individual complaint procedures and the lack of knowledge about these procedures among national lawyers are additional factors limiting the use of these mechanisms. Once it is submitted, the complaint goes to the Minority Rights Committee as a whole body.[27]

In 2008 the Minority Rights Committee reported that it had adopted final opinions on the merits with respect to 25 complaints and found violations of the Minority Rights Treaty in 10 cases. The committee also provided suggestions or recommendations in eight cases, although in these cases it did not establish a formal violation of the Treaty. The Committee has also established a new procedure to follow up on its opinions and recommendations. A special Rapporteur will carry out this follow-up investigation and work with the Committee to enhance state compliance with the recommended actions.[28]

However, even this abridged use of the individual complaint system has had reverberations and demonstrates the potential effectiveness of the new Optional Protocol to the Economic Rights Treaty (discussed in chapter 3). Michael Banton, a member of the Minority Rights Committee from 1986 to 2001 (rapporteur, 1990–1996, and chairperson, 1996–1998), calls attention to the influence of article 14 on states' behavior. Banton notes that if the Minority Rights Committee finds a violation of the convention, the state is to revise its law or practice in the light of the committee's opinion. During Banton's tenure, the Minority Rights Committee considered and adjudicated ten individual complaints/communications in private session. Banton argues that this judicial approach has been successful in affecting state behavior. The Minority Rights Committee,

> like a national court, benefits from the prior refinement of issues and from the adversarial nature of the proceedings. If the petitioner is legally represented there will be a systematic account of the fact alleged, or the relevant national law, and an argument that some part or parts of the Convention have been breached; there will be a legal argument from the state designed to clarify the issues and perhaps a response from the petitioner to the state's submission. If the petitioner is not legally represented the secretariat helps in the process of refining the issues to be put before the Committee which has then simply to adjudicate on them.[29]

Some of these judicial decisions involve issues around the economic and social human rights of minority populations. A Minority Rights Committee decision on an individual complaint in these areas has ramifications beyond the individuals directly affected by the case. It establishes case law that is to be consistently upheld by the state. For example, at its fifty-seventh session, 31 July–25 August 2000, the Minority Rights Committee issued Communication no. 13/1998 concerning a complaint submitted by Anna Koptova against Slovakia. Koptova, a Slovak citizen of Romany ethnicity, was represented by the European Roma Rights Center, a nongovernmental organization (NGO) based in Budapest. In her complaint, Koptova asserted that Slovakia engaged in acts of racial discrimination against her and other Roma and failed to ensure that all public authorities and public institutions refrained from acts or practices of racial discrimination. In the 1980s and 1990s, Koptova alleged that anti-Roma hostility on the part of local officials and/or non-Romany residents forced Romany families to flee causing unemployment and homelessness. She claimed to be a victim based on articles 2, 3, 4, 5, and 6 of the Minority Rights Treaty. The Minority Rights Committee, after ascertaining admissibility, determined that local municipal ordinances prohibiting Roma from settling in Rokytovce and Nagov were a clear violation of the Minority Rights Treaty article 5. However, the committee noted that the Slovak government finally rescinded these resolutions in April 1999 and that article 23 of the constitution of Slovakia guarantees freedom of movement. Thus, the action of the Minority Rights Committee was to recommend that the Slovak government "take the necessary measures to ensure that practices restricting the freedom of movement and residence of Romas under its jurisdiction are fully and promptly eliminated."[30]

Clearly, the Slovak government was under pressure from a variety of sources to revoke discriminatory laws directed against the Roma. Koptova's complaint to the Minority Rights Committee was only one of many actions taken to bring about this change. Yet, the importance of such international pressure should not be dismissed. Koptova's effort brought international attention to the plight of the Roma in Slovakia, impacting on the reputation and international standing of the Slovak government. The efforts of Slovak citizens to enforce their laws on nondiscrimination and freedom of movement received external support from this UN body. In the future, it will be very difficult for these laws to be revoked or ignored. Through working in this manner with individuals and victims in civil society, the UN has a window of opportunity to help enforce human rights.

It is difficult for the UN to force change and adherence to international norms from the outside. Through Minority Rights Treaty article 14, individuals and groups who are victims of racial discrimination can raise their complaints directly to the Minority Rights Committee for arbitration. This is a promising process for the peaceful settlement of these racial and ethnic disputes that cause so much pain and suffering. It is to be hoped that more states will soon accept the jurisdiction of the Minority Rights Committee and accede to article 14 and permit the victims' voices to be heard.

The Minority Rights Committee: States Parties Reports and Concluding Observations

The main work of the Minority Rights Committee, however, is not the arbitration of individual complaints, but the review of states parties reports. Article 9 of the Minority Rights Treaty requires states parties to submit an initial report within one year of the entry into force of the treaty, with periodic reports submitted at two-year intervals.[31] Since 1988, the Minority Rights Committee has nominated one of its members to serve as a country rapporteur for each report. The country rapporteur thoroughly evaluates the state report and prepares a comprehensive list of questions to put to the representative of the reporting state. The Minority Rights Committee makes final recommendations and concluding observations to a great extent on the basis of its examination of country reports. Since 1972, the Minority Rights Committee has invited states to send representatives to respond to questions by committee members. This procedure, not foreseen in the treaty, has subsequently been adopted by all other human rights treaty bodies. The intent is to open a "constructive dialogue" between the reporting state and the Minority Rights Committee. Through such a dialogue, the Minority Rights Committee hopes to exert a positive influence on states' policies to ameliorate racial discrimination.[32]

Obvious weaknesses in this structure include the focus on self-reporting and the lack of enforcement or "power" to bring about positive change. The Minority Rights Committee relies on states parties to follow through on their commitments under the Minority Rights Treaty and to remedy racial injustice in this area of economic and social rights. But if states parties aren't willing to address these issues, there is, in fact, little that the Minority Rights Committee can do. Public pressure and the mobilization of shame may have an impact in dramatic (often media exposed) cases of abuse, such as apartheid, ethnic cleansing, and torture. But it has been less effective in pressuring policy change to address ongoing, systemic abuse—daily practices that lead to a denial of economic and social rights to the world's racial and ethnic minorities.

Some states parties to the Minority Rights Treaty claim that it is contrary to their national law to provide data requested by the Minority Rights Committee; in particular, the demographic composition of the population. Several African states declared the act of gathering data based on ethnicity to be a form of discrimination and contrary to policies of nation building. This can provide a convenient way for majority groups to hide the information that would reveal racial bias.[33]

Many states parties do not even bother to report. The Minority Rights Committee has the ignominious distinction of having the largest number of late reports of any of the treaty bodies. As of July 2009, there were 380 overdue reports to the Minority Rights Committee among the states parties to the Minority Rights Treaty.[34] "Overdue" means nonexistent; these states will not be submitting these past-due reports. The most that can be hoped for at this point is that these delinquent states try to get back on schedule and submit updated reports and meet future deadlines.[35]

When a state party does not fulfill its reporting obligations, the Minority Rights Committee examines the state's practice anyway. The Minority Rights Committee waits at least five years before proceeding on its own. When this occurs, the committee must independently gather information on the delinquent state. For example, if previous reports on the state exist, it will look at them. The committee will also invite the noncomplying state to participate, which may push it to produce a report. Furthermore, outside sources do provide data and, when they do, the committee must then determine the credibility of this information. Likewise, NGOs submit shadow reports on many countries. All of this becomes part of the data that the committee examines.[36]

On 10 October 1994, the United States ratified the Minority Rights Treaty (with reservations), and it entered into force on 20 November 1994. The initial report from the United States was due on 20 November 1995, the second periodic report on 20 November 1997, and the third periodic report on 20 November 1999. The United States did not submit any of these reports. It is perhaps understandable when a small country, which lacks the required technical expertise and resources, submits its report late to the Minority Rights Committee. But it is impossible to justify late reports from the United States.[37]

Finally, in September 2000, the U.S. government submitted the "Initial Report of the United States of America to the Committee on the Elimination of All Forms of Racial Discrimination." The report documents the many ways minority groups in the United States face economic disadvantage and are disproportionately at the bottom of the income distribution curve. U.S. government statistics disclose that members of minority groups are more likely to be poor than are nonminorities, a consequence of persistent discrimination in employment and labor relations, especially in the areas of hiring, salary and compensation, tenure, training, promotion, layoffs, and in the work environment generally. The report also documents violations of minorities' social rights, including the lack of educational opportunities and inadequate access to health insurance and health care. The report notes, for example, that in 1998 the poverty rate among blacks was more than triple the poverty rate of white non-Hispanics. And the poverty rate among Hispanics was not statistically different from that of blacks.[38]

Thus, the U.S. government clearly acknowledges the vast disparities in economic and social rights fulfillment that exist between ethnic and racial groups in the United States. The well-documented report is a useful tool for exposing the effects of ongoing discrimination and bigotry in the United States. However, in the report the U.S. government sidesteps its responsibility to respect, protect, and fulfill economic and social rights.

The U.S. government makes two key points in its discussion of these human rights. First, it makes it clear that it does not view these claims as human rights claims at all. Concerning the Minority Rights Treaty article 5, the U.S. government writes: "Some of these enumerated rights, which may be characterized as economic, social and cultural rights, are not explicitly recognized as legally enforceable 'rights' under U.S. law." By denying their legal status, the United States does not have to accept the state obligations and duties that correspond to these categories of human rights. Within this limited view of human rights, the United States is not legally required to develop strategies to respect, protect, and fulfill the economic, social, and cultural rights of minorities. And, since the Minority Rights Treaty does not require states parties to provide for these rights, but only to prohibit discrimination in their enjoyment, the United States argues it is, in fact, in full compliance with the requirements of the convention.[39]

Second, while the United States does acknowledge severe problems in the economic and social well-being of its minority citizens, it dodges its duty under international law to enact policies to ameliorate this situation.

This position reinforced a key U.S. "reservation" made to the Minority Rights Treaty on ratification in 1994: "[T]he United States does not accept any obligation under this Convention to enact legislation or take other measures under . . . Article 5 with respect to private conduct."[40] While acknowledging that "significant disparities continue," the U.S. government writes in 2000 that "the sources or causes of socio-economic differences are complex and depend on a combination of societal conditions, such as the state of the national and local economies, continued racial and ethnic discrimination in education and employment, and individual characteristics, such as educational background, occupational experiences, and family background."[41] Clearly, all of these areas must be examined. Yet, as a matter of international law, the state remains ultimately responsible for guaranteeing the realization of economic and social human rights. It is the state's responsibility to guarantee the maximum utilization of its available resources to meet the "right of everyone to an adequate standard of living," including rights to food, housing, and clothing.[42] It is unfortunate that the U.S. government does not accept this legal responsibility. The United States has the wealth and prosperity to fulfill its legal and moral duty to protect the vulnerable and to provide a basic level of economic security for all its citizens (as discussed in detail in chapter 8).

In its concluding observations on the 2000 U.S. report, the Minority Rights Committee expressed its concern "about persistent disparities in the enjoyment of, in particular, the right to adequate housing, equal opportunities for education and employment and access to public and private health care. The Committee recommends the State party [the United States] to take all appropriate measures, including special measures . . . to ensure the right of everyone, without discrimination as to race, color, or national or ethnic origin to the enjoyment of the rights contained in article 5 of the Convention."[43]

Between 2001 and 2009, the U.S. submitted four follow-up periodic reports to the Minority Rights Committee, engaging in a "constructive dialogue" over effective policies to alleviate racial discrimination. In the Committee's 2008 "concluding obervations" to the U.S. report, the Committee expressed deep concern "that racial, ethnic and national minorities, especially Latino and African American persons, are disproportionately concentrated in poor residential areas characterized by sub-standard housing conditions, limited employment opportunities, inadequate access to health care facilities, under-resourced schools and high exposure to crime and violence (art. 3)." To address these issues, in 2008 the Committee urged the U.S.

to intensify its efforts aimed at reducing the phenomenon of residential segregation based on racial, ethnic and national origin, as well as its negative consequences for the affected individuals and groups. In particular, the

Committee recommends that the State party: (i) Support the development of public housing complexes outside poor, racially segregated areas; (ii) Eliminate the obstacles that limit affordable housing choice and mobility for beneficiaries of Section 8 Housing Choice Voucher Program; and (iii) Ensure the effective implementation of legislation adopted at the federal and state levels to combat discrimination in housing, including the phenomenon of "steering" and other discriminatory practices carried out by private actors.[44]

Yet, why would the U.S. take these policy recommendations seriously? What are the pressures for the U.S. (and other states) to implement recommendations from the Minority Rights Committee? Do the Minority Rights Committee's concluding observations make a positive difference in the lives of ethnic and racial minorities?

The Minority Rights Committee's Concluding Observations

In its review of states parties' reports, the Minority Rights Committee does not act as a judicial body with the power to determine state violations of international law governing economic and social rights of racial minorities. Rather, the Minority Rights Committee's function is to assist states in their efforts to fulfill their obligations under the Minority Rights Treaty. The point is not to focus on the issue of the compliance or noncompliance of a state with its obligations under the Minority Rights Treaty. Rather, committee members see their role as helping states recognize and ameliorate racial discrimination within their borders.

The concluding observations of the Minority Rights Committee on the states' reports provide a record of the opinions and actions of the committee. These observations summarize the Minority Rights Committee's evaluation of the state party report and contain recommendations the committee hopes the state will follow. The country rapporteur drafts the concluding observations for the committee, which are normally adopted by consensus. The concluding observations represent the most definitive record of the Minority Rights Committee's approach to its mandate.

A review of the Minority Rights Committee's concluding observations over the years reveals a glaring meekness in its approach to the economic and social rights of minority racial groups. Economic and social rights have clearly not been a priority for the committee. The language employed is mild, and there appears to be little pressure placed on states to change policy.

For example, in March 1997 the Minority Rights Committee considered the periodic reports from Panama and adopted the following as part of its concluding observations:

Concern is expressed that some groups living in Panama, such as indigenous people and members of the black and Asian minorities, do not fully benefit from the rights recognized under the Convention. . . . In the light of article 5 of the convention, it is noted with concern that the issue of land rights of indigenous people has remained unsolved in a great majority of cases. These land rights seem also to be threatened by the mining activities which have been undertaken—with the approval of the central authorities—by foreign companies, and also by the development of tourism in these regions.

To overcome these problems, the committee recommended that Panama

take appropriate measures to allow full enjoyment by different groups of society, such as indigenous people or members of the black and Asian minorities, of the rights enumerated by the Convention . . . [and] strongly recommends that the State party actively pursue its current efforts to implement fully the right of indigenous people to own property and land. It especially recommends that the State party investigate and monitor the impact of the work of mining companies, including foreign ones, as well as the impact of the current development of tourism, on the enjoyment of basic rights by indigenous peoples.[45]

It is hard to see how these comments are very helpful to Panama. The Minority Rights Committee has not identified any new specific measures for Panama and merely endorses the government's current efforts regarding property and land rights. The Minority Rights Committee recommendations for "investigating" and "monitoring" corporate activities are superficial and safe.

Keep in mind that the Panamanian government reported in the 1980s and 1990s one of the worst distributions of income in the world, with very high rates of unemployment, and estimates that about half the population of the country lived in poverty. The proportion of the Panamanian population that was undernourished skyrocketed from 12 percent in the early 1970s to 19 percent in the 1990s.[46] The indigenous population, which is composed of five ethnic groups, accounts for between 8 and 10 percent of the population. According to the UN Economic Rights Committee, these ethnic groups were among the poorest and most vulnerable sectors of Panamanian society.[47]

Yet, the Minority Rights Committee does not address the economic plight of these racial minorities. The Minority Rights Committee does not help Panama develop policies that can protect the economic and social rights of these indigenous peoples. The Minority Rights Committee's recommendations should be better informed and specific. It is not that useful just to "express concern" or call for more "monitoring" of the problem. These flimsy and ineffectual reports from the Minority Rights Committee contribute to the sense of futility and cynicism concerning UN human rights efforts.

In 1999, the Minority Rights Committee held its fifty-fourth session (1–19 March) and its fifty-fifth session (2–27 August). During these meetings, the committee considered reports, comments, and information submitted by twenty-eight states parties, independent organizations, and knowledgeable individuals. It is instructive to analyze all the references to economic and social human rights made by the Minority Rights Committee in its twenty-eight concluding observations in response to these state reports in its 1999 sessions. In almost every case, the Minority Rights Committee "expresses its concern" about a given problem and then makes "suggestions and recommendations" for the state party to follow.[48]

The expressions of concern deal with issues of critical importance, such as the absence of sanctions against racial discrimination in the private sector (Austria), discrimination against the Roma (Italy and Romania), the close relationship between socioeconomic underdevelopment and racial discrimination (Peru), the vulnerable status of refugees and immigrants (Costa Rica), and disadvantaged ethnic and tribal minorities (Iran, Mongolia, and Uruguay). The committee often exposes a critical issue of economic and social injustice within the state party. This is a critical first step since exposure can help identify the path forward.

Where the Minority Rights Committee is weak, however, is in helping to find solutions. Its suggestions and recommendations are uniformly unsubstantial. To address these violations of the economic and social human rights of minorities, the committee calls on states parties to "redouble its efforts," take "additional measures," "give more attention" to the issue, "provide information," "take immediate and appropriate measures," "intensify its efforts," "continue to promote" economic development, "take steps to address" economic discrimination, and so on. These "recommendations" are void of any content. What measures should states parties take? What types of policies are effective in addressing economic discrimination? How can a program of economic growth also incorporate policies to address the needs of the most vulnerable minority groups? These questions should be the main focus of the committee.

These weaknesses in the Committee's recommendations persist. For example, in the 2008 concluding observations on the U.S. report, the Committee "recommends that the [U.S.] continue its efforts to address the persistent health disparities affecting persons belonging to racial, ethnic and national minorities, in particular by eliminating obstacles that currently prevent or limit their access to adequate health care, such as lack of health insurance, unequal distribution of health-care resources, persistent racial discrimination in the provision of health care and poor quality of public health-care services." Again, it is hard to see how this is particularly helpful to the U.S. "Eliminating obstacles" to equal access to health insurance and improved care is easier said than done. The Committee, unfortunately, doesn't identify the health policies will bring about these positive results.[49]

Thus, the Minority Rights Committee is adept at identifying the economic and social issues confronting racial minorities within the states parties to the Minority Rights Treaty, but it is not very resourceful in identifying the actions that these nations need to take to address these issues. The Minority Rights Committee's role could be strengthened by spending more time assisting nations in the formulation of effective policy in these areas. It is difficult to construct appropriate and workable policy to ameliorate racial bias in economic development. Yet, as will be seen later on, there are successful programs that can guide policy makers.

These criticisms of the work of the Minority Rights Committee are directed at the complacency of the states parties to the Minority Rights Treaty, and not at the expert members of the committee. These individuals receive no payment for the work they do on the committee and have inadequate research and secretarial assistance. Other difficulties include translation delays and a lack of access to sources of information beyond the state's self-report. Most members have full-time jobs elsewhere, which limits the amount of committee work they can undertake. Overall, committee members' efforts to breathe life into this process have been stymied by a lack of support from nation-states.[50]

The Minority Rights Committee has even had difficulties getting its minimal budget funded. To overcome the committee's financial difficulties resulting from the nonpayment of contributions by states parties, the committee approved an amendment to article 8(6) of the convention, which was later adopted by the General Assembly of the UN. The amendment calls for expenses of the members of the committee to be borne by the regular UN annual budget. However, this amendment is not in force as it awaits the prescribed number (two-thirds) of ratifications by states parties. As of July 2009, only 43 states had ratified this amendment.[51]

In addition, the Minority Rights Committee is set up and funded to meet only twice a year, in the spring and summer. It is hard to imagine how a committee that meets for only three weeks twice a year can effectively monitor the practices of the 173 parties to the convention. This problem is widely acknowledged at the Office of the High Commissioner for Human Rights (OHCHR). Yet, due to the tangible reality of a small staff and a small budget, there is no serious effort to expand the work of the committee.

In fact, there is a large degree of complacency about the weaknesses in the human rights reporting mechanisms. For example, staff members recognize that the only reason that the reporting system as a whole has not collapsed is because all states do not report. If these states did report, the small staff at the OHCHR could not cope. As a result, privately there is an acknowledged sense of relief that all states do not report, and there is no serious political push to get states to report on time. The result is that the reporting system remains ineffectual.[52]

These are serious issues. The Minority Rights Committee gives states the opportunity to say that they are not only concerned with discrimination and racial injustice, but are doing something about it. Yet, the structures and mechanisms theses states have established to address minority rights are underfunded and understaffed, and thus, ineffective.

Strengthening the UN's Approach to Minority Rights

Professionalizing the Minority Rights Committee

Scholars and activists have noted the "splendid isolation" of the human rights treaty bodies from the rest of the UN system.[53] Unfortunately, the Minority Rights Committee has been marginalized and is seen as peripheral to the main work of the UN. Although all Minority Rights Committee reports (including concluding observations) receive general distribution within the UN and are posted on the OHCHR's website, they are read by few and have minimal impact. The Minority Rights Committee submits an extensive yearly report on its meetings and decisions to the UN General Assembly. Yet again, this report does not provoke extensive discussion nor serious actions to address the plight of racial and ethnic minorities.

There are a number of steps that can be taken to strengthen this system. First, the reports from the Minority Rights Committee should go not just to the General Assembly, but to the new UN Economic Security Council recommended in the Global New Deal (see chapter 9). This body could have the administrative staff and technical expertise to help states meet their obligations under the Minority Rights Treaty. This should not only cause the reports themselves to be taken more seriously, but also nudge states to implement policy to ameliorate racial and ethnic bias. States will know that these reports are not simply a bureaucratic assignment to get out of the way as quickly as possible. Rather, the reports will be evaluated and acted on by the main body within the UN system concerned with issues of economic equality—the UN Economic Security Council.

Some reform proposals call for consolidation of the six active treaty bodies into one permanent professional treaty body. In addition to the two already mentioned (Minority Rights Committee and Economic Rights Committee), the other treaty bodies are the Women's Rights Committee, established under the Convention on the Elimination of All Forms of Discrimination against Women; Committee against Torture, established under the Convention against Torture and Other Cruel, Inhuman or Degrading Treatment or Punishment; the Committee on the Rights of the Child, established under the Convention on the Rights of the Child; and the Human Rights Committee, established under the Covenant on

Civil and Political Rights. With a consolidation of these committees, states could harmonize and streamline reports to one body instead of six. There are clear advantages in terms of staff, money, administration, and so on.

However, the danger in such an approach is that the current focus on a single issue will become lost. Discrimination against racial minorities or against women, for example, could get buried in an overall report on state compliance to all international human rights law. Yet, the OHCHR recognized that, to avoid wasteful duplication, some consolidation of reporting was essential. This was accomplished with the adoption by the human rights treaty bodies of the "common core document." State reports to all treaty bodies now include a common core document which provides general information "on the protection and promotion of human rights, as well as general information on non-discrimination and equality and effective remedies in accordance with the harmonized guidelines."[54] This reformed procedure greatly improved efficiency in reporting, while allowing each treaty body to maintain its focus. For example, the Minority Rights Committee can continue to highlight issues of racism and discrimination, and the Women's Rights Committee can continue to address issues of women's rights. The specific mandates and concentrations of each of the six treaty bodies ought to be maintained. These six areas deserve the distinctive specialized attention the individual committees can provide.

There are two measures that can further the professionalization of the committee structure and significantly help the committees achieve their objectives. Rather than starting over, these proposals are intended to enhance and refine the current system. They build on the accomplishments of the committees to date. They also recognize the financial and political constraints facing the UN. They are realistic and doable. These proposals are designed to strengthen the UN treaty body system as a whole and, as a consequence, the functioning of the Minority Rights Committee.

The first proposal is to professionalize the operations of the experts on the committees. States parties elect the experts to sit on a treaty body committee at biannual meetings. Often, experts are elected who do not have the time to conscientiously evaluate government reports and NGO information. Nearly all have full-time employment elsewhere, and thus have difficulty even preparing for meetings. Sometimes political appointments are made and the nominee lacks true expertise in either international law or the subjects of concern to the committee. These problems can be overcome. To guarantee that the persons nominated for election to the committee are qualified to serve, a screening process can be established. The OHCHR, in consultation with relevant NGOs, could review the curriculum vitae of candidates and expose those who are unqualified to serve. Since the individual is to serve with impartiality and "in a personal capacity," this should not involve embarrassing any particular state party. Individual nominees from all countries would have to be experts in the field. And, perhaps more importantly, the experts elected to the committee should be paid to support their hard work. Currently, the members of the Minority Rights Committee work on a pro bono basis.[55] With human rights now a central focus of all UN activities, and with a rising number of states relating to the treaty bodies, it is totally unrealistic to expect members of the committee to be able to fulfill their responsibilities on a volunteer basis. With this structure, membership on the committees is limited to retirees, government officials, or academics subsidized by their governments. With such strong governmental support, the "independence" of the experts becomes questionable. A solution is to pay each committee member a half-time professional salary out of the UN budget for their committee work. This would allow these experts to take a leave of absence for half the year from their full-time jobs. Most professions would allow their employees to take an unpaid leave for six months in order to serve on such a distinguished committee. By funding these salaries for half a year, the UN would be giving the committee members time not only to attend the committee meetings, but also time for adequate preparation and follow-up. Committee members, for example, could then participate in additional working groups, including thematic working groups with members of other treaty bodies. Greater contact with members of other treaty bodies could help lead to joint efforts at eliminating duplication and streamlining operations. In addition, committee members could potentially make visits to states parties for follow-up activities in connection with reports and communications. It is reasonable to expect the UN to fund these part-time salaries to give committee members the time to fulfill their obligations. If the UN is serious about human rights, this minimal financial commitment should be forthcoming.

The second proposal is to professionalize the staff operations in the OHCHR to support the work of the committees. Additional professional staff is needed at the OHCHR to respond to the growing needs of the Minority Rights Committee and the other treaty bodies. For example, staff is needed to conduct a preliminary examination of a state report to the Minority Rights Committee, examine the human rights situation in the particular country, and prepare a working document for the committee. Coordination between treaty bodies can be facilitated with additional staff at the OHCHR. Additional staff is needed to streamline reporting mechanisms to avoid duplication resulting from overlapping instruments, to follow up on reports and communications, to provide technical advice and assistance to states, to draft general comments with one or more members of the committee, and so on. Minimal financial resources could address these concerns.[56]

When Mary Robinson announced that she would not seek an additional term as high commissioner for human rights, she expressed frustration with the UN's lack of financial support for the OHCHR. The OHCHR receives a minute part of the overall UN budget (approximately less than 2 percent), and even this is threatened.[57] This is unacceptable. The minimal funding needs necessary to make the human rights treaty body system work effectively must be forthcoming.

In its contribution to the preparatory process for the 2001 UN World Conference against Racism, Racial Discrimination, Xenophobia and Related Intolerance, the Economic Rights Committee noted: "The full realization of the substantive rights enumerated in the Covenant [on Economic, Social and Cultural Rights]—the rights to education, housing, food, employment, and so on—will go a long way towards the elimination of racism, racial discrimination, xenophobia and related intolerance."[58] Working in conjunction with the Economic Rights Committee, a Minority Rights Committee focus on education and health care for all could significantly contribute toward ending the marginalization and social exclusion of disadvantaged and vulnerable groups.

The Global New Deal and Race

Summary Observations

The work of the Minority Rights Committee can be enhanced with a focus on Sen's capabilities approach (outlined in chapter 2). This strategy can both clarify and simplify the reporting process on economic and social rights and provide policy direction and focus. This approach provides the committee with the tools to help states formulate clear policies to achieve economic and social human rights for all.

Previous chapters have reviewed the policies and programs that states can follow to protect, respect, and fulfill economic and social human rights. The economic and social rights of racial minorities can be achieved through a focus on improving individual capabilities. These economic policies of social development include

Global New Deal Proposals

The Minority Rights Committee needs to break out of the cumbersome traditions that now burden its functioning. Bold and progressive thinking and action can revitalize its work and increase its relevance. The proposal outlined in chapter 9 greatly simplifies the work of the committee in the area of economic and social human rights. The Global New Deal calls for prioritizing the rights of racial and ethnic minorities by focusing on investments in health care and education. Each state should be required to report on how it is addressing these two areas. These priorities are essential to the capabilities approach to human development and indispensable to effective public policy designed to end suffering and protect the vulnera-

expanding basic education and basic health care, including access to clean water, sanitation, and adequate nutrition. The "success stories" of the 1980s and 1990s were those low-income areas and countries (including Karala [India], Botswana, Barbados, and Costa Rica) that achieved levels of health and education comparable to the industrialized states. These recommendations of the Global New Deal are based on the progress of these nations in confronting poverty and suffering.[59]

ble. With this approach, the Minority Rights Committee will be doing more than merely calling for states parties to "redouble [their] efforts," take "additional measures," "give more attention" to the issue, "intensify [their] efforts," "take steps to address" economic discrimination, and so on. Instead, the Minority Rights Committee can work with states to enact specific policies to end racial discrimination in the areas of health and education.

This proposal is also based on the current limitations in staff and funding confronting the Minority Rights Committee. With only limited resources, the committee must focus its attention on where it can be effective. The Minority Rights Committee can have a significant impact if it calls the states parties' attention to these indisputable priorities.

6

Gender and Economic and Social Human Rights

Do socially constructed international human rights advance the economic and social well-being of women? Or do these norms reflect a gender bias that hinders the betterment of women? How are women's economic and social human rights protected in this era of rapid economic globalization? Do particular approaches to international political economy provide a clear guide toward economic and social rights fulfillment for the world's women? How has the UN Committee on the Elimination of Discrimination against Women (Women's Rights Committee) dealt with the economic and social rights of women?

"Men do not want solely the obedience of women, they want their sentiments," wrote John Stuart Mill in 1869 in *The Subjection of Women*. Mill wrote that men desire to have in women "not a forced slave but a willing one. . . . They therefore put everything in practice to enslave their minds . . . turn[ing] the whole force of education to effect their purpose . . . [to show that] it is the duty of women . . . it is their nature, to live for others; to make complete abnegation of themselves, and to have no life but in their affections." Women are taught that "meekness, submissiveness, and resignation of all individual will into the hands of a man is an essential part of sexual attractiveness." Mill contended that "woman" was a social construct and ridiculed the idea that women's then current behavior revealed their "nature." He wrote that this is like planting a tree half in a vapor bath and half in the snow, and then, seeing that one part is flourishing and the other part shriveling, saying that it is the nature of the tree to be that way.[1]

179

Ideas of the social construction of consciousness have an intellectual lineage going back to at least the nineteenth century. Karl Marx labeled this process of manufacturing identity, and the fabrication of male and female human nature, the creation of false consciousness. Marx and Frederick Engels wrote that "consciousness is . . . from the beginning a social product."[2] While postmodernists reject the term "false," since most people believe in the "truth" of their identity, there is agreement among critical scholars on the potent role of culture and power in the social creation of individual understandings of one's identity as a woman or man. For centuries, patriarchal power has depended on a social construction of the idea of a nonthreatening "women's nature" to support an aggressive "natural male." Philip Gourevitch notes that "power largely consists in the ability to make others inhabit your story of their reality."[3] Male power is often contingent on women accepting and inhabiting man's story of their reality.

To a large extent, the international movement to claim women's human rights is an attempt to challenge this oppressive history by forcing men to accept and inhabit women's reality. Working through the UN system, the international women's movement has attempted to articulate the unique claims specific to women. For example, the UN Fourth World Conference on Women held in Beijing adopted a final declaration on 15 September 1995 embracing the collective human rights of women. The broad declaration called on world governments to raise the economic circumstances of women and protect them from increasing levels of violence. At Beijing, governments pledged to act against domestic violence, empower poor women by giving them access to bank services and credit, and give women the right to decide freely all matters relating to their sexuality and childbearing.[4]

But these pledges and norms are also socially constructed, and feminists are divided over the gendered nature of international human rights law. Examine the opposing positions of Hilary Charlesworth and Barbara Stark concerning women's economic and social human rights:

On one hand, Charlesworth states that "the current international human rights structure itself and the substance of many norms of human rights law create obstacles to the advancement of women." She argues that the Economic Rights Treaty[5] is of little help to women because it "does not touch on the economic, social, and cultural contexts in which most women live, since the crucial economic, social, and cultural power relationship for most women is not one directly with the state but with men—fathers, husbands, or brothers—whose authority is supported by patriarchal state structures."[6]

On the other hand, Stark writes that the Economic Rights Treaty is a "postmodern feminist text" that privileges women over men and focuses on the substantive problems traditionally left to women. Stark's argument is that the Economic Rights Treaty recognizes the rights of every human being to be nurtured: "to be cared for, housed, fed, clothed, healed, educated, and made to feel part of a community. These 'nurturing rights' are descriptions of women's work." The Economic Rights Treaty privileges concrete rights over abstract ones in its focus on food, shelter, and health care rather than on abstractions like liberty and equality. These economic and social rights are found in the private arena and can be considered "women's rights."[7]

Human rights are moral claims to a certain standard of treatment that derive solely from the very fact of being human. Women's economic and social human rights strive to prohibit de facto and de jure discrimination through the enactment of measures to provide job training for women, child care, paid leave for childbirth, and so on. All women in all societies can make these claims. However, as Charlesworth points out, unless issues of power are addressed at the same time, these normative pronouncements will be meaningless. Progress does not occur through good will alone, nor simply from good intentions. Women's economic and social human rights will occur when there is structural and economic change for women.

So where does this leave us? There are clear differences in interpretation of the importance and impact of international women's rights as they have been defined in international bodies. However, even accepting Stark's argument that the Economic Rights Treaty privileges women's rights, it is hard to make the case that these rights have been implemented internationally in a conscientious fashion. In fact, there is clear evidence that, as these documents were being drafted, the position of women's economic and social rights deteriorated with deepening economic globalization.[8]

It is therefore imperative to link feminist theories of human rights with feminist theories of international political economy (IPE). Economists, political scientists, and policy makers have struggled for decades to understand the relationship between women/sex/gender and economic development. Neither human rights theories nor human rights law alone can fundamentally address global and national inequities in power based on patriarchy and class. Combined with theories of IPE—which examine these power relations—strategies for the promotion and protection of the economic and social human rights of women can be formulated.

Utilizing Amartya Sen's analysis of freedom and capabilities—the capabilities approach—the Global New Deal articulates a proposal for global and local policy to advance women's economic and social human rights. Such a strategy involves collapsing the conceptual boundaries between international human rights law and international economic policy and those between state sovereignty and transnational law. Central to such a policy is the enactment of gender planning and gender analysis on all levels (local, national, and international) to determine how trading and economic systems, and international and national law, impact women. Or, to use Sen's framework, gender planning involves the enactment of public policy to guarantee women the freedom to achieve well-being.

On the one hand, it is true that human beings construct their social worlds and identities and thus can change them. But on the other hand, it is also true that enduring patterns and institutions make change very difficult. To be effective, a strategy for the protection and promotion of women's international economic and social human rights must therefore address both the social construction of identities/norms and the structural constraints that block change.[9] The capabilities approach, which allows for the integration of IPE (with its focus on structures) to human rights (with its focus on socially constructed norms), provides a way forward.

This chapter analyzes central aspects to these issues in the following sections:

- women's economic and social human rights,
- IPE and women's human rights, and
- linking feminist IPE and feminist human rights theory.

Women's Economic and Social Human Rights

Stark argues that the Economic Rights Treaty is the "marginalized half of international human rights law." The privileged half, the Political Rights Treaty, replicates familiar hierarchies like "male over female" and "abstract over concrete practice." But despite its marginalization, she believes that the Economic Rights Treaty does recognize the specific needs and rights of women. As opposed to documents that call for abstract principles (like "justice" and "equality"), the Economic Rights Treaty specifies a number of clear rights found in both the private and the public arenas.[10]

Examine articles 2.2 , 3, and 10.2:

Article 2.2: "The States Parties to the present Covenant undertake to guarantee that the rights enunciated in the present Covenant will be exercised without discrimination of any kind as to race, color, sex, language, religion, political or other opinion, national or social origin, property, birth or other status."[11]

Article 3: "The States Parties to the present Covenant undertake to ensure the equal rights of men and women to the enjoyment of all economic, social and cultural rights set forth in the present Covenant."[12]

Article 10.2: "Special protection should be accorded to mothers during a reasonable period before and after childbirth. During such period working mothers should be accorded paid leave or leave with adequate social security benefits."[13]

These statements on banning gender discrimination can be interpreted to prohibit de facto as well as de jure discrimination. The state is then legally required to enact measures to remedy existing gender discrimination, for example, by providing job training for women, child care, or paid leave for childbirth and after.

In other words, the Economic Rights Treaty attempts to move the dialogue away from legal formal equality to actual substantive (or de facto) equality. Too often the extension of legal protections against gender discrimination does not in fact create equal opportunities for men and women. Unfortunately, all societies suffer from gender economic disparities and the marginalization of women. As a result, standards that appear to be neutral may in reality reinforce a dominant male power structure. For example, women may have a legal right to full and equal participation in a nation's political system. However, unless measures are taken to overcome the historical relegation of women to the private sphere of the home, this legal right may prove to be of limited use. In fact, de jure or formal equality alone may in fact reinforce inequality, by pushing women and men to accept the status quo as legally "fair" and "just." Those arguing for de facto or substantive equality, on the other hand, are concerned with outcomes and results. From this perspective, what is key is the actual living conditions experienced by women. This approach demands positive action to eliminate the obstacles blocking substantive equality.[14]

Stark's argument is that the Economic Rights Treaty requires states parties to take these positive actions. As noted, this covenant recognizes the rights of every human being to be nurtured: "to be cared for, housed, fed, clothed, healed, educated, and made to feel part of a community."[15] The covenant implies state responsibility in all these areas, which if assumed would imply a corresponding decrease of the burden on women.[16]

The public–private dichotomy has been "central to almost two centuries of feminist writing and political struggle."[17] Women are relegated to the private sphere of home and family while men operate in the public arena of the workplace, politics, law, intellectual life, and so on. In general terms, civil and political rights exist in the public arena—the administration of justice and the conduct of public political life—and historically have been considered "men's rights." Economic and social rights are found in the private arena—the family, health care, food, shelter, clothing, and education—and can be considered "women's rights." There is thus a substantial overlap between women's work and the rights enunciated in the Economic Rights Treaty. Paul Hunt notes that the resistance to incorporating norms and programs to address the private sphere is demonstrated in the well-developed procedures and institutions associated with civil and political rights compared to the weak (and often nonexistent) policies and customs in the social realm. "The juridical marginalization of social rights reflects the public–private dichotomy and the gendered nature of law."[18]

The Economic Rights Treaty is not the only international human rights instrument concerned with women's economic and social rights. The UN approach has been to treat women's rights as a separate issue rather than as part of human rights in general. From the establishment of the Commission on the Status of Women (CSW) in 1947 to the Fourth World Conference on Women in Beijing in 1995, women's rights have been treated as a specialized subset of human rights to be dealt with by distinct bodies. The Women's Rights Treaty (International Convention on the Elimination of All Forms of Discrimination against Women), which came into force in 1981, is of particular importance. As of July 2009, 186 states had ratified the Women's Rights Treaty, making it the second most widely accepted international human rights treaty after the Convention on the Rights of the Child.[19] The Women's Rights Treaty obligates states parties to eliminate discrimination against women. States parties are required to take measures, including legislation, to overcome discrimination in economic and social areas such as employment (article 11), education (article 10), and health care (articles 12 and 14).[20]

As with the Economic Rights Treaty, the Women's Rights Treaty also actively goes beyond formal equality and encompasses substantive equality. Examine articles 1, 4(1), and 4(2):

Article 1: "[T]he term 'discrimination against women' shall mean any distinction, exclusion or restriction made on the basis of sex which has the effect or purpose of impairing or nullifying the recognition, enjoyment or exercise by women, irrespective of their marital status, on a basis of equality of men and women, of human rights and fundamental freedoms in the political, economic, social, cultural, civil or any other field."[21]

Article 4(1): "[Advocates the adoption] by States Parties of temporary special measures aimed at accelerating de facto equality between men and women."[22]

Article 4(2): "[Advocates the adoption] by States Parties of special measures . . . aimed at protecting maternity."[23]

These articles clearly call for equality of result or substantive equality through special measures like affirmative action programs and protection against indirect discrimination. This is the model of equality in international law. Men and women are to be treated equally. This standard is repeated throughout the convention with the phrase "on a basis of equality of men and women." For example, article 11, concerning employment, reads: "States Parties shall take all appropriate measures to eliminate discrimination against women in the field of employment in order to ensure, on a basis of equality of men and women, the same rights."[24]

This phrase "on a basis of equality of men and women" is repeated in all the economic and social areas discussed in the Women's Rights Treaty, including education (article 10), employment (article 11), health care (article 12), economic and social life (article 13), women in rural areas (article 14), and marriage and family relations (article 16).[25]

Charlesworth, Christine Chinkin, and Shelley Wright argue that the underlying assumption of the Women's Rights Treaty's definition of discrimination is that women and men are the same. "But the notion of both equality of opportunity and equality of result accept the general applicability of a male standard (except in special circumstances such as pregnancy) and promise a very limited form of equality: equality is defined as being like a man."[26]

Feminists argue that this approach negates real differences and inequities and, furthermore, ignores real issues of power. "Thus, equality is not freedom to be treated without regard to sex but freedom from systematic subordination because of sex."[27] Thus, the Women's Rights Treaty, while recognizing discrimination as a legal issue, "is premised on the notion of progress through goodwill, education and changing attitudes and does not promise any form of structural, social or economic change for women."[28]

The Women's Rights Treaty establishes the Women's Rights Committee (Committee on the Elimination of Discrimination against Women). The Women's Rights Committee consists of twenty-three members, elected by the states parties for four-year terms, who act in their individual capacities and do not represent particular states. The secretary general is to provide the necessary facilities and staff to service the meetings of the Women's Rights Committee. Unlike other treaty committees, the Women's Rights Committee was not originally serviced by the Office of the High Commissioner for Human Rights (OHCHR), but by the UN's Division for the Advancement of Women. For many years this meant that the sessions of the Women's Rights Committee were not held in Geneva. Until 1993, the Women's Rights Committee met alternatively between Vienna, the headquarters of the Division for the Advancement of Women, and New York. Many observers felt that the separation of the Women's Rights Committee from the other main UN human rights bodies contributed to the marginalization of women's rights issues. In 1993, the Division for the Advancement of Women was relocated to UN Headquarters in New York. And, in 2008 the responsibility for servicing the Women's Rights Committee transferred to the OHCHR in Geneva. As a result the Women's Rights Committee now conducts its work and holds its meetings in New York and at the OHCHR in Geneva. This change has benefited the committee and increased its visibility within the UN system.[29]

The Women's Rights Committee was initially limited by Women's Rights Treaty article 20 to a single two-week annual meeting. However, in 1996 the General Assembly approved an increase in meeting time for the Women's Rights Committee, allowing it to meet for two three-week sessions annually, each preceded by a one-week working group session.[30]

As opposed to every other major institution of the international legal order, the Women's Rights Committee has been staffed primarily by women and not men. With few exceptions, the Women's Rights Committee has almost always been an all-female committee dealing with women's issues. Since its inception, over 100 female and only 4 male experts have served on the committee.[31] The state representatives reporting to the committee, on the other hand, have for the most part been male. Some observers argue that this has resulted in the proceedings becoming adversarial in nature, with the representative feeling victimized and responding defensively.[32] In response to these concerns, the UN Economic and Social Council (ECOSOC) called on the states parties to nominate both female and male experts for election to the Women's Rights Committee. It is instructive to note that ECOSOC did not call on states to correct the much more common dominance of men in all the other human rights supervisory bodies. The Women's Rights Committee rejected ECOSOC's recommendation on the grounds that it could potentially undermine the committee's effectiveness. The committee further called on ECOSOC to attend to equality of representation elsewhere before interfering with its membership.[33]

As with the Minority Rights Committee, the primary responsibility of the Women's Rights Committee is the consideration of states parties' reports. The reporting guidelines are found in article 18 of the Women's Rights Treaty, which, after the initial report, requires periodic reports to be submitted at least every four years and whenever the Women's Rights Committee requests them. On the basis of these reports, the Women's Rights Committee adopts suggestions and recommendations concerning the matters reported to it.

As with the other treaty bodies, the Women's Rights Committee also faces serious problems of states ignoring their legal obligations and refusing to report. The committee, however, has worked diligently with states parties to overcome this problem. While in March 2002 there were 257 overdue state reports to the Women's Rights Committee, as of July 2009, there were only 97 overdue reports.[34]

Since 1982, when the Women's Rights Committee started its work, hundreds of state reports have been submitted. These reports vary in quality and suffer from the inherent problems of subjectivity intrinsic to self-reporting. Yet, often these reports help focus a government on issues of women's rights and stimulate action. For example, in the initial report Guatemala submitted to the Women's Rights Committee, the government noted the difficulty of assembling the report, stating that "studies of this type are only a recent innovation." The task of preparing the report "has also been a positive exercise in thought, analysis and self-appraisal with respect to the position of women in Guatemala . . . [stimulating action to design] strategies and targets . . . to improve the situation encountered in the short and medium term." The report notes that the work of Guatemalan women "is poorly paid or not paid at all and is generally of low productivity owing to lack of access to capital. It is falsely assumed that the man is the one who makes the principal economic contributions to the family, for which reason he is the owner and beneficiary of all payments and services. . . . In the paid work that she does, her salary is inferior to a man's and her instability in the sense of a job is greater." The reporting requirements of the Women's Rights Committee clearly helped the Guatemalan government focus on these issues of gender discrimination and the economic and social well-being of women.[35]

An Optional Protocol to the Women's Rights Treaty was adopted by the CSW on 12 March 1999 and by the General Assembly on 6 October 1999. After receiving ten ratifications, the optional protocol entered into force on 22 December 2000. As of July 2009, ninety-seven states had signed and ratified the optional protocol.[36] This amendment allows for the submission of individual complaints to the Women's Rights Committee and establishes a procedure under which serious and systematic violations of the convention can be investigated. The optional protocol opens the door for women (individuals or groups) to have their voices heard in the UN system. The Women's Rights Committee now initiates inquiries where there are grave or systematic violations of women's rights. These procedures enhance the ability of the Women's Rights Committee to serve as an international forum for women and recommend remedies for violations of women's rights. Individual complaint procedures on other treaty bodies have spurred governments to evaluate means of redress available at the national level (see the discussion of the complaint procedure to the Minority Rights Committee in chapter 5). The optional protocol to Women's Rights Treaty provides an incentive for governments to evaluate the protection of women's rights at the national level.[37]

The Women's Rights Committee also issues general recommendations to states parties that interpret and clarify the legal duties and obligations in the Women's Rights Treaty. The Women's Rights Committee's general recommendations thus serve a similar purpose as the Economic Rights Committee's general comments (reviewed in chapter 3) in the progressive development of international human rights law. A number of the general recommendations have dealt with the economic and social rights of women:[38]

General Recommendation no. 5 (1988) calls on states parties to "make more use of temporary special measures such as positive action, preferential treatment or quota systems to advance women's integration into education, the economy, politics and employment."[39]

General Recommendation no. 13 (1989) urges states parties to ratify International Labor Organization Convention no. 100 concerning equal remuneration for men and women workers for work of equal value.[40]

General Recommendation no. 16 (1991) calls on states parties to include "in their reports to the Committee information on the legal and social situation of unpaid women working in family enterprises . . . [and t]ake the necessary steps to guarantee payment, social security and social benefits for women who work without such benefits in enterprises owned by a family member."[41]

General Recommendation no. 17(1991) encourages states parties to measure and value the unremunerated domestic activities of women, for example, "by conducting time-use surveys as part of their national household survey programmes and by collecting statistics disaggregated by gender on time spent on activities both in the household and on the labour market." States parties are asked to quantify and include the unremunerated domestic activities of women in the gross national product.[42]

General Recommendation no. 18 (1991) addresses the human rights of disabled women and asks states parties to take "special measures to ensure that they have equal access to education and employment, health services and social security, and to ensure that they can participate in all areas of social and cultural life."[43]

General Recommendation no. 24 (1999) addresses state responsibilities in regard to article 12 of the Women's Rights Treaty, which affirms that access to health care, including reproductive health, is a basic human right. This very detailed recommendation calls on states parties to implement a comprehensive national strategy to promote women's health. It is noteworthy that in this general recommendation the Women's Rights Committee explicitly addresses the public–private dichotomy and acknowledges the negative impact on women's nutrition and health resulting from the unequal power relationships between women and men in the home and workplace.[44] This analysis reinforced the 1992 General Recommendation no. 19 on violence against women, which directly confronts discrimination and violations of human rights in public and private acts. "Private" activity includes family violence and abuse, forced marriage, dowry deaths, and female circumcision.[45] Andrew Clapham argues that this 1992 recommendation represented "a giant leap forward in the conceptual thinking surrounding human rights theories and illustrates the crucial importance of collapsing the public/private boundary in the human rights field."[46]

General Recommendation no. 26 (2008) addresses states parties' legal obligations in regards to the human rights of women migrant workers. The committee notes that because "of discrimnation on the basis of sex and gender, women migrant workers may receive lower wages than do men, or experience non-payment of wages, payments that are delayed until departure, or transfer of wages into accounts that are inaccessible to them." "Women migrant workers often suffer from inequalities that threaten their health.

They may be unable to access health services, including reproductive health services, because insurance or national health schemes are not available to them, or they may have to pay unaffordable fees." This general recommendation goes on to provide detailed guidelines on how states can formulate a comprehensive gender-sensitive and rights-based policy on the basis of equality and non-discrimination for women migrant workers. The committee thus provides states with a useful framework to meet their legal human rights obligations in this area.[47]

It is impossible for the Women's Rights Committee in two three-week meetings a year to address the many patriarchal practices that globally subordinate women. In addition, the numerous reservations made by states parties to the Women's Rights Treaty suggest that discrimination against women is still regarded as more acceptable than other practices. Furthermore, the Women's Rights Committee is underfunded and understaffed and lacks effective means to pressure states to correct women's rights violations.

Upendra Baxi writes: "The near-universality of ratification of [the Women's Rights Treaty] . . . betokens no human liberation of women. Rather, it endows the state with the power to tell more Nietzschean lies. . . . 'State' is the name of the coldest of all cold monsters. Coldly, it tells lies, too; and this lie grows out of its mouth: 'I, the state, am the people.'"[48] States can use their ratification of the Women's Rights Treaty to claim "progress" in meeting women's rights while simultaneously implementing public policies that undermine women's economic and social security. Until the Women's Rights Committee is adequately funded and staffed, these global mechanisms to monitor compliance with international women's human rights law will not only remain weak, but could provide the state with "the power to tell more Nietschzean lies." Thus, the earlier recommendations (in chapter 5) to professionalize the operations of the Minority Rights Committee apply equally to the Women's Rights Committee as well.

First, the reports from the Women's Rights Committee deserve more attention. These reports, currently submitted through ECOSOC to the General Assembly, could go directly to the new, proposed UN Economic Security Council recommended in the Global New Deal (see chapter 9). This would cause the reports to be taken more seriously and serve to push states to implement policy to protect women's rights. The reports would then be evaluated and acted on by the main body within the UN system concerned with issues of economic equality—the proposed UN Economic Security Council.

And second, the experts elected to the Women's Rights Committee should be paid to support their hard work. Currently, the members of the Women's Rights Committee receive only a small stipend per year (apart from their daily allowance). As a result, members must keep full-time employment elsewhere and somehow find the time to attend to the committees affairs. A proposed solution (as noted with the Minority Rights Committee) is to pay committee members a half-time professional salary out of the UN budget for their committee work. This would allow these experts to take a leave of absence for half the year from their full-time jobs to serve on the Women's Rights Committee. The member states of the UN can show their commitment to women's rights by approving this minimal funding request to make the Women's Rights Committee functional.

Despite the efforts of the Women's Rights Committee, the economic and social rights of women remain under threat around the world. For example, in 2003 the UNDP reported that literacy rates among young women (15–24 years old) were 60 percent compared to 80 percent for young men. In addition, more women in LDCs suffer from HIV/AIDS and maternal mortality adds a further dimension to women's burdens. Biologically women should live longer than men. Yet, in many developing countries there are millions of, what Amayta Sen labelled, "missing women." These women were killed by infancitide, gender-based abortions, or systematic discrimination in the provision of basic necessities like food and water. As a result, in 2003 the UN estimate was that there were 35–37 million "missing" women in South Asia and an additional 38–40 million "missing" in China.[49]

In addition, women are too often the first to experience the negative consequences of the economic globalization process. In the LDCs, for example, export-processing zones have mushroomed with a preponderance of female workers. According to the Women's Environment and Development Organization (WEDO): "This feminization of employment, often interpreted as a positive outcome of structural adjustment, is in fact a result of international and local demand for cheap and docile labor that can be used in low-skill, repetitive jobs in unsafe and insecure conditions without minimum guarantees."[50] WEDO reports from Malaysia, the Republic of South Korea, the Philippines, India, Sri Lanka, Egypt, and Mexico dramatically illustrate the gendered nature of economic globalization. Egypt, for example, adopted an Economic Reform and Structural Adjustment Program in the 1990s on the basis of agreements with the International Monetary Fund (IMF) and the World Bank. According to WEDO, these programs accentuated poverty and reduced female access to basic social services such as health care and education. Women's overall unemployment in Egypt by the end of the twentieth century was estimated to be around 60 percent. With few employment opportunities, these women remain prime candidates for exploitative working conditions and low wages.[51] The protection and fulfillment of international women's human rights law is fundamentally linked to national and international economic policy.

IPE and Women's Human Rights

It seems that everyone talks of including the voice of women in development planning. Conservative, liberal, and radical perspectives on political economy all now stress the need for including women and/or gender in their analysis. Some of the key feminist IPE theories and approaches to economic and social human rights fulfillment, summarized and analyzed below, include Women in Development (WID), Women and Development (WAD), Gender and Development (GAD), Development Alternatives with Women for a New Era (DAWN), and ecofeminism.

Women in Development

WID represents a liberal feminist approach to development. The assumptions of liberal modernization theory are for the most part accepted. While "traditional" societies are often seen as patriarchal, modern society is regarded as potentially democratic and liberating. The fulfillment of women's rights is envisioned through the integration of women's issues into modernization and development programs. WID brings visibility to women's issues in development thinking. Furthermore, it calls for the integration of women into economic planning and production. WID does not advocate fundamental change in economic structures. According to Nalini Visvanathan, WID has been central to the mainstreaming of gender issues into development agencies.[52]

The aim of WID, following the path-breaking work of Ester Boserup in 1970, was to integrate women into development. Since the fruits of development were not trickling down to women, women should be factored into development programs. Boserup documents the ways in which development programs in the LDCs not only did not benefit women, but actually led to the deterioration of women's economic status. While men were drawn into the "modernized" economic sectors, women remained in subsistence agriculture, which was suddenly viewed as "backward." Only men had access to new technology, credit, and educational opportunities. As men became engaged in commodity production, women continued to produce food for household consumption. Boserup's concern was with equality and integrating women into development models. She brought the issue of gender and development out in the open, and her thinking was essential to the development of WID. She specifically addressed the dynamics inside the home, where family income is often made available to the boys and not the girls of the household.[53]

By the mid-1970s, WID programs had become institutionalized around the world in a variety of departments and projects within donor countries' development agencies. In the 1980s, women's bureaus and ministries were established in the countries of the South. WID became a

---

MEASURING GENDER INEQUALITIES IN HUMAN DEVELOPMENT

In its yearly *Human Development Report*, the UN Development Program (UNDP) publishes the following two indispensable indices that measure gender inequality around the world:

The Gender Development Index
The Gender Development Index (GDI) takes account of inequality of achievement between men and women in longevity, knowledge, and decent standard of living. The "longevity" category compares female and male life expectancy at birth. The "knowledge" category examines two areas: (1) female and male adult literacy rates and (2) female and male combined enrollment ratios. The "decent standard of living" category compares female and male earned income. Gender disparity in basic human development is captured by this index.

In 2007, the UNDP estimated the GDI for 157 countries and found gender inequality everywhere. In thirty-six countries—including India, Mozambique, Pakistan, Turkey, and Yemen—male literacy rates were at least fifteen percentage points higher than female rates.

The Gender Empowerment Measure
The Gender Empowerment Measure (GEM) focuses on whether women can participate in economic and political life. It measures gender inequality in areas of economic and political decision making and participation. It calculates the percentage of women in parliament and the legislature and among senior officials and managers and professional and technical workers. It also reflects the gender disparity in earned income, an indication of economic independence. GEM helps to assess gender inequality in economic and political opportunities.

In 2007, the UNDP estimated GEM for ninety-three countries. In only seventeen countries did women hold 30 percent or more of the seats in parliament. The statistics also reveal that high income is not a prerequisite to equal opportunity for women. The UNDP notes that some developing countries outperformed much richer industrial countries. The Bahamas and Trinidad and Tobago, for example, were ahead of Israel, Japan, and Switzerland.*

---

*UNDP, *Human Development Report 2007/2008* (New York: Palgrave Macmillan, 2007), 326–333.

respectable field of study. Lobbying by WID specialists led to a wider interest in women's role in the development process. The first UN conference on Women and Development was held in 1975 in Mexico City. The years 1976–1985 were declared the Women's Decade, which ended with the Nairobi Women and Development Conference in 1985. The Forward Looking Strategies that emerged from Nairobi called for the full integration of women into mainstream economic development. By the mid-1980s, WID had become thoroughly integrated into the development programs of the leading development international organizations and major government bureaucracies. Women demanded equality: equal access to land and capital, education, and training.[54]

Women and Development

WAD emerged as a critique of WID's acceptance of traditional development economics. Proponents of WAD argue that women were always part of the development process, so the issue is not the integration of women into development. In fact, women's work in the public and private arenas is absolutely critical to the maintenance of modern capitalism. WAD calls for an examination of the nature of the integration of women in development, which has the effect of sustaining existing international structures of inequality.[55]

According to WAD scholars, the WID perspective fails to challenge the capitalist model of development. Gender hierarchies intensified as capitalist systems spread. The public–private cleavage became central. In the public sphere, male labor brought economic rewards, while in the private sphere, female labor was channeled into nonexchange activities, reproduction, and the well-being of the family. Female labor was thus hidden and uncompensated. WAD draws attention to these issues of women's unpaid domestic work and the need for reproductive services.

WAD highlights the gender inequalities that are embedded within current economic and political structures. Gendered market failure occurs when markets fail to invest in and reward women's productive and reproductive work. Gendered public-sector failure occurs when public institutions fail to include women equitably in their services and operations. These are structural failures and not the product of an irrational sexist individual decision maker. WAD focuses on the structural level of gender bias.[56]

Cynthia Enloe eloquently describes the gendered nature of economic structures—that is, banking policies, transnational corporate investments, structural adjustment policies, and so on. Writing about export processing zones, Enloe explains:

> The centerpiece of the bankers' export strategy has been the "Export Processing Zone." Indebted governments set aside territory specifically for factories

producing goods for the international market. Governments lure overseas companies to move their plants to the EPZs by offering them sewers, electricity, ports, runways, tax holidays and police protection. Most attractive of all is the governments' offer of cheap labor. Women's labor has been the easiest to cheapen, so it shouldn't be surprising that in most Export Processing Zones at least 70 per cent of the workers are women, especially young women. The eighteen-year-old woman at the sewing machine—or electronics assembly line or food-processing plant—in Panama's Colon Export Processing Zone has become the essential though unequal partner of the banker in his glass and chrome office in London or Chicago. The risk-taking banker needs the conscientious seamstress to hold his world together. The politician and his technocratic advisor need the seamstress to keep the banker and his home government pacified. If the seamstress rebels, if she rethinks what it means to be a woman who sews for a living, her country may turn up on the list of "unstable regimes" now kept by politically sensitive bankers.[57]

WAD thus draws our attention to the impact of the global economy on the lives of women and structural violence impacting working women. WAD demonstrates how sexual inequality comes hand in hand with capitalist expansion. WAD proponents argue that radical structural reform could be the first step toward addressing women's economic and social human rights. WAD's structuralist focus is a distinct alternative to WID's liberal orientation.

Gender and Development

Why the word "gender" instead of "women"? Beginning in the late 1970s and early 1980s, feminists in GAD rejected an essentialist and universal definition of the category of women. The use of "gender" as opposed to "women" was to eliminate the biological determinism often underlying feminist analysis. Critical theory called for the deconstruction of not only key identities (e.g., men/women and homosexual/heterosexual) but the gendered nature of social institutions as well. As R. Pearson, A. Whitehead, and K. Young wrote in 1984: "[O]ur point of departure was that the relations between men and women are social and therefore not immutable and fixed. The form that gender relations take in any historical situation is specific to that situation and has to be constructed inductively; it cannot be read off from other social relations nor from the gender relations of other societies."[58]

This approach signifies not just a change in language but an understanding that it is gender relations that subordinate women and should be the focus of analysis (as opposed to women per se). GAD calls our attention to this centrality of gender relations in all development activities. This means expanding the focus beyond a concern for "women's issues" (family planning, women's health, women's employment, and so on) to broader issues of macroeconomic planning (structural adjustment programs, debt, environmental degradation, and so on).[59] Through the GAD perspective, development agencies were thus called on to shift their approach from a singular focus on "women's issues" to a deeper understanding of the socially constructed roles of both women and men. Projects should therefore no longer be limited to women, but to overall gender issues in development programs and projects.[60]

Development agencies, including the World Bank and the UN Food and Agriculture Organization, adopted GAD approaches and began training their experts in "gender literacy" and accounting for women's concerns at all levels in their organizations. This involved "screening policy documents, employment policies, planning of projects, sex segregated data collection, monitoring and evaluation procedures, and so on. All development agency staff pass through compulsory training in gender analysis and gender planning."[61]

For example, at the Beijing women's conference, the World Bank made the case for gender on efficiency grounds, linking the interests of women with economic liberalization: "Sound economic policies and well-functioning markets are essential for growth, employment and the creation of an environment in which the returns to investing in women and girls can be fully realized."[62]

As with WID, GAD also does not appear to challenge the prevailing development theory of modernization and economic growth. For example, does GAD pay enough attention to the sexual division of labor? Employment opportunities created for women are often in addition to women's work in the home, and thus serve to deepen female oppression.

A further problem that GAD feminists face is how to define what women have in common while being clear about differences of culture, ethnicity, and class. Sex and gender may be socially constructed ideas that contain different meanings in different societies. The challenge to GAD feminists is to construct an analysis of gender that addresses common oppression women face globally while being sensitive to cultural (and other) differences. The problems of essentialism/universalism versus relativism/difference remain.

If "women" is a socially constructed product strongly influenced by male preferences, then what remains of "women's issues" and "women's rights"? At the nongovernmental organization forum at the Beijing Conference in 1995, speakers asserted that this shift from women to gender had become counterproductive "in that it had allowed the discussion to shift from a focus on women, to women and men and, finally, back to men."[63]

Development Alternatives with Women for a New Era

In the mid-1980s, women from the LDCs organized DAWN, a critique of development's impact on poor women. DAWN's focus on race, class, and gender led to a vision of a world where basic needs become basic rights. The empowerment of poor women through political conscious-ness-raising and education was key to DAWN's outlook.

The feminism of DAWN has its own independent history and was not imposed by Northern, white, middle-class women. DAWN women from the South believe that all women's work should be accounted for in national accounting systems. They question an economic model based on economic growth and call for "equitable development based on the val-ues of co-operation, resistance to hierarchies, sharing, accountability and commitment to peace." They are aware of the multiple nature of the sub-ordination of women in the South—sex, race, class, and their position in the international economic order. Strategies for women's empowerment can only come about by simultaneously examining all of these domains.[64]

DAWN questions whether women in the South want to be integrated into mainstream development models, thereby challenging the WID approach. WID affirms the primacy of the economic growth model. DAWN sees such an approach as fundamentally exploitative of women's paid and unpaid labor. Feminists associated with DAWN thus took the lead in the 1980s and 1990s in opposing the structural adjustment pro-grams (SAPs) of the IMF from a gender perspective. They documented the ways in which SAPs negatively impacted gender equality by forcing governments to cut social-sector investments, especially in education and health, which hit women the hardest. Some DAWN feminists argue that the inability of LDCs to eliminate illiteracy and increase the life expectancy of women can be partially attributed to misguided IMF SAP directives.[65]

Ecofeminism

Ecofeminists draw parallels between male control over nature and over women. Feminist models of sustainable development are put forward as alternatives to the current development models that assault the ecological health of the planet. The global market's destruction of forests and farm-ing systems is contrasted with traditional practices of indigenous peoples.

Vandana Shiva was influential in the development of ecofeminism. In her work, she draws on Hindu religion and philosophy to describe the "femi-nine principle" (prakriti) as the source of all life. The relationship that rural women in India have with nature is seen as the embodiment of the femi-nine principle. For the phrase "sustainable development" to have meaning, it must recover this relationship. Colonialism, "development," and the "green revolution" destroyed small-scale agriculture, created unsustain-able export-oriented agriculture, and marginalized poor women.[66]

Shiva's argument links the violation of nature with the violation of women. Through their role as providers of sustenance, food, and water, women are usually linked to life and nature. Maria Mies calls women's work in producing sustenance the production of life; they make things grow.[67] But women's special relationship with nature can be destroyed under capitalist development. As Shiva writes: "'Productive' man, producing commodities, using some of nature's wealth and women's work as raw material and dispensing with the rest as waste, becomes the only legitimate category of work, wealth and production. Nature and women working to produce and reproduce life are declared 'unproductive.'"[68]

The term "ecofeminism" refers to a range of theoretical positions that draw critical connections between the domination of nature and of women, between feminist and ecological concerns. Two positions found within ecofeminism have been labeled "cultural ecofeminism" and "social ecofeminism." Cultural ecofeminists, located within the essentialist tradition, include contributions by Mary Daly and Susan Griffin. Male culture is seen as aggressive, individualistic, and hierarchical. Women and nature are victims of patriarchal power structures. Women's essential features, such as empathy, caring, and connectedness, are seen as indispensable to the creation of a less violent and more sustainable way of life.[69]

Social ecofeminism is based on the recognition of the social construction of gender. Proponents criticize cultural ecofeminists for reversing hierarchies (putting women on top), which, they believe, in the end is self-defeating. Social ecofeminists stress the connections between gender and class—the relationship between gender roles and the economic organization of production and distribution which undermines ecological balance.[70]

Linking Feminist IPE and Feminist Human Rights Theory

Advocates of these differing perspectives of feminist IPE can find support for their positions within the current international human rights framework.

WID proponents could point to the Women's Rights Treaty's call for states to pledge to embody "the principle of equality of men and women" in their constitutions and other legislation as support for their demand for equality and the equal integration of women into development. The Women's Rights Treaty also calls for legislation against discrimination against women; legal protections of the rights of women on an equal basis with men; measures to eliminate existing discrimination "by any person, organization or enterprise"; and the repeal of all provisions of the penal law that are discriminatory.[71] All of these measures support WID's program of integration.

The radical structural reform called for by WAD mirrors the demand found in the 1986 General Assembly Declaration on the Right to Development: [T]he right of "every human person and all peoples . . . to participate

---

FEMINIST PERSPECTIVES ON
INTERNATIONAL POLITICAL ECONOMY (IPE)

There are many voices speaking through the various feminist perspectives on IPE. Clarifying common elements within each perspective might help us understand their relationship to women's economic and social human rights. At the risk of oversimplification, some common elements can be summarized in the following manner:

- Women in Development (WID) seeks to reform current economic and political structures through the integration of women into development programs and institutions
- Women and Development (WAD) and Development Alternatives with Women for a New Era (DAWN) seek to humble and transform the constraining influence of international economic structures that perpetuate patriarchy and deny women power
- Gender and Development (GAD) and ecofeminism seek positive change for women through an understanding of the human construction of gender roles and the exposure of the male basis to current (mal)development models that undermine environmental sustainability.

---

in, contribute to and enjoy economic, social, cultural and political development, in which all human rights and fundamental freedoms can be fully realized."[72] WAD advocates could also point to article 28 of the Universal Declaration of Human Rights, which states that "[e]veryone is entitled to a social and international order in which the rights and freedoms set forth in this Declaration can be fully realized."[73]

The GAD assault on the socially constructed nature of women's and men's public and private roles in society is supported by the challenge to social and cultural patterns of behavior found in the Women's Rights Treaty, article 5, in which states parties agree to take appropriate measures to "modify the social and cultural patterns of conduct of men and women, with a view to achieving the elimination of prejudices and customary and all other practices which are based on the idea of the inferiority or the superiority of either of the sexes or on stereotyped roles for men and women."[74]

DAWN's focus on the multiple nature of the subordination of women (sex, race, and class) and, in particular, on the attention to both poverty and gender subordination is echoed in both the Women's Rights Treaty and the Minority Rights Treaty. The Minority Rights Treaty calls for "special and concrete measures to ensure the adequate development and protection of certain racial groups or individuals belonging to them for the purpose of guaranteeing them the full and equal enjoyment of human rights and fundamental freedoms."[75] The Women's Rights Treaty, as we have seen, calls for "special measures aimed at accelerating de facto equality between men and women."[76] DAWN's attention to poverty and basic rights is found in the UN's Right to Development, which requires that national development policies aim for the constant improvement of the well-being of the entire population.[77] The UN's Copenhagen Summit on Social Development also addressed these concerns.[78]

Ecofeminists could point to principle 20 of the "Rio Declaration": "Women have a vital role in environmental management and development. Their full participation is therefore essential to achieve sustainable development."[79] The ecofeminist focus on sustainability could draw support from the "Stockholm Declaration"[80] and the UN General Assembly Resolution 37/7 on a World Charter for Nature.[81]

It thus appears that supporters of these different feminist IPE theories can all vindicate their approaches with references to the existing human rights framework and international law. What does it mean that human rights law can validate and support conflicting theoretical analysis? What is the utility of women's human rights to policy makers if these norms can be used to justify opposing perspectives? How can this human rights framework be helpful to those charged with developing economic policy?

Women and the Capabilities Approach

The different feminist approaches to IPE should not be seen as mutually exclusive and contradictory. Since valuable insights are found in all of them, perhaps a more eclectic policy approach is the most fruitful road toward the achievement of women's economic and social human rights. Issues of structure and power can be incorporated into understandings of the social construction of gender and vice versa. These theories can address the ongoing structural dimensions of injustice (i.e. banking policies, structural adjustment programs, and so on) with an analysis of the social construction of patriarchy (i.e., gender hierarchies, female roles, and so on). On the one hand, it is necessary to understand the structural constraints that historically block change and perpetuate mechanisms of exploitation. But, on the other hand, understanding the social construction of identities and/or norms that accept these constraints may provide insights into how to challenge these very structures.

Liberal WID scholars are correct in pointing to the importance of equal treatment. But for equality to be meaningful, issues of class and power must be confronted, as pointed out by proponents of WAD and DAWN. Equal treatment often leads to affirmative action (national and international) and reverse discrimination (national and international) and other programs to support the poor. Gender justice hinges on global attention to basic health care, child care, adequate nutrition, and unemployment insurance. This means challenging the social and economic structures that confine women to the private sphere, as articulated by scholars from GAD and ecofeminists. Women's economic and social human rights depend on attention to all of these dimensions.

Caroline O. N. Moser points to such a multidimensional approach to gender justice in her call for policy makers to incorporate "gender planning" into development schemes. Gender planning takes into account the fact that women and men play different societal roles in the formulation of practical and strategic economic policy. Economic planning must disaggregate households and families within communities on the basis of gender. She points to the "triple role of women" in low-income households in LDCs: reproductive work (the childbearing and rearing responsibilities), productive work (often as secondary earners), and community managing work (the struggle to manage their neighborhoods). If developers are blind to this triple role of poor women, policies will fail to meet women's specific requirements. Moser therefore calls for a more integrative approach in which planning accounts for both income and gender difference. Policy makers will need to identify both strategic and practical gender needs.[82]

Maxine Molyneux identifies key strategic gender needs as including:

- the abolition of the sexual division of labour;
- the alleviation of the burden of domestic labour and childcare;
- the removal of institutionalized forms of discrimination such as rights to own land or property, or access to credit;
- the establishment of political equality;
- freedom of choice over childbearing; and
- the adoption of adequate measures against male violence and control over women.[83]

Moser defines "practical gender needs" as those needs "which are formulated from the concrete conditions women experience, in their engendered position within the sexual division of labour. . . . Therefore in planning terms, policies for meeting practical gender needs have to focus on the domestic arena, on income earning activities and also on community-level requirements of housing and basic services."[84]

There are obviously great disparities in vulnerability between the rich and the poor. A poor woman may not have the option to refuse the economic arrangements presented to her. The weak suffer from those who take advantage of their vulnerable position, and nothing shields them from the consequences of national and global economic forces. These international economic forces are not regulated, yet they can have a devastating impact on the lives of poor women. Poor women cannot alter or change economic structures that hurt them. Low wages, dependence on those who provide credit, patriarchal patterns, and customs of male entitlement within the family all exacerbate the vulnerability of poor women.

Feminist IPE theories attempt to bring into sharp relief the importance of economic power on women's lives. Liberal human rights theories often ignore these powerful forces with proclamations of equality that have no basis in women's real lives. The integration of these perspectives is essential to formulate effective policy for women. Institutional power, international economic structures, and family entitlement customs can be changed and modified to address issues of women's human rights. Only with an incorporation of these issues of power and wealth into the human rights framework can poor women's claims be understood.

A promising incorporation of these issues is found in Sen's capabilities approach (described in chapter 2). What are the actual capacities and opportunities for women to act? This approach acknowledges that people have varying needs for resources: a pregnant woman needs more calories than a nonpregnant woman, a breast cancer patient has unique medical needs, and an unemployed mother in all cultures needs more resources to become productively employed than those not in this situation. The issue is the amount of resources necessary for this person to achieve adequate functioning. As Martha C. Nussbaum writes: "This approach to quality-of-life measurement and the goals of public policy holds that we should focus on the questions: What are the people of the group or country in question actually able to do and to be? Unlike a focus on opulence (say GNP per capita), this approach asks about the distribution of resources and opportunities. In principle, it asks how each and every individual is doing with respect to all the functions deemed important."[85]

Sen's research shows that gender inequality cannot be understood solely in terms of income differences, but should be analyzed in relation to "the extent of relative deprivation of women to the existing inequalities of opportunities (in earning outside income, in being enrolled in schools, and so on). Thus, both descriptive and policy issues can be addressed through this broader perspective on inequality and poverty in terms of capability deprivation."[86]

Nussbaum develops the capabilities approach as a vehicle for overcoming the oppression and exploitation of women. She argues that "international political and economic thought should be feminist, attentive [among other things] to the special problems women face because of sex . . . problems without an understanding of which general issues of poverty and development cannot be well confronted." The denial of basic human needs and basic rights is "frequently caused by their being women."[87]

Nussbaum develops a list of "Central Human Functional Capabilities" that marks the most significant difference between her approach and Sen's: Sen never made such a list. This list of capabilities includes ten broad areas: life; bodily health; bodily integrity; senses, imagination, and thought; emotions; practical reason; affiliation; other species; play; and control over one's political and material environment. Nussbaum's goal is to determine a "decent social minimum" in these areas, contending that "the structure of social and political institutions should be chosen, at least in part, with a view to promoting at least a threshold level of these human capabilities." She argues for protecting a minimum threshold in each of the ten areas of central human functional capabilities as well as for according each of them equal value. The minimum threshold is central to her argument as it trumps culture, family, and religion.[88]

With her Central Human Functional Capabilities list, Nussbaum elaborates a universal set of liberal values to judge and scrutinize all cultures. For example, feminism in India runs up against long-standing cultural practices and religious beliefs. Those who "challenge entrenched satisfactions are frequently charged with being totalitarian and antidemocratic for just this way of proceeding. Who are they to tell real women what is good for them, or to march into an area shaped by tradition and custom with universal standards of what one should demand and what one should desire?" Yet, preferences can be manipulated by tradition and intimidation and "clash with universal norms even at the level of basic nutrition and health." In one desert area in India, women had no feelings of anger or protest about their own severe malnourishment or the lack of a reliable clean water supply: "They knew no other way. They did not consider their conditions unhealthful or unsanitary, and they did not consider themselves to be malnourished." How does a feminist get outside of this box?[89]

A consciousness-raising program changed the situation by challenging entrenched preferences. These same women now fight for clean water, electricity, and a health visitor, all of which enhances their basic capabilities. The power of this story lies in the interface between universal norms and local culture. Despite poverty and suffering, these women seemed to prefer their traditional way of life. Yet, Nussbaum argues, this local preference should not be respected until these women have been given other options. The capabilities approach demands that a woman have a real opportunity to surmount economic deprivations and low expectations. Nussbaum believes that, given the choice, women's preferences in India will shift to universal goods, rather than those preferences that were mere reflections of women's restricted situations. It is the failure of a person to have various basic human capabilities that is important in itself, and not just because the person minds it or complains about it.

Nussbaum's Central Human Functional Capabilities list reinforces existing women's human rights claims. The corpus of international human rights law clarifies the economic, social, cultural, political, and civil rights claims to which all individuals are entitled. It has taken decades of struggle for the international women's movement to achieve clarity and unity around these basic human rights for women. Nussbaum's interpretation of the capabilities approach should be linked directly to these efforts in international law. The capabilities approach is not an alternative to the well-established framework of human rights.[90] Rather, the capabilities approach provides a means to articulate and measure public policy to achieve women's human rights. The capabilities approach gives us the tools to analyze what is preventing women from realizing basic rights to security, subsistence, and freedom, or, to use Sen's phrase, the "freedom to achieve adequate functioning." The capabilities approach helps direct public policy (in education, health care, and so on) to create an environment for women to realize their basic human rights.

The Global New Deal and Gender

Summary Observations

Policies to support economic equality (as defined in chapter 2) are central to the realization of the rights of women enunciated in the Women's Rights Treaty. There is not one feminist theory of IPE (WID, DAWN, and so on) that in itself is adequate in addressing policies for economic equality. Rather, aspects of each theory can be woven together to create policy to respect, protect, and fulfill women's economic and social human rights.

Human rights law has historically been "defined by the criterion of what men fear will happen to them."[91] In the 1980s and 1990s, the women's movement articulated a new conception of human rights that began to take into account what women fear will happen to

Global New Deal Proposals

Central to the Global New Deal is the realization of the economic and social human rights of women through the implementation of the capabilities approach. The Global New Deal in chapter 9 calls for national and international public policy to focus on the education and health of women. The Women's Rights Committee should concentrate on helping states craft policy to meet the education and health care needs of women. The enhancement of women's capabilities in these two areas is key to economic and social rights protection overall. By addressing human capabilities, we expand the real freedoms that women enjoy and create an environment in which women's human rights can be realized.

them. Included in these demands were the ways in which women are denied basic economic and social human rights as a result of both socially constructed gender roles and structural economic forces. Women pushed the human rights framework beyond the public sphere and into the private sphere, which meant holding state and nonstate actors accountable to these norms. Merging this analysis with an eclectic approach to feminist IPE theories can help formulate public policy in the real world to help women realize their rights.

Through a focus on the health care and education of women, two of the priority areas from the Beijing Platform of Action, the Women's Rights Committee can help states formulate national policy to respect, protect, and fulfill economic and social human rights. The Women's Rights Committee could focus like a laser on these issues of women's education and health. Governments would be put on notice: when they come before the Women's Rights Committee they will be particularly questioned on policies to achieve equity in women's education and women's health.

7

Military Spending and Economic and Social Human Rights

What are the economic effects of high levels of military spending on economic well-being? What types of military expenditures create real security for citizens? How does a society provide adequate defense and security without compromising other basic human rights? Are there trade-offs between rights to physical security and rights to subsistence? Do recent proposals from the UN point to a means of achieving a better balance between conflicting sets of human rights claims? Can these concerns be incorporated into a coherent foreign policy agenda?

State institutions exist in the modern world for a variety of broad purposes, including, according to Article 3 of the Universal Declaration of Human Rights (UDHR), the protection of each citizen's "right to life, liberty and security of person." The national defense of the state and the personal security of the individual have been seen as legitimate and essential to the fulfillment of other human rights. In fact, national defense is often described as a pure public good. All citizens, rich and poor, can benefit from a safe environment without detracting from the enjoyment of others. Security, according to Henry Shue, along with subsistence and liberty, is a "basic right."[1]

The U.S. Supreme Court agrees on the critical nature of security and in 1981, citing numerous precedents, declared: "It is 'obvious and unarguable' that no governmental interest is more compelling than the security of the Nation. *Aptheker v. Secretary of State*, [378 U.S. 500, 509 (1964)];

This chapter was coauthored with Diana Fuguitt, professor of economics, Eckerd College.

accord *Cole v. Young*, 351 U.S. 536, 546 (1956); see *Zemel* [*v. Rusk*, 381 U.S. 1, 13–17 (1965)]. Protection of the foreign policy of the United States is a governmental interest of great importance, since foreign policy and national security considerations cannot neatly be compartmentalized."[2]

Yet, in the name of national defense and security, governments have embarked on ambitious military spending programs which unfortunately can jeopardize other human rights. In 2008, for example, global military expenditures totaled approximately one and a half trillion dollars ($1,464 billion), an increase of 4 percent in real terms compared to 2007. More startling, however, is that the 2008 total represented a 45 percent increase in real global military expenditures over the 10 year period of 1999–2008.[3]

This chapter explores the implications of this high level of military spending in relation to economic and social human rights. Is there a trade-off between rights to subsistence and rights to security? Are there direct conflicts between different legitimate rights claims? Western political systems often prioritize civil and political liberties, claiming that these rights "trump" other claims. The pursuit of defense and national security in trubulent times can often override additional priorities including other human rights. To make human rights the cornerstone of domestic and foreign policy means determining the often difficult trade-offs that must be made in order to build a just society. There are conflicts between rights, and resolution of such conflicts might require the accommodation of different values. The metaphor of rights as "trumps" that override all competing considerations is only partially useful. Real life is more complex. The UN, for example, has affirmed both a people's right to self-determination and a people's right to development. In the name of self-defense and liberty, an astounding quantity of military weapons have been purchased around the world. Yet, these military expenditures too often impede economic development. Nations with high levels of military spending risk denying their people basic economic rights in the name of military preparedness to protect the right to self-determination and security.

This chapter explores these issues in the following sections:

- the economic effects of military spending and
- human security and positive peace.

The Economic Effects of Military Spending

Boutros Boutros-Ghali, the former UN secretary general, asserts that "development cannot proceed easily in societies where military concerns are at or near the center of life. Societies whose economic effort is given in substantial part to military production inevitably diminish the prospects of their people for development. . . . Preparation for war absorbs inordinate resources and impedes the development of social institutions."[4] Jack Matlock, a former U.S. ambassador to Moscow, made a similar point in relation to the required weapons spending for new members from Eastern Europe joining NATO in the late 1990s: "It's extraordinarily unwise for these countries to shoulder these costs when they must pay the costs of meeting their social needs."[5]

The secretary general and the ambassador argue that excessive military spending represents a structural choice that accords military priorities and arms a higher priority than meeting other basic human needs. Are these distinguished diplomats right? Are there dire economic consequences to high levels of military spending? And if so, what are the human rights implications of militarization?

The economic effects of military spending can vary across countries, and across time within a given country. In addition, different components of military expenditures (i.e., manpower, procurement of high-tech weapons, and so on) can have different economic effects. An added factor, of course, is whether the military spending is financed through raising taxes, cutting non-defense expenditures, printing money, or through borrowing. Each of these financing routes creates its own economic consequences for the nation.

Those who believe that military spending helps the economy often argue that the employment of military personnel and the awarding of defense contracts generate jobs and incomes. These workers spend their incomes, generating more demand, and stimulating economic growth. In addition, military research and development (R&D) creates useful spin-offs to the society as a whole and thus defense technology complements the civilian sector. The military also provides critical vocational and technical training (pilots, technicians, health professionals) and subsidizes education (GI bill), creating skilled workers for the economy. And finally, the military provides a safe and secure environment that is necessary for fostering economic activity and development.

Yet, critics of excessive military spending will point to the opportunity costs of such high expenditures present in two "trade-offs," often characterized as "guns versus butter" and "guns versus investment." The "guns versus butter" argument implies that high military spending is harmful when it is financed by either (a) reducing public expenditures on health, education, and so on, which deprives citizens of basic social welfare protections, or (b) taxing private incomes which leads to a reduction in private consumption and savings, which slows aggregate demand and thus lowers overall economic growth. The "guns versus investment" argument focuses on the negative consequences of financing military spending through either borrowing or printing new money. Military spending financed through an increase in the budget deficit (borrowing) can lead to an increase in interest rates, which discourages private investment.[6] On the other hand, printing new money to finance military spending can create inflationary pressures in the economy which reduces incentives to invest or save. These harmful dynamics of excessive military spending are explored more fully below.

The negative effects of military spending on society overall are often dramatically shown through analysis of the policies of repressive governments in the less developed world—from Myanmar to Iraq (under Saddam Hussein) to Syria. These dictatorial regimes relied on excessive military expenditures to maintain power and exhibited little concern for human rights. But the often detrimental effect of high levels of military spending goes beyond these imperious regimes. Any country that expends a substantial amount of resources on armaments and armies encounters a potential trade-off between assuring economic and social human rights and these high levels of military spending.

Military Spending in the United States

A useful beginning may be made by examining the effect of military spending on the United States, given the high level of U.S. military expenditures. If significant military expenditures have a positive impact on the U.S. economy, it will be difficult to argue that less developed countries (LDCs) should not pursue such policies. This analysis is particularly important given the role of the U.S. in the global economy. What is the relationship between military expenditure and the state of the U.S. economy? Does such spending accelerate or impede the government's ability to respect, protect, and fulfill economic and social human rights?

The horrifying terrorism of September 11, 2001, in New York City, Washington, D.C., and Pennsylvania shocked the world and altered the security framework. Terrorist threats from individuals and transnational organizations have been elevated above other security issues, including nuclear arms control and missile defense. President George W. Bush pledged in his 2002 State of the Union address to spend "whatever it costs to defend our country."[7] The United States—and even the whole world—experienced seemingly unendurable grief for the thousands of innocents murdered by fanatical terrorists. The United States clearly must act to prevent further terrorism and another "September 11th."

As part of the "global war on terror," George W. Bush led the U.S. into wars in Afghanistan and Iraq. The justifications for these military operations have been fully debated and explored elsewhere. The concern here is solely with the overall economic cost of military spending. According to the widely respected Stockholm International Peace Research Institute (SIPRI): "During the eight-year presidency of George W. Bush, US military expenditure increased to the highest level in real terms since World War II."[8]

The year preceding the Bush administration (FY2000), U.S. military expenditure was $294.4 billion. As Bush left office, military expenditure stood at over $616 billion in FY2008. The last budget submitted by the Bush administration for FY2009 pushed military spending over $690 billion.[9] These figures for U.S. military spending more than doubled during the period of 2000–2009. Furthermore, military spending during these years accounted for a rising share of GDP, increasing from 3.0% in 2000 to 4.5% in 2009. National defense represented a significant portion of the federal budget—approximately 21.7% of total government outlays and 55.4% of discretionary spending in 2009.[10]

In 2008 U.S. military spending represented an astounding 41.5% of total world military expenditures. The nearest competitors were China (5.8%), France (4.5%), U.K. (4.5%), and Russia (4.0%). In fact, U.S. military spending in 2008 was more than the total spent by the rest of the top 15 nations combined.[11]

In addition, rather than raising taxes or cutting non-military spending, the Bush administration financed the wars in Iraq and Afghanistan primarily through government borrowing. Such policies contributed significantly to the transformation of an annual budget surplus of $236 billion in FY2000 to an estimated deficit of $407 billion in FY2009. Soaring budget deficits have led to an explosion of the overall U.S. national debt, with the debt nearly doubling from $5.6 trillion in FY2000 to an estimated $10.4 trillion in FY2009, which SIPRI notes, "is equivalent to 69 per cent of GDP."[12]

The ongoing budgetary costs of the wars in Iraq and Afghanistan are severe. In the most detailed economic analysis to date, Joseph Stiglitz, winner of the Nobel Prize in Economics, and Linda Bilmes estimated that the U.S. budgetary costs of the current wars in Iraq and Afghanistan will total approximately $3.5 trillion ($3,496 billion). This figure includes not only the "emergency supplementals" financing U.S. military operations in the two countries in 2001–2007 but also a "realistic-moderate" assessment of future operations and military costs, future veterans' costs (medical, disability, and social security), and past and future interest paid on the debt incurred to finance these wars. Prior to going to war, officials estimated that the costs in Iraq would be around $50 billion. While Americans were mobilized to support the war, there was no discussion of the economic impact of trillions of dollars of military spending over the years on the health of the U.S. economy.[13]

The U.S. government has long relied on the popular belief that the military budget stimulates the economy. The Keynesian "logic" that military spending can prevent a recession or depression has not been challenged by any administration since World War II. The economic prosperity of the United States during that war left a deep impression. In the 1930s, the country experienced the Great Depression, with unemployment rates hovering around 25 percent. In 1944, the unemployment rate dropped to 1.2 percent.[14] The public's willingness to finance a large military establishment is linked to the perception that these expenditures perform a positive overall economic function in the national economy.

Yet, as Joshua S. Goldstein observed, World War II was characterized by special circumstances—physical war destruction took place predominantly on foreign lands, the productive capabilities of key large U.S. competitors were destroyed, and the U.S. and its allies were victorious in the war—and together these yielded unique economic benefits to the U.S. During the war, production surged in the U.S., while falling by over 50% in Germany and France; "the United States captured world markets and reoriented global production, trade and finance around itself, shaping the rules of the game for the post-1945 era."[15]

Moreover, scholars have found little evidence that military spending since the War has performed the Keynesian function of regulating short-term cycles in economic activity. For example, economist David Gold analyzed data for the "ten business cycle troughs since World War II. In only three of these episodes could military spending be characterized as unambiguously strong in terms of fighting the recession and stimulating the economic recovery." He thus found an "absence of any systematic pattern" in military spending counteracting short-term business cycles.[16]

If not a short-term countercyclical tool, has military spending after World War II continued to provide positive stimulation to the U.S. economy, as popularly believed? In a longitudinal analysis of the U.S. analyzing a century of data (1889–1991), Michael D. Ward, David R. Davis, and Corey L. Lofdahl ran a series of regressions, each for forty-year blocks of time. For every forty-year "window" that included any of the World War II years as a subset, their analysis estimated that military spending had a positive direct stimulative effect on economic growth—certainly affirming the very positive economic effects of World War II military spending. Equally compelling, their results also confirmed the uniqueness of the World War II experience for the United States. For those forty-year periods ending prior to 1943 or beginning after 1947 (i.e., periods without World War II years), they estimated the direct effect of U.S. military expenditures on economic growth consistently to be negative.[17]

In addition, with defense spending consuming such a sizeable percentage (22%–29% annually over 1975–1989)[18] of the federal budget, scholars in the 1980s documented the effect of such expenditures on the federal deficit.[19] During the Reagan years, the United States spent $2 trillion on defense while cutting social welfare programs and taxes. The resulting budget deficits, combined with the Federal Reserve's anti-inflationary restrictive monetary policy, yielded high interest rates, rising dollar values, and large trade deficits—which sent the economy spinning. Furthermore, while the United States in the 1980s devoted around 5 to 6.5 percent of its gross national income (GNI) to defense, its major economic competitors, Japan and Germany, allocated a smaller proportion (approximately 1 and 3 percent, respectively).[20] As a result, the United States consistently had (relatively) less capital to invest in civilian industries. Scholars attribute the relative decline of the U.S. global economic position vis-à-vis Japan and Germany from the 1970s to the early 1990s to this draining of scarce capital from productive civilian industries. Goldstein, as part of his extensive long-cycle analysis published in 1988, estimated "as a rough rule of thumb" that every 1% of GNI devoted to military spending reduced economic growth by about a 0.5 percentage point.[21] Moreover, using statistical regression techniques, Ron Smith, for example, analyzed the determinants of investment for fourteen advanced Western economies for the period of 1954–1973. Estimating the ratio of investment to GNI as a function of the GNI growth rate, unemployment, and military expenditure (as a percentage of GNI), he discovered a robust relationship between increases in defense spending and decreases in investment spending, supporting the argument of a trade-off between military spending and economic growth.[22]

The comparative economic performances shifted when events in Germany and Japan by the close of the twentieth century undercut the competitiveness of these economic adversaries. German reunification—in particular the fixation of too high a par value for the East German currency in terms of the West German one—proved extremely costly. Scholars estimated a seemingly perpetual transfer of about 5 percent of gross domestic product (GDP) to pay for reunification.[23] Moreover, the German government financed reunification by borrowing, thus expanding its budget deficits. With the Bundesbank pursuing tight monetary policy to dampen the budget deficits' likely inflationary impact, together this combination of policies yielded high interest rates which discouraged domestic investment and had the impact of reducing German competitiveness. Japan was criticized for "irresponsible" financial and macroeconomic policy that contributed to a speculative bubble in the stock and property markets; the eventual collapse of these overvalued asset values led to years of lackluster economic performance. As a result, the U.S. economic model was seen by pundits and laissez-faire economists as dramatically superior to welfare state economic models.[24]

Yet, according to economist William K. Tabb in 2001, still "the actual performance of [the European and Japanese] economies over the last thirty or forty years . . . has been much stronger than [that of the U.S. economy]. Over the shorter period since the second half of the 1990s, real GNP growth slowed but still increased as much over the decade in the European Union and Japan as in the United States. Taking the longer view, capital stock increased more, as did the productivity of capital employed per worker, and real wages grew faster in these economies than in the United States." Furthermore, the unemployed in Japan and Western Europe received much better benefits than their counterparts in the United States. In fact, as documented in chapter 8, most workers in the United States saw their standard of living decline in the 1980s and 1990s, despite economic growth.[25]

Ron Smith notes that military spending as a percentage of gross domestic product (GDP) is comparable across countries and sometimes referred to as the "military burden." This share of military spending "is a measure of the priority given to defense, the share of output devoted to the military, not military power or the absolute level of military expenditure. If the growth rate of military expenditure is greater than the growth rate of output, the share will rise."[26]

Due to the overall growth of the U.S. economy, by the mid-1990s there was a decline in the proportion of GDP that the United States devoted to defense. Defense spending increased in the 1990s, but the U.S. GDP increased even more. By 2001, the United States devoted about 3.3% of its GDP to defense, the smallest share since 1940. The Clinton and Bush administrations made this fact central to their arguments for increasing the Pentagon's budget. Both the White House and Congress contended that this decline in the ratio of military spending to GDP justified huge increases in the military budget. As Michael O'Hanlon, a senior fellow at the Brookings Institution, wrote: "Besides, American defense spending— at 3 percent of our gross domestic product—is not unreasonably high. As a percentage of GDP, it was twice as high in the Reagan years and three times as high during the 1950s and 1960s."[27] As we saw above, in 2009 U.S. military spending had grown to 4.5% of its GDP. Defense Secretary Robert Gates and Admiral Mike Mullen argued that even after the wars in Iraq and Afghanistan end, military spending should not drop below 4% of GDP. In February 2008, Geoff Morrell, the Pentagon press secretary stated: "The secretary [Gates] believes that whenever we transition away from war supplements, the Congress should dedicate 4% of our GDP to funding national security. That is what he believes to be a reasonable price to stay free and protect our interests around the world."[28]

The logic of this argument is most peculiar. Its singular focus on this sole yardstick—U.S. defense spending as a percent of the U.S. GDP—misleads and misdirects policy makers and the public. First, as retired Lieutenant Colonel Sayen (U.S. Marine Corps) suggests, "the military budget might instead be determined by the military needs of the nation (the determination of which requires looking outward at potential threats) more than an arbitrarily determined portion of its economy." Assessing threats, prioritizing strategic objectives, and weighing alternative military programs and weapon systems (in terms of both their effectiveness and costs) are essential to designing the most appropriate military as well as to promote sound fiscal management for the nation. Indeed, in his September 2008 speech at the National Defense University, Defense Secretary Gates expressed the importance of such careful planning. He said, "The defining principle driving our strategy is balance. I note at the outset that balance is not the same as treating all challenges as having equal priority. We cannot expect to eliminate risk through higher defense budgets, to, in effect 'do everything, buy everything.'" He continued, "Resources are scarce—and yes, it is a sign I've already been at the Pentagon for too long to say that with a straight face when talking about a half trillion dollar base budget. Nonetheless, we still must set priorities and consider inescapable tradeoffs and opportunity costs."[29]

Second, the argument ignores current comparisons between the United States and its military competitors. Some competitors spend a greater percentage of their national wealth on defense than does the United States, but the absolute level of spending is much lower than that of the United States (as the budget figures on China and Russia quoted earlier demonstrate). Third, this argument dismisses key comparisons between the United States and its economic competitors. The World Bank, for example, reported that in 2007 the United States spent a considerably higher percentage (4.2%) of its GDP on defense than any of its key economic rivals. The United Kingdom, for example, was spending 2.5% of GDP, China 2.0%, Brazil 1.6%, Germany 1.3%, Canada 1.3%, Japan 0.9%, and so on.[30] To stay economically competitive, the United States must pay attention to infrastructure, debt reduction, health care reform, and technology research. Military investments compete for scarce resources with these and other key economic areas. Many scholars and diplomats believe that the critical strategic competition in the world today is in the economic realm and not the military arena. If so, the United States should be pursuing a strategy of reducing its defense GDP share as far as military security obligations will allow. From a political realist position, this also makes sense, since the long-term military strength of the United States depends on a healthy economy.[31]

There are two key points here: the enormity of the military budget and the economic difference between expenditure and productive investment.[32] Key economic thinkers have long viewed military expenditures as an impediment to economic progress because they are merely outlays for goods and services and not investments. Adam Smith in *The Wealth of Nations* probably said it best: "The whole army and navy are unproductive labourers. They are the servants of the public, and are maintained by a part of the annual produce of the industry of other people. Their service, how honourable, how useful, or how necessary soever, produces nothing for which an equal quantity of service can afterwards be procured."[33] Military expenditures are designed to meet an immediate goal. Investments, on the other hand, are designed to increase future resources. Military R&D has created well-publicized inventions and technological innovations of benefit to the civilian economy. But overall, excessive military spending and the diversion of significant amounts of national resources toward nonproductive military expenditures can result in a long-term decline in productive capacity and efficiency.

A key factor in the decline in the living standards of most Americans since the 1970s (as documented in chapter 8) is the amount of capital spent for nonproductive military purposes. Lloyd J. Dumas calculated that in 1990 as the Cold War was concluding, the Department of Defense owned physical capital ("plant equipment, structures, weapons, and related equipment and supplies") with a value equal to more than 80% of the U.S. manufacturing sector's capital equipment and structures.[34] A sizeable portion of these capital expenditures could otherwise have been invested in innovating, expanding, and upgrading civilian productive facilities. Instead, the U.S. experienced a relative decline in competitiveness. For the five largest Western economies, Goldstein reported a negative correlation between military expenditures (as a proportion of GDP) and productivity growth (i.e., increases in GDP per employed person) for 1973–1983. The cross-country variation in average annual productivity growth during this period was notable: only 0.3% in the U.S. in contrast to 1.4% (U.K.), 2.2% (France), 2.3% (West Germany), and 2.8% (Japan).[35] Moreover, concerning the manufacturing sector, for much of the Cold War, manufacturing productivity growth in most European nations averaged twice the U.S. rate, and in Japan was often three times that of the United States.[36]

Investment and R&D are key factors in productivity growth. Yet, during the Cold War years, U.S. military R&D expenditures were high. In the early 1960s federal defense R&D outlays amounted to over 40% of all U.S. R&D expenditures. These federal outlays increased (in total dollars) over the decades, then nearly doubled in real value during the Reagan years; and although their relative share of total U.S. R&D declined after the early 1960s, the percentage remained sizable—still ranging from 22% to 29% of total U.S. R&D over the period 1973–1989.[37] Moreover, in specific fields the percentage was even greater, with the Department of Defense funding about half of U.S. R&D in aerospace and a third of that in electronics.[38] As Robert W. DeGrasse Jr. noted, "Since the military stresses high performance over cost, technologies developed for the military are often too expensive and complex for widespread civilian use. Many of those that do have civilian application . . . had to undergo significant redesign before they were commercially viable."[39] Thus, the prospects of military R&D developing cost-effective techniques or positive technological spinoffs were limited. Furthermore, the military sector competed for technological resources that could otherwise be productively employed in the civilian sector. Indeed, U.S. military R&D and arms production diverted engineers and scientists from civilian projects. Estimates suggest the military sector hired around half of the scientists and engineers in the U.S. during the late 1950s, and around thirty percent over the entire Cold War period.[40] Some of the brightest, most highly skilled people thus did not work directly to increase the productivity and competitiveness of the nation's civilian sector.[41]

Academic studies from the 1980s through the 2000s provide evidence of a complex relationship between military spending and economic growth, as the economic effects of military spending can vary across countries and even within a country across time and different contexts. While there is not a universal relationship, many analyses demonstrate military spending often has a negative effect directly and/or indirectly on economic growth. In his 1985 survey article, Steve Chan, for example, concluded that the evidence is clear for advanced Western economies: military spending does not encourage or facilitate sustained economic growth. In the long run, "these expenditures are more apt to have a negative than a positive impact on investment, inflation, employment, balance of payments, industrial productivity, and economic growth. The evidence on the United States . . . indicates especially significant costs in these regards." He concluded, "Heavy defense spending seems to have a particularly important impact in dampening capital formation and investment, which in turn reduces economic growth in the long run." Chan also noted the "customary preference of officials to finance defense and war by running budget deficits rather than by cutting other programs or raising taxes, [with] much of the cost of this spending shifted to future generations."[42]

In a 1998 study, Uk Heo used thirty-year longitudinal data (generally, 1961–1990) for 80 countries, and estimated a nonlinear model incorporating technological progress to investigate military spending's "direct and immediate effects" on economic growth. His analysis demonstrated that military expenditures had a negative effect in 50 (63%) of the countries (including the United States), a positive effect in only 24 (30%) of the cases, and an inelastic relationship in the remaining six countries. He concluded an "increased defense burden is more likely to deter economic growth"; and conversely, "two thirds of the countries under investigation may expect some kind of a peace dividend, which suggests that defense cutbacks are desirable."[43] In further analysis, Uk Heo and Robert J. Eger III estimated a highly sophisticated multi-equation model using 1951 to 2000 data for the United States. They found that U.S. military spending not only had a negative direct effect on economic growth but also negative indirect and dynamic effects by decreasing investment after a year's lag and decreasing exports immediately through a year later.[44] An earlier two-equation analysis by Alex Mintz and Chi Huang using 1953–1987 data also demonstrated that U.S. military spending had a delayed negative effect on investment (after five years, in their study); Mintz and Huang concluded that "the impact of increased levels of military spending is to significantly decrease investment in the long run" and thereby have a long-term negative effect on economic growth.[45]

Of additional relevance for the United States is Heo's finding that in countries with a high defense burden, military expenditures were more likely to exhibit a negative effect on economic growth. Specifically, his 1998 analysis of 80 countries demonstrated economic effects were negative for 56% of those countries whose military spending was less than 3% of GDP, for 65% of the countries spending 3%–5% of GDP, and for 90% of those spending more than 5% of GDP on the military.[46] These results support the economic desirability of the U.S. keeping its defense burden low.

Dumas's "theory of resource diversion" recognizes that the central purpose of economic activity is to "provide for the material well-being of the population as a whole." A healthy economy produces and distributes consumer goods and services to satisfy material needs (e.g., refrigerators) and producer goods (e.g., machinery and transport equipment) to contribute to the production of future material well-being. Goods or services that do not contribute to material well-being are opportunities lost and therefore represent economic costs. The production of military goods and services is a "noncontributive activity." Of course, national security is a public good that offers substantial benefits, but Dumas's distinction identifies an important opportunity cost of military expenditures. An economy that is persistently dominated by military production will divert critical economic resources to noncontributive activities and experience a long-term decline in productivity. Investment to improve efficiency in the civilian sector will have been stifled.[47] This tendency for defense activities to divert resources away from public and private investments more able to promote growth leads Todd Sandler and Keith Hartley to conclude that the overall impact of military spending on economic growth is negative.[48] When defense activities take scarce resources, including R&D funds, from private investment, long-term growth is impeded.

Many argue that high levels of military spending create jobs. However, according to Robert W. DeGrasse Jr. in 1983, "most industries selling to the Pentagon create fewer jobs per dollar spent than the average industry in the American economy." DeGrasse documented for 1979 that "seven of the 11 manufacturing industries selling the greatest volume of goods to the military—create fewer jobs per dollar than the median manufacturing industry."[49] Three simulations performed in the 1960s and 1970s demonstrated that transferring military expenditures to either civilian government spending or tax cuts (generating additional private spending) created higher employment. An input-output analysis in the early 1980s calculated that shifting $62.9 billion from military purchases to personal consumption expenditures would create an additional 1.5 million jobs.[50] Moreover, the Congressional Budget Office of the U.S. Congress, using two different models of the U.S. economy, concluded in 1992 that the use of the peace dividend to reduce the federal deficit would benefit the economy in the long run.[51]

There is another indirect negative effect of military spending. Alex Mintz and Chi Huang, for example, analyze the indirect impact of arms expenditures on education spending. Their empirical study indicates no negative short-term effects but demonstrates a significant indirect long-term trade-off between spending on defense and on education. The negative effect on education was felt to be attributable to the impact of military policies on investment and growth. Over a "longer time period, military spending crowds out investment, which reduces growth, thereby affecting the amount the government spends on education programs."[52]

And how about now? What are the likely economic effects of multi-year U.S. intervention (war and occupation) in Iraq and Afghanistan? A sophisticated simulation using the Global Insight macroeconomic model forecasts long-run negative impacts. The model begins with an estimate, based on recent budget figures and Congressional Budget Office spending projections, that the additional military spending for these interventions amounts to approximately 1% of GDP per year. The simulation then projects that sustaining this additional military spending annually, without raising taxes, will yield a demand stimulus at first, but then due to higher inflation and interest rates, will discourage investment, reduce economic growth, and increase trade deficits and unemployment. For example, it projects reduced sales in interest-rate sensitive sectors (cars, trucks, new housing construction, and existing housing market) after five, ten, fifteen, and twenty years. As for employment, the model projects jobs will be higher after five years (by 178,700), but then the additional military spending generates unemployment, with jobs less than the baseline scenario by 464,000, 515,300, and 668,100 after ten, fifteen, and twenty years, respectively.[53]

Of further consideration in identifying military spending's economic effects is the extensively documented and widely reported issue of Pentagon waste. Pervasive are Pentagon budget overspending, ineffective and wasteful use of taxpayer resources, and even graft and fraud—which are a disgrace and harmful to the security of the United States. The U.S. General Accounting Office (GAO) in January 2009 identified thirty federal government programs and operations as "at high risk because of vulnerabilities to fraud, waste, abuse, and mismanagement"; half (15) of these "high-risk areas" fall under sole or partial Department of Defense (DOD) responsibility.[54] One of these areas is weapon systems acquisitions, which the GAO has repeatedly listed as "high risk" for the past two decades. In a March 2009 report, the GAO noted "a broad consensus exists that weapon system problems are serious, but efforts at reform have had limited effect." Among the problems, the GAO found the "DOD allows programs to begin development without a full understanding of require-ments and the resources needed to execute them. The lack of early sys-tems engineering, acceptance of unreliable cost estimates based on overly optimistic assumptions, failure to commit full funding, and the addition of new requirements well into the acquisition cycle all contribute to poor outcomes. Moreover, DOD officials are rarely held accountable for poor decisions or poor program outcomes."[55]

The weapons procurement system lacks the necessary systematic checks to ensure the production of military weapons systems is efficient and effectively meets the security needs of the nation. Instead, the pattern is for the DOD to propose and Congress to approve funding for the produc-tion of new military equipment and weapons systems, *prior* to proper and sufficient engineering analyses and tests verifying the designed system's functionality. In effect, the government agrees to buy multi-billion-dollar weapon systems before knowing if the designs are functional—that is, whether the final equipment, once produced, will operate and effectively perform the intended purpose. And the result, perhaps not surprisingly, is a pervasive pattern during the production process of costly redesign, reworking, and repairing this expensive highly sophisticated equipment. The GAO's seventh annual assessment of DOD weapon programs issued in March 2009 reported that the DOD's 96 defense acquisition programs represented a commitment of $1.6 trillion as of 2008. The GAO estimated the costs for these programs had increased by $296.5 billion, or 25%, over the initial total acquisition cost estimates. Such budgetary cost overruns have become characteristic of U.S. weapon development programs, with an estimated 42% of the 2008 programs experiencing at least 25% cost growth.[56] Also, the typical mid-production interruptions unavoidably lead to time delays in the final delivery of the promised weapon systems. For the 2008 program commitments the average schedule delay in deliv-ering initial capabilities was estimated to be 22 months, or nearly two years; as of December 2007, 12 major weapon programs were planning to be late between 25 to 48 months, and another 10 programs expected to be late by more than 48 months, or 4 years. The GAO explained the significance of these time delays. "Acquisition delays can lead to loss of program credibility with stakeholders, increased acquisition costs, new systems not being available to meet the needs of warfighters during combat operations, and the continued use of less capable systems with questionable reliability and high operating costs."[57]

Moreover, once built, a high proportion of the weapon systems in recent years have failed performance tests. As reported by the Defense Science Board, from 2001 through 2006 "approximately 50% of the pro-grams" tested by the DOD in Initial Operational Test & Evaluation were assessed as not operationally effective and/or suitable. These programs were found deficient mainly in Reliability, Availability, and Maintainability (RAM). Of the 228 army systems that completed operational testing from 1997 to 2006, 153 (67%) failed reliability.[58] As this evidence suggests, the wasteful, expensive process that misspends billions of dollars each year is certainly not generating development of the most effective military capability.

Fostering these inefficiencies is a system characterized by insufficient monitoring and enforcement, conflicts of interest and lack of accountability. For instance, at the time of funding proposal, what incentive is there for military officials to reveal the true costs of developing new weapon systems and possibly lose financial support for favorite projects? Or for congressional representatives to require proper testing before funding, and accept delay and possibly eventually canceled production, jobs, and incomes for their districts? Moreover, the ability of former Pentagon and military officials to work in the defense industry and of private defense contractors to perform select government functions (e.g., developing contract requirements) is widely identified as leading to a "revolving door" that generates conflicts of interest.[59] Some well-publicized cases of fraud suggest the risks.

Moreover, the Pentagon's accounting systems do not enable adequate tracking of expenditures or inventory. The Pentagon's own inspector general reported in March 2000 that only $2.6 trillion of a total of $6.9 trillion in accounting entries could be fully documented. Furthermore, $2.3 trillion worth of entries were "not supported by adequate audit trails or sufficient evidence to determine their validity."[60] The U.S. General Accounting Office (GAO) found that the Defense Department cannot "account for billions of dollars of inventory and national defense assets, primarily weapons systems and support equipment." In addition, the GAO determined that the Pentagon already had $37 billion worth of paraphernalia it does not need.[61] Experts estimate that an astounding 70 percent of the defense budget is spent on overhead and infrastructure, with only 30 percent reaching the combat forces in the field. No city in America would allow 7 out of 10 police officers to sit at their desks pushing paper. While the private sector can replace parts in two days, it takes the Pentagon up to three weeks. The list of waste and inefficiency goes on and on.[62]

This squandering of the country's wealth is reminiscent of the extravagant and unrestrained practices of the top-down bureaucracies of the former Soviet Union. Such unchecked, unaccountable, and wasteful actions finally exhausted the Soviet economy. On a daily basis, Pentagon waste pulls down and dampens the U.S. economy.

In summary, there are at least three different ways that excessive military spending restricts economic growth in the United States: first, it leads to a decrease in investment and thus retards the expansion of civilian industry; second, it leads to lower employment and an inefficient use of labor resources; and third, it takes resources away from civilian research and development, impeding nonmilitary innovation and growth and siphoning off highly qualified engineers and labor from the civilian sector.

Military Spending in the Developing World

Excessive military spending, of course, is a global phenomenon. Expensive and sophisticated weapons are sought and purchased everywhere in the name of security and self-determination. As previously noted, world military expenditures in 2008 were estimated to total $1,464 billion, a 45% increase over the period 1999–2008. During that ten-year period, regional military expenditures rose dramatically as well with increases of 94% in North Africa, 50% in South America, 56% in East Asia, 41% in South Asia, and 174% in Eastern Europe.[63] Some of the poorest countries are among those that spend more on military than on education and health. While military spending remains high in these poor countries, investments in areas of human welfare and social and economic security remain low. Consider, for example, the following 2006 public expenditures: Pakistan spent 3.8% of its GDP on its military and only 0.3% on health; the Syrian Arab Republic spent 5.3% of its GDP on military and only 1.9% on education; and Angola spent 3.5% of its GDP on military and only 2.3% on health.[64]

However, at the beginning of the twenty-first century, the UN calculated that in developing countries, the chances of dying from social neglect (from malnutrition and preventable diseases) were around thirty-three times greater than the chances of dying in a war from external aggression.[65] Yet, U.S. arms and military aid continue to flow to countries that face no significant external enemy. As a consequence, too often these well-stocked military forces become instruments for ruling elites to maintain control through internal repression (as was tragically demonstrated in Guatemala throughout the 1980s).

The human cost of excessive military spending in developing countries is enormous. The UN estimated in the mid-1990s that 12 percent of military spending in developing countries could provide funds for primary health care for all, including immunization of all children, elimination of severe malnutrition, reduction of moderate malnutrition by half, and provision of safe drinking water for all. Four percent could reduce adult illiteracy by half by providing universal primary education and educating women to the same level as men. Eight percent could provide basic family planning to all and stabilize the world population by 2015.[66]

As we saw in relation to developed countries, the economic effects of military spending among LDCs can also vary across countries, and across time within a given country. As discussed above, military expenditures can generate jobs and income, and military R&D can potentially create positive spin-offs to society overall. In LDCs, the military can also provide critical vocational and technical training and create skilled workers for the economy. Yet, excessive military spending in LDCs will also lead to the previously described "trade-offs," often characterized as "guns versus butter" and "guns versus investment," and thus serve to harm human development.

There is a considerable debate in the economics literature over the impact of military spending on LDCs. After surveying the many applied and empirical studies on such spending, J. Paul Dunne in 1996 concluded that "while there is no clear consensus on the economic effects of military spending [in LDCs], the most common finding is that [the] military burden has either no significant effect, or a negative effect on economic growth." These results suggested to Dunne "that disarmament need not be costly, and can indeed provide an opportunity for improved economic performance."[67]

In fact, excessive military spending and war preparation in poor countries has contributed to insecurity and actual conflict. Since World War II, the armed conflicts of the world have occurred overwhelmingly in the poor countries, and the devastation of war has been felt by the world's poorest people. For example, the World Bank reported that during 1987–1997 more than 85 percent of all world conflicts were fought within national borders—fourteen were in Africa, fourteen in Asia, and one in Europe. Ninety percent of the war deaths during this time period were civilians. In Rwanda, approximately 800,000 Tutsis and moderate Hutus were killed by Hutu extremists in 1994. These internal wars crippled national economies; public spending was diverted from productive activities and investments often ceased. Skilled workers emigrated abroad. Economists estimate that in a civil war a country's per capita output falls an average of more than 2 percent a year relative to what it would have been without the conflict. The human costs are even greater, especially on the children.[68]

The impact of excessive military spending on the poorest countries thus has the most profound of consequences. As with the United States, such unchecked military spending in the poor countries can divert scarce resources away from productive investment, lower employment, and take resources away from civilian research and development. This can result in a diversion of resources away from sanitation, education, health care, and so on. But the repercussions of militarism dominating these poorest countries goes much further. The internal violence and bloodshed spawned by militarist policies often ravage and overwhelm entire societies.

Costa Rica provides an alternative approach. Costa Rica's success in human development stems from its refusal to accept the "commonsense" security framework that leads nations to develop extensive armies and expensive armaments. For over half a century, Costa Rica has been without an army. Despite its lower-middle-income status, Costa Rica has been able to attain social indicators close to those of an industrialized country, as demonstrated in the following three tables. Table 7.1 presents the ratio of military to social spending in Costa Rica and Latin America; table 7.2 compares key human development indicators for Costa Rica and Latin America; and table 7.3 summarizes primary human development indicators for Costa Rica and Central America.

Since President Figueres abolished the army in 1949, Costa Rica has been able to focus on investments in human development. As seen in table 7.1, these priorities remain. In 2006, while spending basically 0.0% of its GDP on the military, Costa Rica's public expenditures in health and education as a percentage of GDP were 5.3% and 4.7%, respectively. In Latin America as a whole, on the other hand, public expenditures in health and education as a percentage of GDP totaled only 0.7% in health and 3.5% in education. In 2006, the ratio of military to social spending (calculated as military expenditures as a percentage of the combined education and health expenditure) was 28.6% for all of Latin America and the Caribbean—and 0.0% for Costa Rica!

Freed of an oppressive military burden, Costa Rica has for decades invested heavily in human development and the protection and fulfil-

Table 7.1. Public Spending Priorities: Costa Rica and Latin America

	2002	2004	2006
Costa Rica			
Public Spending (% of GDP) on:			
Health[a]	5.7	5.1	5.3
Education[a]	5.1	4.9	4.7
Military[b]	0.0	0.0	0.0
Military Spending as a % of Health & Education			
Spending	0.0	0.0	0.0
Latin America & Caribbean			
Public Spending (% of GDP) on:			
Health[a]	1.1	0.8	0.7
Education[a]	4.3	4.0	3.5
Military[a]	1.4	1.2	1.2
Military Spending as a % of Health & Education			
Spending	25.9	25.0	28.6

Sources: [a]World Bank, World Development Indicators Online, The World Bank Group, 2007, at www.worldbank.org (accessed 28 July 2009); [b]United Nations Development Program (UNDP), *Human Development Reports* (New York: UNDP, yearly).

ment of economic and social human rights. This has resulted in Costa Rica ranking near the top in Latin America in human development. Costa Rica's success is directly linked to its spending priorities. Public spending for all of its social programs, including health, education, water and sewerage, and so on, averaged from 20 to almost 24 percent of its GDP throughout the 1980s and 1990s.[69] Costa Rica frees resources to address the economic and social needs of its people by refusing to militarize its society. At the beginning of the twenty-first century, while spending over 20 percent on social programs, Costa Rica spends minimally on its military.[70] As seen in table 7.2 the results are simply stunning. Since 1960, compared to all of Latin America, Costa Rica has notably lower infant mortalities, longer life expectancy rates, lower illiteracy rates, and much greater access to sanitation facilities.

The Costa Rican success is perhaps most clearly seen in relation to its neighbors, countries of similar size and factor endowments. Table 7.3 contrasts key human development indicators for the five nations of Central

Table 7.2. Human Development in Costa Rica and Latin America

Mortality and Life Expectancy	*1960*	*1985*	*1995*	*2005*
# of Infants Who Die Before One Year old (per 1,000 live births)				
Costa Rica	87	20	14	11
Latin America & Caribbean	110	52	36	24
# of Children Expected to Die by Age Five (per 1,000 live births)				
Costa Rica	123	23	16	12
Latin America & Caribbean	155	67	45	29
# of Years of Life Expectancy at Birth				
Costa Rica	62	75	77	79
Latin America & Caribbean	56	67	70	73

Social Indicators	*1995*	*2006–2007*
% of Adults (age 15 and above) Who Are Illiterate		
Costa Rica	n/a	4
Latin America & Caribbean	n/a	9
% of Population with Access to Improved Water Source		
Costa Rica	96	98
Latin America & Caribbean	87	91
% of Population with Access to Improved Sanitation Facilities		
Costa Rica	95	96
Latin America & Caribbean	72	78

Source: World Bank, World Development Indicators Online, The World Bank Group, 2007 at www.worldbank.org (accessed 31 July 2009).
n/a = data not available

**Table 7.3. Human Development in Central America:
The Costa Rican Success**

	Costa Rica	El Salvador	Guatemala	Honduras	Nicaragua
Probability at birth of not surviving to age 40 (% of cohort), 2000–2005	3.7	9.6	12.5	12.9	9.5
Adult illiteracy rate (% aged 15 and older), 1995–2005	5.1	19.4	30.9	20.0	23.3
Population not using improved water source (%), 2004	3	16	5	13	21
Children under weight for age (% under age 5), 1996–2005	5	10	23	17	10
Births attended by skilled health personnel (%), 1997–2005	99	92	41	56	67
Under-five mortality rate (per 1,000 live births), 2005	12	27	43	40	37

Source: United Nations Development Program (UNDP), *Human Development Report
2007/2008* (New York: Palgrave Macmillan, 2007), 238–240, 247–249, 261–263.

America. The results are startling. For example, in 2005 the under-five
mortality rate per 1,000 live births was 43 in Guatemala but only 12 in
Costa Rica. Betweeen 1997 and 2005, 99% of all births in Costa Rica were
attended by skilled health personnel, while only 56% of mothers in Hon-
duras and only 41% in Guatemala received such care. In 2004, 21% of the
population in Nicaragua did not have access to an improved water source,
while in Costa Rica only 3% lacked safe water. Costa Rica demonstrates
that it is possible for a nation to successfully provide public goods and
promote economic equality through prioritizing spending in health, education, sanitation, and other social programs.

Human Security and Positive Peace

The attitudes that sustain large military forces and deadly armaments did not fall with the Berlin Wall. The logic is mesmerizing: The world is a dangerous place divided into sovereign nation-states, each seeking to improve its position in an anarchic international system. There are few opportunities for cooperation. Each state maintains the right to be free from the scrutiny and intervention of other states in its internal affairs. Each nation is surrounded by danger and must protect itself to survive, which gives rise to a preoccupation with power, particularly military power. Internalizing this acute sense of danger makes it easier to accept high taxation to pay for excessive military expenditures, often at the expense of social development. Yet, such heavy military spending in the name of security can backfire and instead create a condition of insecurity and conflict. Furthermore, such expenditures can limit the ability of nations to fulfill other international human rights, in particular economic and social rights. "Security" defined solely as the heavily armed defense of one's borders can subvert the secure lives of the people living within those borders. How does a nation provide a basic right to physical security without compromising other human rights?

Feminist researchers and peace studies scholars distinguish between negative peace and positive peace. Negative peace and negative security stem from a desire to inhibit the existence of a destructive entity. Deterrence and the conventional "realist" power-politics paradigm are examples of negative peace. Here, security is the result of canceling one threat by another: threats and counterthreats cancel out the actual use of force and create "negative" peace. The goal is to be able to threaten someone else, as in a householder's purchase of a gun for protection from crime. A secure state is therefore one that is able to counter any military threat it may face. Negative peace refers to the absence of war and other direct violence.[71]

Positive peace and positive security, on the other hand, reflect the desire to eliminate the threat by addressing its cause. The objective is not to counter the threat but to end all threats by addressing the source of the problem. The goal is to cure the disease rather than to simply address its symptoms. Central to positive peace is not just the absence of war and violence, but also the protection of human rights and social justice. The elimination of underdevelopment and institutionalized poverty are considered signs of peace.[72] Positive security, for example, would embrace serious arms control negotiations and agreements. The proliferation of all types of arms (conventional, biological, chemical and nuclear) makes conflict more volatile and escalation more likely. When the U.S., Russian, French, British, and German governments subsidize arms exporters and fail to take the lead in disarmament measures, they exacerbate the threat and undercut their own security.

In the pursuit of positive peace, territorial security is seen as only a component of a people's overall security needs, which are conceptualized to include both security through armaments and security through sustainable human development. The *1994 Human Development Report,* for example, outlines seven main categories of threats to human security: economic, food, health, environmental, personal, community, and political. The critical security threats are often poverty and malnutrition, inadequate education, environmental degradation, population pressures, and inadequate health care.[73] Proponents of positive peace describe conditions of insecurity in pollution, war, sickness, oppression, and poverty. Peace is thus not merely the resolution of isolated conflicts and a return to a prewar condition. Rather, peace involves attention to conditions of cultural destruction, malnutrition, disease, poverty, and discrimination based on race, gender, and sexual orientation. Peace studies therefore focus not only on rights to self-determination and freedom, but on economic and social human rights as well.

A human rights agenda can also only be implemented within a framework of positive peace. Excessive military spending, based on the idea of negative peace, has led to neither peace nor stability. In fact, an overemphasis on military superiority can undermine attempts to build regimes of trust and harmony among the world's nations. Large militaries and extensive arms programs are usually symptoms of deep conflict. The underlying causes of these conflicts are not addressed through further military spending. Arms control and disarmament and the demobilization of armed forces are therefore often prerequisites to providing a cooperative framework within which nations may pursue the implementation of international human rights law.

International security and stability are dependent on domestic security and stability. The roots of conflict within domestic societies are often the result of economic, social, and environmental pressures that cause poverty and unemployment and pit one community, class, sex, or ethnic group against another. Human rights as the core of domestic and foreign public policy can provide a route for the achievement of peace and stability. Preoccupations with "balance of power" and military prowess can only continue to produce a world of insecurity and war. Policies based on outmoded notions of realpolitik (i.e., power politics) exacerbate insecurities. The irony is that human rights policies and the provision of global public goods offer the clearest road to achieve the "realist" objectives of security and stability. Long-term interests in international stability should compel governments to explore human security and positive peace.

It is commonly accepted that totalitarianism and human rights are incompatible. The negative impact of excessive military spending on basic human rights must also be understood. The collective human right to self-determination and the individual human right to personal security are fundamental needs of every human community. For this reason, proposals for immediate and unilateral disarmament consistently fail. As long as societies and individuals feel threatened, the need will be felt to possess armaments to keep aggressors at bay. But steps could be taken to limit excessive military spending which, as we have seen, causes so many problems in developed and developing nations. Moreover, to move towards positive peace, successful multilateral disarmament requires mutual trust and a sense of common security. Key to the effort of establishing positive peace is to curb the massive arms sales that promote larger and larger military budgets. Actions to limit arms sales are a critical first step toward the creation of frameworks of trust and common security.

Limiting Arms Sales

The sheer volume of arms sales by the U.S., the world's largest arms supplier, is staggering. In 2007, the U.S. accounted for over 45% of all weapons transferred globally. U.S. Foreign Military Sales (FMS) totaled over $23 billion in 2007 and $32 billion in 2008. By 2007, the U.S. was selling weapons to over 174 states and territories, including the Democratic Republic of the Congo, Liberia, Indonesia, Iraq, Afghanistan, India, Kyrgyzstan, Pakistan, and Uzbekistan. The U.S. has sold weapons to undemocratic regimes and human rights abusers. Such actions often fuel regional arms races and promote the very instablity they are intended to reduce.[74]

It has proven to be very difficult to curb the U.S. weapons industry. This was dramatically demonstrated in 1997 when the Clinton administration decided to lift a nineteen-year-old ban on weapon sales to Latin America. Reversing the ban imposed by President Jimmy Carter in 1978, the administration announced that it would now allow arms sales on a case-by-case basis. The reversal was a huge victory for military contractors like the Lockheed Martin Corporation and the McDonnel Douglas Corporation.[75] From Thucydides to present-day political scientists, it has been noted that the influx of new weapons into a region sets off arms races and rekindles traditional rivalries. Nations either acquire arms or form alliances with distant states to balance out the perceived military power of their neighbors. The Clinton administration, however, in an Orwellian twist, asserted the opposite: its spokesperson claimed that lifting the ban would stabilize the region and promote democracy. Instead, it stimulated an arms race; as we saw above, military spending in Latin America increased 50% between 1998 and 2008.[76]

According to William Hartung and Frida Berrigan, "[m]ore than half (13) of the top 25 U.S. arms recipients in the developing world during

2006/07 were either undemocratic governments or regimes that engaged in major human rights abuses. . . . Total U.S. arms transfers to undemocratic governments and/or major human rights abusers totaled more than $16.2 billion in 2006/07." Hartung and Berrigan note further that "of the 27 major conflicts under way during 2006/07, 20 involved one or more parties that had received arms and training from the United States." An additional negative and tragic consquence of the massive U.S. arms sales abroad is the "boomerang" effect. This occurs when U.S. weapons and technology fall into the hands of adversaries and terrorists, as happened in Afghanistan, Iran, and Iraq.[77]

These arms sales are usually justified by political and strategic foreign policy priorities, often framed in terms of "balance of power" objectives. But, economic arguments are also utilized. For example, in 1992, President George H.W. Bush lobbied for the sales of F-16 combat aircraft to Taiwan and F-15 jets to Saudi Arabia by stating that "in these times of economic transition, I want to do everything I can to keep Americans at work." The negative, strategic consequences of Bush's actions were severe. The F-16 sales to Taiwan provoked China to pull out of talks at the UN Security Council aimed at limiting weapons transfers to regions of conflict around the world.[78]

U.S. taxpayer money supports this weapons trade. In 2001, for example, the arms industry received approximately $7.5 billion in federal support including grants, subsidized loans, and marketing assistance. This represented the second largest subsidy program for business in the federal budget (after agricultural price supports). A first step toward limiting arms sales is to end these corporate subsidies. This will not be easy. The weapons industry fights hard to keep its privileges and government largess. In the 1990s, these international arms dealers poured more than $59 million into federal campaigns. Such investments continue to bring dividends. In November 2000, Congress quietly passed a bill that would give $300 million in new tax breaks to U.S. arms exporters—on top of the $7.5 billion federal support they already received.[79]

The consequences of these arms sales abroad are shameful. U.S. arms were supplied to Saddam Hussein in Iraq and to Osama bin Laden while he was organizing al-Qaeda.[80] U.S. weapons transfers have supported brutal dictators from the Shah of Iran to Ferdinand Marcos in the Philippines to Mobutu in Zaire (Democratic Republic of the Congo). U.S. weapons helped arm the Guatemalan death squads and the Somali warlords, including Siad Barre. Weapon sales to governments who abuse the human rights of their people are a moral disgrace. It is shameful for U.S. taxpayer money to subsidize such sales.

A legitimate use of taxpayer money, on the other hand, would be to help the arms industry convert to production for peaceful ends, transforming these military industries to civilian enterprises. The government can play a key role in helping industries make this transformation. This process can begin with restrictions placed on arms exports. Such weapons sales can no longer be justified as a means of preserving jobs and stemming economic decline. Clearly, cooperative security, positive peace, and human development are not enhanced by the sale of high-tech weapons systems. Our advanced defense technologies can be redirected toward productive civilian ends.[81]

Positive Peace and Human Security

The demise of the former USSR and the end of the Cold War created wide expectations for a reduction in world military spending and the emergence of new cooperative global security agreements. However, terrorist attacks in nations around the world, wars in Afghanistan and Iraq, numbing violence in the Congo and Sudan, and the seemingly perpetual conflict between the Palestinians and Israelis dashed these hopes. As a result, excessive levels of military spending continue to infect every continent and appear to be on a perpetual upward spiral.

However, as we have seen throughout this chapter, real human security cannot be attained through armies and armaments alone, and instead requires that attention also be paid to global public goods, including health and environmental security, rebuilding decaying infrastructure, and so on. It is possible, for example, for the U.S. to maintain adequate military forces to protect against all conceivable threats from national military organizations and independent terrorist groups while redirecting resources away from expensive and outdated military programs and arms and toward human development. For example, Business Leaders for Sensible Priorities (BLSP) is an organization committed to changing U.S. government spending priorities that they believe are undermining economic security. This organization is made up of over 650 of the most successful business leaders in the country. These top American businesspeople believe that federal government spending priorities are undermining U.S. national security. BLSP members include present or former CEOs of Bell Industries, Black Entertainment Television, Goldman Sachs, Men's Wearhouse, and Phillips Van Heusen. These business professionals describe how reductions in Pentagon spending can enhance economic security while still protecting America's borders. For example, the BLSP note that by eliminating 6,500 nuclear weapons (which still leaves the U.S. nuclear arsenal with the equivalent of 23,000 Hiroshima bombs) the U.S. would save $17 billion per year, enough money to hire 425,000 teachers to reduce class sizes in schools across the United States. Or, decommissioning 75,000 troops stationed overseas would save $4 billion per year, and could pay for 971,000 eligible kids, who currently cannot take part due to inadequate funding, to participate in Head Start.[82]

The over three trillion dollars the U.S. is spending on the wars in Iraq and Afghanistan could have funded many other human needs. Drawing on the National Priorities Project, Stiglitz and Bilmes write: "A trillion dollars could have built 8 million additional housing units, could have hired some 15 million additional public school teachers for one year; could have paid for 120 million children to attend a year of Head Start; or insured 530 million children for health care for one year; or provided 43 million students with four-year scholarships at public universities. Now multiply these numbers by three."[83]

It is startling to realize that the U.S. cost of two weeks of fighting in Iraq and Afghanistan—some $8 billion—would meet the world Millennium Development Goal of eradicating illiteracy by 2015. In addition, the trillions of dollars spent on these wars, according to Stiglitz and Bilmes, would have fulfilled U.S. commitments to the poorest countries for the next third of a century. At a minimum, the money could have provided a tax cut or health care for hard-pressed middle-income Americans. There are countless ways in which the money for these wars could have been spent more productively and left the U.S. more secure.[84]

The Global New Deal and Military Spending

Summary Observations

For the vast majority of individuals on the planet, human rights remain a fantasy, a utopian dream, aspirations for some long-distant future. To these individuals, human rights just do not seem feasible in today's world of intractable geopolitical rivalries, massive arms races, terrorism, and unspeakable human suffering. Furthermore, the vast resources mobilized for national defense and war preparation seem to indicate that the world's leaders expect a future filled with further anguish and conflict.

War and excessive military spending are bad for the economy. Although defense spending can generate jobs, train workers, and generate income, excessive

Global New Deal Proposals

To achieve a significant global cutback in military spending, it is necessary to develop new international institutions specifically committed to demilitarization and human rights. Since the end of the Cold War, a plethora of proposals for the restructuring of the UN have been produced.[86] The Global New Deal embraces the construction of two new global institutions dedicated to overcoming the destructive legacy of excessive military spending and establishing a framework of common security: an International Verification Agency and a Global Demilitarization Fund. These proposals described in chapter 9 provide an institutional framework for achieving positive

military spending also leads to the previously described "trade-offs," characterized as "guns versus butter" and "guns versus investment," and thus serve to harm human development. Such extreme spending can stunt, rather than stimulate, economic growth. Excessive military spending utilizes scarce economic resources that could otherwise be put to more productive use in civilian industries. Massive military spending leads to an inefficient use of labor resources and siphons off highly qualified engineers and labor from the civilian sector. Economic and social rights fulfillment in all nations depends on a shift in resources away from excessive military spending and toward human development.[85]

For international human rights to move beyond the realm of utopia and serve as the cornerstone of domestic and foreign public policy, military spending must be contained.

peace. The International Verification Agency can ensure compliance with disarmament agreements, thereby creating a global framework for monitoring and verification, thus providing the assurance and confidence that all will disarm. The Global Demilitarization Fund can help to finance a proactive conversion policy to shift military industries to civilian production to sustain employment, incomes, and consumption. The fund could respond not only to disarmament efforts, but also to other human security needs—such as famine relief and merciful responses to natural disasters (see chapter 9).

A human rights public policy agenda means moving toward positive peace and common security. If the global community is serious about protecting human rights, bold and dramatic action is needed. It is no longer enough just to point out the interrelationships between peace, demilitarization, and human rights. Human rights strategies must direct public policy away from excessive military spending and toward sustainable human development.

8

The United States and
Economic and Social Human Rights
A Contrast with Europe

Why has the United States resisted a human rights approach to economic and social human rights? How effective is the European human rights system in protecting the economic and social human rights of its citizens? Have the Europeans or the Americans been more successful in preventing suffering among the poor and vulnerable? What are the advantages to the American people for the United States to adopt and implement the Economic Rights Treaty, the American Convention on Human Rights, and the "Protocol of San Salvador" which affirms economic, social, and cultural rights?

Since the end of the Cold War, significant differences have erupted between key European states and the United States over the proper role of the United Nations and the importance of multilateral diplomacy. On a variety of issues—from war crimes and the International Criminal Court to environmental degradation and the Kyoto Protocol—Europeans and Americans vigorously disagreed and ultimately parted ways. These tensions boiled over into outright hostility over the U.S. decision to invade and occupy Iraq.

One area of severe disagreement between the United States and most of Europe (that has received inadequate attention in the media and the academy) is the issue of economic and social human rights. While the United States rejects a human rights approach to economic development and planning, European states have embraced this direction. While the United States resists incorporating economic and social human rights norms into their domestic legal structure, Europe has established the world's strongest

233

regional human rights system. These differences manifest themselves in policy outcomes with higher protections in Europe for the poor, the vulnerable, and the weak. If a poor person could control where she was born, it would be in her interest (i.e., economic well-being) to enter the world in most nations of Western Europe and not the United States. At the base of the disagreements between the United States and key European states is a fundamental dispute over the responsibility of the government to respect, protect, and fulfill economic and social human rights.

After summarizing the major differences between key European states and the United States regarding the utility of a human rights–based approach to development, I analyze how concretely each region addresses the "right to subsistence"—that is, claims to basic needs of food, clothing, housing and medical care made by the sick, unemployed, aged, disabled, widowed, and others faced with circumstances beyond their control. This review reveals the vitality and strength of the European human rights system to provide for the basic needs of defenseless groups. The U.S. approach of limited state action and responsibility, on the other hand, appears to create insecurity and vulnerability for the needy.

This chapter analyzes these issues in the following sections:

- the U.S. approach,
- the European approach,
- the right to subsistence,
- better to be poor in Europe than in the United States, and
- human rights and human development in the United States.

The U.S. Approach

Since the 1940s the United States has passed legislation to guarantee key economic and social entitlements, including social security, Medicare, and unemployment benefits. However, President Franklin D. Roosevelt (FDR) is probably the only U.S. president to fully embrace and act on the conception of "economic and social human rights." In 1941 FDR first articulated his commitment to these rights claims in his famous "Four Freedoms" speech. Roosevelt further elaborated a clear vision of economic and social rights for America in his call for an "Economic Bill of Rights" in his State of the Union address of 1944.

It is interesting to note the many ways in which these rights received later articulation in the Universal Declaration of Human Rights (UDHR) and the International Covenant on Economic, Social and Cultural Rights (Economic Rights Treaty). Roosevelt's 1940s vision is codified in these key UN human rights documents which include the following economic and social human

---

FRANKLIN D. ROOSEVELT'S ECONOMIC BILL OF RIGHTS

Franklin D. Roosevelt (FDR) called for an Economic Bill of Rights in his State of the Union address of 1944:

We have come to a clear realization of the fact that true individual freedom cannot exist without economic security and independence. "Necessitous men are not freemen." People who are hungry and out of a job are the stuff of which dictatorships are made.

In our day these economic truths have become accepted as self-evident. We have accepted, so to speak, a second Bill of Rights under which a new basis of security and prosperity can be established for all—regardless of station, race or creed.

Among these are:

The right to a useful and remunerative job in the industries, or shops or farms or mines of the Nation;

The right to earn enough to provide adequate food and clothing and recreation;

The right of every farmer to raise and sell his products at a return which will give him and his family a decent living;

The right of every businessman, large and small, to trade in an atmosphere of freedom from unfair competition and domination by monopolies at home or abroad;

The right of every family to a decent home;

The right to adequate medical care and the opportunity to achieve and enjoy good health;

The right to adequate protection from the economic fears of old age, sickness, accident, and unemployment;

The right to a good education.

All of these rights spell security. And after this war is won, we must be prepared to move forward, in the implementation of these rights, to new goals of human happiness and well-being.*

---

*Franklin D. Roosevelt, *State of the Union Address of 1944*, 90 Cong. Rec. 55, 57 (1944).

rights claims: the right to work, the right to just and favorable remuneration, the right to housing, the right to health care, the right to social security and unemployment insurance, and the right to education.

Through his "New Deal," FDR was able to push through legislation enacting public policy in areas from social security to unemployment benefits to jobs programs. State intervention was seen as key to the success of

---

FDR AND INTERNATIONAL HUMAN RIGHTS

Economic and social human rights embraced by Franklin D. Roosevelt (FDR) and later codified in the Universal Declaration of Human Rights (UDHR) and the International Covenant on Economic, Social and Cultural Rights (Economic Rights Treaty) include:

The Right to Work
"The right to a useful and remunerative job in the industries, or shop or farms or mines of the Nation" (FDR); "Everyone has the right to work, to free choice of employment, to just and favorable conditions of work and to protection against unemployment" (UDHR, Art. 23); "The States Parties to the present Covenant recognize the right to work . . ." (Economic Rights Treaty, Art. 6).

The Right to Just and Favorable Remuneration
"The right to earn enough to provide adequate food and clothing and recreation" (FDR); "Everyone who works has the right to just and favorable remuneration ensuring for himself and his family an existence worthy of human dignity, and supplemented, if necessary, by other means of social protection" (UDHR, Art. 23); ". . . remuneration which provides all workers, as a minimum, with . . . a decent living for themselves and their families . . . rest, leisure and reasonable limitation of working hours . . ." (Economic Rights Treaty, Art. 7).

The Right to Housing
"The right of every family to a decent home" (FDR); "Everyone has the right to a standard of living adequate for the health and well-

---

these policies, as it was often "market failure" that had led to exorbitantly high rates of unemployment and a general mal-distribution of income. Yet, during the Cold War, "rights" language came to be seen as problematic. Claims of a "right" to employment, health care, and housing seemed to run counter to the American ethos of individualism, personal responsibility, hard work, and individual initiative. The Cold War politicized this debate. Economic and social rights were associated with the values of Communism, while civil and political rights were said to reflect the ideals of liberal U.S. capitalism and democracy.

All presidents since FDR, Republican and Democrat alike, have refused to expend needed political capital to make the case for economic and

being of himself and his family, including food, clothing, housing . . ."
(UDHR, Art. 25); ". . . recognize the right of everyone to an adequate
standard of living for himself and his family, including adequate
food, clothing and housing, and to the continuous improvement of
living conditions" (Economic Rights Treaty, Art. 11).

The Right to Health Care
"The right to adequate medical care and the opportunity to achieve
and enjoy good health" (FDR); "Everyone has the right to a standard
of living adequate for the health and well-being of himself and his
family, including food, clothing, housing and medical care and necessary social services . . ." (UDHR, Art. 25); "The States Parties to the
present Covenant recognize the right of everyone to the enjoyment of
the highest attainable standard of physical and mental health" (Economic Rights Treaty, Art. 12).

The Right to Social Security and
Unemployment Insurance
"The right to adequate protection from the economic fears of old
age, sickness, accident, and unemployment" (FDR); "Everyone, as a
member of society, has the right to social security . . ." (UDHR, Art.
22); "The States Parties to the present Covenant recognize the right
of everyone to social security, including social insurance" (Economic
Rights Treaty, Art. 9).

The Right to Education
"The right to a good education" (FDR); "Everyone has the right to
education" (UDHR, Art. 26); "The States Parties to the present Covenant recognize the right of everyone to education" (Economic Rights
Treaty, Art. 13).

social human rights. President Carter is a slight exception. In October
1977, President Carter did transmit the Economic Rights Treaty to the U.S.
Senate for its consent. In doing so, however, Carter proposed reservations
to the treaty to clarify that the United States understood the provisions
of the Economic Rights Treaty to be "goals to be achieved progressively
rather than through immediate implementation" and that the provisions
of the Covenant were "not self-executing."[1] In other words, even if the
Senate had ratified the Economic Rights Treaty, the U.S. government
would not have been required to immediately implement its obligations
under the treaty.[2] Even these strong reservations were not enough to
obtain Senate ratification.

The Reagan Administration of the 1980s reversed many human rights policies of the Carter years, including presidential support for the Economic Rights Treaty. More fundamentally, Reagan sought to recast the vocabulary of the human rights debate. The phrase "human rights" was meant to refer to only political rights and civil liberties. In fact, there was a move away from "human rights" as a term, and instead, the Reagan administration spoke of "individual rights," "political rights," and "civil liberties." Their strategy was simply to define "economic rights out of existence."[3] Assistant Secretary of State Elliott Abrams defended this approach in a congressional hearing when he argued that recognition of economic and social human rights "tends to create a growing confusion about priorities in the human rights area and a growing dispersion of energy in ending human rights violations." Abrams argued that economic and social human rights were "easily exploited to excuse violations of civil and political rights."[4]

Abrams's testimony crystallized the growing conservative sentiment in the United States that the very concept of economic and social rights was antithetical to American principles. Abrams stated, "The great men who founded the modern concern for human rights . . . established separate spheres of public and private life. . . . Social and economic and cultural life was left in the private sphere." He concluded that "the rights that no government can violate [i.e., civil and political rights] should not be watered down to the status of rights that governments should do their best to secure [i.e. economic, social, and cultural rights]."[5]

This rejection of the very idea of economic and social human rights became even more consolidated throughout the 1980s. This dismissal, for example, was dramatically on display in November 1988, when the U.S. representative told the Third Committee of the UN General Assembly that responsible adults select their own careers, obtain their own housing, and arrange for their own medical care. The state should foster a legal framework which encourages fairness and prohibits fraud and then get out of the way to allow individuals to live their lives as they see fit. She went on to criticize UN bodies for departing from "the traditional concern for civil and political rights" and having "from time to time . . . decreed the existence of so-called social and economic rights."[6]

The Clinton administration in the 1990s made only minimal efforts in the area of economic and social human rights and did not press for ratification of the Economic Rights Treaty. Under Clinton, the United States did affirm the indivisibility of all international recognized human rights (economic, social, cultural, civil, and political) at the 1993 World Conference on Human Rights in Vienna. The United States endorsed the Vienna Declaration and Program of Action, which states:

> All human rights are universal, indivisible and interdependent and inter-
> related. The international community must treat human rights globally in

a fair and equal manner, on the same footing, and with the same emphasis. While the significance of national and regional particularities and various historical, cultural and religious backgrounds must be borne in mind, it is the duty of States, regardless of their political, economic and cultural systems, to promote and protect all human rights and fundamental freedoms.[7]

Yet, despite this endorsement of the totality and indivisibility of all human rights, the United States continued under Clinton to deny the validity of economic and social human rights. Recall, for example, the U.S. response to the Minority Rights Treaty and the Minority Rights Committee discussed in chapter 5. In this report, the U.S. government during the Clinton years clearly acknowledged the vast disparities in economic and social rights fulfillment that exist between ethnic and racial groups in the United States. Yet, at the same time, the government sidestepped its responsibility to respect, protect, and fulfill economic and social human rights. The government made clear that it did not view these claims as rights at all and denied any legal responsibility to ameliorate the economic injustices facing minority communities in the United States.

In contrast to Europe, there is no strong regional human rights system monitoring compliance with economic and social human rights in the Americas. The United States has played a marginal role in both the Inter-American Commission on Human Rights and the Inter-American Court of Human Rights, not ratified the "American Convention on Human Rights," and neither signed nor ratified the "Additional Protocol to the American Convention on Human Rights in the Area of Economic, Social and Cultural Rights" ("Protocol of San Salvador"). The Protocol of San Salvador, which entered into force on 16 November 1999,[8] is the attempt by the countries of the Americas to strengthen and consolidate the economic and social human rights laws of the region. Building on the Economic Rights Treaty, the Protocol of San Salvador addresses the right to work, just conditions of work, trade union rights, the right to social security, the right to health, the right to a healthy environment, the right to food, and the right to education. The intent of the Protocol of San Salvador, similar to that of the European "Social Charter" (described below), is to strengthen regional compliance with key economic and social human rights. Through its refusal to participate, the United States has belittled this regional endeavor.[9]

As of August 2009, the United States has neither ratified the Economic Rights Treaty nor the Protocol of San Salvador and appears unlikely to do so in the foreseeable future.

The European Approach

As opposed to the U.S. reluctance to embrace economic and social human rights, the democratic states of Europe have overwhelmingly accepted this framework. These European states have joined together in the Council of Europe to create the world's strongest regional human rights system. They have adopted enforceable economic and social human rights in the European Social Charter. In addition, these states have been actively engaged with the UN Office of the High Commissioner for Human Rights in Geneva in the adoption and enforcement of international human rights law. These states have ratified the Economic Rights Treaty and participated in the reporting and enforcement mechanisms set up by this treaty. A review of these European efforts reveals the stark difference between U.S. and European approaches to economic and social human rights.

The Council of Europe and the European Social Charter

The member states of the Council of Europe have accepted the legal obligations in international law to respect, protect, and fulfill economic and social human rights. Scholars have defined "a human rights system" as consisting of (1) clear lists of internationally guaranteed human rights, (2) permanent institutions, and (3) compliance or enforcement procedures.[10] The Council of Europe has created such a human rights system with economic and social rights clearly defined, institutions established, and compliance procedures in operation.

Beginning with ten Western European states in 1949,[11] the Council of Europe has expanded its membership to forty-seven states by 2009.[12] Membership in the council is conditioned *de facto* upon adherence to the European Convention on Human Rights and Fundamental Freedoms (ECHR) and its eleven protocols. The European system was pathbreaking in its creation of an international court for the protection of human rights and the establishment of procedures for individual complaints and denunciations of human rights violations. Over time the institutional structures and normative guarantees have been strengthened.

Progress has been particularly impressive in the European approach to economic and social human rights. The three components of the European human rights system (clearly enunciated rights, permanent institutions, and enforcement procedures) have evolved and developed in the following manner.

Clear List of Internationally Guaranteed Human Rights

In 1961 the European Social Charter (ESC) was adopted with the revised version entering into force on 1 July 1999.[13] The ESC is an extensive validation of the key economic and social rights found in the Economic Rights Treaty. Key rights guaranteed by the ESC include the following:

Housing: a commitment to universal access to decent, affordable housing and a reduction in the number of homeless persons;

Health: a commitment to provide accessible, effective health care facilities for the entire population;

Education: a pledge to provide free primary and secondary education, free vocational guidance services, and a ban on work by children under the age of 15;

Employment: all individuals have the right to earn their living in an occupation freely entered into, and each state will design a social and economic policy to ensure full employment;

Social Protections: everyone is guaranteed the right to social security, social welfare, and social services, and to be protected against poverty and social exclusion.

Permanent Institutions

The European Committee of Social Rights (ECSR) was established to determine whether member states honor their commitments in the ESC. This committee is composed of thirteen independent and impartial members elected by the Council of Europe for six-year terms, renewable once. The ECSR advises on whether or not national law and practice by the States Parties are in conformity with the Charter.

Enforcement Procedures

States Parties submit yearly reports on how they are implementing the ESC both in law and practice. The ECSR examines the reports and publishes its conclusions on whether or not the country concerned is in conformity with the ESC. If a state ignores the recommendations and remains out of compliance with the ESC, the Committee of Ministers will recommend changes in law or in practice to the violating state. In addition, a collective complaints procedure came into force in 1998, through which individuals and organizations are entitled to raise State Party violations of the ESC directly to the ECSR.

A review of these enforcement procedures illustrates their strengths.

ECSR State Reports and Conclusions: States Parties to the ESC submit yearly reports to the ECSR on how they implement the ESC in law and in practice.[14] The ECSR examines the reports to determine whether the country concerned is in compliance with the ESC. Its conclusions on state practices are published every year. If a state takes no action to come into compliance with the ESC, the Committee of Ministers sends a recommendation to that state asking it to change the situation in law or in practice. In addition, a Governmental Committee made up of representatives of the States Parties to the ESC, in consultation with representatives of the European social organizations participating as observers, considers decisions of non-compliance. The State concerned is expected to establish measures it will take to remedy the situation and provide a timetable for achieving compliance. If a State fails to take these actions, the Governmental Committee may recommend that the Committee of Ministers address a further recommendation to the State concerned to take appropriate measures to remedy the situation. The Governmental Committee reports to the Committee of Ministers yearly on its actions, including delinquent states and issues/areas of noncompliance.[15]

ECSR Collective Complaint Procedure: The vitality of the European human rights system in relation to economic and social human rights can be demonstrated through an examination of the collective complaints procedure. Since 1998, when this procedure came into operation, there have been a total of fifty-five complaints lodged with the ECSR against the following countries: France (19), Portugal (9), Greece (7), Bulgaria (6), Italy (3), Belgium (2), Croatia (2), Finland (2), Ireland (2), The Netherlands (1), Slovenia (1), and Sweden (1). The ECSR has reached final decisions on most of these cases with strong recommendations for changes to the state parties involved.[16] In most cases changes were made at the national level to protect citizens' economic and social human rights. This trajectory of complaint, hearing, decision, state deliberation and, often, compliance is impressive evidence of a strong human rights system.

For example, in response to a complaint filed by the International Federation of Human Rights in 2000, the ECSR found Greece to be in violation of the prohibition of forced labor in Article 1.2 of the ESC. The Greek government responded with a legislative decree to bring their laws in conformity with the ESC and reported on further legislative and administrative action taken to bring the country into compliance with Article 1.2. This impressive and speedy action by the Greek government is a clear example of the responsiveness of European states to this regional human rights system.[17]

European States and the Economic Rights Treaty

In addition to the ESC, the nations of Europe also participate actively in the mechanisms established by the United Nations to monitor economic and social human rights. European states have signed and ratified the Economic Rights Treaty (which, as noted above, the United States has not ratified). Substantive provisions in part three of the Economic Rights Treaty include rights to the following: an adequate standard of living, including food, clothing, and housing; physical and mental health; education; scientific and cultural life; the opportunity to work; just and favorable conditions of work; rest and leisure; social security; special protection for the family, mothers, and children; and the right to form and join trade unions and to strike.

As discussed in chapter 3, the group of independent experts charged with implementation responsibility of the Economic Rights Treaty is the

Economic Rights Committee. This committee is composed of eighteen independent experts elected by the UN Economic and Social Council for four-year terms. The reporting procedure is similar to that of the ECSR and involves a dialogue between the state party and the Economic Rights Committee. Regular country reports are submitted by states parties, deliberations are held, and general comments are published.

Most European states follow through on their reporting requirements to the Economic Rights Committee and appear to take the work of the committee seriously. These states are concerned about their reputations, and they thus respond to committee requests. The convention calls for progressive compliance with demonstrable progress. The Economic Rights Committee thus looks for steady improvement and does not accept a nation standing still or going backward.

The European states' participation in this human rights machinery set up by the United Nations has strengthened the protection of economic and social human rights of the vulnerable in these respective countries. The United Kingdom, for example, has consistently reported to the Economic Rights Committee and been responsive to the "Concluding Observations" of these experts. The UK established an "extensive and elaborate administrative infrastructure" to facilitate giving effect to the provisions of the Economic Rights Treaty. And, furthermore, the UK enacted the European Convention on Human Rights into domestic legislation, which constituted a considerable departure from the traditional approach not to incorporate international human rights treaties in UK domestic law. Such a legal framework allows for issues of discrimination based on race or gender to be adjudicated.

A further example of this human rights impact on national legislation is in Spain.

After the Economic Rights Committee asked Spain to continue efforts to ensure effective equality between men and women, in particular with regard to access to education and jobs and equal pay for equal work, Spain took on this task with the Plan of Equal Opportunities, 1997–2000. After the Economic Rights Committee pushed Spain to take all appropriate preventive and penal measures to combat effectively all forms of racial discrimination, Spain passed a new penal code which went into force on 26 May 1996. This code recognizes racism and anti-Semitism as aggravating circumstances in offenses against persons and property. Additional offenses include the provocation of discrimination, hatred, or violence on racist grounds, illegal foreign labor, clandestine immigration, and job discrimination on ethnic or racial grounds.[18]

How are we to evaluate the impact of this United Nations Economic Rights Treaty on the domestic level? "Impact" can be understood to reflect influence on the realization of human rights norms in individual countries. In the cases of the UK and Spain it is probably impossible to draw a direct causal link between the treaty body reporting system for the Economic Rights Treaty and legislative or policy reform. However, this system clearly reinforces and supports efforts underway within the UK and Spain to respect, protect, and fulfill economic and social human rights. It would be an exercise in speculation and guesswork to try to quantify the impact of this human rights system with any precision. It is more important to see the ways in which this legal framework changes the terms of the debate, supports local initiatives, and enhances an overall human rights framework in this area of economic and social rights. In these respects, this system is having an important impact in reinforcing and strengthening economic and social human rights in Europe.

The Right to Subsistence

The conflicting approaches between the United States and Europe over public policy to provide a minimum level of subsistence for the poor reveal starkly the profound chasm between them over the validity of a human rights approach to poverty alleviation and the protection of the vulnerable.

Article 25(1) of the UDHR declares: "Everyone has the right to a standard of living adequate for the health and well-being of himself and of his family, including food, clothing, housing and medical care and necessary social services, and the right to security in the event of unemployment, sickness, disability, widowhood, old age or other lack of livelihood in circumstances beyond his control." The respect for human dignity thus includes a minimum level of subsistence necessary to support the continuation of human life at a decent level.

The United States and Europe have different interpretations of the role of the state in providing this level of basic subsistence. To a large degree the debate revolves around the extent to which this social assistance should be understood as a legal "right." The U.S. limits, while the European states expand, state responsibility to guarantee sufficient resources to all citizens as the ultimate guarantor of the right to subsistence.

The United States and the Right to Subsistence

U.S. federal courts have determined that the poor have no constitutional human rights claims to subsistence. Consider, for example, the 1970 decision of the Supreme Court of the United States in *Dandridge v. Williams*. The case concerned the operation of the state of Maryland's welfare system which established an upper limit of $250 a month per household in the Aid to Families with Dependent Children (AFDC) program. The litigants had large families and argued that this maximum grant limitation operated to discriminate against them merely because of the size of their families. In deciding for the State of Maryland, the Supreme Court declared:

> [A] solid foundation for the regulation can be found in the State's legitimate interest in encouraging employment. . . . [T]he intractable economic, social, and even philosophical problems presented by public welfare assistance programs are not the business of this Court. The Constitution may impose certain procedural safeguards upon systems of welfare administration. But the Constitution does not empower this Court to second-guess state officials charged with the difficult responsibility of allocating limited public welfare funds among the myriad of potential recipients.[19]

The Supreme Court's decision to uphold the Maryland maximum grant rule is a clear demonstration of the lack of federal protection for subsistence rights in the United States. Social and economic rights are not constitutionally protected. This decision is in violation of the Economic Rights Treaty as interpreted by the Economic Rights Committee (see in particular General Comment 3, paragraph 10). But, since the United States has not ratified the Economic Rights Treaty, the country is not technically in violation of international law.[20]

The executive and legislative branches of the U.S. government have also acted to limit the economic and social rights claims of the poor. Under the banner of welfare reform, the government enacted legislation limiting direct assistance and promoting individual initiative and personal responsibility. After a tumultuous debate, in 1996 the United States enacted the Personal Responsibility and Work Opportunity Reconciliation Act (PRWORA).[21] President Clinton designed this statute to "end welfare as we know it." The PRWORA abolished the Aid to Families with Dependent Children (AFDC) program, a federal entitlement to subsistence aid for eligible families. To replace AFDC, PRWORA established the Temporary Assistance to Needy Families (TANF) program, which neither guaranteed assistance to needy families nor required the states to do so. An examination of this radical restructuring of U.S. social welfare policy in relation to the legal obligations of the Economic Rights Treaty is instructive. Many of the features of PRWORA are in clear violation of the legal duties of states enunciated in the Economic Rights Treaty. If the United States had ratified this treaty, it is hard to see how they could have defended PRWORA before the Economic Rights Committee. Examine the following:

1. Benefits under PRWORA are not guaranteed to all eligible recipients, but limited by the number of applicants and the amount of appropriation. While this limitation was imposed, the United States continued to spend billions of dollars on space exploration and outdated and esoteric military projects. This is a clear violation of Article 2.1 of the Economic Rights Treaty, which calls on states to utilize the "maximum of its available resources" to progressively

achieve the full realization of the economic and social rights of its citizens. It is also a violation of Article 10 which calls for the "widest possible protection and assistance" for the family, particularly the "care and education of dependent children," and Article 11 which recognizes the right of everyone to an adequate standard of living including "adequate food, clothing and housing, and to the continuous improvement of living conditions."

2. Individual states could interpret PRWORA as requiring recipients to accept whatever job is offered them, and canceling their benefits if they decline. This is a clear violation of Article 6.1 of the Economic Rights Treaty which recognizes the right "of everyone to the opportunity to gain his [or her] living by work which he [or she] freely chooses or accepts." Article 6.2 requires state parties to take steps including "technical and vocational guidance and training programs, policies and techniques to achieve steady economic, social and cultural development and full and productive employment under conditions safeguarding fundamental political and economic freedoms to the individual."

3. PRWORA imposes a five-year limit on benefits for most recipients and is a deliberate retreat from a legal guarantee of subsistence benefits to families in need. This is a clear violation of Articles 2.1, the commitment to seek to achieve progressively "the full realization of the rights recognized in the present Covenant by all appropriate means," and 5.2, limiting derogations from the Covenant.

While the federal government and the U.S. Constitution do not provide protections of subsistence rights to the poor, the constitutions of at least twenty states include references and language on the care of the needy and the protection of the health of state residents. These state constitutions can be interpreted as imposing a duty on the states to aid, in particular, poor children. Bert Lockwood, R. Collins Owens, and Grace Severyn point out that many state constitutions contain substantive provisions that deal explicitly with poverty, housing, shelter, and nutrition. Examples include New York's requirement that the legislature provide for "aid, care and support of the needy" and Alabama's obligation to provide "adequate provision for the maintenance of the poor." The plaintiffs in *Daugherty v. Wallace* argued that Ohio's constitutional guarantee of the right of "obtaining safety" encompasses the right of poor citizens to receive subsistence assistance from the state, in an amount sufficient to enable them to avoid homelessness and to obtain basic health care.[22]

Lockwood, Owens, and Severyn argue that state constitutional provisions regarding safety and/or happiness can serve as the basis for a constitutional right to public assistance sufficient to meet basic needs. In their view, the right to obtain happiness and safety is meaningless for the unemployed, disabled, and poor unless interpreted as imposing an affirmative right to assistance sufficient to provide shelter and medical care. Individual states' constitutional guarantees to happiness and safety can be interpreted to encompass a right to basic subsistence, defined as protection against deprivations of the food, clothing, shelter, and medical care necessary for a decent life. Given that many state constitutions have clauses declaring as inalienable the right to seek and/or obtain happiness and/or safety, these clauses may serve as a source of a positive right to basic needs. A strategy of litigating the happiness and safety clauses of state constitutions may be adapted by advocates of the poor facing serious reductions in public assistance. State constitutions may then serve as a better vehicle than the U.S. Constitution for responding to the needs of the impoverished.[23]

European States and the Right to Subsistence

As already noted, the ESC validates a rights-based approach to development and guarantees basic subsistence rights for all citizens, including rights to housing, health, education, employment, and social protection. These economic and social human rights have been incorporated into the constitutional and legal systems of the member states of the Council of Europe. Examine, for example, the legal frameworks of Germany and Switzerland.

Germany: Article 1(1) of the post-war German Constitution states: "Human dignity shall be inviolable. To respect and to protect it shall be the duty of all state authority." The Federal Administrative Court determined that the principle of human dignity required that provisions for the support of the poor be available as a matter of enforceable individual right, not merely as a matter of administrative policy. The Federal Constitutional Court supported this decision by adopting the position that Article 1(1), in combination with the principle that the Federal Republic of Germany is a "social state" (Article 20(1)), signifies a guarantee of security of livelihood. This court further directed that income tax legislation should provide an exemption for the minimum level of income necessary to ensure an existence consistent with human dignity for the taxpayer's family.[24]

Switzerland: Although not part of the E.U., Switzerland is a member of the Council of Europe and has signed the ESC. The Swiss have adopted a rights-based approach to economic and social welfare and development. For example, the Federal Court of Switzerland in 1995 stated the following:

> The security of elemental human necessities like food, clothing and shelter is *the* precondition for human existence and development. It is simultaneously

an indispensable element of a community based on democracy and the rule of law. Therefore security of livelihood satisfied the requirements for being guaranteed as an unwritten constitutional right.

The principle that a citizen who falls into economic need must be supported (by his home municipality) has long been known in Swiss law; it dates back to the Sixteenth Century. The Federal Court for its part has explained in older decisions on the subject of intercantonal disputes over care of the poor that it is both a humanitarian obligation and a duty inherent in the purpose of the modern state to preserve persons found within its territory against physical ruin when necessary.

In scholarly writings a fundamental right to security of livelihood is almost unanimously recognized. . . . The view primarily expressed in scholarship is that it involves an unwritten constitutional right. Various other constitutional starting points have also been invoked: the constitutional principle of human dignity, which guarantees to every person what she may expect from the community by virtue of her humanity; the right to life as the core of personal freedom, which would no longer be preserved if the most minimal prerequisites of survival were not ensured.[25]

The Swiss Federal Court thus declares that the security of elemental human necessities such as food, clothing, and shelter are an indispensable element of a democratic community and the rule of law. The court states categorically that the fundamental "right to security of livelihood satisfies [the] criteria for justiciability." The court emphasized the human rights basis to this decision and the inherent legal duties imposed upon the state to protect persons against "physical ruin when necessary."[26]

Better to Be Poor in Europe than in the United States

Due to European states' commitment to economic and social human rights, the poor in Europe are better provided for and taken care of than their counterparts in the United States. An individual in the bottom rungs of economic wealth would undoubtedly prefer to be born in Europe than in the United States. These conclusions are drawn from the 2004 study by Alberto Alesina and Edward Glaeser examining the differences in family benefits, health care, sickness and accidental injury benefits, disability benefits, poverty relief, and workers' rights and labor legislation between Germany and Sweden, on the one hand, and the United States on the other.

Family benefits:

- Germany and Sweden: Child benefits are available without regard to income until the child reaches eighteen (Germany) or sixteen (Sweden), but these limits can be extended if the child pursues higher education. Using 1999 PPP (purchasing power parity) adjusted dollars, each child entitles the representative German household to monthly benefits of $136 (Germany) or $87 (Sweden).

- United States: Family allowances do not exist in the United States. Each child entitles the representative U.S. household to monthly benefits of zero. The United States does have a fixed child yearly tax credit of $600 per child (in 2001).[27]

Health care:

- Germany and Sweden: Both countries provide universal coverage, with unlimited benefits including payments for doctors' fees, hospitalization, and the cost of pharmaceutical products.
- United States: The United States does not provide universal health care coverage for its citizens. The U.S. Medicare program targets the elderly, while Medicaid serves low-income households and people with disabilities. Unemployed workers have no coverage. Employed workers must rely on their employer to offer health insurance as part of their compensation package.[28]

Sickness and accidental injury benefits:

- Germany and Sweden: German and Swedish legislation guarantees sickness benefits to replace the loss of earnings due to sickness for all persons in paid employment. These benefits replace up to 70 percent (Germany) and 80 percent (Sweden) of gross earnings.
- United States: There are no federal sickness and accidental injury benefits in the United States. Only five states in the United States offer any kind of sickness benefit at all.[29]

Disability benefits:

- Germany and Sweden: Germany requires five years of employment and Sweden three years of employment, before a worker can receive benefits to replace income due to inability to engage in gainful activity. The Swedish scheme provides a basic minimum pension, enhanced with an income-based supplement and care and handicap allowances. The German benefit is calculated using the level of income and the number of years of contribution.
- United States: The United States requires at least five years employment to qualify and the disability benefit is based on the worker's average monthly earnings. The U.S. benefits are much smaller than their European counterparts. While the average benefit in the United States corresponds to approximately 43 percent of the worker's average wage, in Sweden the corresponding figure is 80 percent.[30]

Poverty relief:

- Germany and Sweden: These two countries rely on unlimited and unconditional plans (called Sozialhilfe and Socialbidrag, respectively) to alleviate poverty. These government programs are directed at persons unable to support themselves and not covered by other schemes (e.g., disability benefits, etc.).
- United States: The United States does not have a plan aimed at the poor as a general category. Instead, there is an array of programs targeting different groups. At the beginning of the twenty-first century, for example, U.S. Supplemental Security Income (SSI) targeted aged, blind, and disabled persons with annual gross incomes below about $14,500. The TANF program continues to be limited to two years of assistance and recipients who are able to work must find a job at the end of that period. Low-income households can also receive food and nutrition assistance (food stamps) and some housing assistance.[31]

Workers' rights and labor legislation:

- Overall in the European Union, the minimum wage is 53 percent of the average wage, against 39 percent in the United States. But this figure only tells a small part of the difference in attitudes towards workers' rights between the two. In almost all categories of workers' protections, from fair labor standards, employment protection policies, minimum annual leave policies, and benefit replacement and duration ratios, Alesina and Glaeser found the United States to be at the bottom compared to European states.[32]

Human Rights and Human Development in the United States

As noted in chapter 3, the 2008 HPI-2 reveals that the United States ranks in the bottom categories of human development in comparison to the industrialized, developed countries of Europe. For example, out of all of these twenty wealthy countries, the United States has the highest percentage of people living below the income poverty line (17.0%) and the highest percentage of people who will probably not live to the age of 60 years (11.6%). The HPI-2 further reveals that 20 percent of adults in the United States (age 16–65) lack "functional literacy skills." This statistic alone is alarming, as it means that over 20 percent of Americans cannot read the back of a prescription bottle and give the correct amount of medicine to their children.[33]

It is hard not to conclude from this data that the alleviation of the suffering of the vulnerable and the protection of the economic and social human rights of the bottom 20–25 percent of the population is not a top priority for the United States. These dismal outcomes can be linked to the refusal of the United States to accept the legitimacy of a rights-based framework for development. If one judges a nation and its economic system by the way it treats its most fragile and weak citizens, the United States fails miserably.

In hard power resources the United States is doing quite well with the world's largest economy (with a GDP of $12,417 billion and a per capita income of $41,890 in 2005)[34] and the world's largest military (with a military budget for FY2009 over $690 billion).[35] But these robust figures of economic and military power are misleading. What they ignore is the decline in living standards and the growing social insecurity, breeding despair and hopelessness, found in every U.S. city. Since the 1980s the U.S. economy has been working against the interests of the bottom third of the population and these tendencies are deepening.

Consider the following trends in human development in the United States from the 1980s to 2010. In the 1980s:

- The U.S. government documented the decline in the U.S. standard of living from the mid-1970s through the 1980s. Despite positive production and income growth in the national economy, it became harder to climb out of poverty in the United States during this period. The Census Bureau reported that the percentage of full-time workers with low earnings grew sharply in the 1980s, despite the economic expansion that brought increased prosperity to the affluent. The bureau defined low earnings as $12,195 per year, expressed in 1990 dollars (thus adjusted for inflation). At the end of the 1970s, 12.1% of all full-time employees earned below the equivalent of $12,195; by 1990, that figure had risen to 18%.[36]
- The number of American children living in poverty grew by more than 1 million during the 1980s, and in 1989 about 18% of children in the United States lived in families with incomes below the federal poverty line, including 39.8% of all African American children, 38.8% of Native American children, 32.2% of Hispanic children, 17.1% of Asian American children, and 12.5% of Caucasian children.[37]

These trends continued throughout the 1990s:

- Inflation-adjusted wage rates for the median worker fell in the 1980s and continued to decline sharply in the 1990s. From 1989 to 1997, real wages for the majority of workers in the middle—the vast U.S.

middle class—continued to erode, with the median worker's wage falling 5 percent since 1989.[38]

- Average weekly earnings fell sharply: in constant dollars, earnings went from $312 in 1973 to $256 in 1996, a decline of 19 percent.[39]
- A Congressional Budget Office study documented that the gap between the rich and the poor more than doubled from 1979 to 2000. This gulf was so large in 2000 that the richest 1 percent of U.S. citizens as a group had more money to spend after taxes than the entire bottom 40 percent of the population.[40]
- The proportion of the nation's income received by the poorest fifth of U.S. families declined dramatically, while the proportion held by the richest families increased. The respected Gini Index calculates that this form of inequality worsened from 1970 to the end of the 1990s.[41] Consider that in 1980 the top 5 percent of all families received 14.6% of the nation's aggregate income. By 2001, this elite group of 5 percent was getting 21.0% of all income. On the other side, the already small share of the nation's income going to the bottom fifth of families fell by 20.8 percent during these years.[42]
- The proportion of the U.S. population lacking health insurance increased over the same time: 15.6 percent, a total of 41.7 million Americans, had no health insurance in 1996, up from 10.9 percent in 1976.[43]
- In September 2000, the U.S. Agriculture Department revealed the depths of hunger in America: 31 million Americans were hungry and faced food insecurity.[44]
- Sterile economic figures should not hide the human tragedy represented by these economic conditions. For example, the percentage of children under eighteen living in poverty increased from 14.9% in 1970 to 19.89% in 1996, a 33 percent increase.[45]

These trends continued throughout the first decade of the twenty-first century:

- The Census Bureau reported that the number of Americans living in poverty increased in 2002 by 1.7 million and the median household income declined by 1.1 percent.[46]
- Academic studies in 2003 concluded that one in four U.S. workers earn $8.70 an hour or less; the high end of this range ($8.70 hourly) works out to $18,100 a year, roughly the current official poverty level in the United States for a family of four. For most of these workers, job mobility is nonexistent; there is no career ladder for home health care workers, poultry processors, retail clerks, housekeepers, and janitors. These workers lack health insurance, child care, and receive little or no vacation.[47]

- New York City reported in early 2004 that nearly one of every two black men between 16 and 64 was jobless and not working.[48]

And finally, the social health of the United States today, according to the *American Human Development Report 2008–2009*, is as follows:

- While spending more per capita on health care than any nation in the world, roughly $5.2 billion every day, Americans live shorter lives than citizens of many other nations, including virtually every Western European and Nordic country. In addition, the U.S. infant mortality rate is on par with that of Croatia, Cuba, Estonia, and Poland. "If the U.S. rate were equal to that of first-ranked Sweden, twenty-one thousand more American babies would have lived to celebrate their first birthday in 2005."[49]
- The United States ranked forty-second in global life expectancy and first among the world's twenty-five richest countries in the percentage of children living in poverty.[50]
- Fundamental deprivations in food and housing are far too prevalent. The U.S. Department of Agriculture reports, for example, that "on a typical day in November 2005, an estimated 531,000 to 797,000 households experienced very low food security" and were unable to have a normal eating pattern due to a lack of money or other resources. And, over the course of a year, at least 1.35 million children are at some point homeless. Sarah Burd-Sharps, Kristen Lewis, and Eduardo Borges Martins summarize: "More families with children are homeless today than at any time since the Great Depression. For the hungry and homeless, the American Dream is especially elusive. It is hard to dream on an empty stomach, with no roof over your head or living in fear of violence."[51]

Conclusion

The argument is often made by U.S. economists that the problem with Europe's social welfare approach is its negative effects on overall economic growth. These scholars maintain that when an economy is enfeebled by high taxes and restrictive regulations, business incentives disappear, investments decline, and the economy slows. A slow-growth economy brings in fewer tax revenues, resulting in the government being unable to pay for all the promised social benefits. To avoid painful cuts in these social welfare programs, governments practice deficit spending which further harms the economy. Expensive retirement programs, health benefits, and social security protections end up being a drag on economic growth. Since everyone suffers with slow economic growth, social spending on this level is thus counter-productive to the protection of the needs of the society as a whole, including the welfare of the vulnerable and poor.

Recent academic reports challenge these assumptions. In one study, for example, Professor Peter H. Lindert, former president of the Economic History Association and an associate of the National Bureau of Economic Research, examined levels of taxes, public investments in education, transportation and health care, and social transfers like Social Security. His findings disputed this widely accepted view that welfare state policies harm a nation's productivity. He writes: "It is well known that higher taxes and transfers reduce productivity. Well known—but unsupported by statistics and history."[52] He focuses his study on social programs and compares the level of social spending over nine decades up to the year 2000 in nineteen developed nations, including most of Western Europe, Japan, Australia, the United States, and Canada. His conclusion is that high spending on these social programs creates no statistically measurable deterrent to the growth of productivity or per capita GDP. Since WWII, despite the implementation of welfare state policies, European economies continued to grow faster than the United States, a nation with low social spending. "Nine decades of historical experience fail to show that transferring a larger share of GDP from taxpayers to transfer recipients has a negative correlation with either the level or the rate of growth of GDP per person."[53]

In fact, Lindert finds that when we switch from GDP per person, the usual measure of income and productivity, to GDP per hour worked, a better measure of labor productivity, the high social spending countries do quite well. "Countries like the Netherlands, France, and Germany have caught up with the United States in output per labor hour. In fact, in GDP per hour worked, the United States ranked below eight other countries in 1992. Six of these eight countries with higher output per hour worked were continental welfare states."[54]

Lindert explains his conclusion that high levels of social spending prove no deterrent to economic growth by noting the following three points: First, he observes that the tax systems of countries with high social spending are not "anti-growth" because they derive much of their tax revenues from regressive consumption taxes. These nations do not penalize profits or capital investment any more than the United States, and possibly even less. Second, the European social programs with high welfare benefits usually include everyone. Since benefits are not cut off as income grows, there is no penalty for finding work or investing. And third, a lot of this social spending (for example, spending in education and health) is conducive to economic growth. In nations with comprehensive public health programs, people are healthier and live longer and are thus more productive. He also shows how government support for child care and requirements to re-employ women after maternity leave at the same job can enhance economic growth.[55]

The United States and Economic and Social Human Rights

Summary Observations

It is unfortunate that the mythology of the negative impact of social spending on economic growth continues as conventional wisdom in the United States. This wrongheaded view reinforces the U.S. resistance to internationally recognized economic and social human rights. The U.S. reluctance to accept legal obligations to provide a basic right of subsistence to its citizens has helped to create a country where inequality is skyrocketing and the poor are ignored. Perhaps the United States can learn from the European experience and come to see that the national interest corresponds with the establishment and implementation of a strong human rights system for all citizens.

The United States can also follow the lead of the Latin American states and actively work with the Inter-American Commission on Human Rights. The Latin American states have attempted to construct a human rights system modeled after the remarkably successful European system. The United States can join this effort and actively help to create a robust human rights commission in the Americas committed to economic and social human rights.

Global New Deal Proposals

A human rights approach to economic justice gives the United States a way forward. Such an approach prioritizes the needs of the most vulnerable sectors of the population and pays attention to the "negative externalities" and destructive aspects of all known economic growth models. A U.S. commitment to respect, protect, and fulfill economic and social human rights could be the first step towards the construction of a framework of human rights protections for all U.S. citizens.

The "global new deal" in chapter 9 calls on the United States to ratify the Economic Rights Treaty, the American Convention on Human Rights, and the Protocol of San Salvador which affirms economic, social, and cultural rights. The United States can assume global leadership in the campaign for economic and social human rights. It is tragic that the basic human rights of millions of Americans go unmet year after year after year. The good news is that there are programs to address the amelioration of this suffering caused by economic dislocations and the functioning of the global economy. It would be refreshing to the people

The other alternative, of course, is for the United States to continue on its current path of extreme mal-development—a path that is failing to serve a growing percentage of the U.S. population.

of the world for the United States to place the needs of the poor as the nation's number one priority. Ratifying these three basic human rights treaties would be a tremendous step forward toward the creation of a true human rights system in the Americas to assist the needy and vulnerable.

9

The Global New Deal

To overcome human suffering at the height of the Great Depression, U.S. President Franklin Delano Roosevelt proposed a New Deal for America. Roosevelt's New Deal embraced a series of policy proposals to overcome market failure and to protect the economic and social human rights of the most vulnerable. Some of these policies succeeded while others failed. Yet, the premise behind his actions, that governments have a duty to mobilize resources to act for the public welfare, continues to inspire. The public institutions and economic reforms created out of the New Deal gave the government the ability to establish a basic level of economic security to its citizens. These institutions and reforms were designed to provide short-term relief and the eventual implementation of a long-term economic safety net for all Americans. While Roosevelt's New Deal failed to adequately meet the needs of African Americans and the very poor, these public policies, including social security, literally prevented millions from falling into poverty and destitution.

Today, we need a Global New Deal. Suffering in every nation is linked not only to national economies, but also to the global economy. The denial of basic public goods and market failure are often the result of forces outside the control of an individual nation-state. Public policy at the international level is needed to correct these insufficiencies. To provide for the public welfare, governments must work through international law and international organizations to correct the maldevelopment currently accompanying globalization. Roosevelt gives us an inspiring example of state mobilization at the national level. Today, mobilization is needed at

THE GLOBAL NEW DEAL

Promote Economic Equality
Establish a UN Economic Security Council
Rivet on the twenty-twenty proposal

Finance Global Public Goods
Launch a Global Public Goods Fund
Implement the Tobin Tax

Hear the Victims' Voices
Adjudicate violations of economic and social human rights
Enhance the power of the UN Economic Rights Committee
Ratify the Optional Protocol to the Economic Rights Treaty

Maintain Ecological Balance
Set up a World Environment Organization

Prioritize the Rights of Racial and Ethnic Minorities
Focus policy on primary health care
Focus policy on basic education

Prioritize Women's Rights
Focus policy on primary health care
Focus policy on basic education

Reduce Military Spending
Found an International Verification Agency
Institute a Global Demilitarization Fund

Affirm International Human Rights Law
U.S. Ratify the Economic Rights Treaty and the American Convention on Human Rights

the global level to implement international public policy to protect the innocent. This book is an attempt to take up this responsibility and to identify international public policy to safeguard the general welfare.

The Global New Deal is formulated within the normative framework of human rights. Since World War II, the international community at the

UN has successfully defined, articulated, and elaborated the content of international economic and social human rights. The Global New Deal is an attempt to identify and develop policy to fulfill these basic economic and social human rights.

The Global New Deal is neither a fanciful dream nor a radical, revolutionary proposal. On the contrary, these ideas are realistic and doable. Furthermore, given the common environmental and social vulnerabilites of all peoples everywhere, this plan of action is in the interests of both the rich and powerful and the poor and weak. Global cooperation through international law to promote human rights and protect public goods is a reasonable path away from a world of conflict, exploitation, inequality, and injustice and toward a global, sustainable, and just future for all.

The Global New Deal

Promote Economic Equality

Establish a UN Economic Security Council

The existing UN Security Council is the most powerful organ in the UN system. It is charged with maintaining international peace and security and has the power to enforce collective security through economic sanctions and military force. The violent deaths of at least 50 million people in World War II forced the international community to try a new framework for peace. The UN Security Council is mandated to act with force to uphold international law and punish aggressors who commit interstate violence. Since its founding, the UN's role in the area of peace and security has evolved over the years to include peacekeeping, peacebuilding, and peacemaking. Although failures and setbacks have occurred, it is widely recognized that the active role of the UN Security Council in the area of peace and security has fundamentally altered the fabric of international relations.

Today, we need a new security council, a UN Economic Security Council (ESC), to alter the fabric of international economic relations.[1] The needless suffering of millions around the world demands nothing less. As previously noted, half of the world's people—3.1 billion—live on less than $2.50 a day, and 1.4 billion live on less than $1.25 a day. In poor countries, as many as 50 percent of all children are malnourished.[2] More than 26,000 children die every day from mainly preventable causes.[3]

Just as the startling violence of World War II compelled states to join together to try a new peace system, so today the astonishing brutality of our unregulated global economic system should lead us to a new framework for economic cooperation. This is not a utopian proposal. It is in every individual state's national interest to support the establishment of an ESC. Rich and poor states can all benefit from a cooperative international organization committed to the idea of promoting global economic equality. Such cooperation could help the LDCs overcome the historical legacy of underdevelopment and focus on the expansion of the human development and human capabilities of their people. Meanwhile, the developed nations would benefit from expanded trade and investment opportunities created through successful sustainable development in LDCs.

Tinkering with existing international organizations that work on global economic affairs (from the UN Development Program [UNDP] to the International Monetary Fund [IMF]) is not adequate. Strong, bold action by the international community is necessary. As the late Mahbub ul Haq, the chief architect of the UNDP's annual *Human Development Report,* wrote: "Often, a courageous step helps focus the collective human mind, while minor adjustments in arrangements go unnoticed and have little impact."[4]

Bureaucratic malaise and political deadlock on these central issues can be overcome. The political courage that Roosevelt demonstrated at the height of the Great Depression should be our guide. Member states of the UN are constantly called on to demonstrate the "political will" necessary to effectively address daunting global challenges from global poverty to the destruction of the earth's biosphere. Responsible, caring leaders must show not only political will, but also political courage by taking the risks that always accompany proposals for fundamental change.

Haq and the UNDP were among the first to propose the formation of an ESC within the UN. Haq envisioned an expansive ESC that would implement a program based on security in its fullest sense: security for people, from food security to ecological security. Haq's ESC was conceived to provide leadership in resolving global economic crises. His proposed ESC would also provide an "early warning system" to plan assistance in internal conflicts. The UNDP mentioned five quantitative indicators for an early warning system for human security: income and job security, food security, human rights violations, ethnic and other conflicts, and the ratio of military to social spending. The UNDP also hoped that this expansive ESC would work to strengthen the UN development system.[5] The Haq–UNDP proposal has considerable merit. However, perhaps we should begin with a more focused mandate for the ESC.

A streamlined and efficient ESC could focus primarily on the promotion of economic equality. Economic equality, as defined in chapter 2, refers to universal and equal access to global public goods, including basic education, a healthy environment, food and water, primary health care and sanitation, and housing. We have seen the ways in which globalization and "market failure" threaten these public goods and contribute to global human misery (so clearly described by the World Bank and the UNDP).

The ESC can center on measures to end this needless suffering through the promotion of economic equality. It could do this by concentrating on what is called the "twenty-twenty compact" for human development.

ESC Mandate: Promote Economic Equality

The ESC can fulfill its mandate of promoting economic equality by riveting on the twenty-twenty compact for human development proposed by the United Nations Children's Fund (UNICEF) and the UNDP. The ESC could require yearly reports from all member states on individual progress toward achieving twenty-twenty. The ESC could hold states accountable to implement the twenty-twenty agreement.

The twenty-twenty compact calls for 20 percent of foreign economic aid budgets and 20 percent of LDCs' national budgets to be allocated to the provision of basic needs for all in the developing world. Almost all the member states of the UN agreed to the final declaration from the World Summit for Social Development in Copenhagen in 1995, which adopted the UNICEF–UNDP proposed twenty-twenty compact for human development. These nations pledged to ensure the provision of at least the very basic human development levels for all people. Most LDCs can achieve minimum levels of nutrition, safe drinking water, primary health care, population stabilization, and access to basic education by adjusting existing developmental priorities. However, some of the poorer countries will require international assistance in addition to their own domestic efforts. At Copenhagen, the UNDP estimated that these additional costs would be $30 to $40 billion per year over ten years.[6] Five years later in 2000, it was estimated that the fulfillment of these basic social services was approximately $206 to $216 billion, while the funds channeled to those areas totaled about $136 billion. As a result, an increase of at least $70 to $80 billion annually was estimated to be needed to provide full coverage.[7]

The twenty-twenty compact illustrates how most of these funds can be found within existing budgets. At the beginning of the twenty-first century, developing countries devoted on average approximately 13 percent of their national budgets to these basic human development concerns. Raising this figure to 20 percent would provide the equivalent of additional billions of dollars in resources. This money could be diverted primarily from wasteful military spending and prestigious development projects. This restructuring is doable; achieving the budgetary goal of 20 percent is feasible. Developed donor countries, at the same time, allocated only 8 to 9 percent of their foreign economic aid to these human priorities (health care, basic education, mass-coverage water supply systems, and so on). If these donors would readjust their aid allocation for these human priority goals, this would provide additional billions of dollars to these human rights priorities. This would require donor nations to not use political criteria in the allocation of 20% of their aid funds, and instead award this aid to meet these human development priorities in the poorest countries. Combined, the twenty-twenty compact could potentially produce most of the required $80 billion. It should be emphasized that these funds are already part of government budgets, and no new taxes are envisioned. These needs can be met through a restructuring of existing budget priorities.[8]

In developing countries, average spending on these social services unfortunately remains very low. One study in 2000, for example, indicated that spending averaged between 12 to 14 percent in these critical areas for thirty developing countries. Defense spending and debt service continued to be given priority. Few developing countries allocated the minimum 20 percent to basic social services. Some allocations were astonishingly low: 4% in Cameroon, 7.7% in the Philippines, and 8.5% in Brazil.[9]

The ESC could focus primarily on the twenty-twenty compact. It could be responsible for pressuring industrialized and less-developed states to implement twenty-twenty. Some developing states are now living up to their side of twenty-twenty and allocating 20 percent of public spending to basic social services. But, according to the UNDP, at the beginning of the twenty-first century no donor state was living up to its commitment to allocate 20 percent of its aid budget to basic social services.[10] Historically, the UN has often been successful when it engaged in a constructive dialogue with states and helped them come into compliance with international norms. The ESC could similarly engage nation-states on ways to fulfill their obligations under twenty-twenty, and help to mobilize public pressure to support this effort. As mentioned, states would be required to report yearly on their progress toward achieving twenty-twenty. The ESC could pressure international financial institutions (i.e., World Bank, IMF) and trade organizations (i.e., WTO) to focus their policies on helping states achieve twenty-twenty. The ESC could spur rich and poor nations to support twenty-twenty by cutting back on wasteful military spending and investing in the protection of public goods. Twenty-twenty shows that it is possible to readjust priorities and develop policies to meet basic needs and promote economic equality. With this clear and straightforward mandate, the ESC could play a principal leadership role in global economic governance.

The composition of the new ESC should reflect the new balance of economic and political power in the world today with all important geographical regions or political constituencies represented. Permanent members of the ESC could be the most populous nations and those with the largest economies. This would include Bangladesh, Brazil, China, France, Germany, India, Indonesia, Japan, Nigeria, Pakistan, Russia, South Africa, United Kingdom, and United States. Other nations and regions could be represented on a rotating basis. For example, rotating members of the UN Security Council are elected from the following regions: three from Africa; two from Asia; three from Europe; and two from Latin America. The ESC could establish a similar scheme to ensure global representation. It would be important to keep the membership relatively small and manageable—thirty members or less would be ideal. Decisions should be made only in a way that reassures both the developed and underdeveloped countries. Thus, a majority of the representatives of both areas would be required to agree (modeled after the successful governance system established in the GEF described in chapter 4). And finally, the ESC would need a competent, professional secretariat. The final composition of the ESC will have to be carefully negotiated. But the establishment of a balanced and functional ESC dedicated to the principles of economic equality is clearly feasible, practical, and necessary.[11]

Finance Global Public Goods

Launch a Global Public Goods Fund

Economic and social human rights depend on the protection and provision of public goods. As discussed in chapter 2, global public goods include basic education, a healthy environment, food and water, primary health care and sanitation, and housing. Elements of these goods are all nonexcludable and nonrivalrous in consumption, and these goods are frighteningly undersupplied. Individual nations can provide equal access to these public goods for each of their citizens only through multilateral action in international law and international organization.

The twenty-twenty proposal is a clear beginning, but it will not raise sufficient funds to achieve universal and equal access to global public goods. The second proposal of the Global New Deal is thus to establish a Global Public Goods Fund. This fund would raise the capital necessary for the protection and fulfillment of these public goods. For example, the Copenhagen World Summit for Social Development estimated that a poverty eradication program would cost an additional $40 billion per year.[12] The proposed Global Public Goods Fund could provide this financing.

The fund could also be used to finance international responses to crises including earthquakes, hurricanes, resource depletion, famines, and other natural disasters and human emergencies. Funding is needed to respond adequately and effectively to such crisis conditions that often affect millions of people. The crisis list is extensive and includes the rebuilding of war-torn societies (from Haiti to Afghanistan to Rwanda to Sudan and the Congo) and resettling the millions of refugees whose lives have been disrupted by wars. Emergency funding of this nature has historically been inadequate and raised in an ad hoc manner. The Global Public Goods Fund could become the permanent international agency ready to respond to these emergency situations.

In addition, the fund could play a central role in financing the global transition to sustainable development and the preservation of the global commons. As discussed in chapter 4, the UN Conference on the Environment and Development in Rio de Janeiro in 1992 produced an action plan called "Agenda 21." Implementation of this global program of environmental protection and renewal was estimated to cost about $125 billion per year in external financing alone.[13] The fund could provide this financing.

The twenty-twenty proposal is a start. But clearly as the costs of providing global public goods and responding to global emergencies continue to rise, more funding is necessary. The Global Public Goods Fund is intended to fill this financing gap and could be administered by the ESC.

The Tobin Tax

One of the most widely debated proposals for raising the capital to support global public goods is called the "Tobin Tax." James Tobin, winner of the Nobel Prize for Economics in 1981, first suggested a small tax on the international movement of speculative capital as a means for stablizing global finance and investments. In his Janeway Lectures at Princeton in 1972, Tobin viewed the tax as a means to enhance the efficacy of macroeconomic policy. This idea, as Tobin said, "sank like a rock" and was anathema to central bankers. Yet, the proposal received a strong boost at the World Social Summit in Copenhagen in 1995 where it was endorsed and promoted by a number of distinguished economists and politicians, including the former President of France, François Mitterrand. (Conservatives and bankers would like the Tobin Tax to go away. One central banker commented, "Oh, that again. It's the Loch Ness Monster, popping up once more!")[14]

Estimates at the Copenhagen Summit were that a tax rate of only .05 percent on the international movement of speculative capital from 1995–2000 could raise over $150 billion each year. The volume of foreign exchange transactions worldwide reached $1.3 trillion per day in 1995, a total of $312 trillion in a year of 240 business days. Thus, a small tax of .10 percent would yield approximately $312 billion, and a tax of .05 percent well over $150 billion.[15]

Tobin cautions, however, that these figures should be scaled back with more modest expectations predicted. First, the tax itself will reduce the overall volume of such international transactions and thus reduce revenues. And second, the job of tax collection would fall to member states themselves. It would be desirable to allow small, underdeveloped countries to retain shares of the collected revenues, sometimes up to 100 percent. These countries clearly need these funds to provide access to public goods. Furthermore, it might "sweeten the pill if each nation were allowed to retain at least 50 percent of the proceeds and to choose—among internationally agreed alternatives—where the tax revenues would go."[16]

Accepting these conditions on splitting the revenue from the Tobin Tax, Inge Kaul and John Langmore forecast that most of the revenue would be retained nationally—up to 100 percent for low-income countries. Even if this is the case, these scholars estimated in 1996 that a tax of just .10 percent minus these conditionalities would still raise $27 billion a year for international purposes.[17]

It should be noted that Tobin's main motivation was never to raise revenue. In his mind, the central benefit of this tax on the movement of speculative capital was to reduce short-term speculation and increase national policy autonomy. The volatilities and ongoing financial crisis in the global economy have led many to agree with the need for some control on financial markets. The Mexican and Asian crises of the 1990s, in particular, convinced many of the need for some regulation of speculative capital. The 2009 global recession led others to endorse similar types of financial regulation. And this is the beauty of the Tobin Tax. For not only does it potentially raise the funds needed to finance and provide global public goods, it also pushes, as Tobin writes, "exchange rates [to] reflect to a larger degree long-run fundamentals relative to short-range expectations and risks." Tobin estimates that 80 percent of foreign exchange transactions involve "round trips of seven days or less. Most occur within one day." As seen in Mexico, Indonesia, and elsewhere, the human suffering caused by such rapid capital flight is horrifying. The Tobin Tax would lessen the incentive for such irresponsible action.[18]

Hear the Victims' Voices

Adjudicate Violations of Economic and Social Human Rights

One of the central dilemmas in the development of a workable system of global governance in the area of human rights is the concept of sovereignty. In international law, states have certain sovereign rights and peoples have rights to self-determination. Attempts at the enforcement of human rights from above, a top-down approach, often appear in conflict with principles of nonintervention and the prerogatives of a local community. UN attempts to "mobilize shame" and enforce sanctions against violating states often provoke a local backlash. Who is the UN to come in and tell a native people what to do? And furthermore, international organizations are often out of touch with the reality of forces on the ground. This has led to misjudgments and secondary effects of actions (like sanctions) hurting the vulnerable population the action was intended to help.

However, the successes in international action in support of human rights provide a direction for future action. One such success was the international campaign against apartheid in South Africa. The international "mobilization of shame" and global economic sanctions did contribute to the successful effort of the African National Congress to end this racist system of governance. A fundamental reason these international actions were effective was because they were done in conjunction with a local movement for national liberation. The international community was following the lead of the people of South Africa and responding to their requests. The UN was not imposing sanctions against the will of the people. The people organizing and fighting for human rights in South Africa requested the UN support and asked for the economic sanctions. NGOs, intergovernmental organizations (IGOs), and individual states responded and imposed harsh sanctions to help force the government of South Africa to adhere to the basic standards of human dignity found within international human rights law.[19]

The third part of the Global New Deal draws on these lessons and endorses a proposal that is responsive to the voices of the victims and coordinated with efforts for change being conducted at the local level. As opposed to a top-down effort that could potentially undermine local reform efforts (as critics argue is embodied in the proposed "social clause" to the WTO reviewed in chapter 3), the Global New Deal calls for the enhancement of the power of the Economic Rights Committee to be able to hear and respond to the voices of the oppressed.

The UN General Assembly approved an optional protocol to the Economic Rights Treaty on 10 December 2008. The idea behind the protocol is to link the Economic Rights Committee directly to individuals and groups in civil society who are denied economic and social rights protection. The purpose of the optional protocol is to give legal standing to victims of abuse and those organizing for social change. The voices of those individuals who are denied economic and social human rights deserve to be heard.

The approved optional protocol provides the basic framework for a workable system.[20] The Economic Rights Committee has formulated clear procedures for the submission of complaints from individuals and groups. The protocol spells out how the Economic Rights Committee is to process and adjudicate these complaints. As noted in chapter 3, the Economic Rights Committee already reviews the self-reporting by states parties on their compliance with the terms of the Economic Rights Treaty. But self-reporting is obviously inadequate, as most states will want to present the best case possible. The protocol is a means for the Economic Rights Committee to obtain more reliable and objective information. It will allow individuals and affected groups to present to the Economic Rights Committee evidence on state policies that fail to uphold the obligation to respect, protect, and fulfill economic and social human rights. Victims will be able to appeal directly to the Economic Rights Committee to pressure their state to uphold its commitment to international law.

However, in this era of globalization, individuals and groups should also be able to raise violations of international law by IFIs, trade organizations, powerful individuals, and transnational corporations (TNCs) as well as states. The often negative impact of economic globalization on the poor has been documented and discussed. IFIs, trade organizations, and TNCs should be held accountable to international human rights law and global workers rights standards. Citizens from both developed and underdeveloped countries need an avenue to voice their complaints against IFIs, trade organizations, and TNCs. Through the protocol, the Economic Rights Committee will provide the means for these victims to speak and the legal support for their case to be heard. In addition, the protocol includes an inquiry mechanism through which parties may permit the committee to investigate, report on, and make recommendations on "grave or systematic violations" of the Economic Rights Treaty. Such an inquiry mechanism may allow the Economic Rights Committee to examine the work of IFIs, trade organizations, and TNCs as well as states. Currently, the Economic Rights Committee has no legal basis on which to assess the impact of IFIs and TNCs on economic and social human rights. The optional protocol may change this and give the Economic Rights Committee this authority.[21]

There should also be a mechanism in international society for individuals and groups to file complaints of unjust and inequitable trading and investment practices that harm the economic and social rights of a nation's citizens. The Economic Rights Committee is the logical body to hear and resolve such complaints. Citizens and organizations within the developed and underdeveloped states would have the authority to register such complaints. The impetus for these actions would thus come from the local community, the citizens themselves. There would be no imposition of norms from outside, but rather a cooperative movement to protect social justice. This Global New Deal proposal, in effect, consolidates the social clause idea into this expansive view of the optional protocol to the Economic Rights Treaty. In this interpretation of the protocol, the Economic Rights Committee is empowered to hear complaints against all economic actors, including states, TNCs, trade organizations, and IFIs.

The current optional protocol to the Political Rights Treaty has not led to an overwhelming and unworkable magnitude of individual complaints. The Human Rights Committee procedures weed out frivolous complaints. Individuals must first exhaust all local remedies. These same procedures are in place with the new optional protocol to the Economic Rights Treaty. The hope is that the mere existence of these procedures will cause states, IFIs, trade organizations, powerful individuals, and TNCs to show more respect for economic and social human rights. In addition, NGOs and individuals in civil society can use the judgments and rulings of the Economic Rights Committee in their work to help mold public opinion. All of this is key to global governance and central to the creation of a new international environment that protects, respects, and fulfills economic and social human rights.

The dispute settlement procedures of the WTO give real power to this intergovernmental organization. Member states must adhere to the decisions of the dispute settlement bodies of the WTO or face penalties, including economic sanctions. Ideally, similar enforcement measures in the area of economic and social rights should also be in place. If states can now be punished for violating principles of free trade, why should they also not be subject to sanctions for violating the economic and social human rights of their citizens? Eventually, such a system may evolve. But in the current international environment, it is hard to envision states giving this much power to the UN or other international organizations committed to social justice.

However, it is realistic to think that states would approve an avenue for the voices of the victims to be heard. It is realistic to believe that the optional protocol to the Economic Rights Treaty will be ratified by the states parties to the Economic Rights Treaty. The people of the developed and underdeveloped worlds have a joint interest in correcting injustices in the global economy. Enhancing the powers of the Economic Rights Committee provides a way to shine a bright light on these human adversities and mobilize political support for change within affected states. The Global New Deal urges state ratification of the optional protocol.

Maintain Ecological Balance

Set Up a World Environment Organization

A myriad of proposals have been drafted to strengthen international environmental governance. Some suggest upgrading the UN Environment Program's (UNEP) status from a program to an organ of the UN General Assembly, similar to the UNDP. Others assert that a new functional commission of ECOSOC or standing committee on the environment should be established. Additional ideas call for transforming the UN Trusteeship Council into an environmental security council or remodeling the UN Security Council to allow global environmental issues to be integrated more fully into the UN's functioning.[22] The Global New Deal embraces the need for streamlined and improved global environmental governance and calls for the creation of a new World Environment Organization (WEO).

In 1994, Daniel C. Esty proposed such a WEO to provide the comprehensive international coordination needed to respond to environmental threats. He called for the creation of a single organization with a mandate and resources to coordinate worldwide efforts to protect the environment. Such an organization could provide an environmental balance to the WTO's sole focus on liberalizing trade. Esty believes that free traders and environmentalists would both benefit from the creation of an international institution committed to the development of effective policy to ameliorate long-term environmental harms. Esty writes:

> Like the GATT [WTO], a [WEO] . . . would provide a bulwark against domestic pressures that undermine long-term thinking and make sensible policies hard to achieve. Such a body could serve as an honest broker in transnational environmental disputes, assessing risks and benefits from environmental threats and allocating costs and cleanup responsibilities. Just as the GATT built on the core concept of nondiscrimination as a means to trade liberalization, a [WEO]. . . would establish guidelines, centered on the polluter pays principle, to promote international cooperation in addressing environmental matters and the integration of economic and environmental policy goals.[23]

Michael W. Doyle and Rachel I. Massey believe that Esty's hypothetical WEO is optimistic. They argue instead that any new international environmental organization should have more limited goals. Their idea is to begin with a pragmatic mandate, achieve measurable success, and then grow over time.[24] Other scholars fear that a strong, centralized WEO could take pressure off other UN agencies to integrate environmental protection into their programs. To address these concerns, some advocate the creation of a high commissioner for environmental protection within the UN system. The high commissioner could coordinate international environmental policy and force long-range planning. The prestige and clout of the Office of the High Commissioner—the highest rank in the UN system under the secretary general—would hopefully bring more credibility and thus more action on environmental priorities. The high commissioner would be appointed by the UN General Assembly and could receive and assess communications from states, private organizations, and private individuals concerning compliance with or violation of international environmental law. Perhaps both a high commissioner and the new WEO are needed to lead the global transition to sustainability and the protection of the global commons.[25]

Hilary French, however, notes that debates over form should not distract us from the more critical questions of function. There is a pressing need for centralizing global environmental governance. A WEO, for example, could serve an important monitoring and implementing role in international environmental law. The current dispersed collection of treaty bodies could be brought under one roof. The WEO would need to be given sufficient financial resources to monitor treaty compliance and stimulate innovative programs. French points to the precedent set by the International Labor Organization (ILO), which has successfully strengthened hundreds of labor standards such as workplace safety and child labor. The ILO also reviews members' compliance with its standards and provides technical assistance to help them with this task. Through its investigations alone, the ILO often generates enough pressure to bring an errant country into line. The tripartite governing structure of the ILO of labor, business, and government may also be a model for a WEO to emulate.[26]

A strong WEO with authority and funding could address the difficult situation LDCs face of "institutional overload." P. M. Haas, R. O. Keohane, and M. A. Levy note that there are so many organizations and treaties in existence relating to the environment that governments are spread too thin and have difficulty complying with them all. International environmental protection thus suffers from "institutional overload."[27] An effective and well-funded WEO could resolve this conundrum. Rather than having to relate to multiple organizations, governments would be able to work with the WEO on environmental matters. The WEO could consolidate the reporting procedures of international environmental treaties and work with developing states to ease their reporting and compliance burdens.

In addition to UNEP, the CSD, and the Global Environment Facility (GEF), there are now an overwhelming number of environmental IGOs. The Food and Agriculture Organization, UNDP, UN Industrial Development Organization, World Bank, and World Meteorological Organization all have significantly expanded activities related to monitoring or protecting the environment. There are also issue-specific treaty secretariats for many environmental conventions, including biodiversity, hazardous wastes, oceans and seas, climate, and the ozone. All bureaucracies fight for larger budgets, bigger projects, and a central, leading role. The result is that these environmental organizations often compete with each other for management responsibility and limited international financing. A strong WEO could help resolve disputes and streamline reporting and monitoring. The less developed countries, in particular, would benefit from the central coordination of these reporting, monitoring, and managing functions. The WEO would not be replacing these other environmental IGOs. Rather, it would be ending redundancy, simplifying reporting, and hopefully establishing efficiency.

In regards to the global trading system, the WEO should be given powers equal to the WTO. Trade measures could be evaluated by the WTO for efficiency and by the WEO for environmental protection. Currently, WTO rules are enforced through binding dispute resolution procedures. If a national law is found in violation of WTO rules, a dispute resolution panel has the power to require the offending country to either pay a financial penalty (equal to the foregone trade) or amend its legislation. The WEO should be given the same compulsory power to enforce international environmental law as the WTO has to enforce international trade law.

Furthermore, when trade liberalization and environmental protection collide, the two organizations should be required to resolve the dispute collectively before any action is taken. Both WEO and the WTO, for example, would evaluate and determine whether a national environmental law was either a "nontariff barrier to trade" or a legitimate tool to protect the environment. A trade organization, like the WTO, should not be able to trump an environmental organization, like the proposed WEO. The preservation and restoration of our planet's fragile ecosystem would be the responsibility of the WEO.

As the lead environmental organization, the WEO could also coordinate the work of the other environmental IGOs, including UNEP, CSD and GEF. This coordination function is critical to prevent overlap and redundancy. WEO should not try to gather all these organizations under one roof. As outlined earlier, these organizations serve clear purposes and functions and their existing capabilities and usefulness should not be undermined. By clarifying responsibilities and facilitating communication, WEO should help these other environmental organizations do their jobs well.

A beginning point for WEO is to learn from the experience of the General Agreement on Tariffs and Trade (GATT). GATT was organized around a few basic principles of liberal economics, such as nondiscrimination, reciprocity, and liberalization. Esty argues that a WEO should begin the same way, by organizing its work around a few basic environmental principles, including the polluter pays principle and the precautionary principle.[28]

With adequate financial backing, the WEO could reinvigorate and put some teeth into "Agenda 21," which still represents the most ambitious and comprehensive framework ever devised by governments for global environmental policy making. The intent of "Agenda 21" was to stimulate cooperation on 120 separate initiatives for environmental and economic improvement. However, every chapter's finance and implementation sections were weak, and political support for implementing the measures waned when financing was not forthcoming. Rather than starting over, the WEO could begin from the framework established at the Rio Conference and develop a financing and implementation program to turn those promises into reality.

The WEO could help subsidize research and development in energy efficiency, renewable energy, and zero-emission cars. Many believe, for example, that the only feasible alternative to our environmentally destructive fossil fuel or carbon–based energy economy is a solar/hydrogen-based economy. Solar/hydrogen-based energy sources include wind power, solar photovoltaics, geothermal power, and direct sunlight. Wind and solar cells are thought to be the cornerstones of a new local energy-based economy. The WEO could help nations make the transition to a solar/hydrogen-based economy.[29]

The WEO must have the financial clout needed to fight for the world's environmental security. Many commentators have noted the social consequences of ecological decay. As the per capita availability of water, fish, and land continues to decline, regional instabilities are bound to produce conflict. Ecological devastation often leads to massive homelessness by creating thousands of "environmental refugees" around the world. The WEO could hopefully give humanity a chance to create real economic and environmental security.

Funding for the WEO could come from the Global Public Goods Fund (already described) and the proposed Global Demilitarization Fund defined later in this chapter.

Prioritize the Rights of Racial and Ethnic Minorities

Focus Policy on Primary Health Care

The Minority Rights Committee could monitor the degree to which states parties ensure primary health care and sanitation to their entire populations, including all racial minorities.

The plight of the aboriginal people in Canada is illustrative. At the beginning of the twenty-first century, aboriginal people had seven years less life expectancy than the overall Canadian population and almost twice as many infant deaths. The link here between social conditions and health could not be more stark. The poor health of indigenous people in Canada is directly related to the social environment (i.e., access to health care, sanitation, and so on). Canada as a nation is proud of being consistently ranked at or near the top on the UNDP Human Development Index (HDI). Yet, if on-reserve native peoples of Canada were a nation ranked on the HDI, they would place at approximately a shocking sixty-third. Aboriginal people are among the poorest of Canadians.[30]

The less developed and least developed countries have the ability to address basic medical needs. At the beginning of the new century, health experts estimated, for example, that almost half of the preventable deaths of infants under five years old in poor countries were the result of diarrheal and respiratory illness, exacerbated by malnutrition. These conditions can be most effectively dealt with through preventive measures at local facilities. The Minority Rights Committee can examine if a nation is implementing cost-effective strategies for serving the entire population, rather than only the well off, or only a particular racial group. In some countries, for example, a single teaching hospital can take 20 percent or more of the government's health budget. Almost all developing countries can point to examples of major hospitals whose operational costs resulted in the curtailment of health clinics and preventive services. The right to health involves access to standard or primary medical care that must be taken to be more basic than the "freedom" to receive costly surgical procedures. Vulnerable populations in poor countries have the right to insist on access to basic medical care. The Minority Rights Committee should examine the distribution of health benefits and the provision of health services for all racial and ethnic groups.[31]

The policies of nonstate actors, however, will also have to be examined by the Minority Rights Committee. In Brazil, for example, in the 1990s IMF-mandated cuts of 40.5% in social expenditures led to reductions of 12.3% in education, 6.6% in health, 83.1% in the Social Action Sanitation Program, and 50% in the retraining programs for unemployed workers. These forced cuts made it difficult for Brazil to meet its economic and social obligations under international law. It became difficult for Brazil to achieve universal and equitable access by all people to primary health care. The poorest sectors of the population have not had access to the expensive, technologically complex health care in the urban areas. Inequality and social exclusion are the result as a double network of social services is created—one for the rich and the other for the poor.[32]

Focus Policy on Basic Education

The Minority Rights Committee could monitor the degree to which states parties ensure basic education to their entire populations, including all racial minorities. International human rights law requires states to ensure basic education for their citizens. Poverty again is not an excuse for failing to implement policies and practices toward these ends. UNICEF has documented the ways in which poor countries can achieve remarkable results with commitment and farsightedness. In Asia, for example, the Indian state of Kerala entered the twenty-first century with a 90 percent literacy rate. This is far in excess of the 58 percent literacy rate in Punjab, which has more than double Kerala's per capita income.[33] Or compare Vietnam and Pakistan. In 2008, Pakistan, with a much greater per capita income, has a 49 percent adult literacy rate compared to Vietnam's 90 percent.[34] Pleas of poverty preventing adequate education expenditures ring particularly false when military spending in South Asia continues unabated.

It is within the Minority Rights Committee's charge to regulate states parties' compliance with the provisions of the Minority Rights Treaty requiring access to education without discrimination. Indigenous and racial minorities consistently face unequal educational opportunities around the world. In Peru, for example, at the beginning of the twenty-first century the national average illiteracy rate was 13 percent, but among the indigenous population it reached 33 percent, and in the case of indigenous women 44 percent. In Uruguay, the black population had a greater dropout rate at all levels of schooling, and attained on average a year and a half less schooling than white people.[35] In 1984 in Slovakia, 80 percent of Roma children attended kindergarten, but only 15 percent did so in 2000. In the 1990s in India, the adult literacy rate among women of established tribes was 24 percent, compared with 39 percent for all Indian women.[36] The Minority Rights Committee can push Peru, Uruguay, Slovakia, and India to confront these issues and correct these inequities in educational opportunities.

National governments have far more resources to devote to education than are currently allocated. Governments need to be roused to recognize the priority of education. For many states, education just is not a priority. In 1999 UNICEF reported that only fourteen of the seventy African countries (20 percent) participating in the European Community's Lomé IV aid agreement (covering 1990–1999) ranked education and training a high priority. The overwhelming majority, forty-five countries, saw it as a low priority and six had no education or training programs at all.[37]

Yet, the social and economic value to a society of investing in basic education is unassailable. The role of UN treaty bodies is to hold nations accountable to their human rights obligations. The Minority Rights Committee can push states parties to assure that all citizens have access to primary health care and basic education.

Prioritize Women's Rights

The UNDP's Gender Development Index (GDI) measures differences between men and women in life expectancy, educational attainment, and earned income. The *Human Development Report 2007–2008* calculated the GDI for 157 countries and found gender inequality in every single society. However, some very diverse countries did show an improvement in the GDI rankings, including Denmark, Estonia, and Belize. This demonstrates once again that human development and gender equality can be achieved in different income levels, stages of development, and cultures.[38]

The 1995 Beijing Platform of Action called on governments to prepare national plans of action outlining implementation strategies to achieve the goals of the women's conference. By January 2000, a total of 116 states had submitted national action plans to the UN Division for the Advancement of Women. NGOs and other actors in civil society contributed to the documentation and analysis of many of these national reports. The UN Development Fund for Women reported that the majority of these reports focused on four critical areas: education and training, women in power and decision making, women and health, and violence against women. Only a few of the reports established time-bound targets and indicators for monitoring progress. When asked to assess achievements, most stated that a shortage of resources was a major obstacle to progress in all areas.[39]

Through a focus on primary health care and basic education of women, two of the priority areas from the Beijing Platform of Action, the Women's Rights Committee can help states formulate national policy to respect, protect, and fulfill economic and social human rights.

Focus Policy on Primary Health Care

Gender inequality in the provision of basic health care is devastating to the world's women. According to UN reports in 2008, over half a million women in developing countries died annually in childbirth or of complications from pregnancy. Only 35% of women giving birth in the least developed countries were attended to by a skilled health professional, leading millions to suffer serious long-term complications. In addition, hundreds of thousands of women, including teenage girls, died every year as a result of unsafe, illegal abortions. And women accounted for approximately half of all new cases of HIV infection. Basic health care is central to the capabilities approach—providing women with the opportunity and freedom to achieve well-being.[40]

The Women's Rights Committee's General Recommendation no. 24 on women and health is a valuable resource for states parties to utilize in the formulation of public policy for women. In this very detailed general recommendation, the Women's Rights Committee asks states parties to report on their understanding of (1) how policies and measures on health care address the health rights of women from the perspective of women's needs and interests and (2) how they address the distinctive features that differ for women in comparison to men, such as biological factors, socioeconomic factors, psychosocial factors, and confidentiality. The general recommendation outlines the states parties' obligations to respect, protect, and fulfill women's human right to basic health care. The obligation to respect requires states to refrain from obstructing action taken by women in pursuit of their health goals. For example, women's access to health services should not be restricted on the grounds that women do not have the authorization of husbands, partners, parents, or health authorities or because they are unmarried. The obligation to protect requires states to take action to prevent gender-based violence, a critical health issue for women. The obligation to fulfill imposes on states the duty to use the maximum of its available resources to ensure that women realize their rights to health care.

The committee then calls on states parties to

> implement a comprehensive national strategy to promote women's health throughout their lifespan. This will include intervention aimed at both the prevention and treatment of diseases and conditions affecting women, as well as responding to violence against women, and will ensure universal

access for all women to a full range of high-quality and affordable health care, including sexual and reproductive health services. States parties should allocate adequate budgetary, human and administrative resources to ensure that women's health receives a share of the overall health budget comparable with that for men's health, taking into account their different health needs.[41]

These reports, combined with the national action plans for implementing the programs from the Beijing Conference, provide the Women's Rights Committee and national governments the information needed to craft policy to meet the health needs of women. The Women's Rights Committee can press states to change policy and/or follow up on promises.

Focus Policy on Basic Education

Gender inequity in the provision of education is also devastating to the world's women. At the beginning of the twenty-first century, in all developing countries there were still 80 percent more illiterate women than illiterate men.[42] This meant that of the estimated 960 million illiterate adults in the world, about two-thirds were women. In some communities, more than half the female population aged fifteen and over could neither read nor write. Female literacy differed among regions. In Latin America and the Caribbean, overall female literacy was 85%, in Sub-Saharan Africa 49%, in northern and western Africa 45%, and in South Asia 38%. There are also major differences within countries and regions. For example, in the Arab world female literacy was slightly over 50%, but it ranged from lows of 20% in Yemen and 22% in Morocco to highs of 89% in Lebanon and 73% in Jordan and Kuwait. Rural and urban differences were often stark. In rural India, female literacy was only 30%, compared with 64% in urban areas. It is imperative for the Women's Rights Committee to monitor the degree to which states parties strive to ensure basic education to women.[43]

UN Millennium Development Goal 3 on gender equality includes the following target: "Eliminate gender disparity in primary and secondary education, preferably by 2005, and in all levels of education no later than 2015." In 2008, the UN reported progress toward this goal: "School doors have swung open for girls in nearly all regions as many countries have successfully promoted girls' education as part of their efforts to boost overall enrolment. Girls' primary enrolment increased more than boys' in all developing regions between 2000 and 2006. As a result, two out of three countries have achieved gender parity at the primary level. Despite impressive gains, girls account for 55 percent of the out-of-school population." The UN reported that while boys and girls from the richest households and urban areas in LDCs had near equal primary school attendance, this was not the case in the rural areas and poorest households. Interventions, such as the elimination of school fees, the provision of school meals and the promotion of later marriage, are needed to boost girls' primary school attendance.[44]

UN and World Bank statistics confirm that women deprived of education face serious obsticles to raising healthy and productive children. Uneducated women tend to have more children than they wish which can often compound financial problems and family difficulties. Better-educated women are able to use contraception more effectively and communicate better with their spouse about the desired family size. Studies also consistently show that women's education improves child survival. And furthermore, longitudinal studies in the United States and the United Kingdom show that, controlling for other household-level factors, a mother's education is associated with better child cognitive development.[45]

Women's education is linked to women's health. Education makes it possible and easier for women to obtain medical care, comply with instructions, and follow up with health care providers. Low education makes it more difficult for women to obtain health care information, prevent illness, and care for the sick.[46]

Cross-country analysis by the World Bank released in 2000 indicated that countries that invest in girls' education have higher rates of economic growth. The results were remarkable across all geographical regions and levels of economic development. Closing the gender gap in schooling is critical to successful human development. For example, analysis from Kenya suggested that giving women farmers the same education and inputs as men increased yields by as much as 22 percent. An analysis from Burkina Faso indicated that output could increase by 6 to 20 percent through a more equitable allocation of productive resources between men and women.[47]

The Women's Rights Committee could focus like a laser on these issues of women's education. The committee should draft a general recommendation on education, similar to the one on health care, to crystalize the committee's expectations in this important area. Governments would be put on notice that when they come before the Women's Rights Committee they will be questioned in particular on policies to achieve equality in women's education. Hopefully, since their reputation is on the line, these governments will enact policies to protect women's rights. The concluding observations and other reports from the Women's Rights Committee could be forwarded to the new ESC. The central role and prominence of the proposed ESC should result in abundant publicity of its proceedings. This attention should put additional pressure on states to prioritize public policy for the health and education of women.

Respecting, protecting, and fulfilling the economic and social rights of women is central to the success of the Global New Deal.

Reduce Military Spending

Found an International Verification Agency and a
Global Demilitarization Fund

The creation of a new International Verification Agency, proposed by Michael Renner, could help create confidence that disarmament enhances rather than undermines security. Ronald Reagan's quip to Mikhail Gorbachev, "trust but verify," holds true internationally. Effective inspections and monitoring arrangements are essential to verify compliance with disarmament agreements. This new agency would be charged with inspection responsibilities for nuclear, chemical, biological, and conventional disarmament. The new International Verification Agency could draw on the successful experience of existing disarmament agencies and agreements and expand the verification function to cover other armaments.[48]

For example, the Convention on the Prohibition of the Development, Production, Stockpiling and Use of Chemical Weapons and on Their Destruction (CWC) entered into force on 29 April 1997. The CWC was the first multilateral disarmament agreement to provide for the elimination of an entire category of weapons of mass destruction within a fixed time frame and under a universal verification mechanism. By August 2009, 188 states parties had ratified or acceded to the CWC.[49] The CWC established the Organization for the Prohibition of Chemical Weapons (OPCW) to verify global adherence to the treaty. In its first 22 months of operation, the OPCW conducted 500 inspections, totaling 28,000 inspection days, at nearly 260 sites on the territories of 29 states parties. By the end of March 1999, the OPCW had also conducted a total of 170 inspections at 63 former chemical weapon production facilities and 33 chemical weapon storage sites.[50] OPCW inspections accelerated in the first decade of the twenty-first century.

In 2007 the OPCW verified the destruction of thousands of metric tons of chemical warfare agents in key states parties, including Albania, India, Russia, and the U.S. The agency was able to verify that in 2007 Albania had destroyed their entire stockpile of chemical weapons. India in 2007 completed the destruction of 93% of its declared chemical weapons stockpile. And, as of 31 December 2007 the U.S. had destroyed a total of 14,074,585 metric tonnes of chemical-warfare agents (51% of its declared stockpile), on schedule to meet the agreed 2012 deadline for the complete destruction by the U.S. of all its chemical weapons. At the end of 2007 only five states parties remained with declared chemical weapons. This record of the OPCW demonstrates that it is possible for the international community to successfully monitor the spread of weapons of mass destruction and verify their elimination.[51]

The Convention on the Prohibition of the Use, Stockpiling, Production and Transfer of Anti-Personnel Land Mines and on their Destruction entered into force on 1 March 1999. The treaty had been ratified by 156 governments by August 2009.[52] This global treaty banning the use of land mines has achieved remarkable levels of success, despite the nonparticipation of the United States and China. A year and a half after the treaty went into effect, 10 million stockpiled antipersonnel mines had been destroyed, trade in these weapons had almost completely halted, and no shipments of land mines were recorded.[53] By the end of 2007, more than 42 million stockpiled mines had been destroyed, the number of mine-producing states had dropped to thirteen, and trade in land mines was virtually nonexistent.[54]

Similar verification measures are established in the Comprehensive Test Ban Treaty (CTBT) to halt nuclear weapons proliferation. As of August 2009, 148 states had ratified the treaty. For the treaty to enter into force, all forty-four states listed in annex 2 to the treaty must deposit their ratifications with the UN secretary general. These annex 2 states are those that possess nuclear power or research reactors. As of August 2009, of these forty-four states, forty-one had signed and thirty-five had ratified the treaty, including Russia. The treaty will enter into force only when the delinquent final 9 states in annex 2 submit their ratifications. Despite Russia's ratification of the CTBT, the United States, China, Israel, Pakistan, and India have refused to participate in this international effort to make the world a safer place.[55]

On 13 October 1999, after a brief debate and rushed vote, the U.S. Senate rejected ratification of the CTBT by a vote of 51 to 48. Senators voting against the treaty argued that it was unverifiable. Yet, the facts speak otherwise. The headquarters of the CTBT in Vienna has established an effective global verification regime, consisting of a global network of 337 facilities: 170 seismic, 60 infrasound, 11 hydroacoustic, and 80 radionuclide stations supported by 16 radionuclide laboratories. These facilities are located in eighty-nine countries around the world.[56] With this level of global monitoring and verification, it is very hard to imagine how a renegade state or terrorist group could successfully violate the CTBT and not get caught. Nuclear explosions are hard to hide. This strong and convincing case for a workable verification regime was not seriously studied or debated by the U.S. Senate. This U.S. Senate's action against this measure made it much more difficult to limit the spread of weapons of mass destruction and certainly made the world a more dangerous place.[57] President Barack Obama recognized the importance of the CTBT and announced in 2009 that his administration would "immediately and aggresively" seek ratification of the treaty. Obama described nuclear weapons as "the most dangerous legacy of the Cold War," and argued that the U.S. had a "moral responsibility" to lead global efforts for a world free of nuclear weapons.[58]

The CWC, Land Mines Convention, and the CTBT demonstrate that global monitoring and verification can be effective. A new International

Verification Agency can build on these efforts and work to create a global framework for disarmament and peace. It is in every nation's interest to slow down and eventually halt weapons proliferation, particularly weapons of mass destruction. The most powerful nations, including the United States, can do little to halt the spread of these insidious weapons through unilateral action. It is only through international law and multilateral action that true progress toward positive peace can be achieved.

The International Verification Agency could be funded through the creation of a Global Demilitarization Fund, as proposed years ago by Nobel Peace Prize winner Oscar Arias. Arias called on the nations of the world, both rich and poor, to commit themselves to at least a 3 percent a year reduction in their military spending levels. The rich would be asked to earmark only one-fifth of these savings toward the demilitarization fund, and the developing countries would contribute around one-tenth. The money raised could address not only disarmament efforts, but also other human security needs—such as famines, natural disasters, and resource depletion. The fund could be the key to adequate financing of the WEO.[59]

In preparation for the UN Copenhagen Conference on Social Development in 1995, the UNDP estimated that a 3 percent reduction in global military spending would yield about $460 billion over five years, of which around $385 billion would be generated in the industrial world and around $75 billion in the developing world. Eighty to ninety percent of these funds would remain in each nation's budget, to be used to finance industry conversion, sustain employment and incomes, and/or reduce taxes or budget deficits or government debt. However, if the rich nations were to allocate only 20 percent and the poor nations 10 percent of this "peace dividend" to the new Global Demilitarization Fund, this would generate at least $85 billion over five years, or about $14 billion per year.[60] This fund can be used to finance the verification sites and programs of the International Verification Agency. With adequate funding, international organizations can successfully monitor and control the spread of weapons of war.

Recently, Nobel Laureate Arias noted that "[t]his year [2009] alone, the governments of Latin America will spend nearly $50 billion on their armies. That's nearly double the amount spent five years ago, and it is a ridiculous sum in a region where 200 million people live on fewer than $2 a day and where only Colombia is engaged in an armed conflict. More combat planes, missiles and soldiers won't provide additional bread for our families, desks for our schools or medicine for our clinics. All they can do is destabilize a region that continues to view armed forces as the final arbiter of social conflicts."[61]

A Global Demilitarization Fund can help nations break the dangerous cycle of constantly expanding military spending. As Arias stated: "Only global cooperation can foster the security we have sought for so long, but which has eluded us so frequently. Let us make a definitive effort to use the peace dividend for the construction of just, prosperous and demilitarized societies. And let us capitalize on the benefits of disarmament to promote and guarantee the rewards of peace."[62]

Affirm International Human Rights Law

U.S. Ratification of the Economic Rights Treaty and the American Convention on Human Rights

Many U.S. citizens assume that the United States is in the forefront of the global movement for human rights. Yet only Presidents FDR and Carter spent key political capital to push forward an international human rights agenda. As a consequence, the U.S. is actually one of the world's laggards regarding the ratification and implentation of key human rights treaties. For example, the U.S. has not ratified the following treaties: Convention on the Rights of the Child, Women's Rights Treaty, Economic Rights Treaty, American Convention on Human Rights, and many others. We have seen throughout this book the importance of a human rights approach to the myriad of issues surrounding economic and social justice. U.S. active participation in this international human rights framework could further enhance this successful work and create mechanisms for the alleviation of the suffering of the poor and vulnerable inside America and around the world.

The Economic Rights Treaty is one of the central instruments of international law, ratified by 160 nations. As demonstrated in chapter three, the Economic Rights Committee has successfully defined the core obligations of states to respect, protect, and fulfill economic and social human rights. Furthermore, the monitoring and implementation mechanisms established by this committee have been surprisingly effective in pushing states to adopt national laws to protect the vulnerable. The United States should join this effort.

The World Health Organization reported in 2005 that the annual death toll from poverty-related causes was around 18 million, or one-third of all human deaths. Thomas Pogge noted that this added up to approximately 270 million deaths since the end of the Cold War.[63] Yet, as should be clear to readers of this book, this problem is not insurmountable. As Pogge wrote:

Though constituting 44 percent of the world's population, the 2,735 million people the World Bank counts as living below its more generous $2 per day international poverty line consume only 1.3 percent of the global product, and would need just 1 percent more to escape poverty so defined. The high-income countries, by contrast, have about 81 percent of the global product. With our average per capita income nearly 180 times greater than that of the poor (at market exchange rates), we could eradicate severe poverty world-wide if we chose to try—in fact, we could have eradicated it decades ago.[64]

The institutional structure established to monitor and implement the policies advocated by Pogge and others to end severe poverty have been established through the Economic Rights Treaty, the Economic Rights Committee, and the Office of the High Commissioner for Human Rights. As the world's wealthiest nation, the U.S. has an ethical duty to participate in this structure and help the global community alleviate severe economic injustice.

As demonstrated in chapter 8, the nations of Europe have established the world's most successful regional human rights regime through the European Convention on Human Rights, the European Social Charter, the European Committee on Social Rights, and the European Human Rights Court. The impact of these bodies on the protection of the economic and social human rights of the citizens of Europe has been profound. In case after case, national governments throughout Europe have brought their policies into compliance with the economic and social standards that meet the minimum requirements of international human rights law.

Efforts to establish similar human rights structures in the Western Hemisphere have unfortunately been stymied. The U.S. has not ratified the American Convention on Human Rights, which was adopted by the nations of the Americas meeting in San José, Costa Rica, in 1969. By not ratifying this treaty, the U.S. is not a member of the Inter-American Court of Human Rights and thus not a serious partner in the promotion and protection of fundamental human rights in the Western Hemisphere.

In addition, the U.S. has neither signed nor ratified the "Additional Protocol to the American Convention on Human Rights in the area of Economic, Social, and Cultural Rights (known as the "Protocol of San Salvador"). The Protocol of San Salvador seeks to follow the European Social Charter and clarify and enshrine protections in the economic, social, and cultural spheres in such areas as the right to work, the right to health, the right to food, and the right to education. The robust European human rights approach to poverty alleviation has been one of the most significant and profound human achievements of the late twentieth century. Every nation seriously concerned with these issues can learn from this experience and incorporate these succssful approaches into national policies. A first step is to recognize the importance of a regional approach to economic and social human rights protection in this era of economic interdependence. The American Convention on Human Rights and the Protocol of San Salvador provide the institutional vehicles to begin to emulate the successful European approach in the Western Hemisphere.

The Global New Deal in Action

Let me take a difficult example of the reality of global capitalism and see how economic and social human rights could be protected in the proposed Global New Deal. In 1995, garment workers in El Salvador earned fifty-five cents an hour sewing cotton tops and khaki pants for the GAP, a U.S. TNC. Workers were made to spend eighteen-hour days in unventilated factories with undrinkable water. Workers who complained were denied bathroom breaks and made to sweep outside all morning in the boiling sun. After an international outcry against sweatshops, including organizing by groups like the National Labor Committee (a union-backed, workers' advocacy group based in New York), the GAP made some changes. By 2001, garment workers for the GAP received coffee and lunch breaks, bathrooms were unlocked, the factory cleaned up, and employees could complain to a group of independent monitors. The GAP clearly was embarrassed by its glaring abuse of employee dignity and rights. Yet, in 2001 these GAP garment workers in El Salvador earned only sixty cents an hour, merely five cents more an hour than six years earlier. GAP garment workers endured long hours and had to meet high production quotas. Their small earnings still did not provide enough compensation on which to live.[65]

Can anything be done? Not according to the *New York Times* reporters who wrote:

> Yet the real alternative in this impoverished nation is no work. And government officials won't raise the minimum wage or even enforce labor laws too rigorously for fear that employers would simply move many jobs to another poor country. The lesson from the GAP's experience in El Salvador is that competing interests among factory owners, government officials, American managers and middle-class consumers—all with their eyes on the lowest possible cost—make it difficult to achieve even basic standards, and even harder to maintain them.[66]

In other words, there is no alternative! Without these exploitative, low-paying GAP jobs, there would be no jobs at all!

The GAP's profits in 2000 were $877 million.[67] The GAP could pay liveable, decent wages to its workers and still reap profits for its shareholders.[68] The GAP clearly has benefited from the unwillingness of the government of El Salvador to raise the minimum wage. The government and the GAP have focused on investments and profits and not on the rights of the most vulnerable. The GAP can blame the government of El Salvador for not enforcing labor laws. The government can blame the forces of the global economy that cause it to keep wages low. The UN, afraid to challenge state "sovereignty," accepts the status quo. And consumers are left in the dark and buy products often created under conditions of inhumanity.

How could the Global New Deal address these issues of economic and social human rights in El Salvador? How would the Global New Deal hold governments, TNCs (like the GAP, Nike, and Reebok), IFIs, trade organizations, and other actors answerable to international human rights law?

First, the ESC would hold the government of El Salvador account-able to keep its part of the twenty-twenty proposal. The government would have to report on what actions it had taken to promote economic equality—that is, how much public investment was made in education, health care, nutrition, sanitation, and so on. Public policy to promote economic equality and protect public goods would be promoted by the council. The government would be called on to protect a minimum living wage for all workers, including TNC employees. The impact of the poli-cies of the IMF, World Bank, and other global institutions on economic equality and the living standards of the people of El Salvador would also be assessed. In the past, IFI pressure for fiscal austerity has often led to government cuts in basic social services for the poor. The ESC could work with the IFIs to modify their austerity programs that have had such a devastating impact on the most vulnerable sectors.

Second, the ESC would hold aid donors responsible to keep their part of the twenty-twenty proposal. At least 20 percent of all existing aid to the country should go toward the provision of basic needs, including nutrition, sanitation, primary education, and so on. However, the Global Public Goods Fund (thanks to the Tobin Tax) could also help El Salvador fund such global public goods as the eradication of disease, poverty alle-viation, and environmental sustainability. All of these public policies and programs would enhance the quality of life for all workers in El Salvador, including TNC employees.

Third, the UN Economic Rights Committee would accept complaints from TNC employees through its new optional protocol. These employees would have the opportunity to demonstrate the ways in which their eco-nomic and social human rights had been violated. Any UN actions of rights enforcement would then be in response to the voices of the victims. Through this mechanism, the TNC could be held accountable to pay a living wage and uphold the basic economic and social human rights affirmed in international law. A decision by the Economic Rights Com-mittee in support of the requested changes by the TNC employees could help mobilize political support in El Salvador for such actions. TNCs, as well as states, could then be held accountable to human rights law.

Fourth, the WEO would work with the government of El Salvador to protect its natural capital and bring its national law into compliance with international environmental treaties. With managing and monitoring functions centralized in the WEO, it will be easier for El Salvador to meet its reporting obligations under international environmental law. In addition, the environmental impact of trade agreements would be assessed. Thanks to capital from the Global Demilitarization Fund, the WEO could help finance El Salvador's transition to a solar/hydrogen-based economy, the clear alternative to the environmentally destructive fossil fuel or carbon–based energy economy.

Fifth, the UN Minority Rights Committee would monitor the degree to which El Salvador ensures basic medical care and basic education to all of its citizens, including all racial minorities. The Minority Rights Committee would push for equal employment opportunities for all citizens, including access to jobs at TNCs. The Minority Rights Committee would work with the government of El Salvador to design public policy that guarantees economic and social rights for all without discrimination based on race or ethnicity.

Sixth, the UN Women's Rights Committee would look closely at the treatment of women in El Salvador, with a particular focus on education and health care. The Women's Rights Committee would work with El Salvador to develop time-bound targets and indicators for measuring progress in respecting, protecting, and fulfilling women's economic and social human rights. The impact of TNCs in El Salvador on women workers would be a particular concern. Policy designed to foster well-paying jobs for women would be promoted.

Seventh, the International Verification Agency, having established inspection and monitoring arrangements throughout Central America, would report to El Salvador on the level of compliance with disarmament treaties in the region. With this verified information, El Salvador could proceed with significant cuts in its military budget. Funds from this disarmament effort could be directed toward fulfilling the twenty-twenty priorities (outlined earlier). These programs of nutrition, basic education, health care, and sanitation benefit all workers in the country, including TNC employees.

It is only through this type of comprehensive approach that public policy for the protection of the economic and social human rights of the people of El Salvador or any country can be attained. Human rights fulfillment depends on holding all economic actors to these ethical standards.

Globalization from Below: NGOs and the Global New Deal

A prominent component of Roosevelt's New Deal was the ubiquitous blue eagle indicating public participation in the National Recovery Act.[69] The Roosevelt administration understood the importance of widespread support and broad participation in its program of reform and recovery.

Far-reaching popular collaboration is also indispensable for the success of the Global New Deal in the twenty-first century. Decisions that affect the quality of our lives and well-being cannot be left to remote global institutions that have historically suffered from a lack of transparency and accountability. Democratizing global governance is key to the success of the Global New Deal.

The sole mention of NGOs in the UN Charter is a single sentence in article 71 concerning the operations of the Economic and Social Council. The founders of the UN intended the organization to be a forum for sovereign states and never envisaged a central role for individuals from civil society operating through NGOs and transnational networks. Yet, through a focus on universal and timeless values combined with hard work and dedication, NGOs were able to overcome this statist bias and open up international organizations to new levels of public accountability. In addition, NGOs have developed alternative perspectives on global governance that often challenge the status quo and raise the concerns of the vulnerable and powerless.

By the 1990s, strong transnational organizations and movements for social justice, human rights, and ecological balance had emerged. It is thus impossible to really understand international relations today without analyzing the work and impact of these NGOs. According to the Brussels-based Union of International Associations, by 2007 there were more than 60,000 NGOs operating across international borders.[70] NGO scholars have estimated that half of all international social change NGOs work on three central issues: human rights, the environment, and women's rights.[71] These new global actors have fundamentally changed the fabric of international politics. They provide a vehicle for increasing public participation in global governance.

NGOs have joined together in powerful transnational networks and participated actively in all the major UN conferences on the environment, human rights, population, women, cities, and racism. Individuals and NGOs were instrumental in the initiation, promotion, and adoption of the 1997 Ottawa treaty that banned antipersonnel land mines and the 1998 agreement in Rome to create a UN International Criminal Court. Working from the bottom up, national, transnational, and global NGOs can bring about fundamental change in international relations.

There are a myriad of initiatives in civil society relevant to the concerns of the Global New Deal (see Pivotal NGOs Working on Economic and Social Human Rights: Building Democratic Participation in chapter 3). Individual and transnational NGOs are already working for many of the proposals of the Global New Deal, such as the twenty-twenty proposal, the Tobin Tax, and a WEO.

This active popular support for these initiatives is central to their eventual adoption. In fact, the institutional and procedural changes at the global level proposed in the Global New Deal depend on broad widespread support among people in all nations, in all races, and in all classes. It is only with such support that these initiatives will be adopted. And it is only with the active involvement of global civil society that global institutions will be held accountable to implement and uphold the Global New Deal program of reform.

Final Thoughts

At the beginning of this book, I quoted a student of mine who wanted to believe in the possibility of a world based on human rights, peace, and ecological balance, but given current arrangements of economic and political power, he just didn't "honestly see how we can make the jump from here to there." The Global New Deal was written to articulate a first step on the path from here to there. I hope that the feasible alternatives for global humane governance are now clearer to my student and to all who are infected with "realist" pessimism. We no longer need to accept needless suffering. The public policy proposals of the Global New Deal illustrate that there are alternatives; the human community does have options. There is nothing preordained by either the structure of the international system of states or the economic system of the market that makes economic and social human rights a dream. They are not a utopian fantasy. They can be achieved. The question is: Do we have the courage to walk this path?

Notes

Introduction to Second Edition

1. Gordon Brown, "The Special Relationship Is Going Global," *The Sunday Times* (timesonline.co.uk), 1 March 2009.

2. United Nations, *Millennium Declaration*, UN Doc.A/RES/55/2, 18 September 2000.

3. Current information on the Millennium Development Goals is available at www.un.org/millenniumgoals (accessed 18 June 2009).

4. United Nations Development Program (UNDP), *Human Development Report 1994* (New York: Oxford University Press, 1994), 6.

5. Joseph E. Stiglitz, *Globalization and Its Discontents* (New York: Norton, 2002), 23.

6. Juan Forero, "Still Poor, Latin Americans Protest Push for Open Markets," *New York Times*, 19 July 2002, 1(A).

7. Jean-Paul Sartre, Preface to *The Wretched of the Earth* by Frantz Fanon (New York, Grove, 1963), 22.

8. United Nations, *The Millennium Development Goals Report 2008*, 4; available at www.un.org/millenniumgoals/pdf/The%20Millennium%20Development%20Goals%20Report%202008.pdf (accessed 18 June 2009).

9. "The Crisis at Home and Abroad," *New York Times*, 4 March 2009, 26(A).

10. Anthony Faiola, "U.S. Downturn Dragging World into Recession, *Washington Post*, 9 March 2009, 1(A).

11. "More Than 1 Billion Go Hungry, the World Food Program Says," *New York Times*, 13 June 2009.

12. Shaohua Chen and Martin Ravallion, "The Developing World Is Poorer Than We Thought, but No Less Successful in the Fight against Poverty," Policy Research Working Paper 4703, The World Bank Development Research Group, August 2008.

13. Jan Vandemoortele, "Are We Really Reducing Global Poverty?" in Peter Townsend and David Gordon (eds.), *World Poverty: New Policies to Defeat an Old Enemy* (Bristol: The Policy Press, 2002), 378.

14. See, for example: Martin Wolf, *Why Globalization Works* (New Haven, CT: Yale University Press, 2005); Jagdish Bhagwati, *In Defense of Globalization* (New York: Oxford University Press, 2004).

15. Benjamin M. Friedman, "Globalization: Stiglitz's Case," *The New York Review of Books*, 15 August 2002, 52.

16. United Nations Development Program (UNDP), "Measuring Income Poverty: Where to Draw the Line," *Human Development Report 2003* (New York: Oxford University Press, 2003), 42.

17. The World Bank, "New Data Show 1.4 Billion Live on Less Than US$1.25 a Day, but Progress against Poverty Remains Strong," 26 August 2008; Chen and Ravallion, "The Developing World Is Poorer Than We Thought, but No Less Successful in the Fight against Poverty."

18. The World Bank, "New Data Show 1.4 Billion."

19. Jan Vandemoortele, "Are We Really Reducing Global Poverty?" 380 (emphasis in original).

20. David Gordon, "The International Measurement of Poverty and Anti-Poverty Policies," in Peter Townsend and David Gordon (eds), *World Poverty: New Policies to Defeat an Old Enemy* (Bristol: The Policy Press, 2002), 63.

21. Jan Vandemoortele, "Are We Really Reducing Global Poverty?" 382.

22. See Wolfgang Sachs, *The Development Dictionary* (London: Zed Books, 1992).

23. Thomas W. Pogge, Howard Nye, and Sanjay Reddy, "What Is Poverty?" *The New York Review of Books*, 21 November 2002.

24. Sanjay G. Reddy and Thomas W. Pogge, "How Not to Count the Poor" (version 6.2), 29 October 2005, 30–33. Available at www.columbia.edu/~sr793/count .pdf (accessed 18 June 2009).

25. Robert Bissio, "Rights in the Time of Crisis," *Social Watch Report 2008* (Montevideo, Uruguay: Instituto Del Tercer Mundo, 2008), 3–5.

26. "The MDGs, Easier Said Than Measured," *Social Watch Report 2008* (Montevideo, Uruguay: Instituto Del Tercer Mundo, 2008), 6.

27. United Nations Development Program (UNDP), *Human Development Report 1996* (New York: Oxford University Press, 1996), 27–28.

28. United Nations Development Program (UNDP), *Human Development Report 2000* (New York: Oxford University Press, 2000), 151.

29. United Nations Development Program (UNDP), *Human Development Report 2006* (New York: Palgrave Macmillan, 2006), 22.

30. Johan Galtung, *Human Rights in Another Key* (Cambridge: Polity Press, 1994); see William Felice, *Taking Suffering Seriously: The Importance of Collective Human Rights* (Albany, NY: SUNY Press, 1996), 21.

31. Christian Bay, "Taking the Universality of Human Needs Seriously," in J. Burton, ed., *Conflict: Human Needs Theory* (New York: St. Martin's, 1990); see William Felice, *Taking Suffering Seriously: The Importance of Collective Human Rights* (Albany, NY: SUNY Press, 1996), 21, 80.

32. Henry Shue, *Basic Rights: Subsistence, Affluence, and U.S. Foreign Policy* (Princeton, N.J.: Princeton University Press, 1980), 32; see William Felice, *Taking Suffering Seriously: The Importance of Collective Human Rights* (Albany, NY: SUNY Press, 1996), 82–83.

33. Thomas Pogge, "Poverty and Human Rights," in Rhona K. M. Smith and Christien van den Anker, eds., *The Essentials of Human Rights* (London: Hodder Arnold, 2005), 286–88.

34. Thomas Pogge, *World Poverty and Human Rights* (Malden, MA: Polity, 2002).

35. Pogge, *World Poverty and Human Rights*.

36. Alston further notes that the existing arrangements for reporting on progress made in relation to the MDGs remains "primitive and not especially convincing by most standards." The main "consumer" of the national reports appears to be the UNDP while their overall impact on national policy remains murky. In addition, there is a neglect of the human rights perspective and human rights standards in this reporting which instead remains "galvanized around the relatively bureaucratically formulated MDGs." Philip Alston, "Ships Passing in the Night: The Current State of the Human Rights and Development Debate Seen through the Lens of the Millennium Development Goals, *Human Rights Quarterly* 27 (2005): 814–15.

37. See Alston, "Ships Passing," 823–25.

Chapter 1

1. World Bank, "Understanding Povery," 2008, available at: http://web.world bank.org/WBSITE/EXTERNAL/TOPICS/EXTPOVERTY/EXTPA/0,,contentMD K:20153855~menuPK:435040~pagePK:148956~piPK:216618~theSitePK:430367,00. html (accessed 8 June 2009); World Bank, *World Development Report 2000/2001: Attacking Poverty* (New York: Oxford University Press, 2001), 3. See also: Adam W. Parsons, "World Bank Poverty Figures: What Do They Mean?" Share the World's Resources, 15 September 2008, available at: http://www.stwr.org/globalization/ world-bank-poverty-figures-what-do-they-mean.html (accessed 8 June 2009).

2. UNICEF, *State of the World's Children 2008* (New York: UNICEF, 2008), see http://www.unicef.org/sowc08/profiles/child_survival.php (accessed 8 June 2009).

3. The phrase "there is no alternative" has been attributed to Margaret Thatcher. See Douglas H. Boucher, *The Paradox of Plenty: Hunger in a Bountiful World* (Oakland, Calif.: Food First, 1999), 274. Pundits now refer to the phrase "there is no alternative" as "TINA."

4. Anti-Slavery International, "What Is Modern Slavery," available at: http:// www.antislavery.org/homepage/antislavery/modern.htm (assessed 8 June 2009). Barbara Crossette, "What It Takes to Stop Slavery," *New York Times*, 22 April 2001, 5(4); See also: "Slavery in the 21st Century," available at: http://www. vilaweb.cat/www/diariescola/noticia?id=2627878 (assessed 9 June 2009).

5. Barry Bearak, "Lives Held Cheap in Bangladesh Sweatshops," *New York Times*, 15 April 2001, 1(1); National Garmet Workers' Federation, "Sweatshops in Bangladesh," available at: http://www.waronwant.org/overseas-work/sweatshops -and-plantations/sweatshops-in-bangladesh (assessed 8 June 2009). In an earlier era, such economic exploitation was called "imperialism." Now it is often called the negative externalities of "globalization." Economist William K. Tabb provides a clear explanation of imperialism: "Imperialism is not simply about territorial acquisition, but more broadly involves gaining political and economic control over other peoples and lands, whether by military force or more subtle means. It is a matter of state policy and practice extending power and domination, often by economic means." See William K. Tabb, *The Amoral Elephant: Globalization and the Struggle for Social Justice in the Twenty-First Century* (New York: Monthly Review, 2001), 80.

6. Elisabeth Rosenthal, "Without 'Barefoot Doctors,' China's Rural Families Suffer," *New York Times*, 14 March 2001, 1(A). "Missing the Barefoot Doctors—Rural China (The State of Rural China)," *The Economist* (US), 13 October 2007.

7. UNICEF, *State of the World's Children 2008* (New York: UNICEF, 2008), available at http://www.unicef.org/sowc08/index.php; statistics summarized at: http://www.unicef.org/sowc08/profiles/child_survival.php (accessed 8 June 2009).

8. Elizabeth Olson, "Nations Cutting Aid to the Jobless, Study Says," *New York Times*, 22 June 2000, 4(C); One World South Asia, "ILO Predicts Global Unemployment Growth by 20 Million," 22 October 2008, available at: http://southasia.oneworld.net/todaysheadlines/ilo-predicts-global-unemployment-growth-by-20-million (accessed 8 June 2009).

9. Rachel Swarns, "Drug Makers Drop South Africa Suit over AIDS Medicine," *New York Times*, 20 April 2001, 1(A).

10. Melody Petersen, "Lifting the Curtain on the Real Costs of Making AIDS Drugs," *New York Times*, 24 April 2001, 1(C).

11. AVERT, "AIDS, Drug Prices and Generic Drugs," available at: http://www.avert.org/generic.htm (accessed 8 June 2009).

12. See "Note to the Reader on Terminology and Acronyms" in this book. Throughout the book, I will refer to each of the treaties and their relevant committees by subject matter. Thus, the International Covenant on Economic, Social and Cultural Rights becomes the Economic Rights Treaty and the committee established under it becomes the Economic Rights Committee. Hopefully, this language will be more accessible than the use of the standard UN acronyms to refer to the treaty and committee (CESCR and CESCR Committee). Thus, the International Convention on the Elimination of All Forms of Racial Discrimination becomes the Minority Rights Treaty and the committee established under it becomes the Minority Rights Committee, and so on.

13. Joel Cohen, *How Many People Can the Earth Support?* (New York: Norton, 1995), 54.

14. "More Than 1 Billion Go Hungry, the World Food Program Says," *New York Times*, 13 June 2009.

15. See Douglas Boucher, ed., *The Paradox of Plenty* (Oakland, Calif.: Food First, 1999); Partha Dasgupta, *An Inquiry into Well-Being and Destitution* (New York: Oxford University Press, 1993); *Poverty and Hunger: Issues and Options for Food Security in Developing Countries* (Washington, D.C.: World Bank, 1986); *The Hunger Project, Ending Hunger: An Idea Whose Time Has Come* (New York: Praeger, 1985).

16. For example, see the following suggestions: Richard Falk and Andrew Strauss's proposal for a "Global Parliament" in their "Toward a Global Parliament," *Foreign Affairs* 80, no. 1 (January–February 2001): 212–218; Richard Falk's outline for "Global Humane Governance" in his *On Humane Governance* (University Park: Pennsylvania State University Press, 1995); Al Gore's proposal for "A Global Marshall Plan" in his *Earth in the Balance: Ecology and the Human Spirit* (New York: Penguin, 1992); Mark Hertsgaard's plea for a "Global Green Deal" in his *Earth Odyssey: Around the World in Search of Our Environmental Future* (New York: Broadway, 1998).

17. See the chapter "The Morality of the Depths: The Right to Development As an Emerging Principle of International Law," in William F. Felice, *Taking Suffering Seriously: The Importance of Collective Human Rights* (Albany: SUNY Press, 1996), 69–90.

Chapter 2

1. Milton Friedman, *Capitalism and Freedom* (1962; reprint, Chicago: University of Chicago Press, 1982); James Caporaso and David Levine, *Theories of Political Economy* (New York: Cambridge University Press, 1992), 33–54; Dudley Dillard, "Capitalism," in *The Political Economy of Development and Underdevelopment*, ed. Charles Wilber and Kenneth Jameson (New York: McGraw-Hill, 1992), 85–93.

2. Dillard, "Capitalism," 88; see also P. T. Bauer, *Equality: The Third World and Economic Delusion* (Cambridge, Mass.: Harvard University Press, 1981).

3. Michael Joseph Smith, *Realist Thought from Weber to Kissinger* (Baton Rouge: Louisiana State University Press, 1986), 103.

4. Smith, *Realist Thought*, 99–133. Smith's chapter on Reinhold Niebuhr, "The Prophetic Realism of Reinhold Niebuhr," is exceptionally valuable.

5. See Jennifer L. Hochschild, *Facing up to the American Dream: Race, Class, and the Soul of the Nation* (Princeton, N.J.: Princeton University Press, 1996).

6. In a "perfect" market, a unique price for each good will arise out of all welfare-improving transactions. This price is a result of independent and voluntary actions of individuals pursuing the maximization of individual private satisfaction. If prices are free to respond to these independent actions, they will tend to settle at levels that allow for maximum welfare-improving transactions. The "free market" thus yields an optimum of social welfare. This type of group welfare has been termed "Pareto optimum" after its discoverer Vilfredo Pareto. See Caporaso and Levine, *Theories of Political Economy*, 82–83.

7. See Friedrich A. von Hayek, *The Road to Serfdom* (1944; reprint, Chicago: University of Chicago Press, 1994).

8. Robert Skidelsky, "Keynes's Middle Way," in *Readings in International Political Economy*, ed. David Balaam and Michael Veseth (Upper Saddle River, N.J.: Prentice Hall, 1996), 45–54.

9. Skidelsky, "Keynes's Middle Way," 49–50.

10. Mel Gurtov provides a useful and interesting comparison of realists and "corporate globalists." See Mel Gurtov, *Global Politics in the Human Interest*, 4th ed. (Boulder, Colo.: Rienner, 1999), 23.

11. Gurtov, *Global Politics*, 46–55.

12. Joel Cohen, *How Many People Can the Earth Support?* (New York: Norton, 1995), 272.

13. John Madeley, *Big Business, Poor Peoples: The Impact of Transnational Corporations on the World's Poor* (London: Zed, 1999), 72.

14. See Stanley Hoffmann, *World Disorders: Troubled Peace in the Post–Cold War Era* (Lanham, Md.: Rowman & Littlefield, 1998), 108–122.

15. See Bertell Ollman, *Alienation: Marx's Conception of Man in Capitalist Society* (New York: Cambridge University Press, 1971), 73–84.

16. See William F. Felice, *Taking Suffering Seriously: The Importance of Collective Human Rights* (Albany: SUNY Press, 1996), 131–150.

17. André Gunder Frank, *Capitalism and Underdevelopment in Latin America* (New York: Monthly Review, 1967); André Gunder Frank, *Latin America: Underdevelopment or Revolution* (New York: Monthly Review, 1969).

18. Samir Amin, *Delinking: Towards a Polycentric World* (London: Zed, 1985); Samir Amin, *Maldevelopment: Anatomy of a Global Failure* (London: Zed, 1990).

19. Paul A. Samuelson, "The Pure Theory of Public Expenditure," *Review of Economics and Statistics* (November 1954): 387–389. Please note that "good" refers to good or service.

20. Paul A. Samuelson, "Aspects of Public Expenditure Theories," *Review of Economics and Statistics* (November 1958): 335. For clear explanations of "nonexcludability" and "nonrivalrous consumption," see Ruben P. Mendez, *International Public Finance: A New Perspective on Global Relations* (New York: Oxford University Press, 1992), 53–66; and Inge Kaul, Isabelle Grunberg, and Marc A. Stern, eds., *Global Public Goods: International Cooperation in the 21st Century* (New York: Oxford University Press, 1999), 2–16.

21. Adam Smith, *The Wealth of Nations* (Indianapolis, Ind.: Liberty Classics, 1976), 723.

22. Samuelson, "Aspects of Expenditure Theories," 335.

23. With exclusion, there is no free rider problem. So why does a market tend to yield allocative inefficiency in this case? The zero marginal cost of providing a nonrivalrous good to an additional individual would suggest the allocatively efficient price is zero, while the good being subject to congestion would justify a price equal to the marginal congestion cost that an individual's consumption would impose on others. It is unlikely that a firm would charge a price that exactly reflects these principles, thus leading to suboptimal provision of the good.

24. Elinor Ostrom, Joanna Burger, Christopher B. Field, Richard B. Norgaard, and David Policansky, "Revisiting the Commons: Local Lessons, Global Challenges," *Science* (April 1999): 278–282.

25. For the classic analysis of a fishery as a common resource, see H. Scott Gordon, "The Economic Theory of a Common-Property Resource: The Fishery," *The Journal of Political Economy* (April 1954): 124-142.

26. Garrett Hardin, "The Tragedy of the Commons," *Science* 162 (13 December 1968).

27. Mendez, *International Public Finance*, 55.

28. See Thomas Dietz, Elinor Ostrom, and Paul C. Stern, "The Struggle to Govern the Commons," *Science* (12 December 2003): 1907–1912; Daniel W. Bromley, ed., *Making the Commons Work: Theory, Practice, and Policy* (San Francisco: Institute for Contemporary Policy, 1992); Elinor Ostrom, *Governing the Commons: The Evolution of Institutions for Collective Action* (New York: Cambridge University Press, 1990).

29. Kaul, Grunberg, and Stern, *Global Public Goods*, 509.

30. Samuelson, "The Pure Theory of Public Expenditure," 389.

31. Kaul, Grunberg, and Stern, *Global Public Goods*, xx-xxi.

32. Kaul, Grunberg, and Stern, *Global Public Goods*, 11, 509–510.

33. Kaul, Grunberg, and Stern, *Global Public Goods*, 24–25, 454–455.

34. Partha Dasgupta, *An Inquiry into Well-Being and Destitution* (New York: Oxford University Press, 1993), 149.

35. For example, see Robert Taylor, "Economics, Ecology, and Exchange: Free Market Environmentalism," *Humane Studies Review* 8, no. 1 (Fall 1992).

36. Dasgupta, *Inquiry into Well-Being*, 530, 540.

37. Dasgupta, *Inquiry into Well-Being*, 144.

38. Dasgupta, *Inquiry into Well-Being*, 40, 54.

39. Richard Jolly, "Profiles in Success: Reasons for Hope and Priorities for Action," in *Development with a Human Face: Experiences in Social Achievement and Economic Growth*, ed. Santosh Mehrotra and Richard Jolly (Oxford: Clarendon, 1997), 8.

40. Santosh Mehrotra, "Social Development in High-Achieving Countries: Common Elements and Diversities," in *Development with a Human Face*, ed. Santosh Mehrotra and Richard Jolly (Oxford: Clarendon, 1997), 29.

41. Amartya Sen, "Agency and Well-Being: The Development Agenda," in *A Commitment to the World's Women: Perspectives on Development for Beijing and Beyond*, ed. Noeleen Heyzer with Sushma Kapoor and Joanne Sandler (New York: UN Development Fund for Women, 1995).

42. Mehrotra, "Social Development," 40.

43. Mehrotra, "Social Development," 41.

44. Mehrotra, "Social Development," 48; see also William F. Felice, "Militarism and Human Rights," *International Affairs* 74, no. 1 (January 1998).

45. Mehrotra, "Social Development," 49.

46. Instituto Del Tercer Mundo, *Social Watch Report 2008: Rights Is the Answer* (Montevideo, Uruguay: Instituto Del Tercer Mundo, 2008).

47. Instituto Del Tercer Mundo, *Social Watch Report 2008*, 116; See also: Instituto Del Tercer Mundo, *Social Watch Report No. 2* (Montevideo, Uruguay: Instituto Del Tercer Mundo, 1998), 33.

48. United Nations Development Program (UNDP), *Human Development Report 2007/2008*, (New York: Palgrave Macmillan, 2007), 229–231; 238–240.

49. See Amartya Sen, *Inequality Reexamined* (Cambridge, Mass.: Harvard University Press, 1992), 12–13.

50. See Robert Nozick, "Distributive Justice," *Philosophy and Public Affairs* 3 (1973); Robert Nozick, *Anarchy, State and Utopia* (New York: Basic, 1974).

51. See John Rawls, *A Theory of Justice* (Cambridge, Mass.: Harvard University Press, 1971).

52. See Karl Marx, *Critique of the Gotha Program* (1891; reprint, New York: International, 1977).

53. For example, see conservative economist P. T. Bauer's rejection of the "unholy grail of equality" in Bauer, *Equality*.

54. Cohen, *How Many People*, 293.

55. Amartya Sen, *Development As Freedom* (New York: Knopf, 1999), 108.

56. Peter Singer, *Practical Ethics*, 2nd edition, (Cambridge: Cambridge University Press, 1993), 21.

57. John Arthur and William Shaw, "What Is Justice," in *Poverty Amidst Plenty: World Political Economy and Distributive Justice*, ed. Edward Weisband (Boulder, Colo.: Westview, 1989), 26–27.

58. David Beetham, "What Future for Economic and Social Rights," in *Politics and Human Rights*, ed. David Beetham (Oxford: Blackwell, 1995), 46.

59. Beetham, "What Future," 47.

60. Henry Shue, *Basic Rights: Subsistence, Affluence and US Foreign Policy* (Princeton, N.J.: Princeton University Press, 1980), 27.

61. Shue, *Basic Rights*, 32.

62. Rosa Luxemburg, *The National Question and Autonomy* (1909), reprinted in Micheline R. Ishay, ed., *The Human Rights Reader: Major Political Essays, Speeches, and Documents from the Bible to the Present* (New York: Routledge, 1997), 290–299.

63. Asbjørn Eide, "Realization of Social and Economic Rights and the Minimum Threshold Approach," in *Human Rights and the World Community*, ed. Richard Claude and Burns Weston (Philadelphia: University of Pennsylvania Press, 1992), 159–169. Eide argues that a state's obligation to fulfill the expectations of all for the enjoyment of the right to food may take two forms: "[A]ssistance in order to provide opportunities for those who have not; direct provisions of food or resources which can be used for food (direct food aid, or social security) when no other possibility exists, for example, (1) when unemployment sets in (such as under recession); (2) for the disadvantaged and the elderly; (3) during sudden situations of crisis or disaster . . . , and (4) for those who are marginalized (e.g., due to structural transformations in the economy and production)."

64. Haile Selassie quote, and 1 Thess. 3:10, quoted in Sen, *Inequality Reexamined*, 77.

65. UNDP, *Human Development Report 1996* (New York: Oxford University Press, 1996), 52–54.

66. Sen states: "Egalitarian policies to undo the inequalities associated with human diversity are much less problematic from the point of view of incentives than policies to undo inequality arising from differences in effort and application, on which much of the incentive literature has tended to focus. Thus, the importance of human diversity in inequality evaluation . . . may also have some considerable bearing on the nature and force of the incentive problem in pursuing egalitarian policy (particularly in the context of moving towards less inequality of elementary capabilities). This is not a trivial issue, in so far as antecedent diversities (e.g. in gender, age, class) are among the central factors behind unequal freedoms that people have in the world in which we live." See Sen, *Inequality Reexamined*, 143.

67. See Eide, "Realization of Social and Economic Rights," 163.

68. "The Limburg Principles on the Implementation of the International Covenant on Economic, Social and Cultural Rights," UN Doc. E/CN.4/1987/17, Annex, comprising 1–103, which were agreed on by the twenty-nine participants of the symposium held from 2–6 June 1986 at the University of Limburg, Maastricht, Netherlands.

69. John Kenneth Galbraith, *Economic Development* (Cambridge, Mass.: Harvard University Press, 1964).

70. Mary Robinson, "Development and Rights: The Undeniable Nexus," UN Office of the High Commissioner for Human Rights, 26 June 2000.

71. UNDP, *Human Development Report 2000*, 20.

72. Sen, *Inequality Reexamined*, 4–5, 39.

73. Sen, *Inequality Reexamined*, 49, 81.

74. Sen, *Inequality Reexamined*, 81–82.

75. Sen, *Inequality Reexamined*, 33, 38.

76. Sen, *Inequality Reexamined*, 151.

77. Sen notes, for example, that the capability deprivation of African Americans cannot be explained solely through an examination of income figures. It is rather the result of a variety of factors, including problems of health care, education, and urban crime. Residents of Harlem have a higher income than the average Bangladeshi citizen. Yet, according to the *New England Journal of Medicine*, men in the Harlem region of rich New York City have less of a chance to reach the age

of forty than Bangladeshi men. Information on incomes doesn't explain this phenomena. Nor does it explain for the country as a whole why African Americans in the age group thirty-five to fifty-five have 2.3 times the mortality rate as do whites in the United States. Low income is just one factor among many explaining these conditions. Sen points to other aspects of the social environment, including the inadequacy of health facilities, the violent modes of inner-city living, and the absence of social care. See Sen, *Inequality Reexamined*, 114–115.

78. Richard N. Cooper, "The Road From Serfdom: Amartya Sen Argues that Growth Is Not Enough," *Foreign Affairs*, January/February 2000, Vol. 79, No. 1, 165.

79. James North, "Sen's Sensibility," *The Nation*, 6 December 1999, 41.

80. Sen, *Development As Freedom*, 20–21.

81. Sen, *Development As Freedom*, 3.

82. Joseph E. Stiglitz, "Knowledge As a Global Public Good," in Inge Kaul, Isabelle Grunberg, and Marc A. Stern, *Global Public Goods: International Cooperation in the 21st Century* (New York: Oxford University Press, 1999) 309, 310.

83. Ruben P. Mendez, *International Public Finance: A New Perspective on Global Relations* (New York: Oxford University Press, 1992), 66–69.

84. The Convention on Biological Diversity, Article 2, available at: http://www.cbd.int/convention/articles.shtml?a=cbd-02 (accessed 9 July 2009).

85. Charles Perrings and Madhav Gadgil, "Conserving Biodiversity: Reconciling Local and Global Public Benefits" in Inge Kaul, et. al., *Providing Global Public Goods: Managing Globalization* (New York: Oxford University Press, 2003), 532–533.

86. David Hunter, James Salzman, Durwood Zaelke, *International Environmental Law and Policy* (New York: Foundation Press, 2007), 489–490.

87. Hunter, Salzman, and Zaelke, *International Environmental Law*, 2, 22–23.

88. Committee on Economic, Social and Cultural Rights, *General Comment no. 15* (2002), "The Right to Water," UN Doc. E/C.12/2002/11 (20 January 2003), 2.

89. Committee on Economic, Social and Cultural Rights, *General Comment no. 12* (1999), "The Right to Adequate Food," UN Doc. HRI/GEN/1/Rev.4 (7 February 2000), 75.

90. United Nations Development Program (UNDP), *Human Development Report 2006: Beyond Scarcity: Power, Poverty and the Global Water Crisis* (New York: Palgrave Macmillan, 2006), 3.

91. "More Than 1 Billion Go Hungry, the World Food Program Says," *New York Times*, 2 June 2009.

92. UNDP, *Human Development Report 2006*, 5.

93. Inge Kaul, Isabelle Grunberg, Marc A. Stern, *Global Public Goods: International Cooperation in the 21st Century* (New York: Oxford University Press, 1999), 12.

94. Kaul, Grunberg, Stern, *Global Public Goods*, 13.

95. Mark W. Zacher, "Global Epidemiological Surveillance: International Cooperation to Monitor Infectious Diseases," in Inge Kaul, Isabelle Grunberg, and Marc A. Stern, *Global Public Goods: International Cooperation in the 21st Century* (New York: Oxford University Press, 1999), 266–267.

96. Zacher, "Global Epidemiological Surveillance," 268.

97. Ruben P. Mendez, *International Public Finance* (New York: Oxford University Press, 1992), 63.

98. Inge Kaul, Isabelle Grunberg, and Marc A. Stern, "Defining Global Public Goods," in Kaul, Grunberg, & Stern, *Global Public Goods: International Cooperation in the 21st Century* (New York: Oxford University Press, 1999), 10–11.

99. Inge Kaul, Pedro Conceição, Katell Le Goulven, and Ronald U. Mendoza, "How to Improve the Provision of Global Public Goods," in Kaul, et. al., *Providing Global Public Goods: Managing Globalization* (New York: Oxford University Press, 2003), 45-46.

100. Zacher, "Global Epidemiological Surveillance," 275–276.

101. Sylvia C. Martinez, "The Housing Act of 1949: Its Place in the Realization of the American Dream of Homeownership," *Housing Policy Debate*, Vol. 11, No. 2 (2000), 467. Available at: http://www.innovations.harvard.edu/showdoc.html?id=3043 (accessed 8 July 2009).

102. Press Briefing by Special UN Rapporteur on Right to Adequate Housing, 11/05/2005. Available at: http://www.un.org/News/briefings/docs/2005/kotharibrf050511.doc.htm (accessed 8 July 2009).

103. Press Briefing by Special UN Rapporteur on Right to Adequate Housing, 11/05/2005. Available at: http://www.un.org/News/briefings/docs/2005/kotharibrf050511.doc.htm (accessed 8 July 2009).

Chapter 3

1. See the chapter "The Morality of the Depths: The Right to Development as an Emerging Principle of International Law," in William F. Felice, *Taking Suffering Seriously: The Importance of Collective Human Rights* (Albany: SUNY Press, 1996), 69–90.

2. The International Bill of Human Rights encompasses the Universal Declaration of Human Rights, the International Covenant on Civil and Political Rights (Political Rights Treaty), and the International Covenant on Economic, Social and Cultural Rights (Economic Rights Treaty).

3. Julia Hausermann, "The Realisation and Implementation of Economic, Social and Cultural Rights," in *Economic, Social and Cultural Rights: Progress and Achievement*, ed. Ralph Beddard and Dilys M. Hill (New York: St. Martin's, 1992), 49.

4. David Hunter, James Salzman, and Durwood Zaelke, *International Environmental Law and Policy, Third Edition* (New York: Foundation Press, 2007), 1284–1286. See also: Kathryn S. Fuller, "Balancing Trade and Sea Turtles," *International Herald Tribune*, 16–17 May 1998.

5. The 1998 WTO Appellate Body ruling in the shrimp–turtle case, however, may have opened a door linking trade and environmental protection in the future. Article 20 of the General Agreement on Tariffs and Trade allows for certain environmental exceptions to trade rules. Traditionally, environmental laws that protected the environment outside the enacting country's borders had been ruled out. The 1998 ruling may have changed this by requiring merely a "sufficient nexus" between the law and the environment of the enacting state. Thus, transboundary impacts on air and water and on endangered and migratory species might provide such a nexus. See UN Environment Program, *Environment and Trade: A Handbook* (Winnipeg, Canada: International Institute for Sustainable Development, 2000), 30.

6. Address by President Bill Clinton to the World Trade Organization, Geneva, Switzerland, 18 May 1998.

7. BBC News, "Dismay at Collapse of Trade Talks, 30 July 2008. Available at http://news.bbc.co.uk/2/hi/business/7532302.stm (accessed 27 June 2009).

8. Norberto Bobbio, *The Age of Rights* (Cambridge, Mass.: Polity, 1996), 53.

9. An emerging approach to international relations theory is called "constructivism." Constructivists examine how language is used to "construct" the social world. The social construction of legal rules and norms (like human rights laws and norms) are a particular focus due to their mediating role between people and society. See John Gerard Ruggie, *Constructing the World Polity: Essays on International Institutionalization* (New York: Routledge, 1998).

10. Virginia A. Leary, "The Paradox of Workers' Rights As Human Rights," in *Human Rights, Labor Rights, and International Trade*, ed. Lance A. Compa and Stephen F. Diamond (Philadelphia: University of Pennsylvania Press, 1996), 28. It is notable that the United States has ratified only one of the ILO's basic human rights conventions: Convention no. 105 on the Abolition of Forced Labor. The ILO Conventions and ratification information is available at http://www.ilo.org/ilolex/english/convdisp1.htm (accessed 1 July 2009).

11. Paul Hunt, *Reclaiming Social Rights: International and Comparative Perspectives* (Hants, England: Dartmouth, 1996), 2.

12. Asbjørn Eide, "Economic, Social and Cultural Rights as Human Rights," in *Economic, Social and Cultural Rights: A Textbook*, ed. Asbjørn Eide, Catarina Krause, and Allan Rosas (Dordrecht, Netherlands: Kluwer Academic, 1995), 31.

13. See Center for Economic and Social Rights (CESR), "Economic, Social and Cultural Rights: A Guide to the Legal Framework" (January 2000): 6, at www.cesr.org/text%20files/escrguide.PDF (accessed 15 July 2001). See also *CESR's Basic Primer on ESC Rights*, available at http://cesr.live.radicaldesigns.org/article.php?id=275 (accessed 1 July 2009).

14. Eide, "Economic, Social and Cultural Rights"; CESR, "Economic, Social and Cultural Rights: A Guide to the Legal Framework."

15. "The Limburg Principles on the Implementation of the International Covenant on Economic, Social and Cultural Rights," UN ESCOR, Commission on Human Rights, 43rd sess., Agenda Item 8, UN Doc. E/CN.4/1987/17/Annex (1987), reprinted in "The Limburg Principles on the Implementation of the International Covenant on Economic, Social and Cultural Rights," *Human Rights Quarterly* 9, no. 2 (1987): 122–135.

16. "The Maastricht Guidelines on Violations of Economic, Social and Cultural Rights," *Human Rights Quarterly* 20, no. 3 (1998): 691–704.

17. See Danilo Turk, Special Rapporteur of the Sub-commission on Prevention of Discrimination and Protection of Minorities, "The Full Realization of Economic, Social and Cultural Rights (Final Report)," UN ESCOR, Commission on Human Rights, 48th sess., Agenda Item 8, UN Doc. E/CN.4/Sub.2/1992/16 (1992); Vienna Declaration and Programme of Action, UN GAOR, World Conference on Human Rights, 48th sess., 22d plenipotentiary meeting, UN Doc. A/CONF.157/24 (1993); "UN Seminar on Appropriate Indicators to Measure Achievements in the Progressive Realization of Economic, Social and Cultural Rights," UN GAOR, World Conference on Human Rights, 4th sess., Provisional Agenda Item 6, UN Doc. A/CONF.157/PC/73 (1993).

18. "Maastricht Guidelines," 692.

19. Henry Shue, *Basic Rights: Subsistence, Affluence, and U.S. Foreign Policy* (Princeton, N.J.: Princeton University Press, 1980).

20. "Center for Human Rights, Right to Adequate Food As a Human Right," UN Doc. E/CN.4/Sub.2/1987/23, UN Sales no. E.89.Xiv.2 (1989).

21. "Maastricht Guidelines," 693–694.

22. "Maastricht Guidelines," 694.

23. "Maastricht Guidelines," 697.

24. "Maastricht Guidelines," 696. For a comprehensive overview of the UN's approach to economic and social rights, see Scott Leckie, "Another Step towards Indivisibility: Identifying the Key Features of Violations of Economic, Social and Cultural Rights," *Human Rights Quarterly* 20, no. 1 (1998).

25. See Philip Alston, "The Committee on Economic, Social and Cultural Rights," in *The United Nations and Human Rights*, ed. Philip Alston (New York: Oxford University Press, 1992), 473–475.

26. See Matthew Craven, *The International Covenant on Economic, Social, and Cultural Rights: A Perspective on Its Development* (Oxford: Clarendon, 1995).

27. The United States has not ratified the First Optional Protocol to the Political Rights Treaty.

28. Ratification information available at http://treaties.un.org/Pages/Treaties .aspx?id=4&subid=A&lang=en (accessed: 2 July 2009).

29. United Nations, "Report of the Human Rights Committee, Volume I: 91st session (15 October–2 November 2007), 92nd session (17 March–4 April 2008), 93rd session (7–15 July 2008)," A/63/40 (Vol. I), available at: http://daccessdds. un.org/doc/UNDOC/GEN/G08/439/42/PDF/G0843942.pdf?OpenElement (accessed 26 June 2009). See also Office of the United Nations High Commissioner for Human Rights (OHCHR), *Human Rights*, no. 2 (Spring 1998): 13.

30. Mercedes Morales, Human Rights Officer, OHCHR, interview by author, Geneva, Switzerland, 22 May 1998. (Note: Other UN observers estimate a much higher level of state compliance with decisions of the Human Rights Committee.)

31. OHCHR, *Human Rights*, 15–16.

32. OHCHR, *Human Rights*, 16.

33. Ratification information available at http://treaties.un.org/Pages/Treaties. aspx?id=4&subid=A&lang=en (accessed 2 July 2009).

34. Louis Henkin, *The Age of Rights* (New York: Columbia University Press, 1990), 33.

35. Henry J. Steiner and Philip Alston, *International Human Rights in Context* (Oxford: Clarendon, 1996), 316.

36. Craven, *International Covenant*, 104.

37. See Aryeh Neir, "Social and Economic Rights: A Critique," in H. J. Steiner, P. Alston, and R. Goodman, *International Human Rights in Context: Law, Politics, Morals, 3rd Edition* (Oxford: Oxford University Press, 2008), 283–285; See also E.G. Vierdag, "The Legal nature of the Rights Granted by the International Covenant on Economic, Social and Cultural Rights," *Netherlands Yearbook of International Law*, Vol. 9, 103.

38. Philip Alston, "Putting Economic, Social, and Cultural Rights Back on the Agenda of the United States," in W. Schulz (ed.), *The Future of Human Rights: U.S. Policy for a New Era* (Philadelphia: University of Pennsylvania Press, 2008), 129;

See also V.B. Gomes, "The Future of Economic, Social and Cultural Rights," in R. Smith and C. den Anker (eds.), *The Essentials of Human Rights* (London: Hodder, 2005).

39. Abdullahi Ahmed An-Na'im, *Human Rights in Cross-cultural Perspectives: A Quest for Consensus* (Philadelphia: University of Pennsylvania Press, 1992), 5.

40. International Conference on Popular Participation in the Recovery and Development Process in Africa, *African Charter for Popular Participation in Development and Transformation* (Arusha, Tanzania, 1990) E/ECA/CM.16/11/Corr. 1.

41. UNDP, *Human Development Report 1997* (New York: Oxford University Press, 1997), 16.

42. UNDP, *Human Development Report 1996* (New York: Oxford University Press, 1996), 27.

43. UNDP, *Human Development Report 1996*, 27–28.

44. UNDP, *Human Development Report 1997*, 18.

45. UNDP, *Human Development Report 2000* (New York: Oxford University Press, 2000), 147.

46. UNDP, *Human Development Report 2000*, 147.

47. UNDP, *Human Development Report 2000*, 150–151.

48. UNDP, *Human Development Report 2007/2008* (New York: Palgrave Macmillan, 2007), 238–240.

49. UNDP, *Human Development Report 2003* (New York: Oxford University Press, 2003), 2.

50. UNDP, *Human Development Report 2000*, 151, 157–158.

51. UNDP, *Human Development Report 2000*, 159–150, 170–171.

52. UNDP, *Human Development Report 2007/2008*, 241.

53. UNDP, *Human Development Report 2000*, 153.

54. Virginia Dandan, Chairperson of the Committee on Economic, Social and Cultural Rights, interview by author, Geneva, Switzerland, 7 June 2000.

55. Dandan interview.

56. Dandan interview.

57. Dandan interview.

58. Scott Leckie, "The Committee on Economic, Social and Cultural Rights: Catalyst for Change in a System Needing Reform," in *The Future of UN Human Rights Treaty Monitoring*, ed. Philip Alston and James Crawford (Cambridge: Cambridge University Press, 2000), 134. Examples of NGO reports that have been strongly reflected in the concluding observations adopted by the Economic Rights Committee include "A Report to the UN Committee on Economic, Social and Cultural Rights on Housing Rights Violations and the Poverty Problem in Hong Kong" (November 1994), prepared by the Society for Community Organisation and the Hong Kong Human Rights Commission; "Housing for All? Implementation of the Right to Adequate Housing for the Arab Palestinian Minority in Israel: A Report for the UN Committee on Economic, Social and Cultural Rights on the Implementation of Article 11(1) of the UN Covenant on Economic, Social and Cultural Rights" (April 1996), prepared by the Arab Coordinating Committee on Housing Rights, Israel (ACCHRI); and "El Derecho a la Vivienda en Mexico" (March 1994), prepared by Casa y Ciudad, Cenvi, Copevi and Fosovi.

59. Kitty Arambulo Wilson, Human Rights Officer, OHCHR, interview by author, Geneva, Switzerland, 9 June 2000.

60. Dandan interview.

61. Philippines, UN Doc. E/C.12/1995/18; Belgium, UN Doc. E/C.12/1994/20, quoted in Leckie, "The Committee on Economic, Social and Cultural Rights," 136–137.

62. Committee on Economic, Social and Cultural Rights, "Globalization and Economic, Social and Cultural Rights" (May 1998), reprinted in Economic Rights Committee, "Note on the Eighteenth Session" (27 April–15 May 1998), at www .unhchr.ch/html/menu2/6/EconomicRightsTreatynote.htm#note18th (accessed 16 July 2001).

63. Committee on Economic, Social and Cultural Rights, "Statement of the UN Economic Rights Treaty Committee to the Third Ministerial Conference of the World Trade Organization (Seattle, 30 November to 3 December 1999)," UN Doc . E/C.12/1999/9 (26 November 1999).

64. Dandan interview.

65. World Bank, *World Development Report 2000/2001: Attacking Poverty* (New York: Oxford University Press, 2001), 15.

66. Committee on Economic, Social and Cultural Rights, "Globalization and Economic, Social and Cultural Rights."

67. For example, see Sarah Anderson, ed., *Views from the South: The Effects of Globalization and the WTO on Third World Countries* (Oakland, Calif.: Institute for Food and Development Policy, 2000).

68. Arambulo Wilson interview.

69. Dandan interview.

70. Committee on Economic, Social and Cultural Rights, "The Incorporation of Economic, Social and Cultural Rights into the United Nations Development Assistance Framework (UNDAF) Process" (15 May 1998), at www.unhchr.ch/html/ menu2/6/EconomicRightsTreatynote.htm#note18th (accessed 16 July 2001).

71. See United Nations, "Guidelines: Common Country Assessment (CCA)" (April 1999); United Nations, "Guidelines: United Nations Development Assistance Framework (UNDAF)" (April 1999).

72. UN High Commissioner for Human Rights, Research and Right to Development Branch, "Note on the United Nations Development Assistance Framework (UNDAF) Process (draft)" (May 2000).

73. United Nations, "Guidelines," 17–21.

74. Sylvie Saddier, Human Rights Officer, Research and Right to Development Branch, OHCHR, interview by author, Geneva, Switzerland, 8 June 2000.

75. These examples are from an internal OHCHR review of CCA and UNDAF country team documents.

76. Saddier interview. See also "2009 CCA/UNDAF Guidelines," available at: http://www.undg.org/index.cfm?P=226 (accessed 1 July 2009); and "Results-Based Management in UNDAFs," available at: http://www.undg.org/docs/7960/ Results%20Based%20Management%20in%20UNDAFs.pdf (accessed 1 July 2009).

77. UNDP–OHCHR, Human Rights Strengthening–HURIST, Program Document.

78. Saddier interview. See also "Background—HURIST and the Mid-Term Review," available at: http://www.unhchr.ch/development/hurist.html (accessed 1 July 2009).

79. Stefanie Grant, Chief, Research and Right to Development Branch, OHCHR, interview by author, Geneva, Switzerland, 8 June 2000.

80. OHCHR, Fact Sheet no. 16 (Rev. 1), "The Committee on Economic, Social and Cultural Rights," 22, at www.unhchr.ch/html/menu6/2/fs16.htm (accessed 11 March 2001). For a comprehensive and thoughtful critique of the proposal for an individual complaint procedure for the Economic Rights Committee, see Kitty Arambulo, Strengthening the Supervision of the International Covenant on Economic, Social and Cultural Rights: Theoretical and Procedural Aspects (Antwerpen: Intersentia, 1999).

81. Vienna Declaration and Programme of Action, adopted by the UN World Conference on Human Rights, 25 June 1993, UN Doc. A/CONF.157/24; reprinted in 32 ILM 1661 (1993), see paragraph 75.

82. The Netherlands Institute of Human Rights published the proceedings of the Expert Meeting on the Adoption of an Optional Protocol to the Economic Rights Treaty. See Fons Coomans and Fried van Hoof, eds., *The Right to Complain about Economic, Social and Cultural Human Rights* (Utrecht: Netherlands Institute of Human Rights, 1995).

83. Commission on Human Rights, "Draft Optional Protocol to the International Covenant on Economic, Social and Cultural Rights," UN Doc. E/CN.4/1997/105 (18 December 1996): 4–5.

84. Arambulo Wilson interview; Dandan interview.

85. Erika de Wet, "Labor Standards in the Globalized Economy: The Inclusion of a Social Clause in the General Agreement on Tariff and Trade/World Trade Organization," *Human Rights Quarterly* 17, no. 3 (1995): 450.

86. de Wet, "Labor Standards," 453.

87. Christian Barry and Sanjay G. Reddy, *International Trade and Labor Standards: A Proposal for Linkage* (New York: Columbia University Press, 2008), 79, 81.

88. Population Council, "Female Garment Workers Study in Bangladesh," New York: Population Council (1998): 1–8.

89. For a useful and thorough analysis of these issues, see David M. Smolin, "Strategic Choices in the International Campaign against Child Labor," *Human Rights Quarterly* 22, no. 4 (2000): 942–987.

90. Dan Cunniah, "The Dangers of Complacency in the Face of a Global Social Crisis," *Social Development Review* 2, no. 2 (June 1998): 18.

91. Stephen Herzenberg, "In from the Margins: Morality, Economics, and International Labor Rights," in *Human Rights, Labor Rights and International Trade*, ed. Lance A. Compa and Stephen F. Diamond (Philadelphia: University of Pennsylvania Press, 1996), 100–101, 108.

92. Denis MacShane, "Human Rights and Labor Rights: A European Perspective," in *Human Rights, Labor Rights, and International Trade*, ed. Lance Compa and Stephen Diamond (Philadelphia: University of Pennsylvania Press, 1996), 52.

93. See "The Social Clause—No Panacea for Workers' Rights," in UNDP, *Human Development Report 2000*, 85.

94. See Bruno Simma, "The Implementation of the International Covenant on Economic, Social and Cultural Rights," in *The Implementation of Economic and Social Rights: National, International and Comparative Aspects*, ed. Franz Matscher (Arlington, Va.: Engel Verlag, 1991), 88–94.

95. Committee on Economic, Social and Cultural Rights, General Comment no. 3 (1990), UN Doc. E/1991/23, Annex III.

96. Matthew Craven, *The International Covenant on Economic, Social, and Cultural Rights: A Perspective on Its Development* (Oxford: Clarendon, 1995), 143.

97. Craven, International Covenant, 143.

98. Sigrun I. Skogly, *The Human Rights Obligations of the World Bank and the International Monetary Fund* (London: Cavendish, 2001), 133–134.

99. Committee on Economic, Social and Cultural Rights, General Comment no. 4, "The Right to Adequate Housing" (Art. 11[1] of the Covenant) (6th sess., 1991), in United Nations, "Compilation of General Comments and General Recommendations Adopted by Human Rights Treaty Bodies," UN Doc. HRI\ GEN®\Rev. 1 at 53 (1994).

100. Economic Rights Committee, General Comment no. 4.

101. Craven, *International Covenant*, 336.

102. Craven, *International Covenant*, 336.

103. Committee on Economic, Social and Cultural Rights, General Comment no. 5, "Persons with Disabilities" (11th sess., 1994), UN Doc E/C.12/1994/13 (1994).

104. Economic Rights Committee, General Comment no. 5.

105. Economic Rights Committee, General Comment no. 5.

106. Committee on Economic, Social and Cultural Rights, General Comment no. 6, "The Economic, Social and Cultural Rights of Older Persons" (13th sess., 1995), UN Doc. E/C.12/1995/16/Rev. 1 (1995), 4.

107. Committee on Economic, Social and Cultural Rights, General Comment no. 6, 4–5.

108. Committee on Economic, Social and Cultural Rights, General Comment no. 7, "The Right to Adequate Housing" (article 11[1] of the Covenant), UN Doc. E/C.12/1997/4 (1997), 1–2.

109. Committee on Economic, Social and Cultural Rights, General Comment no. 7, 3, 4.

110. Committee on Economic, Social and Cultural Rights, General Comment no. 8 (1997), "The Relationship between Economic Sanctions and Respect for Economic, Social and Cultural Rights," UN Doc. E/C.12/1997/8 (12 December 1997), 2.

111. Committee on Economic, Social and Cultural Rights, General Comment no. 8, 3.

112. Committee on Economic, Social and Cultural Rights, General Comment no. 9 (1998), "The Domestic Application of the Covenant," UN Doc. HRI/ GEN/1/Rev. 4 (7 February 2000), 48–52. The committee refers to article 27 of the Vienna Convention on the Law of Treaties: "[A] party may not invoke the provisions of its internal law as justification for its failure to perform a treaty."

113. Committee on Economic, Social and Cultural Rights, General Comment no. 10 (1998), "The Role of National Human Rights Institutions in the Protection of Economic, Social and Cultural Rights," UN Doc. HRI/GEN/1/Rev. 4 (7 February 2000), 53–54.

114. Committee on Economic, Social and Cultural Rights, General Comment no. 13 (1999), "The Right to Education," UN Doc. HRI/GEN/1/Rev. 4 (7 February 2000), 75.

115. Committee on Economic, Social and Cultural Rights, General Comment no. 13, 68–69.

116. Committee on Economic, Social and Cultural Rights, General Comment no. 11 (1999), "Plans of Action for Primary Education," UN Doc. HRI/GEN/1/Rev. 4 (7 February 2000), 54–56.

117. Committee on Economic, Social and Cultural Rights, General Comment no. 12 (1999), "The Right to Adequate Food," UN Doc. HRI/GEN/1/Rev. 4 (7 February 2000), 59.

118. Committee on Economic, Social and Cultural Rights, General Comment no. 12, 60.

119. Committee on Economic, Social and Cultural Rights, General Comment no. 12, 61.

120. Committee on Economic, Social and Cultural Rights, General Comment no. 12, 58, 61.

121. Committee on Economic, Social and Cultural Rights, General Comment no. 14 (2000), "The Right to the Highest Attainable Standard of Health," UN Doc.E/C.12/2000/4 (4 July 2000), 2.

122. Committee on Economic, Social and Cultural Rights, General Comment no. 14, 3–4.

123. Committee on Economic, Social and Cultural Rights, General Comment no. 14, 13.

124. Committee on Economic, Social and Cultural Rights, General Comment no. 14, 14.

125. Committee on Economic, Social and Cultural Rights, General Comment no. 14, 14.

126. Committee on Economic, Social and Cultural Rights, General Comment no. 15 (2002), "The Right to Water," UN Doc. E/C.12/2002/11 (20 January 2003), 1–2.

127. Committee on Economic, Social and Cultural Rights, General Comment no. 15, 9.

128. Committee on Economic, Social and Cultural Rights, General Comment no. 15, 9.

129. Committee on Economic, Social and Cultural Rights, General Comment no. 15, 10.

130. Committee on Economic, Social and Cultural Rights, General Comment no. 15, 12.

131. Committee on Economic, Social and Cultural Rights, General Comment no. 16 (2005), "On the Equal Rights of Men and Women," UN Doc. E/C.12/2005/4 (11 August 2005), 5.

132. Committee on Economic, Social and Cultural Rights, General Comment no. 17 (2005), "Scientific, Literary or Artistic Production," UN Doc. E/C.12/GC/17 (12 January 2006), 2.

133. Committee on Economic, Social and Cultural Rights, General Comment no. 17, 10–11.

134. Committee on Economic, Social and Cultural Rights, General Comment no. 18 (2005), "The Right to Work," UN Doc. E/C.12/GC/18 (6 February 2006), 3.

135. Committee on Economic, Social and Cultural Rights, General Comment no. 18, 7–8.

136. Committee on Economic, Social and Cultural Rights, General Comment no. 19 (2007), "The Right to Social Security," UN Doc. E/C.12/GC/19 (4 February 2008), 3.

137. Committee on Economic, Social and Cultural Rights, General Comment no. 19, 3, 13–14.

138. Committee on Economic, Social and Cultural Rights, General Comment no. 20 (2009), "Non-Discrimination in Economic, Social and Cultural Rights (art. 2, para. 2)," UN Doc. E/C.12.GC/20 (25 May 2009), 3–4.

139. Committee on Economic, Social and Cultural Rights, General Comment no. 20, 5–10.

Chapter 4

1. Antonio Augusto Cançado Trindade, "Human Rights and the Environment," in *Human Rights: New Dimensions and Challenges*, ed. Janusz Symonides (Paris: UN Educational, Scientific, and Cultural Organization, 1998), 118.

2. David Hunter, James Salzman, and Durwood Zaelke, *International Environmental Law and Policy*, 3rd edition (New York: Foundation Press, 2007), 197.

3. Craig S. Smith, "150 Nations Start Groundwork for Global Warming Policies," *New York Times*, 18 January 2001, 7(A).

4. Intergovernmental Panel on Climate Change (IPCC), *Climate Change 2007: Synthesis Report*, approved at IPCC Plenary XXVII, Valencia, Spain, 12–17 November 2007. Available at: http://www.ipcc.ch/pdf/assessment-report/ar4/syr/ar4_syr_spm.pdf (accessed 15 July 2009).

5. Bill McKibben, "Too Hot to Handle," *New York Times*, 5 January 2001, 17(A).

6. CNN, "Obama: Leaders Will Work Together on Climate, 9 July 2009. Available at: http://www.cnn.com/2009/WORLD/europe/07/09/g8.summit/index.html (accessed 14 July 2009). See also Mark Hertsgaard, "A Global Green Deal," *The Nation*, 16 March 2009.

7. International Union for Conservation of Nature and Natural Resources (IUCN), *The IUCN Red List of Threatened Species*, 2008. Available at: http://www.iucnredlist.org/static/stats (accessed 14 July 2009).

8. Aaron Sachs, *Eco-Justice: Linking Human Rights and the Environment*, World-Watch Paper 127 (Washington, D.C.: Worldwatch Institute, 1995).

9. Michael R. Anderson, "Human Rights Approaches to Environmental Protection: An Overview," in *Human Rights Approaches to Environmental Protection*, ed. Alan E. Boyle and Michael R. Anderson (New York: Oxford University Press, 1996), 1–4.

10. The International Bill of Human Rights encompasses the Universal Declaration of Human Rights, the International Covenant on Civil and Political Rights (Political Rights Treaty), and the International Covenant on Economic, Social and Cultural Rights (Economic Rights Treaty).

11. African Charter on Human and Peoples' Rights, Banjul, 26 June 1981, entered into force 21 October 1986, OAU Doc. CAB/LEG/67/3 Rev. 5.

12. Robin Churchill, "Environmental Rights in Existing Human Rights Treaties," in *Human Rights Approaches to Environmental Protections*, ed. Alan E. Boyle and Michael R. Anderson (New York: Oxford University Press, 1966), 105–107.

13. Additional Protocol to the American Convention on Human Rights in the Area of Economic, Social and Cultural Rights, OAS Treaty Series no. 69, reprinted at 28 ILM 156 (1989), enacted at San Salvador in November 1988, at http://www .oas.org/juridico/english/treaties/a-52.html (accessed 15 July 2009).

14. Ratification information is available at http://www.oas.org/juridico/ english/Sigs/a-52.html (accessed 15 July 2009).

15. Churchill, "Environmental Rights," 99–100.

16. "Convention on the Rights of the Child," UN Doc. A/Res/44/49, at www .unhchr.ch/html/menu3/b/k2crc.htm (accessed 15 July 2009).

17. Antonio Augusto Cançado Trindade, "Human Rights and the Environment," in *Human Rights: New Dimensions and Challenges*, ed. Janusz Symonides (Paris: UN Educational, Scientific, and Cultural Organization, 1998).

18. Extracts of the constitutional provisions on environmental rights and duties are reproduced in Edith Brown Weiss, *In Fairness to Future Generations: International Law, Common Patrimony, and Intergenerational Equity* (Tokyo: United Nations University Press, 1989), 297–327. The constitution of Brazil is on 298.

19. Article 24 of the Constitution of the Republic of South Africa, as adopted on 8 May 1996 and amended on 11 October 1996 by the Constitutional Assembly. Available at: http://www.info.gov.za/documents/constitution/1996/96cons2. htm#12 (accessed 15 July 2009).

20. "Stockholm Declaration of the United Nations Conference on the Human Environment," UN Doc. A/CONF.48/14 (16 June 1972), at http://www.unep .org/Documents.Multilingual/Default.asp?DocumentID=97&ArticleID=1503 (accessed 15 July 2009).

21. Charter of Economic Rights and Duties of States, adopted by the UN General Assembly, 12 December 1974, GA Res. 3281, UN GAOR, 29th sess., Supp. no. 31, at 50, UN Doc. A/9631 (1975); 14 ILM 251 (1975).

22. UN General Assembly Resolution on a World Charter for Nature, 37 UN GAOR (Supp. no. 51) 17 (28 October 1982).

23. UN General Assembly Resolution 44/228 of 1989.

24. "Agenda 21," UN Doc. A/CONF.151/26, at http://www.unep.org/ Documents.Multilingual/Default.asp?DocumentID=52 (accessed 15 July 2009).

25. "Rio Declaration on Environment and Development; at http://www.unep org/Documents.Multilingual/Default.asp?documentID=78&articleID=1163 (accessed 15 July 2009).

26. "Vienna Declaration and Programme of Action," 32 ILM 1661 (1993) (see in particular point eleven), at http://www1.umn.edu/humanrts/instree/l1viedec. html (accessed 15 July 2009).

27. Fatma Zohra Ksentini, "Human Rights and the Environment," Final Report of the Special Rapporteur, UN Doc. E/CH.4Sub.21994/9 (6 July 1994).

28. Draft Principles on Human Rights and the Environment, UN Commission on Human Rights, Sub-commission on Prevention of Discrimination and Protection of Minorities, Final Report of the Special Rapporteur, UN Doc. E/CN.4/ Sub.2/1994/9 (6 July 1994).

29. Draft Principles on Human Rights and the Environment.

30. "Johannesburg Declaration on Sustainable Developlment; at http:// www.un.org/esa/sustdev/documents/WSSD_POI_PD/English/POI_PD.htm (accessed 15 July 2009).

31. UN General Assembly 60/1 on 2005 World Summit Outcome, 24 October 2005; available at: http://daccessdds.un.org/doc/UNDOC/GEN/N05/487/60/PDF/N0548760.pdf?OpenElement (accessed 15 July 2009).

32. UN General Assembly Resolution 2997 on Institutional and Financial Arrangements for International Environmental Co-Operation, 27 UN GAOR (Supp. no. 30) 43 (15 December 1972).

33. Hilary French, *Vanishing Borders: Protecting the Planet in the Age of Globalization* (New York: Norton, 2000), 157–158.

34. David Hunter, James Salzman, and Durwood Zaelke, *Internatinonal Law and Policy*, 3rd edition (New York: Foundation Press, 2007), 222–223.

35. Governing Council of the United Nations Environment Programme, "Global Civil Society Statement to the Twenty-Third Session of the Governing Council/Global Ministerial Environment Forum," 20 January 2005, UNEP/GC.23/INF/16.

36. Hunter, Salzman, and Zaelke, *International Environmental Law and Policy*, 3rd edition, 224.

37. UN General Assembly Resolution 37/7 on a World Charter for Nature, 37 UN GAOR (Supp. no. 51) 17 (28 October 1982).

38. Declaration of Environmental Policies and Procedures Relating to Economic Development, adopted by the African Development Bank, Arab Bank for Economic Development in Africa, Asian Development Bank, Caribbean Development Bank, Inter-American Development Bank, World Bank, Commission of European Communities, Organization of American States, UN Development Program, and UN Environment Program, 1 February 1980, 19 ILM 524 (1980).

39. Alexander Timoshenko and Mark Berman, "The United Nations Environment Programme and the United Nations Development Programme," in *Greening International Institutions*, ed. Jacob Werksman (London: Earthscan Publications, 1996), 40.

40. Philip Shabecoff, *A New Name for Peace: International Environmentalism, Sustainable Development, and Democracy* (Hanover, N.H.: University Press of New England, 1996), 47–49.

41. David L. Downie and Marc A. Levy, "The UN Environment Programme at a Turning Point: Options for Change," in *The Global Environment in the Twenty-First Century: Prospects for International Cooperation*, ed. Pamela S. Chasek (Tokyo: United Nations University Press, 2000), 358.

42. United Nations, "Review and Appraisal of the Implementation of Agenda 21: Contribution of the United Nations Environment Programme to the Special Session," UN Doc. A/S-19/5, section II B (1997), at un.org/00/ga/docs/S-19/plenary/As19-5.EN (accessed 19 June 2001).

43. UN Environment Program, "Implementation by UNEP of Agenda 21: Note by the Executive Director" (prepared for the 19th sess., Nairobi, 17 January–7 February 1997, Item 5 of provisional agenda, "Preparations for the 1997 Review and Appraisal of Agenda 21"), UN Doc. UNEP/GC.19/INF 17, quoted in Downie and Levy, "UN Environment Programme," 360.

44. Downie and Levy, "UN Environment Programme," 366.

45. Chris Mensah, "The United Nations Commission on Sustainable Development," in *Greening International Institutions*, ed. Jacob Werksman (London: Earthscan Publications, 1996), 21.

46. Resolution on Institutional Arrangement to Follow up the United Nations Conference on Environment and Development, UNGA Res. 47/191, GAOR, 47th sess., UN Doc. A/RES/47/191 (1993).

47. UN Department for Policy Coordination and Sustainable Development, "Terms of Reference: Commission on Sustainable Development" (1993), at www .un.org/dpcsd/dsd/csdback.thm (accessed 19 June 2001).

48. Pamela S. Chasek, "The UN Commission on Sustainable Development: The First Five Years," in *The Global Environment in the Twenty-First Century: Prospects for International Cooperation*, ed. Pamela S. Chasek (Tokyo: United Nations University Press, 2000), 383.

49. Mensah, "United Nations Commission," 24.

50. Hilary F. French, *Partnership for the Planet: An Environmental Agenda for the United Nations* (Washington, D.C.: Worldwatch Institute, 1995), 32–34.

51. French, *Vanishing Borders*, 161–162.

52. Chasek, "UN Commission," 384.

53. Chasek, "UN Commission," 385.

54. UN Chronicle 34, no. 2 (Summer 1997): 34.

55. Chasek, "UN Commission," 386.

56. Andrew C. Revkin, "Sustainability for Rich and Poor," *The New York Times News Blog*, 10 May 2007. Available at http://thelede.blogs.nytimes.com/2007/05/10/ sustainability-for-rich-and-poor/?scp=16&sq=commission%20on%20sustainable %20development&st=cse (accessed 16 July 2009).

57. Helen Sjöberg, "The Global Environment Facility," in *Greening International Institutions*, ed. Jacob Werksman (London: Earthscan Publications, 1996), 149.

58. Hunter, Salzman, and Zaelke, *International Environmental Law and Policy*, 3rd edition, 1584–1585.

59. "Instrument for the Establishment of the Restructured Global Environment Facility" (1994), paragraphs 2 and 3, at www.gefweb.org/Documents/Instrument/ instrument.html (accessed 19 June 2001), also quoted in Hunter, Salzman, and Zaelke, *International Environmental Law and Policy*, 3rd edition, 1584.

60. Sjöberg, "Global Environment Facility," 151.

61. Sjöberg, "Global Environment Facility," 157–158.

62. French, *Vanishing Borders*, 154–155.

63. French, *Vanishing Borders*, 153.

64. Erika Kinetz, "Spotlight: Monique Barbut of the UN Global Environment Facility, *New York Times*, 4 May 2007. Available at: http://www .nytimes.com/2007/05/04/business/worldbusiness/04iht-wbspot05.1.5567223 .html?pagewanted=1&sq=global%20environment%20facility&st=cse&scp=1 (accessed 16 July 2009).

65. Kinetz, "Spotlight: Monique Barbut."

66. Hunter, Salzman, and Zaelke, *International Environmental Law and Policy*, 3rd edition, 1584.

67. Kinetz, "Spotlight: Monique Barbut."

68. See Zoe Young, "NGOs and the Global Environmental Facility: Friendly Foes?" *Environmental Politics* (Spring 1999). See also Hunter, Salzman, and Zaelke, *International Environmental Law and Policy* (1st edition), (New York: Foundation Press, 1998), 1485, 1489.

69. See Paul Wapner, *Environmental Activism and World Civic Politics* (Albany: SUNY Press, 1996); Paul Wapner, "The Transnational Politics of Environmental NGOs: Governmental, Economic, and Social Activism," in *The Global Environment in the Twenty-First Century: Prospects for International Cooperation*, ed. Pamela S. Chasek (Tokyo: United Nations University Press, 2000), 87–108.

70. World Commission on Environment and Development, *Our Common Future* (Oxford: Oxford University Press, 1987), 43.

71. Andrew Dobson, *Justice and the Environment: Conceptions of Environmental Sustainability and Theories of Distributive Justice* (New York: Oxford University Press, 1998), 33.

72. Anthony D'Amato, "World Conferences and the Cheapening of International Norms," *St. Louis-Warsaw Transatlantic Law Journal* 1 (1995), reprinted in Anthony D'Amato and Kirsten Engle, eds., *International Environmental Law Anthology* (Cincinnati, Ohio: Anderson, 1996), 29.

73. Sharachandra Lélé, "Sustainable Development: A Critical Review," *World Development* 19, no. 6 (1991): 607–621, quoted in Dobson, *Justice and the Environment*, 33.

74. See, for example, James Gustave Speth, *The Bridge at the Edge of the World: Capitalism, the Environment, and Crossing from Crisis to Sustainability* (New Haven: Yale University Press, 2008), 46–66.

75. "Sustainable Development: A New Consensus," Final Report of the President's Council on Sustainable Development, quoted in Leslie Paul Thiele, *Environmentalism for a New Millennium* (New York: Oxford University Press, 1999), 53.

76. Bill McKibben, *Deep Ecology: The Wealth of Communities and the Durable Future* (New York: Holt and Company, 2007), 5–45.

77. Herman Daly, "The Steady-State Economy: Toward a Political Economy of Biophysical Equilibrium and Moral Growth," in *Toward a Steady-State Economy* (San Francisco: Freeman, 1973), 167, quoted in Thiele, *Environmentalism for a New Millennium*, 55.

78. John Nichols, interview in *The Workbook* (Southwest Research and Information Center), (Spring 1992): 20–21, quoted in Thiele, *Environmentalism for a New Millennium*, 41–42.

79. Thiele, *Environmentalism for a New Millennium*, 58–59.

80. Edith Brown Weiss, *In Fairness to Future Generations: International Law, Common Patrimony, and Intergenerational Equity* (Tokyo: United Nations University Press, 1989), 2.

81. David Reed, ed., *Structural Adjustment, the Environment, and Sustainable Development* (London: Earthscan Publications, 1996), 32–37. Reed outlines the economic, social, and environmental components to sustainable development on these pages.

82. In June 2001, for example, a *New York Times*–CBS News Poll showed that 57 percent of Americans were willing to pay higher prices for electricity and gasoline if it meant protecting the environment. See Richard L. Berke and Janet Elder, "Bush Loses Favor Despite Tax Cut and Overseas Trip," *New York Times*, 21 June 2001, 1(A).

83. Paul Hawken, Amory Lovins, and L. Hunter Lovins, *Natural Capitalism: Creating the Next Industrial Revolution* (New York: Little, Brown, 1999), 2–3.

84. Hawken, Lovins, and Lovins, *Natural Capitalism*, 4.

85. Hawken, Lovins, and Lovins, *Natural Capitalism*, 3.

86. Hawken, Lovins, and Lovins, *Natural Capitalism*, 4.

87. These proposals are outlined in great detail in Hawken, Lovins, and Lovins, *Natural Capitalism*. This exceptional book is a notable contribution to the development of workable solutions to our massive environmental problems.

88. Francisco Orrego Vicuña, "State Responsibility, Liability, and Remedial Measures under International Law: New Criteria for Environmental Protection," in *Environmental Change and International Law: New Challenges and Dimensions*, ed. Edith Brown Weiss (Tokyo: United Nations University Press, 1992), 151.

89. Orrego Vicuña, "State Responsibility," 132–133.

90. "Rio de Janeiro Declaration on Environment and Development," UN Doc. A/CONF.151/26 (13 June 1992), at www.unep.org/Documents/Default.asp ?DocumentID=78&ArticleID=1163 (accessed 18 July 2009).

91. Quoted in Thiele, *Environmentalism for a New Millennium*, 84.

92. Kyoto Protocol to the UN Framework Convention on Climate Change, at http://unfccc.int/kyoto_protocol/items/2830.php (accessed 18 July 2009).

93. Vandana Shiva, "Ecological Balance in an Era of Globalization," in *Principled World Politics: The Challenge of Normative International Relations*, ed. Paul Wapner and Lester Edwin J. Ruiz (Lanham, Md.: Rowman & Littlefield, 2000), 130, 137.

Chapter 5

1. See William F. Felice, *Taking Suffering Seriously: The Importance of Collective Human Rights* (Albany: SUNY Press, 1996).

2. International Convention on the Elimination of All Forms of Racial Discrimination (Minority Rights Treaty), adopted and open for signature and ratification by General Assembly resolution 2106 (XX) of 21 December 1965, and entered into force 4 January 1969, in accordance with article 19, at http://www2.ohchr.org/english/law/cerd.htm (accessed 20 July 2009); also reprinted in Natan Lerner, *The UN Convention on the Elimination of All Forms of Racial Discrimination* (Alphen aan den Rijn, Netherlands: Sijthoff and Noordhoff, 1980), 217–230.

3. Rüdiger Wolfrum, ed., *United Nations: Law, Policies and Practice* (Dordrecht: Martinus Nijhoff, 1995), 1005–1006.

4. Natalie Angler, "Do Races Differ? Not Really, Genes Show," *New York Times*, 22 August 2000, 1(F).

5. Kevin Danaher, "Getting at Hunger's Roots: The Legacy of Colonialism and Racism," in *The Color of Hunger: Race and Hunger in National and International Perspective*, ed. David L. Shields (Lanham, Md.: Rowman & Littlefield, 1995), 89–91.

6. Philip Gourevitch, *We Wish to Inform You That Tomorrow We Will Be Killed with Our Families* (New York: Farrar, Straus, and Giroux, 1998), 47–48.

7. See Centre for Human Rights, Report of the Seminar on the Political, Historical, Economic, Social and Cultural Factors Contributing to Racism, Racial Discrimination and Apartheid (New York: United Nations, 1991), HR/PUB/91/3. "The Seminar affirms that racial discrimination means any distinction, exclusion, restriction or preference based on race, colour, descent, or national or ethnic origin which has the purpose or effect of nullifying or impairing the recognition, enjoyment or

exercise, on an equal footing, of human rights and fundamental freedoms in the political, economic, social, cultural or any other field of public life" (23).

8. James Gustave Speth, "The Plight of the Poor: The United States Must Increase Development Aid," *Foreign Affairs* 78, no. 3 (May–June 1999): 14.

9.World Bank, "Understanding Povery," 2008, available at http://web .worldbank.org/WBSITE/EXTERNAL/TOPICS/EXTPOVERTY/EXTPA/0 ,,contentMDK:20153855~menuPK:435040~pagePK:148956~piPK:216618~the SitePK:430367,00.html (accessed 8 June 2009).

10. CIA food distribution world maps available at http://www.theglobal educationproject.org/earth/human-conditions.php (accessed 19 July 2009); The World Food Program hunger map is available at http://www.wfp.org/hunger/ map (accessed 19 July 2009); "More Than 1 Billion Go Hungry, the World Food Program Says," *New York Times*, 13 June 2009; see also Christopher S. Wren, "UN Report Maps Hunger 'Hot Spots,'" *New York Times*, 9 January 2001, 8(A); see also Map of Global Hunger, 1997 (fig. 1.1), in *Hunger in a Global Economy* (Washington, D.C.: Bread for the World Institute, 1997), 11.

11. "Blacks Lead the Way in Income Growth," *St. Petersburg Times*, 10 October 1998, 1(E).

12. Sylvia Nasar with Kirsten B. Mitchell, "Booming Job Market Draws Young Black Men into Fold," *New York Times*, 23 May 1999, 1(1).

13. Fox Butterfield, "More Blacks in Their 20's Have Trouble with the Law," *New York Times*, 5 October 1995, 18(A).

14. Fox Butterfield, "Number of Inmates Reaches Record 1.8 Million," *New York Times*, 15 March 1999, 14(A). See also Marc Miringoff and Marque-Luisa Miringoff, *The Social Health of the Nation: How America Is Really Doing* (New York: Oxford University Press, 1999), 66–71, 80–85.

15. Sarah Burd-Sharps, Kristen Lewis, and Eduardo Borges Martins, *The Measure of America: American Human Development Report 2008–2009* (New York: Columbia University Press, 2008), 12, 39.

16. "Report: Low Pay, Benefits Still Plague U.S. Hispanics," *St. Petersburg Times*, 5 July 2000, 3(A).

17. Burd-Sharps, et. al., *Measure of America*, 39.

18. Ratification information is available at http://treaties.un.org/Pages/ ViewDetails.aspx?src=TREATY&mtdsg_no=IV-2&chapter=4&lang=en (accessed 19 July 2009).

19. Michael Banton, "Decision-Taking in the Committee on the Elimination of Racial Discrimination," in *The Future of UN Human Rights Treaty Monitoring*, ed. Philip Alston and James Crawford (Cambridge: Cambridge University Press, 2000), 60.

20. See Minority Rights Treaty, articles 1 and 5.

21. Cecilia Möller, Human Rights Officer, Committee on the Elimination of All Forms of Racial Discrimination, interview by author, Geneva, Switzerland, 6 June 2000.

22. Karl Josef Partsch, "The Committee on the Elimination of Racial Discrimination," in *The United Nations and Human Rights*, ed. Philip Alston (New York: Oxford University Press, 1992), 360.

23. See Drew Mahalic and Joan Gambee Mahalic, "The Limitation Provisions of the International Convention on the Elimination of All Forms of Racial Discrimination," *Human Rights Quarterly* 9 (1987): 82–83.

24. Theodor Meron, "The Meaning and Reach of the International Convention on the Elimination of All Forms of Racial Discrimination," *American Journal of International Law* 79 (1985): 287, emphasis added.

25. Meron, "Meaning and Reach," 288–289.

26. Ratification information is available at http://treaties.un.org/Pages/ViewDetails.aspx?src=TREATY&mtdsg_no=IV-2&chapter=4&lang=en (accessed 19 July 2009).

27. Möller interview.

28. Committee on the Elimination of All Forms of Racial Discrimination, *Report of the Committee on the Elimination of Racial Discrimination, Seventy-Second Session (18 February–7 March 2008) and Seventy-Third Session (28 July–15 August 2008)*, General Assembly, Official Records, 63rd session, Supplement No. 18 (A/63/18), 107.

29. Banton, "Decision-Taking," 57.

30. Committee on the Elimination of All Forms of Racial Discrimination (Minority Rights Committee), Communication no. 13/1998: Slovakia, CERD/C/57/D/13/1998 (1 November 2000).

31. Minority Rights Treaty, article 9. The Minority Rights Committee decided in 1990 that after the submission of an initial comprehensive report, states should submit further comprehensive reports every four years and brief updating reports in the intervening two-year periods.

32. Office of the High Commissioner for Human Rights (OHCHR), *Manual on Human Rights Reporting* (Geneva: United Nations, 1997), 267–304.

33. Möller interview; see also Banton, "Decision-Taking," 67.

34. Data on "late reports" is available at the UN High Commissioner for Human Rights website www.unhchr.ch/tbs/doc.nsf/newhvoverduebytreaty?OpenView (accessed 19 July 2009).

35. It should be noted that the Minority Rights Committee is the oldest treaty body committee, which partially explains its large number of overdue states parties' reports in comparison with the other treaty body committees. The treaty body committee with the second most overdue reports is the Economic Rights Committee, with 200 late as of July 2009. See www.unhchr.ch/tbs/doc.nsf/newhvoverduebytreaty?OpenView (accessed 19 July 2009).

36. Möller interview.

37. See Stefanie Grant, "The United States and the International Human Rights Treaty System: For Export Only?" in *The Future of UN Human Rights Treaty Monitoring*, ed. Philip Alston and James Crawford (Cambridge: Cambridge University Press, 2000), 317–329.

38. United States, "Initial Report of the United States of America to the United Nations Committee on the Elimination of Racial Discrimination" (September 2000), 17–18, 76, at www1.umn.edu/humanrts/usdocs/cerdinitial.html (accessed 21 March 2001).

39. United States, "Initial Report," 66, 40–41.

40. "U.S. Reservations, Understandings and Declarations, International Convention on the Elimination of All Forms of Racial Discrimination," 140 Cong. Rec. 14326 (1994). U.S. adherence effective 20 November 1994. Available in Louis Henkin et al., *Human Rights: Documentary Supplement* (New York: Foundation, 2001), 192–193.

41. United States, "Initial Report," 75–76.

42. International Covenant on Economic, Social and Cultural Rights (Economic Rights Treaty), adopted at New York 16 December 1966, and entered into force 3 January 1976, UNGA Res. 2200 (XXI), 21 UN GAOR, Supp. (no. 16) 49, UN Doc. A/6316 (1967), see, in particular, article 11.

43. "Concluding Observations of the Committee on the Elimination of Racial Discrimination: United States of America," CERD/C/59/Misc.17/Rev. 3 (14 August 2001).

44. Committee on the Elimination of All Forms of Racial Discrimination, *Report of the Committee on the Elimination of Racial Discrimination, Seventy-Second Session (18 February–7 March 2008) and Seventy-Third Session (28 July–15 August 2008)*, General Assembly, Official Records, 63rd session, Supplement No. 18 (A/63/18), 92.

45. Minority Rights Committee, 50th sess., "Concluding Observations of the Committee on the Elimination of Racial Discrimination: Panama," CERD/C/304/Add. 32 (23 April 1997).

46. Food and Agriculture Organization, *Mapping Undernutrition—An Ongoing Process* (Rome: Food and Agriculture Organization, 1996); see also Bread for the World Institute, *Hunger in the Global Economy* (Silver Springs, Md.: Bread for the World Institute, 1998), 100.

47. Committee on Economic, Social and Cultural Rights (Economic Rights Committee), "Concluding Observations: Report on the Technical Assistance Mission: Panama," E/C.12/1995/8, 12th sess. (20 June 1995).

48. Minority Rights Committee, "Report of the Committee on the Elimination of Racial Discrimination, Fifty-Fourth Session (1–19 March 1999) and Fifty-Fifth Session (2–27 August 1999)," A/54/18 (29 September 1999).

49. Minority Rights Committee, *Report of the Committee on the Elimination of Racial Discrimination, Seventy-Second Session (18 February–7 March 2008) and Seventy-Third Session (28 July–15 August 2008)*, General Assembly, Official Records, 63rd session, Supplement No. 18 (A/63/18), 98.

50. See Banton, "Decision-Taking," 71.

51. Ratification information is available at http://treaties.un.org/Pages/ViewDetails.aspx?src=TREATY&mtdsg_no=IV-2-a&chapter=4&lang=en (accessed 19 July 2009); OHCHR, *Manual on Human Rights Reporting*, 294–295.

52. Interviews at the OHCHR, Geneva, Switzerland, June 2000; see also Philip Alston, "Final Report on Enhancing the Long-Term Effectiveness of the United Nations Human Rights Treaty System," UN Doc. E/CN.4/1997/74 (7 March 1997). Alston estimates that somewhere between seven and twenty-four years would be required to review the overdue state reports, if they were all to be submitted.

53. Andrew Clapham coined the phrase "splendid isolation" to describe the separation of the treaty bodies from the rest of the UN system. See Andrew Clapham, "UN Human Rights Reporting Procedures: An NGO Perspective," in *The Future of UN Human Rights Treaty Monitoring*, ed. Philip Alston and James Crawford (Cambridge: Cambridge University Press, 2000), 175–198.

54. Minority Rights Committee, *Guidelines for the CERD-Specific Document to be Submitted by States Parties Under Article 9, Paragraph 1, of the Convention*, CERD/C/2007/1, 13 June 2008, 2. Available at http://daccessdds.un.org/doc/UNDOC/GEN/G08/426/49/PDF/G0842649.pdf?OpenElement (accessed 20 July 2009).

55. Philip Alston reports: "[M]embers of the Human Rights Committee, the Committee on the Elimination of Discrimination Against Women and the Committee on the Rights of the Child will receive US$3,000 per year (apart from their daily allowance) and others (members of the Committee on Economic, Social and Cultural Rights, the Committee on the Elimination of Racial Discrimination and the Committee Against Torture) will receive nothing (apart from the same allowances)." See Final Report of Philip Alston, UN Doc. E/CN.4/1997/74 (7 March 1997), para. 84.

56. Elizabeth Evatt, "Ensuring Effective Supervisory Procedures: The Need For Resources," in *The Future of UN Human Rights Treaty Monitoring*, ed. Philip Alston and James Crawford (Cambridge: Cambridge University Press, 2000), 471.

57. The *New York Times* reported that there was a movement among some states at the UN to abolish the OHCHR after Mary Robinson left office. See Barbara Crossette, "Kofi Annan: An Idealist Who Took the Heat, Shook up the UN and Keeps Top Post," *New York Times*, 28 June 2001, 8(A).

58. Preparatory Committee, World Conference against Racism, Racial Discrimination, Xenophobia and Related Intolerance, "Contribution of the Committee on Economic, Social and Cultural rights to the Preparatory Process for the World Conference Against Racism, Racial discrimination, Xenophobia and Related Intolerance," A/CONF.189/PC.1/14, 1st sess. (29 February 2000).

59. Santosh Mehrotra, "Social Development in High-Achieving Countries: Common Elements and Diversities," in *Development with a Human Face*, ed. Santosh Mehrotra and Richard Jolly (Oxford: Clarendon, 1997), 29, 32.

Chapter 6

1. John Stuart Mill, *Three Essays: On Liberty [1859], Representative Government [1861], and The Subjection of Women [1869]* (London: Oxford University Press, 1912), 443–444, 451–452.

2. See Karl Marx and Frederick Engels, *The German Ideology* (1931; reprint, New York: International, 1970), 51.

3. Philip Gourevitch, *We Wish to Inform You That Tomorrow We Will Be Killed with Our Families* (New York: Farrar, Straus, and Giroux, 1998), 181.

4. Beijing Declaration, adopted by the Fourth World Conference on Women, 15 September 1995, UN Docs.A/CONF.177/20 (17 October 1995) and A/CONF.177/20/Add. 1 (27 October 1995).

5. International Covenant on Economic, Social and Cultural Rights (Economic Rights Treaty), concluded at New York 16 December 1966, and entered into force 3 January 1976, 993 UNTS 3.

6. Hilary Charlesworth, "Human Rights As Men's Rights," in *Women's Rights, Human Rights: International Feminist Perspectives*, ed. Julia Peters and Andrea Wolper (New York: Routledge, 1995), 108.

7. Barbara Stark, "The 'Other' Half of the International Bill of Rights As a Postmodern Feminist Text," in *Reconceiving Reality: Women and International Law*, ed. Dorinda Dallmeyer (Washington, D.C.: American Society of International Law, 1993), 20–21, 27, 33.

8. For example, see Jessica Stern, "Women in the Labour World: What about the Commitment?" in *Social Watch 1999*, ed. Roberto Bissio (Montevideo, Uruguay: Instituto Del Tercer Mundo, 1999), 72–76.

9. R. J. Barry Jones coined the term "structural constructivism" to call our attention to both "structures" and "social construction." See R. J. Barry Jones, "Globalization and Change in the International Political Economy," *International Affairs* 75, no. 2 (1999): 361.

10. Stark, "'Other' Half," 20–21.

11. Economic Rights Treaty, article 2.2.

12. Economic Rights Treaty, article 3.

13. Economic Rights Treaty, article 10.2.

14. Paul Hunt, *Reclaiming Social Rights: International and Comparative Perspectives* (Aldershot, Hants: Dartmouth, 1996), 88.

15. Stark, "'Other' Half," 27.

16. Stark notes that there are countless examples of states relieving women of some burdens. For example, "Sweden assures benefits for disabled children; Norway has established an ombudsman (sic) for children 'to deal with complaints of child abuse, physical conditions of children, child care, and schools'; and Belarus provides subsidies for children's clothing." See Stark, "'Other' Half," 31.

17. Carole Pateman, "Feminist Critiques of the Public/Private Dichotomy," in *Public and Private in Social Life*, ed. S. Benn and G. Gaus (London: Croom Helm, 1983), 281.

18. Hunt, *Reclaiming Social Rights*, 87.

19. Ratification information is available at: http://treaties.un.org/Pages/ViewDetails.aspx?src=TREATY&mtdsg_no=IV-8&chapter=4&lang=en (accessed 20 July 2009).

20. International Convention on the Elimination of All Forms of Discrimination against Women (Women's Rights Treaty), concluded at New York, 18 December 1979, and entered into force 3 September 1981, 1249 UNTS 13.

21. Women's Rights Treaty, article 1.

22. Women's Rights Treaty, article 4.1.

23. Women's Rights Treaty, article 4.2.

24. Women's Rights Treaty, article 11.

25. Women's Rights Treaty.

26. Hilary Charlesworth, Christine Chinkin, and Shelley Wright, "Feminist Approaches to International Law," *American Journal of International Law* 85 (1991): 631–632.

27. Charlesworth, Chinkin, and Wright, "Feminist Approaches," 632.

28. Charlesworth, Chinkin, and Wright, "Feminist Approaches," 634.

29. See "Committee on the Elimination of Discrimination Against Women—Mandate" available at: http://www2.ohchr.org/english/bodies/cedaw/mandate.htm (accessed 21 July 2009). See also Mara R. Bustelo, "The Committee on the Elimination of Discrimination against Women at the Crossroads," in *The Future of UN Human Rights Treaty Monitoring*, ed. Philip Alston and James Crawford (Cambridge: Cambridge University Press, 2000), 82.

30. Bustelo, "Committee," 82.

31. The four male members of the Women's Rights Committee were Mr. Johan Nordenfelt of Sweden (1982 to 1984); Mr. Göran Melander of Sweden (2001–2004);

Mr. Cornelius Flinterman of The Netherlands (2003–2010); Mr. Niklas Bruun of Finland (2008–2012). Also see Bustelo, "Committee," 80. Committee membership list available at: http://www2.ohchr.org/english/bodies/cedaw/membership. htm (accessed 20 July 2009).

32. Roberta Jacobson, "The Committee on the Elimination of Discrimination against Women," in *The United Nations and Human Rights*, ed. Philip Alston (New York: Oxford University Press, 1992), 459.

33. Charlesworth, Chinkin, and Wright, "Feminist Approaches," 624.

34. Data on "late reports" is available at http://www.unhchr.ch/tbs/doc.nsf/newhvoverduebytreaty?OpenView (accessed 20 July 2009).

35. "Initial Report of Guatemala Submitted to the Women's Rights Treaty Committee," Women's Rights Treaty/C/Gua/1–2 (2 April 1991), reprinted in Henry J. Steiner and Philip Alston, eds., *International Human Rights in Context: Law, Politics, Morals* (New York: Oxford University Press, 1996), 888–891.

36. Ratification information is available at http://treaties.un.org/Pages/Treaties.aspx?id=4&subid=A&lang=en (accessed 21 July 21, 2009).

37. The text of the optional protocol to Women's Rights Treaty is available http://www2.ohchr.org/english/law/cedaw-one.htm (accessed 21 July 2009).

38. United Nations, "Compilation of General Comments and General Recommendations Adopted by Human Rights Treaty Bodies," HRI/GEN/1/Rev. 4 (7 February 2000), 154–201.

39. "Compilation of General Comments and General Recommendations," 156.

40. "Compilation of General Comments and General Recommendations," 160–161.

41. "Compilation of General Comments and General Recommendations," 164.

42. "Compilation of General Comments and General Recommendations," 165.

43. "Compilation of General Comments and General Recommendations," 166.

44. "Compilation of General Comments and General Recommendations," 194–201.

45. "Compilation of General Comments and General Recommendations," 168.

46. Andrew Clapham, *Human Rights in the Private Sphere* (Oxford: Clarendon, 1993), 100.

47, Women's Rights Committee, *General Recommendation No. 26 on Women Migrant Workers*, CEDAW/C/2009/WP.1/R (5 December 2008), 6. Available at: http://www2.ohchr.org/english/bodies/cedaw/docs/GR_26_on_women_migrant_workers_en.pdf (accessed 21 July 2009).

48. Upendra Baxi, "Voices of Suffering, Fragmented Universality, and the Future of Human Rights," in *The Future of International Human Rights*, ed. Burns H. Weston and Stephen P. Marks (Ardsley, N.Y.: Transnational, 1999), 123; Walter Kaufmann, *The Portable Nietzsche* (New York: Viking Penguin, 1959), 160–161.

49. United Nations Development Program, *Human Development Report 2003* (New York: Oxford University Press, 2003), 86.

50. Women's Environment and Development Organization (WEDO), *Mapping Progress* (New York: Women's Environment and Development Organization, 1998), 13.

51. WEDO, *Mapping Progress*, 67–68.

52. Nalini Visvanathan, "Introduction to Part 1," in *The Women, Gender and Development Reader*, ed. N. Visvanathan et al. (London: Zed, 1997), 20.

53. Ester Boserup, *Women's Role in Economic Development* (New York: St. Martin's, 1970).

54. Rosi Braidotti et al., *Women, the Environment and Sustainable Development* (London: Zed, 1994), 80.

55. Visvanathan, "Introduction," 18–19.

56. Anne Marie Goetz, "Introduction: Getting Institutions Right for Women in Development," in *Getting Institutions Right for Women in Development*, ed. Anne Marie Goetz (London: Zed, 1997), 5.

57. Cynthia Enloe, *Bananas, Beaches and Bases: Making Feminist Sense of International Politics* (Berkeley: University of California Press, 1990), 159–160.

58. R. Pearson, A. Whitehead, and K. Young, "Introduction: The Continuing Subordination of Women in the Development Process," in *Of Marriage and the Market: Women's Subordination Internationally and Its Lessons*, ed. K. Young, C. Wolkowitz, and R. McCullagh (London: Routledge and Kegan Paul, 1984), x.

59. Ruth Pearson and Cecile Jackson, "Introduction: Interrogating Development," in *Feminist Visions of Development*, ed. C. Jackson and R. Pearson (New York: Routledge, 1998), 5.

60. Rounaq Jahan, *The Elusive Agenda: Mainstreaming Women in Development* (London: Zed, 1995), 21.

61. Braidotti et al., *Women*, 82.

62. Sally Baden and Anne Marie Goetz, "Who Needs [Sex] When You Can Have [Gender]?" in *Feminist Visions of Development*, ed. C. Jackson and R. Pearson (New York: Routledge, 1998), 24.

63. Baden and Goetz, "Who Needs [Sex]," 21.

64. Braidotti et al., *Women*, 117–118.

65. Jahan, *Elusive Agenda*, 78–79.

66. R. Braidotti et al., "Women, the Environment and Sustainable Development," in *The Women, Gender and Development Reader*, ed. N. Visvanathan et al. (London: Zed, 1997), 57–58.

67. Maria Mies, *Patriarchy and Accumulation on a World Scale* (London: Zed, 1986), 16–17, 55.

68. Vandana Shiva, "Women in Nature," in *Staying Alive* (London: Zed, 1989), quoted in N. Visvanathan et al., eds, *The Women, Gender and Development Reader* (London: Zed, 1997), 63.

69. Braidotti et al., *Women*, 162–163. See also Miriam Abramovay and Gail Lerner, "Introduction: Gender and Sustainable Development in Latin America and the Caribbean," in *Gender and Sustainable Development, a New Paradigm: Reflecting on Experience in Latin America and the Caribbean*, ed. Ana Maria Brasileiro (New York: UN Development Fund for Women, 1996), 11–12; Margaret Snyder, *Transforming Development: Women, Poverty and Politics* (London: Intermediate Technology Publications, 1995).

70. Bina Agarwal, "The Gender and Environment Debate: Lessons from India," *Feminist Studies* 18, no.1 (1992).

71. Women's Rights Treaty, article 2.

72. Declaration on the Right to Development, adopted by the UN General Assembly, 4 December 1986, GA Res. 41/128 (Annex), UN GAOR, 41st sess., Supp. no. 53, at 186, UN Doc. A/41/53 (1987).

73. Universal Declaration of Human Rights, adopted by the UN General Assembly, 10 December 1948, Resolution 217 A, UNGAOR, 3rd sess., pt. 1, Resolutions, at 71, UN Doc. A/810 (1948).

74. Women's Rights Treaty, article 5.

75. International Convention on the Elimination of All Forms of Racial Discrimination (Minority Rights Treaty), adopted and open for signature and ratification by General Assembly resolution 2106 (XX) of 21 December 1965, and entered into force 4 January 1969, in accordance with article 19.

76. Women's Rights Treaty, article 4.1.

77. Declaration on the Right to Development, article 2.3.

78. World Summit For Social Development, Copenhagen 1995, "Copenhagen Declaration and Programme of Action," available at: http://www.un.org/esa/socdev/wssd/index.html (accessed 21 July 2009).

79. "Rio de Janeiro Declaration on Environment and Development," UN Doc. A/CONF.151/26 (13 June 1992).

80. "Stockholm Declaration of the United Nations Conference on the Human Environment," UN Doc. A/CONF.48/14 (16 June 1972), at www.unep.org/ (accessed 19 June 2001).

81. World Charter for Nature, adopted by the UN General Assembly, 28 October 1982, GA Res. 37/7 (Annex), UN GAOR, 37th sess., Supp. no. 51, at 17, UN Doc. A/37/51.

82. Caroline O. N. Moser, "Gender Planning in the Third World: Meeting Practical and Strategic Needs," in *Gender and International Relations*, ed. Rebecca Grant and Kathleen Newland (Bloomington: Indiana University Press, 1991), 83–88.

83. Maxine Molyneux, "Mobilization without Emancipation? Women's Interests, State and Revolution in Nicaragua," *Feminist Studies* 11, no. 2 (1985), quoted in Moser, "Gender Planning," 90.

84. Moser, "Gender Planning," 90–91.

85. Martha C. Nussbaum, *Sex and Social Justice* (New York: Oxford University Press, 1999), 34.

86. Amartya Sen, *Development As Freedom* (New York: Knopf, 1999), 109.

87. Martha C. Nussbaum, *Women and Human Development: The Capabilities Approach* (Cambridge: Cambridge University Press, 2000), 4.

88. Nussbaum, *Women and Human Development*, 75.

89. Nussbaum, *Women and Human Development*, 113–114.

90. Nussbaum too often presents the capabilities approach as an alternative to human rights. She painstakingly details how this approach is supposedly superior to a human rights focus. It does not carry the "baggage" of "rights" language, which is understood in many different ways and is often seen as privileging Western culture. Furthermore, people differ about both the basis of a rights claim (e.g., rationality, artifacts of law, or mere life) and whether rights are held by individuals or groups. Her solution is to propose that the best way of thinking about rights is to see them as "combined capabilities." Yet, in the end, she agrees that we still need the language of rights "despite its unsatisfactory features." She acknowledges the power of a human rights claim to a certain type of treatment. See Nussbaum, *Women and Human Development*, 100.

91. Hilary Charlesworth, "What Are 'Women's International Human Rights?'" in *Human Rights of Women: National and International Perspectives*, ed. Rebecca J. Cook (Philadelphia: University of Pennsylvania Press, 1994), 71.

Chapter 7

1. Henry Shue, *Basic Rights: Subsistence, Affluence, and U.S. Foreign Policy* (Princeton: Princeton University Press, 1980), 20–22. Universal Declaration of Human Rights is available at: http://www.un.org/en/documents/udhr/ (accessed 28 July 2009).

2. *Haig v. Agee*, 453 U.S. 280 (1981) in Louis Henkin, Gerarld L. Neuman, Diane F. Orentlicher, and David W. Leebron, *Human Rights* (New York: Foundation Press, 1999), 207.

3. Sam Perlo-Freeman, Catalina Perdomo, Elisabeth Sköns and Petter Stälenheim, "Military Expenditure," in *SIPRI Yearbook 2009: Armaments, Disarmament and International Security*, chapter 5, 179, available at: http://www.sipri.org/yearbook (accessed 28 July 2009).

4. Boutros Boutros-Ghali, *An Agenda for Development* (New York: United Nations Publication, 1995), 20.

5. Jeff Gerth and Tim Weiner, "Arms Makers See Bonanza by Selling NATO Expansion," *New York Times*, 29 June 1997, 1(1).

6. As William J. Baumol and Alan S. Blinder write: "Consider what happens in financial markets when the government engages in deficit spending. When it spends more than it takes in, the government must borrow the rest. It does so by selling bonds, which compete with corporate bonds and other financial instruments for the available supply of funds. As some savers decide to buy government bonds, the funds remaining to invest in private bonds must shrink. Thus, some private borrowers get "crowded out" of the financial markets as the government claims an increasing share of the economy's total saving." William J. Baumol and Alan A. Blinder, *Macroeconomics: Principles & Policy*, 11th edition (Mason, Ohio: South-Western Cengage Learning, 2009), 310.

7. George W. Bush, State of the Union Address, 29 January 2002, at www.whitehouse.gov/news/releases/2002/01/20020129-11.html (accessed 22 March 2002).

8. Perlo-Freeman, et. al., *SIPRI Yearbook 2009*, 184.

9. U.S. Office of Management and Budget, *Budget of the United States Government: Fiscal Year 2010, Historical Tables* (Washington DC: US GPO, 2009), table 3.2 at www.gpoaccess.gov/usbudget/fy10/sheets/hist03z2.xls (accessed 25 July 2009).

10. Perlo-Freeman, et. al., *SIPRI Yearbook 2009*, 184, 188.

11. Perlo-Freeman, et. al., *SIPRI Yearbook 2009*, 182.

12. Perlo-Freeman, et. al., *SIPRI Yearbook 2009*, 189. Please note that the estimated U.S. budget deficit in FY2009 of $407 billion does not include either a) the Obama administration's economic stimulation measures which were approved by Congress or b) the supplemental funding approved for the expansion of the war in Afghanistan. As a result, the FY2009 budget deficit will likely exceed this conservative projection.

13. Joseph Stiglitz and Linda Bilmes, *The Three Trillion Dollar War: The True Cost of the Iraq Conflict* (New York: Norton & Co., 2008), 59.

14. U.S. unemployment rates are available at the U.S. Bureau of Labor Statistics: http://stats.bls.gov/ (accessed 29 July 2009).

15. Joshua S. Goldstein, *Long Cycles: Prosperity and War in the Modern Age* (New Haven, Conn.: Yale University Press, 1988), 265, 267; Joshua S. Goldstein, "How Military Might Robs an Economy," *New York Times*, 16 October 1988, F3.

16. David Gold, "Does Military Spending Stimulate or Retard Economic Performance? Revisiting an Old Debate." The New School International Affairs Working Paper 2005-01, Paper prepared for presentation at the Annual Meeting of the Allied Social Sciences Associations, Philadelphia, 8 January 2005 at www.newschool.edu/internationalaffairs/docs/wkg_papers/Gold_2005-01.pdf (accessed 25 June 2009).

17. Michael D. Ward, David R. Davis, and Corey L. Lofdahl, "A Century of Tradeoffs: Defense and Growth in Japan and the United States," *International Studies Quarterly* 39, no. 1 (1995): 27–50.

18. U.S. Office of Management and Budget, *Budget of the United States Government: Fiscal Year 2010*, Historical Tables (Washington DC: US GPO, 2009), table 3.2 at www.gpoaccess.gov/usbudget/fy10/sheets/hist03z2.xls (accessed 25 July 2009).

19. See David P. Calleo, *Beyond American Hegemony: The Future of the Western Alliance* (New York: Basic, 1987), 109–126; Paul Kennedy, *The Rise and Fall of the Great Powers* (New York: Random House, 1987), 514–535.

20. Ruth Leger Sivard, *World Military and Social Expenditures*, 16th ed. (Washington, DC: World Priorities, 1996), 48–53; Ruth Leger Sivard, *World Military and Social Expenditures*, 14th ed. (Washington, DC: World Priorities, 1991), 54–56.

21. Goldstein, "How Military Might"; Goldstein, *Long Cycles*.

22. Ron Smith, "Military Expenditure and Investment in OECD Countries, 1954–1973," Journal of Comparative Economics 4 (1980): 19–32; For an analysis confirming this negative trade-off for the United States using 1946–1978 data, see Karen Rasler and William Thompson, "Defense Burdens, Capital Formation, and Economic Growth," *Journal of Conflict Resolution* 32, no. 1 (1988): 61–86.

23. William K. Tabb, *The Amoral Elephant: Globalization and the Struggle for Social Justice in the Twenty-First Century* (New York: Monthly Review, 2001), 54.

24. Tabb, *Amoral Elephant*, 54–55.

25. Tabb, *Amoral Elephant*, 77.

26. Ron Smith, *Military Economics* (London: Palgrave Macmillan, 2009), 91.

27. Michael O'Hanlon, "What Price for Military Readiness?" *New York Times*, 27 June 2001.

28. Thom Shanker, "Proposed Military Spending Is Highest Since WWII," *New York Times*, 4 February 2008.

29. Lt. Col. John Sayen, "Introduction & Historic Overview: The Overburden of America's Outdated Defenses" in *America's Defense Meltdown: Pentagon Reform for President Obama and the New Congress* (Stanford Security Studies), ed. Winslow Wheeler (Stanford, CA: Stanford University Press, 2009), 2; Robert M. Gates, Speech delivered at the National Defense University (Washington, DC: U.S.

Department of Defense, 29 September 2008) at http://www.defenselink.mil/speeches/speech.aspx?speechid=1279 (accessed 10 August 2009).

30. World Bank Group, "World Development Indicators Online," military expenditures (% of GDP), available at: www.worldbank.org (accessed 28 July 2009).

31. Carl Conetta, "Toward a Smaller, More Efficient, and More Relevant US Military," PDA Briefing Memo 17 (October 2000), at www.comw.org/pda/0010bm17.html (accessed 7 April 2001).

32. See Lloyd J. Dumas, "Finding the Future: The Role of Economic Conversion in Shaping the Twenty-First Century," in *The Socio-Economics of Conversion from War to Peace*, ed. Lloyd J. Dumas (Armonk, N.Y.: Sharpe, 1995).

33. Adam Smith, *The Wealth of Nations* (New York: Modern Library, 1937), 315.

34. Lloyd J. Dumas, "Bang for the Buck: The Real Effects of Military Spending on Security," paper prepared for the Annual Meeting of the Allied Social Science Associations, Philadelphia, 8 January 2005, p. 5 at www.utdallas.edu/~ljdumas/BangBuck.doc (accessed 31 July 2009).

35. Goldstein, *Long Cycles*, 266–267.

36. Robert W. DeGrasse Jr., *Military Expansion, Economic Decline* (New York: Council on Economic Priorities, 1983), Chart 2.6, 82.

37. These numbers would be even higher if the portions of space R&D that supported the U.S. military were included. U.S. Office of Management and Budget, *Budget of the United States Government: Fiscal Year 2010*, Historical Tables (Washington DC: US GPO, 2009), table 9.7 at www.gpoaccess.gov/usbudget/fy10/sheets/hist03z2.xls (accessed 25 July 2009); National Science Foundation *Science and Engineering Indicators 2008* (Arlington, VA: National Science Board, NSB 08-01A, January 2008), Appendix table 4-3 at http://www.nsf.gov/statistics/seind08/append/c4/at04-03.xls (accessed 25 July 2009).

38. Ethan Barnaby Kapstein, *The Political Economy of National Security: A Global Perspective* (Columbia, S.C.: University of South Carolina Press, 1992), 51.

39. DeGrasse, *Military Expansion*, 105–106.

40. Gold, "Does Military Spending"; Dumas, "Bang for the Buck," 5.

41. DeGrasse, *Military Expansion*, 28–106.

42. Steve Chan, "The Impact of Defense Spending on Economic Performance: A Survey of Evidence and Problems," *Orbis* (Summer 1985): 413–414.

43. Uk Heo, "Modeling the Defense-Growth Relationship around the Globe," *The Journal of Conflict Resolution* 42, no. 5 (October 1998): 647, 652.

44. Uk Heo and Robert J. Eger III, "Paying for Security: The Security-Prosperity Dilemma in the United States," *The Journal of Conflict Resolution* 49, no. 5 (October 2005): 792–817.

45. Alex Mintz and Chi Huang, "Defense Expenditures, Economic Growth, and the 'Peace Dividend,'" *American Political Science Review* 84, no. 4 (1990): 1289.

46. Heo, "Modeling," 649.

47. Dumas, "Finding the Future," 7; Dumas, "Bang for the Buck," 3–7; quote on 3.

48. Todd Sandler and Keith Hartley, *The Economics of Defense* (Cambridge: Cambridge University Press, 1995), 220.

49. DeGrasse, *Military Expansion*, 29.

50. DeGrasse, *Military Expansion*, 23–36.

51. Congressional Budget Office, *The Economic Effects of Reduced Defense Spending* (Washington, D.C.: Congressional Budget Office, 1992), 9.

52. Alex Mintz and Chi Huang, "Guns and Butter: The Indirect Link," *American Journal of Political Science* 35, no 3 (1991): 752.

53. Dean Baker, "The Economic Impact of the Iraq War and Higher Military Spending," Center for Economic and Policy Research, May 2007. Available at http://www.cepr.net/index.php/publications/reports/the-economic-impact-of-the-iraq-war-and-higher-military-spending/ (accessed 2 August 2009).

54. GAO (U.S. Government Accountability Office), *Defense Acquisitions: DOD Must Prioritize Its Weapon System Acquisitions and Balance Them with Available Resources*, GAO-09-501T (Washington, DC: 18 March 2009), p.2, at www.gao.gov (accessed 12 July 2009).

55. GAO, *Defense Acquisitions: DOD Must Prioritize*, GAO Highlights.

56. GAO, *Defense Acquisitions: Assessments of Selected Weapon Programs*, GAO-09-326SP (Washington, DC: 30 March 2009), p.7, at www.gao.gov (accessed 12 July 2009).

57. GAO, *Defense Acquisitions: Assessments*, 7, 10–11.

58. Defense Science Board, *Task Force on Developmental Test & Evaluation* (Washington, DC: Office of the Under Secretary of Defense for Acquisition, Technology and Logistics, May 2008), pp. 2–3, 13, at http://www.acq.osd.mil/dsb/reports/2008-05-DTE.pdf (accessed 12 July 2009).

59. For example, see William D. Hartung and Bernie Sanders, "Time to End Waste at the Pentagon" *Politico* 24, June 2008, at www.newamerica.net (accessed 12 July 2009).

60. John Isaacs and Dan Koslofsky, "Trim Pentagon Fat," *Bulletin of the Atomic Scientists* 57, no. 1 (January–February 2001): 26.

61. Isaacs and Koslofsky, "Trim Pentagon Fat," 26.

62. William A. Owens and Stanley A. Weiss, "An Indefensible Military Budget," *New York Times*, 7 February 2002, 23(A).

63. Perlo-Freeman, et. al., *SIPRI Yearbook 2009*, 180.

64. World Bank Group, "World Development Indicators Online," military, health, & education expenditures (% of GDP), available at: www.worldbank.org (accessed 28 July 2009).

65. UNDP, *Human Development Report 1994*, 50.

66. UNDP, *Human Development Report 1994*, 50.

67. J. Paul Dunne, "Economic Effects of Military Expenditure in Developing Countries: A Survey," in *The Peace Dividend*, eds. Nils Gleditsch, Olav Bjerkholt, Adne Cappelen, Ron Smith, and J. Paul Dunne (Amsterdam: Elsevier, 1996), 455, 459.

68. World Bank, *World Development Report 2000/2001*, 50.

69. Leonardo Garnier et al., "Costa Rica: Social Development and Heterodox Adjustment," in *Development with a Human Face: Experiences in Social Achievement and Economic Growth*, ed. Santosh Mehrotra and Richard Jolly (New York: Oxford University Press, 1997), 372.

70. World Bank, *World Development Report 2000/2001*, 306.

71. Maria Stern, *Security Policy in Transition* (Stockholm: Padriger, 1991), 26–28; Robert Elias and Jennifer Turpin, "Introduction: Thinking about Peace," in *Rethinking Peace*, ed. Robert Elias and Jennifer Turpin (Boulder, Colo.: Rienner, 1994), 4; Johan Galtung, "Violence, Peace and Peace Research," *Journal of Peace Research 6*, no. 3 (1969): 167–191.

72. Elias and Turpin, "Thinking about Peace," 4–5.

73. UNDP, *Human Development Report 1994*, 24–25.

74. William D. Hartung and Frida Berrigan, "U.S. Weapons at War 2008," New American Foundation, December 2008. Available at: http://www.newamerica. net/publications/policy/u_s_weapons_war_2008 (accessed 12 July 2009).

75. Steven Lee Myers, "U.S. Lifts a Ban on Weapon Sales to Latin America," *New York Times*, 2 August 1997, 1(1).

76. On 30 January 2002, the government of Chile announced that it would buy ten F-16 fighter jets from the United States for $660 million. This transaction represented the first time in two decades that Washington had approved the transfer of sophisticated weapons to a Latin American country. Brazil, Peru, Bolivia, and Argentina felt pressured to respond in kind and the arms race on the continent took off. See Christopher Marquis, "In Unusual Deal, Chile Will Buy Advanced U.S. Fighter Jets," *New York Times*, 31 January 2002, 8(A).

77. Hartung and Berrigan, "U.S. Weapons at War 2008."

78. William D. Hartung, "An Unstoppable Arms Trade?" *World Policy Journal*, Fall 2008. Available at: http://www.newamerica.net/publications/articles/ 2008/unstoppable_arms_trade_8265 (accessed 12 July 2009).

79. William D. Hartung, "Stop Arming the World," *Bulletin of the Atomic Scientists 57*, no. 1 (January–February 2001): 35.

80. See Steve Coll, *Ghost Wars* (New York: Penguin Books, 2004); Chalmers Johnson, *Blowback* (New York: Henry Holt, 2000); Chalmers Johnson, *The Sorrow of Empire* (New York: Henry Holt, 2004).

81. See Domenick Bertelli, "Military Contractor Conversion in the United States," in *The Socio-Economics of Conversion from War to Peace*, ed. Lloyd J. Dumas (Armonk, N.Y.: Sharpe, 1995).

82. Business Leaders for Sensible Priorities, "Does the Pentagon Need Another $10,000,000,000?" *New York Times*, 24 March 1999, 21(A).

83. Stiglitz and Bilmes, *The Three Trillion Dollar War*, xv. See also: www.costof-war.com.

84. Stiglitz and Bilmes, *The Three Trillion Dollar War*, xvi-xvii.

85. For example, see J. Lynch, ed., *Economic Adjustment and Conversion of Defense Industries* (London: Westview, 1987); Alejandro E. Nadal, "Military R&D: The Economic Implications of Disarmament and Conversion," *Defense and Peace Economics 5*, no. 2, (1994): 131–151; United Nations, *Economic Aspects of Disarmament: Disarmament as an Investment Process* (New York: United Nations Publications, 1993); Anthony Voss, *Converting the Defense Industry* (Oxford: Oxford Research Group, 1992).

86. For example, see Boutros Boutros-Ghali, *An Agenda for Peace*, 1995 (New York: United Nations Publications, 1995); Richard Falk, *On Humane Governance: Toward a New Global Politics* (University Park: Pennsylvania State University Press, 1995), 207–240; Saul H. Mendlovitz and Burns H. Weston, eds., "Symposium:

Preferred Futures for the United Nations," *Transnational Law and Contemporary Problems* 4, no. 2 (Fall 1994).

Chapter 8

1. Louis Henkin, Gerald L. Neuman, Diane F. Orentlicher, and David W. Leebron (eds), *Human Rights* (New York: Foundation Press, 1999), 1112.
2. Gerhard von Glahn explains this issue: "In the United States, a self-executing treaty becomes domestic law as soon as the instrument enters into force internationally. Non-self-executing agreements require implementing legislation before they come into effect domestically. In the United States and elsewhere, the courts look at that implementing legislation in arriving at a decision in relevant cases" (Gerhard von Glahn, *Law Among Nations*, 6th edition (New York: Macmillan Publishing Co., 1992), 568.
3. Philip Alston , "U.S. Ratification of the Covenant on Economic, Social and Cultural Rights: The Need for an Entirely New Strategy," *American Journal of International Law* 84 (1990): 365, 372–75.
4. Elliott Abrams, "Statement of Elliott Abrams, Assistant Secretary of State, Bureau of Human Rights and Humanitarian Affairs," *Review of State Department Country Reports on Human Rights Practices for 1981: Hearing Before the Subcommittee on Human Rights and International Organizations of the House Committee on Foreign Affairs,* 97th Cong., 2nd Sess. 7 (1982).
5. Abrams, "Statement," 1982.
6. Patricia M. Byrne, "Statement by Ambassador Patricia M. Byrne to the Third Committee of the UN General Assembly," Nov. 9, 1988, Department of State Press Release USUN 129-(88). Reprinted Henkin, et. al, *Human Rights,* 1114.
7. *Vienna Declaration and Programme of Action* (1993) 32 ILM 1661 (see in particular point 5). Available at www.unhchr.ch/huridocda/huridoca.nsf/ (Symbol)/A.CONF.157.23.En?OpenDocument (accessed 22 May 2009).
8. Ratification information is available at the Inter-American Commission on Human Rights website: http://www.cidh.oas.org/Basicos/English/Basic4 .Amer.Conv.Ratif.htm (accessed 23 May 2009).
9. The "Additional Protocol to the American Convention on Human Rights in the Area of Economic, Social and Cultural Rights" is available at http://www .cidh.oas.org/Basicos/English/basic5.Prot.Sn%20Salv.htm (accessed on 23 May 2009).
10. J. B. Ruhl, "The Fitness of Law: Using Complexity Theory to Describe the Evolution of Law and Society and Its Practical Meaning for Democracy," *Vanderbilt Law Review* 49 (1996): 1407.
11. The Statute of the Council of Europe was signed in London on 5 May 1949, on behalf of Belgium, Denmark, France, Ireland, Italy, Luxembourg, the Netherlands, Norway, Sweden, and the United Kingdom.
12. Ratification information on the Statute of the Council of Europe is available at http://www.coe.int/T/e/com/about_coe/member_states/default.asp (assessed 25 April 2009).

13. The texts of the European Social Charter of 1961 and all relevant protocols are available at http://conventions.coe.int/Treaty/Commun/QueVoulezVous .asp?NT=035&CM=8&DF=4/25/2009&CL=ENG (assessed 25 April 2009).

14. In odd years, the state reports concern the hard-core provisions (Articles 1,5,6,7,12,13,16, 19, and 20), and in even years the other provisions.

15. Information on ECSR state reporting procedures is available at http://www .coe.int/t/dghl/monitoring/socialcharter/Reporting/StateReports/Reports_ en.asp (accessed 26 April 2009).

16. Collective complaint information available at http://www.coe.int/t/dghl/ monitoring/socialcharter/ComplaintSummaries/CCSummariesMerits2009_en .pdf (accessed 26 April 2009).

17. *Twelfth Report on the Implementation of the European Social Charter Submitted by the Government of Greece*, RAP/Cha/GR/XII(2001), Strasbourg, 3 December 2001. Available at: http://www.coe.int/T/E/Human%5FRights/Esc/4%5FRep orting%5Fprocedure/1%5FState%5FReports/Social_Charter/XVI_1/Greece%20 12th%20report.pdf (accessed 17 June 2004).

18. Christof Heyns and Frans Viljoen, *The Impact of the United Nations Human Rights Treaties on the Domestic Level* (The Hague, The Netherlands: Kluwer Law International, 2002), 598.

19. Supreme Court of the United States, *Dandridge v. Williams*, (1970) 397 U.W. 471.

20. Committee on Economic, Social and Cultural Rights, General Comment no. 3 (1990), UN Doc.E/1991/23, Annex III. Paragraph 10 states that "a minimum core obligation to ensure the satisfaction of, at the very least, minimum essential levels of each of the rights is incumbent upon every State Party. Thus, for example, a State Party in which any significant number of individuals is deprived of essential foodstuffs, of essential primary health care, of basic shelter and housing, or of the most basic forms of education is, *prima facie*, failing to discharge its obligations under the Covenant."

21. PRWORA, "Personal Responsibility and Work Opportunity Reconciliation Act," (1996) Pub. L. 104–193, 110 Stat. 2105.

22. Bert Lockwood, Jr., R. Collins Owens, III, and Grace Severyn, G., "Litigating State Constitutional Rights to Happiness and Safety: A Strategy for Ensuring the Provision of Basic Needs to the Poor," *William and Mary Bill of Rights Journal* 2.1 (1993), 4, 5, 8.

23. Lockwood, Owens, and Severyn, "Litigating State Constitutional Rights," 9, 28.

24. Henkin, Newman, Orlentlicher, and Leebron, *Human Rights*, 1171.

25. Federal Court of Switzerland, "V. v. Municipality X. and Council of the Canton of Bern," (1995), BGE 122 I 367.

26. Federal Court of Switzerland, "V. v. Municipality X."

27. Alberto Alesina and Edward Glaeser, *Fighting Poverty in the U.S. and Europe: A World of Difference* (Oxford: Oxford University Press, 2004), 21–22.

28. Alesina and Glaeser, *Fighting Poverty*, 22.

29. Alesina and Glaeser, *Fighting Poverty*, 22–23.

30. Alesina and Glaeser, *Fighting Poverty*, 23.

31. Alesina and Glaeser, *Fighting Poverty*, 23–24.

32. Alesina and Glaeser, *Fighting Poverty*, 38, 40.

33. United Nations Development Program (UNDP), *Human Development Report 2007/2008* (New York: Palgrave Macmillan, 2007), 241.

34. UNDP, *Human Development Report 2007/2008*, 229, 277.

35. U.S. Office of Management and Budget, Budget of the United States Government: Fiscal Year 2010, Historical Tables (Washington DC: US GPO, 2009), table 3.2 at www.gpoaccess.gov/usbudget/fy10/sheets/hist03z2.xls (accessed 25 July 2009).

36. Jason DeParle, "Report, Delayed Months, Says Lowest Income Group Grew," *New York Times*, 12 May 1992, 15(A).

37. "Children in Poverty: 1 Million More in 80's," *New York Times*, 8 July 1992, 20(A).

38. Alan B. Krueger, "The Truth about Wages," *New York Times*, 31 July 1997, 23(A).

39. Marc Miringoff and Marque-Luisa Miringoff, *The Social Health of the Nation: How America Is Really Doing* (New York: Oxford University Press, 1999), 98.

40. Lynnley Browning, "U.S. Income Gap Widening, Study Says," *New York Times*, 25 September 2003, 2(C).

41. Miringoff and Miringoff, *Social Health*, 104.

42. Andrew Hacker, "The Underworld of Work," *The New York Review of Books*, 12 February 2004.

43. Miringoff and Miringoff, *Social Health*, 92.

44. *New York Times*, "Millions Still Going Hungry in the U.S., Report Finds," 10 September 2000, 26(1).

45. Miringoff and Miringoff, *Social Health*, 80.

46. Lynette Clemetson, "More Americans in Poverty in 2002, Census Study Says," *New York Times*, 27 September 2003, 1(A).

47. Beth Shulman, *The Betrayal of Work: How Low-Wage Jobs Fail 30 Million Americans* (New York: The New Press, 2003), 25–44.

48. Janny Scott, "Nearly Half of Black Men in City Are Jobless, Study Finds," *The New York Times*, 28 February 2004, 15(B).

49. Sarah Burd-Sharps, Kristen Lewis, and Eduardo Borges Martins, *The Measure of America: American Human Development Report 2008–2009* (New York: Columbia University Press, 2008), 4.

50. Burd-Sharps, Lewis, & Martins, *The Measure of America*, 12.

51. Burd-Sharps, Lewis, & Martins, *The Measure of America*, 19.

52. Peter H. Lindert, *Growing Public: Social Spending and Economic Growth Since the Eighteenth Century* (Cambridge: Cambridge University Press, 2004), 227.

53. Lindert, *Growing Public*, 17–18.

54. Lindert, *Growing Public*, 18.

55. Lindert, *Growing Public*. See also Jeff Madrick, "Economic Scene," *New York Times*, 15 April 2004, 2 (C).

Chapter 9

1. For a discussion of weaknesses of current UN structures, including the Economic and Social Council see Maurice Williams, "Beyond Development Cooperation: Toward a New Era of Global and Human Security" (opening statement to the

international conference Beyond Development Co-Operation: Toward a New Era of Global and Human Security, Ottawa, Canada, 15–16 October 1993).

2. World Bank, "Understanding Povery," 2008, available at http://web .worldbank.org/WBSITE/EXTERNAL/TOPICS/EXTPOVERTY/EXTPA/0 ,,contentMDK:20153855~menuPK:435040~pagePK:148956~piPK:216618~the SitePK:430367,00.html (accessed 8 June 2009).

3. UNICEF, *State of the World's Children 2008* (New York: UNICEF, 2008), see http://www.unicef.org/sowc08/profiles/child_survival.php (accessed 8 June 2009).

4. Mahbub ul Haq, *Reflections on Human Development* (New York: Oxford University Press, 1995), 187.

5. Haq, *Reflections on Human Development*, 91, 186–199.

6. William F. Felice, *Taking Suffering Seriously: The Importance of Collective Human Rights* (Albany: SUNY Press, 1996), 85–86; see also UNDP, *Human Development Report 1994* (New York: Oxford University Press, 1994), 7, 50, 77.

7. UNDP, *Human Development Report 2000*, 9; see also UNDP, UNESCO, UNFPA, UNICEF, WHO, and the World Bank, *Implementing the 20/20 Initiative: Achieving Universal Access to Basic Social Services* (New York: UNDP et al., 1998).

8. UNDP, *Human Development Report 2000*, 9.

9. UNDP, *Human Development Report 2000*, 9.

10. UNDP, *Human Development Report 2000*, 120.

11. See Haq, *Reflections on Human Development*, 197–198.

12. Inge Kaul and John Langmore, "Potential Uses of the Revenue from a Tobin Tax," in *The Tobin Tax: Coping with Financial Volatility*, ed. Mahbub ul Haq, Inge Kaul, and Isabelle Grunberg (New York: Oxford University Press, 1996), 263.

13. Kaul and Langmore, "Potential Uses," 263.

14. James Tobin, "Prologue" to *The Tobin Tax: Coping with Financial Volatility*, ed. Mahbub ul Haq, Inge Kaul, and Isabelle Grunberg (New York: Oxford University Press, 1996), x.

15. It is worth noting that Tobin himself suggested a higher tax rate of 0.5% on the international movements of speculative capital. The higher rate would serve Tobin's goal of slowing these often disruptive and unproductive invesments. Tobin, "Prologue," xvii; UNDP, *Human Development Report 1994*, 9, 59, 70; see also Felice, *Taking Suffering Seriously*, 86–87.

16. Tobin, "Prologue," xvii.

17. Kaul and Langmore, "Potential Uses," 267.

18. Tobin, "Prologue," xii.

19. It is often difficult for outsiders to determine the legitimacy of self-proclaimed "freedom fighters" and the validity of an organization's claim to represent a people's struggle for human rights. In Iraq, for example, opportunists were able to manipulate outside states and gain their support. Yet, the South Africa example demonstrates that with care outside state and nonstate actors can have a positive impact on a peoples' struggle for independence and dignity.

20. For an outstanding summary and evaluation of the Optional Protocol to the Economic Rights Treaty, see Kitty Arambulo, *Strengthening the Supervision of the International Covenant on Economic, Social and Cultural Rights* (Antwerpen: Intersentia, 1999).

21. "Optional Protocol to the International Covenant on Economic, Social and Cultural Rights," General Assembly Resolution A/RES/63/117, on 10 December 2008. Available at http://www2.ohchr.org/english/bodies/cescr/docs/A-RES-63-117.pdf (accessed 25 July 2009).

22. Ved P. Nanda, "Environment," in *United Nations Legal Order*, vol. 2, ed. Oscar Schachter and Christopher C. Joyner (Cambridge: Cambridge University Press, 1995), 667.

23. Daniel C. Esty, *Greening the GATT: Trade, Environment, and the Future* (Washington, DC: Institute for International Economics, 1994), 230. Esty named his proposed environmental IGO the Global Environmental Organization. To avoid confusion, I have kept the name WEO throughout the book.

24. Michael W. Doyle and Rachel I. Massey, "Intergovernmental Organizations and the Environment: Looking towards the Future," in *The Global Environment in the Twenty-First Century: Prospects for International Cooperation*, ed. Pamela S. Chasek (Tokyo: United Nations University Press, 2000), 421–422.

25. Alexandre Kiss, "An Introductory Note on a Human Right to Environment," in *Environmental Change and International Law: New Challenges and Dimensions*, ed. Edith Brown Weiss (Tokyo: United Nations University Press, 1992), 203.

26. Hilary French, *Vanishing Borders* (New York: Norton, 2000), 159–160.

27. P. M. Haas, R. O. Keohane, and M. A. Levy, eds., *Institutions for the Earth: Sources of Effective International Environmental Protection* (Cambridge: MIT Press, 1993).

28. Esty, *Greening the GATT*, 80–81.

29. See Bill McKibben, *Deep Economy: The Wealth of Communities and the Durable Future* (New York: Holt, 2007), 129–176.

30. Roberto Bissio, ed., *Social Watch 1999* (Montevideo: Instituto Del Tercer Mundo, 1999), 125. For the current Human Development Index, Canada ranks fourth highest. UNDP, *Human Development Report 2007/2008* (New York: Palgrave, 2007), 229.

31. Santosh Mehrotra, "Health and Education Policies in High-Achieving Countries: Some Lessons," in *Development with a Human Face*, ed. Santosh Mehrotra and Richard Jolly (New York: Oxford University Press, 1997), 64–65.

32. Bissio, *Social Watch 1999*, 118.

33. UN Children's Fund (UNICEF), *The State of the World's Children 1999* (New York: UN Children's Fund, 1999), 80.

34. UNDP, *Human Development Report 2007/2008*, 230–231.

35. Bissio, *Social Watch 1999*, 178, 210.

36. UNDP, *Human Development Report 2000*, 33.

37. UNICEF, *State of the World's Children 1999*, 81.

38. UNDP, *Human Development Report 2007–2008*, 326–328.

39. UN Development Fund for Women, *Progress of the World's Women 2000* (New York: UN Development Fund for Women, 2000), 110–111.

40. UNDP, *Human Development Report 2007–2008*, 250; UN Dept. of Economic & Social Affairs, *The Millennium Development Goals Report 2008*, 4, available at: http://www.un.org/millenniumgoals/pdf/The%20Millennium%20Development%20Goals%20Report%202008.pdf (accessed 26 July 2009); see also

Naomi Neft and Ann E. Levine, *Where Women Stand: An International Report on the Status of Women in 140 Countries, 1997–1998* (New York: Random House, 1997), 5.

41. Women's Rights Committee, *General Recommendation no. 24* (20th session, 1999), in United Nations, "Compilation of General Comments and General Recommendations Adopted by Human Rights Treaty Bodies," HRI/GEN/1/Rev. 4 (7 February 2000), 194–201.

42. UNDP, *Human Development Report 2000,* 96.

43. Neft and Levine, *Where Women Stand,* 29–30.

44. UN Dept. of Economic & Social Affairs, *The Millennium Development Goals Report 2008,* 18, available at: http://www.un.org/millenniumgoals/pdf/The%20 Millennium%20Development%20Goals%20Report%202008.pdf (accessd 26 July 2009).

45. UNFPA, "Poverty, Inequality and Population," *State of the World Population 2008* (chapter 5), available at: http://www.unfpa.org/swp/2008/en/05_ poverty_inequality.html (accessed 26 July 2009); World Bank, *World Development Report 2000/2001,* 119.

46. World Bank, *World Development Report 2000/2001,* 119.

47. World Bank, *World Development Report 2000/2001,* 119.

48. Michael Renner, "Budgeting for Disarmament: The Costs of War and Peace," *Worldwatch Paper 122* (November 1994): 44.

49. CWC ratification record can be found at http://www.opcw.org/about -opcw/member-states/ (accessed 12 August 2009).

50. Derek Boothby, "Arms Control and Disarmament," in *A Global Agenda: Issues before the 55th General Assembly of the United Nations,* ed. John Tessitore and Susan Woolfson (Lanham, Md.: Rowman & Littlefield, 2000), 86.

51. Oganization for the Prohibition of Chemical Weapons (OPCW), "Report of the OPCW on the Implementation of the Convention on the Prohibition of the Development, Production, Stockpiling and Use of Chemical Weapons and on their Destruction in 2007," C-13/4, 3 December 2008, available at: http://www .opcw.org/documents-reports/annual-reports/ (accessed 26 July 2009). Note the information summarized in the text is in reference to OPCW Category 1 chemical weapons.

52. Ratification information on the "Convention on the Prohibition of the Use, Stockpiling, Production and Transfer of Anti-Personnel Mines and on their Destruction" is available at: http://treaties.un.org/Pages/ViewDetails.aspx?src =TREATY&mtdsg_no=XXVI-5&chapter=26&lang=en (accessed 12 August 2009).

53. "Early Success Is Reported for Global Treaty Banning Land Mines," *New York Times,* 7 September 2000, 3(A).

54. See Landmine Monitor, "Landmine Monitor Report 2008: Toward a Mine-Free World," available at: http://lm.icbl.org/index.php/publications/ display?url=lm/2008/ (accessed 26 July 2009).

55. Ratification information on the Comprehensive Test Ban Treaty (CTBT) is available at http://www.ctbto.org/the-treaty/status-of-signature-and-ratification/ (accessed 12 August 2009).

56. Details of the international verification and monitoring system are available at http://www.ctbto.org/verification-regime/background/overview-of-the -verification-regime/page-2/ (accessed 26 July 2009).

57. Boothby, "Arms Control," 77; See also William J. Broad, "Useful Legacy of Nuclear Treaty: Global Earphones," *New York Times*, 19 June 2001, 1(F).

58. See "CTBT in the Limelight at the Carnegie Conference on Nonproliferation, 8 April 2009 at http://www.ctbto.org/press-centre/press-releases/2009/ctbt-in -the-limelight-at-thecarnegie-conference-onnonproliferation/ (accessed 26 July 2009); see also Katerine Ling, "Obama's Nuclear Nonproliferation Plan Heralds Changes for DOE Labs," *New York Times*, 6 April 2009, available at http://www .nytimes.com/gwire/2009/04/06/06greenwire-obamas-nonproliferation-plan -heralds-changes-f-10439.html?scp=1&sq=Obama%20nuclear%20Prague&st=cse (accessed 26 July 2009).

59. UNDP, *Human Development Report 1994*, 59.

60. UNDP, *Human Development Report 1994*, 9.

61 Oscar Arias, "Fuel for a Coup: The Perils of Latin America's Oversized Militaries," *Washington Post*, 9 July 2009.

62. UNDP, *Human Development Report 1994*, 59.

63. Thomas Pogge, "World Poverty and Human Rights,"*Ethics and International Affairs* 19, no. 1 (2005), 1.

64. Pogge, "World Poverty," 1.

65. Leslie Kaufman and David Gonzalez, "Labor Progress Clashes with Global Reality," *New York Times*, 24 April 2001, 1(A).

66. Kaufman and Gonzalez, "Labor Progress Clashes with Global Reality," 1(A).

67. Leslie Kaufman, "GAP: Scrambling to Regain Its Cool," *New York Times*, 24 February 2002, 1(3).

68. In response to public pressure, the GAP continues to modify and adjust some of its labor policies. For example, in 2004 the GAP announced its support for a unionized clothing factory in El Salvador. See Jenny Strasburg, "Gap, Inc. Agrees to Union Factory," *San Francisco Chronicle*, 20 April 2004, available at http://www.sfgate.com/cgi-bin/article.cgi?f=/c/a/2004/04/20/BUG7J67JFO1 .DTL (accessed 4 August 2009).

69. My thanks to the publisher's anonymous reviewer for calling to my attention Roosevelt's use of the blue eagle to promote the New Deal.

70. Thomas Richard Davies, "The Rise and Fall of Transnational Civil Society: The Evolution of International Non-Governmental Organizations Since 1839," Working Paper on Transnational Politics, Centre for International Politics, City University, London. Available at http://www.city.ac.uk/intpol/dps/Working Papers/T_Davies%20The%20Rise%20and%20Fall%20of%20Transnational%20 Civil%20Society.pdf (accessed 4 August 2009).

71. Margaret Keck and Kathryn Sikkink, *Activists beyond Borders: Advocacy Networks in International Politics* (Ithaca, N.Y.: Cornell University Press, 1998), ix.

Index

About the Author

William F. Felice is professor of political science and head of the International Relations and Global Affairs discipline at Eckerd College. Dr. Felice was named the 2006 Florida Professor of the Year by the Carnegie Foundation for the Advancement of Teaching. In addition, Felice has received Eckerd College's John M. Bevan Teaching Excellence and Campus Leadership Award, and he has been recognized by the students as Professor of the Year and by the faculty as the Robert A. Staub Distinguished Teacher of the Year.

Felice is the author of *Taking Suffering Seriously: The Importance of Collective Human Rights* (1996), *The Global New Deal: Economic and Social Human Rights in World Politics* (2003), *How Do I Save My Honor?: War, Moral Integrity, and Principled Resignation* (2009), and numerous articles on the theory and practice of human rights. He has published articles in the *Cambridge Review of International Affairs*, *Ethics and International Affairs*, *Human Rights Quarterly*, *International Affairs*, *Social Justice*, and other journals.

Felice received his Ph.D. from the Department of Politics at New York University. He has served as a trustee on the board of the Carnegie Council for Ethics in International Affairs. He was also the past president of the International Ethics Section of the International Studies Association.

Breinigsville, PA USA
21 September 2010
245797BV00001B/2/P